Mad or Bad?

A Critical Approach to Counselling and Forensic Psychology

Sara Miller McCune founded SAGE Publishing in 1965 to support the dissemination of usable knowledge and educate a global community. SAGE publishes more than 1000 journals and over 800 new books each year, spanning a wide range of subject areas. Our growing selection of library products includes archives, data, case studies and video. SAGE remains majority owned by our founder and after her lifetime will become owned by a charitable trust that secures the company's continued independence.

Los Angeles | London | New Delhi | Singapore | Washington DC | Melbourne

Mad or Bad?

A Critical Approach to Counselling and Forensic Psychology

Edited by

Andreas Vossler
Catriona Havard
Graham Pike
Meg-John Barker
Bianca Raabe

Los Angeles | London | New Delhi
Singapore | Washington DC | Melbourne

Los Angeles | London | New Delhi
Singapore | Washington DC | Melbourne

SAGE Publications Ltd
1 Oliver's Yard
55 City Road
London EC1Y 1SP

SAGE Publications Inc.
2455 Teller Road
Thousand Oaks, California 91320

SAGE Publications India Pvt Ltd
B 1/I 1 Mohan Cooperative Industrial Area
Mathura Road
New Delhi 110 044

SAGE Publications Asia-Pacific Pte Ltd
3 Church Street
#10-04 Samsung Hub
Singapore 049483

Editor: Susannah Trefgarne
Editorial assistant: Lucy Dang
Production editor: Rachel Burrows
Marketing manager: Camille Richmond
Cover design: Lisa Harper-Wells
Typeset by: C&M Digitals (P) Ltd, Chennai, India
Printed by CPI Group (UK) Ltd, Croydon, CR0 4YY

First published 2017

Library of Congress Control Number: 2016955859

British Library Cataloguing in Publication data

A catalogue record for this book is available from the British Library

ISBN 978-1-4739-6351-1
ISBN 978-1-4739-6352-8 (pbk)

At SAGE we take sustainability seriously. Most of our products are printed in the UK using FSC papers and boards. When we print overseas we ensure sustainable papers are used as measured by the PREPS grading system. We undertake an annual audit to monitor our sustainability.

CONTENTS

LIST OF IMAGES

ABOUT THE EDITORS AND CONTRIBUTORS

Dr Andreas Vossler is Director of the Foundation Degree in Counselling and Senior Lecturer in Psychology at the Open University. He is also a systemic trained couple and family psychotherapist. His current research activities focus on therapeutic work with couples and families, infidelity, internet infidelity, and counselling and psychotherapy. Andreas is co-editor of the *Counselling and Psychotherapy Research Handbook* (2014) and *Understanding Counselling and Psychotherapy* (2010; both Sage). He has authored three textbooks and published 17 book chapters and 20 articles in peer-reviewed papers on topics related to counselling and psychotherapy (family therapy, infidelity, online counselling, health psychology, psychiatry) and research methods. Andreas is on the editorial board of *Counselling Psychology Quarterly* and *Forum Community-Psychology*.

Dr Catriona Havard is a Senior Lecturer at the Open University. She has investigated how accurate people are at recognising faces, in the forensic context of eyewitness identification from line-ups. The aim of her research is to make eyewitness evidence more reliable, especially for children and older adult (over 60 years) witnesses, and to reduce misidentifications that could lead to wrongful convictions.

Dr Meg-John Barker is a Senior Lecturer in Psychology at the Open University and a UKCP accredited psychotherapist. Meg-John has published many academic books and papers on topics including mindfulness, relationships, sexuality and gender, as well as co-editing the journal *Psychology & Sexuality*. They chaired production of the main counselling module at the Open University and co-edited the accompanying textbook *Understanding Counselling and Psychotherapy*, as well as writing further books on *Mindful Counselling and Psychotherapy*, and on *Sexuality and Gender for Mental Health Professionals*. Their main focus is on writing for the general public, drawing on academic and psychotherapeutic theories and research. They published the mindfulness-influenced self-help relationship book *Rewriting the Rules* in 2013, and 2016 saw the publication of *The Secrets of Enduring Love* (with Jacqui Gabb), a comic introduction to queer (with Julia Scheele), and a practical guide to sex (with Justin Hancock). Meg-John also informs UK policy and practice around sexuality and gender, and they are involved in running many public events, including Critical Sexology. They blog about all these topics on www.megjohnbarker.com. Twitter: @megjohnbarker.

Professor Graham Pike is an academic with interests in forensic psychology, critical criminology and applied cognition, whose research focuses on issues of evidence and harm within the criminal justice system. He is Professor of Forensic Cognition at the Open University, Deputy Director of the Harm and Evidence Research Collaborative and Associate Director for the National Centre for Policing Research and Professional Development. His research has led to changes in the PACE Codes of Practice, numerous guidelines for policing practice and also development of the VIPER identification system and E-FIT software. He has a passion for public engagement, whether it be producing Apps (see Photofit-me and OU Brainwave in the Apple and Android stores), MOOCs (www.futurelearn.com/courses/forensic-psychology), blogs (oucriminology.wordpress.com) or participating in public lecture tours (see www.crimiknowledge.com). Twitter: @Graham_Pike.

Dr Bianca Raabe is an academic with interests in Social, Developmental and Counselling Psychology, whose research interests have focused on young people's constructions of citizenship and identity, and is currently interested in 'wild' therapy, and therapy in open spaces. In maintaining her therapeutic practice Bianca is involved in both short-term (three session counselling) and long-term psychotherapy. She is a Staff Tutor based in the North East of England, at the Open University, Gateshead. In her role as a Staff Tutor she has particular interest in collaborative teaching and learning and working with complex group dynamics.

Joanne H. Alexander is a psychology graduate researcher at the University of Northampton. She has worked on local, national and international research projects, centred on domestic violence, housing provisions for victims of violence, referral practices in children's social care, models of early help, and care leavers' access to Higher Education. Her doctoral research explores the intergenerational transmission of family violence.

Dr Clare Bingham is a Consultant Clinical Psychologist and Head of Psychology at the John Howard Centre, a medium secure inpatient service in Hackney. She trained in systemic approaches at the Tavistock and Portman NHS Foundation Trust between 2005 and 2007 and was involved in setting up a family therapy clinic for the Forensic Directorate of East London NHS Foundation Trust. She lectures on Doctoral Clinical Psychology training courses across the North Thames region and her teaching includes lectures on systemic work in forensic settings.

Dr Matt Bruce graduated in 2005 from University College London as a Clinical Psychologist and has since acquired a specialism in dangerousness and severe personality disorder across various security settings and providers in the UK and USA. In the UK he was clinical lead for a pilot programme funded by the Department of Health and Ministry of Justice, to treat high-risk of high-harm offenders with severe personality disorders. Dr Bruce is also an honorary faculty member at the Institute of Psychiatry, Psychology and Neuroscience at Kings College London and has published peer-reviewed articles and book chapters on the subject of forensic psychology. In the USA, he has worked as a Clinical Psychologist at Saint Elizabeths Hospital, Department of Behavioral Health, Washington, DC and currently holds an Assistant Professor appointment on the postgraduate Forensic Psychology program at George Washington University.

Professor Jane E.M. Callaghan is a psychologist at the University of Northampton, where she leads the Centre for Family Life and undertakes applied psychology research. Her specialist interests include violence in the family, child and adolescent mental health, as well as gender and identity, and professionalism.

Dr Troy Cooper is a Senior Lecturer in Psychology at the Open University. Her first research was in eating disorders and addiction to alcohol and illegal drugs, and her first job was at the Addictions Research Unit (now National Addictions Centre) at the Institute of Psychiatry in London. Troy began a career at the Open University in the mid-1990s tutoring, teaching and writing on psychology modules, and developed research interests in online learning, the place of reflection in learning, and student well-being and success. Recently she gained a DipHE in Childhood and Adolescent counselling, and has worked with bereaved children. Troy's current main scholarship and practice interests are in the social construction and mediation of mental illness, and working with older people and in the broader context of issues at the end of life.

Dr Simon Cross is Senior Lecturer in Media and Culture at Nottingham Trent University, UK. Simon has published widely on media analysis of public policy issues. He is the author of *Mediating Madness: Mental Distress and Cultural Representation* (Palgrave Macmillan, 2010). Current research includes work on psychiatric and prison architecture and the legacy of the Jimmy Savile sexual abuse scandal.

Dr Emily Glorney is a Senior Lecturer in Forensic Psychology at Royal Holloway, University of London, where she is the Programme Director for the MSc Forensic Psychology. She is also a Chartered and Registered Forensic Psychologist with extensive experience in the assessment and treatment of offenders in forensic mental health and prison settings. Emily's applied research interests focus on the mental health of offenders in hospitals and prisons. Emily has published research on traumatic brain injury and violence among female prisoners, peer mentoring, and religion and spirituality in recovery pathways of forensic mental health service users, substance misuse and mental illness, forensic mental health service delivery, and comparison of characteristics of sexual killers. Forthcoming work focuses on mental health and risk reduction in prisons, such as self-harm among male prisoners. Emily is on the editorial board for the *Journal of Aggression, Conflict and Peace Research* and is a reviewer for several international peer-reviewed journals publishing high-quality research related to forensic psychological issues and mental health.

Mary Haley is the Head of Psychotherapy at HMP Grendon, a prison comprised entirely of democratically run therapeutic communities. She is also the Wing Therapist on one of the six communities there. She is a UKCP registered Integrative Psychotherapist whose main area of interest is Attachment Theory, particularly in its relevance to forensic patients. Prior to working in HMP Grendon, Mary worked as an individual psychotherapist as part of the Mental Health In-Reach Team at HMP Whitemoor for over 12 years and before that was a prison governor grade, holding various management roles in several prisons over a period of 17 years. These included management of residential wings, security risk assessment, management of life sentenced prisoners, working in the women's estate policy unit and design and delivery of operational and management training. She has a small private practice and has done work for TV programmes doing psychological assessments for participants in some reality TV shows.

Dr Daniel Holman is a Research Associate in the Department of Sociological Studies at the University of Sheffield. He completed his PhD in 2012 at the University of Essex under the supervision of

Professor Joan Busfield, which was entitled Social Class and the Use of Talking Treatments. He has published peer-reviewed papers and appeared on national radio, based on this research. Daniel then took up a Research Associate post at the University of Cambridge to work on a large-scale Type 2 diabetes peer support randomised controlled trial. His current post focuses on understanding the links between health inequalities, ageing and social quality, especially through the application of social policy-oriented cross-national comparative research.

Amanda O'Donovan BA, MPsych, C Clin Psych is a Consultant Clinical Psychologist and specialises in psychological medicine and clinical health psychology in areas such as HIV, sexual health and well-being, sexual assault, chronic pain and Chronic Fatigue Syndrome (CFS). She has worked in the NHS for 19 years and is Head of Psychology at St Bartholomew's Hospital and the Royal London Hospital in Infection and Immunity and an Honorary Lecturer at Queen Mary London, University College London, University of East London and the Tavistock Centre for Couples and Relationships, London. Amanda has a longstanding interest in mindfulness, CBT, systemic approaches and compassion-focused work. She is editor and co-author of *Sex and Sexuality: A Manual for Therapists and Trainers* (Routledge, 2009) and co-founder of the My Body Back clinic and Café V in London for women who have experienced sexual violence.

David Pilgrim PhD is Honorary Professor of Health and Social Policy at the University of Liverpool and Visiting Professor of Clinical Psychology at the University of Southampton. He trained and worked in the NHS as a clinical psychologist before completing a PhD in psychology and then a Masters in sociology. With this mixed background, his career was split then between clinical and academic work as a health policy researcher. His publications include *Understanding Mental Health: A Critical Realist Exploration, A Sociology of Mental Health and Illness* (Open University Press, 2005 – winner of the 2006 BMA Medical Book of the Year Award), *Mental Health Policy in Britain* (Palgrave, 2002) and *Mental Health and Inequality* (Palgrave, 2003) (all with Anne Rogers). All of this work is approached from the position of critical realism and so the philosophy of science and social science is an overarching framework in relation to any topic. Currently he is writing a book on child sexual abuse and public policy.

Dr Andrew Reeves is a Senior Lecturer in Counselling and Psychotherapy at the University of Chester and a Senior Accredited Counsellor/Psychotherapist at the University of Liverpool. Andrew has undertaken research into counselling and psychotherapy interventions with people who present at risk of suicide, and who self-injure, for many years and has written extensively in this area. He worked for many years in secondary care mental health services as a social worker and therapist. He is the former Editor-in-Chief of *Counselling and Psychotherapy Research* journal.

Dr Joan A. Reid is an Assistant Professor at the University of South Florida St Petersburg and a Licensed Mental Health Counselor in the State of Florida. Her research concerns include human trafficking, sexual violence, child maltreatment, victimology and recovery of crime victims. Her recent research has appeared in *Sexual Abuse: A Journal of Research and Treatment*, *Child Maltreatment* and *Criminal Behaviour and Mental Health*.

Dr Tara N. Richards is an Assistant Professor in the School of Criminal Justice at the University of Baltimore. Her primary areas of research include intimate partner violence, sexual assault and the role of gender in criminal justice system processes. Her recent empirical work is featured in *Crime & Delinquency*, *Violence Against Women* and *Child Abuse & Neglect*, and she is the co-editor of the book *Sexual Victimization: Then and Now* (Sage, 2014).

Hári Sewell is founder and director of HS Consultancy, and is a former executive director of health and social care in the NHS. HS Consultancy specialises in training and consultancy in social justice, equalities and mental health. Hári is Honorary Senior Research Fellow at University of Central Lancashire and is an Associate of the Centre for Citizenship and Community. He is widely published on subjects of race equality in mental health, equalities and social care perspectives. Hári was former editor of the journal *Inequalities in Health and Social Care* and was part of the Marmot Review of health inequalities post-2010. Hári was equalities lead in the Department of Health's Mental Health Development Unit and has been central in campaigning around equalities and mental health.

Brigitte Squire MBE is a Consultant Clinical Psychologist and Programme Director of the Multi-Systemic Therapy (MST) Services of Cambridgeshire County Council and Cambridgeshire and Peterborough Foundation Trust. Originally qualified in Belgium in 1981, she advanced her career in England since 1990 working for the NHS and obtained an MA in Systemic Therapy at the City of London University in collaboration with the Tavistock Clinic in 1994. For the past 14 years she has driven the commissioning and progression of MST within the Cambridgeshire and Northampton County Council and led on four

MST Adaptations for specialist client groups (serious adolescent substance abuse, child abuse and neglect, family integrated transitions and adolescent sexual problem behaviour). She was a Sector Advisor for the Department of Health for four years, assisting in setting up new similar teams in the UK. Brigitte received a Cambridge Justice Award for outstanding contribution to Cambridgeshire's Criminal Justice System in 2007 and was a finalist for a national NHS Leadership Award under the category NHS Innovator of the Year in 2009. In 2010 she was awarded an Honorary MBE for her services to Youth Justice.

Henry Strick van Linschoten is a psychotherapist in private practice, based in London. He is an attachment-based psychoanalytic psychotherapist, specialising in relationships, sexual, gender and relational diversity, trauma and dissociation. He has contributed to the online offerings of Confer UK, where he is also an Advisor, and has a strong internet presence. He has worked for three years at HMP Holloway, the high-security prison for women in London. He is a registered member of the UK Council for Psychotherapy (UKCP), a member of the European Society for Trauma and Dissociation (ESTD) and registered with Pink Therapy. In his earlier career he graduated in Development Economics, Econometrics and Statistics, and was an international businessman.

Dr Paul Taylor is Deputy Head of the Department of Social and Political Science and a Senior Lecturer in Criminology at the University of Chester, UK. Paul writes in the area of mental health and criminal justice, being the lead editor of *A Companion to Criminal Justice, Mental Health and Risk* (Policy Press, 2014). He is also currently researching and writing on topics of well-being among authorised police firearms officers, and a military veteran's experience as a victim of domestic violence and abuse. Paul is the Associate Editor of the Sage journal *Illness, Crisis and Loss* and sits on a number of sociology and health-related academic journal editorial boards.

Dr Jemma Tosh is a Chartered Psychologist based in Vancouver, Canada. Her research interests include gender, sexuality, sexual violence, critical psychology and intersectionality. She is the author of *Perverse Psychology: The Pathologization of Sexual Violence and Transgenderism* (Routledge, 2015) and *Psychology and Gender Dysphoria: Feminist and Transgender Perspectives* (Routledge, 2016). Jemma has published numerous papers, book chapters and commentaries on gender, sexual violence and psychology. She is a researcher at the Faculty of Health Sciences at Simon Fraser University where she completes projects related to gender, violence, natural resource extraction and climate change. She is also the Director of Psygentra Consulting Inc and is the Editor for their publication, *Journal of Psychology, Gender & Trauma*.

Dr Allan Tyler is a writer and researcher in LGBT mental health, sex and intimacy. He is a visiting lecturer in the Psychology Division of the School of Applied Sciences, London South Bank University, the Department of Geography, Environment, and Development Studies at Birkbeck College, University of London, and at the School of Psychotherapy and Psychology at Regent's University London. His PhD research explored some of the experiences, representations and identities of men who sell sex to men through advertising and social media in contemporary London. He has worked with community-based organisations to develop critical understanding and knowledge with minority and hard-to-reach populations. He has written several book chapters exploring the psychological, social, cultural and political aspects of embodiment, gender, sexuality and media, particularly for gay and bisexual men and trans* people and people selling sex. He also supervises research projects exploring various aspects of addiction counselling and forensic psychology. He tweets from @aptTyler.

Dr Nadia Wager is currently a Reader in Forensic Psychology at the University of Huddersfield and a visiting lecturer in Forensic Psychology and Victimology at Royal Holloway University of London. She was awarded a BSc (Hons) in Psychology and Criminology in 1998, after spending almost 20 years in various social support roles (e.g. community mental health, young people with profound physical and learning disabilities, the elderly and pre-school children). She was awarded a PhD in Social Psychology in 2002 by Brunel University and completed Stage 1 of the British Psychological Society's Diploma in Forensic Psychology in 2009. She has been teaching about the causes, consequences and possibilities for intervention with regard to sexual violence for 15 years to undergraduates, Masters and Doctoral students. Her research interests include investigating the causal mechanisms that potentiate risk for sexual revictimisation, evaluation of the services for survivors of sexual violence, exploring responses to disclosures of sexual victimisation and creating an understanding of conditions that facilitate disclosure, the use of restorative justice in the context of sexual and domestic violence, exploration of young men's understanding of consent for sexual intimacy and evaluation of the efficacy of psycho-educational programmes to prevent sexual revictimisation.

Dr Zoe Walkington is a Senior Lecturer at the Open University. She has a PhD in the area of forensic psychology. Zoe is involved in researching several areas of forensic and investigative psychology, including police suspect interviews, witness interpretations of crime scenes and the use of reading initiatives for increasing empathic responding towards offenders. Zoe regularly provides simulation-based training to police officers, specialising in the psychology of advanced suspect interviewing.

Dr Katherine D. Watson is a history lecturer at Oxford Brookes University. Her research focuses on areas where medicine, crime and the law intersect. She is the author of *Poisoned Lives: English Poisoners and their Victims* (Hambledon and London, 2004) and *Forensic Medicine in Western Society: A History* (Routledge, 2011), and the editor of *Assaulting the Past: Violence and Civilization in Historical Context* (Cambridge Scholars Publishing, 2007). She is currently working on a monograph on medico-legal practice in England and Wales 1700–1914, based on a project funded by the Wellcome Trust.

ACKNOWLEDGEMENTS

As editors of *Mad or Bad?* we want to say a heartfelt 'thank you' to all the people who have help to put this book together. Lucy Dang, Charlotte Meredith, Susannah Trefgarne and Rachel Burrows from SAGE have been both very supportive and patient with us. All of the chapter authors are owed a huge debt of gratitude for their excellent contributions to *Mad or Bad?*, as are the Open University students and staff members who provided the artwork for the book. We also personally want to thank our colleagues at the Open University for their support during the book production, especially Androulla Corbin, Sue Cheval, Amanda Vaughan, Gary Kitchen and Ian Fribbance. Last but not least, a big 'thank you' goes out to our friends and families – two-legged and four-legged – who coped with us during the work on the book.

INTRODUCTION

Welcome to *Mad or Bad? A Critical Approach to Counselling and Forensic Psychology*. We hope you will enjoy reading this book and come to understand more about counselling and forensic psychology in general, as well as about the fascinating relationship between them. As our title suggests, our particular focus in this book is on the overlaps between counselling and forensic psychology and between mental health and criminal behaviour. This means that we will reflect a good deal on questions of who is seen as 'mad' or 'bad' by professionals and by wider society, what this means for how they are treated, and what we can learn from that.

To explore the areas where the debates around counselling/psychotherapy and crime coincide we have brought together leading experts from the UK and USA in the fields of counselling and psychotherapy, forensic psychology, criminal justice and criminology. The twenty chapters written by these experts will critically examine the various intersections between the disciplines of counselling/psychotherapy and forensic psychology and their related fields of practice.

While there is no shortage of academic books and other publications on both counselling/psychotherapy and forensic psychology, this book takes a new and innovative approach in looking at commonalities and disparities in those areas where these disciplines overlap. We hope that you will find this approach is relevant and attractive whether you are a student, a practitioner, or just somebody who is intrigued by these areas. Interest in both counselling/psychotherapy and forensic psychology – and in therapeutic work in forensic settings – is soaring at the moment, yet trainees and professionals on each side are often unaware of the discourses and practices in the other field, and may feel unskilled and poorly equipped for work in challenging therapeutic and forensic environments. Informed by contemporary research and debates, this book will hopefully help you as reader to develop a critical understanding of the themes and issues related to crime and therapy that are highly relevant for theory and practice, yet often ignored or neglected.

Why 'Mad or Bad?'?

You might wonder why we have chosen the question of *'Mad or Bad?'* as the title for this book. As with other terms in this book that need further analysis or consideration, the quotation marks indicate that both 'mad' and 'bad' are often used as a shorthand term to express popular misconceptions of criminality and mental health/illness. It is therefore important to understand that we use the title *'Mad or Bad?'* as a provocative question aimed at challenging common prejudices that are unfortunately all too often embedded in media stories and the production of policy.

The meanings that are commonly attached to 'mad' and 'bad' suggest that these concepts are rooted in different paradigms. 'Mad' is a casual term from psychiatric discourse often used in a pejorative manner for mental health problems, whereas 'bad' refers to the law and values inherent to the legal and criminal justice system. While not necessarily related or in opposition to each other (e.g. one can be seen as 'mad' and 'bad' at the same time), the pairing points to underlying differences and tensions in terms of the values, cultures and practices developed in the fields of counselling and forensic psychology that we will explore in this book.

The question of *'Mad or Bad?'* is indicative of a debate that has a long history and often surfaces in media reports and court cases. The debate centres around questions regarding whether someone with mental health problems should be considered as fully responsible for their offences, and if certain behaviours should be treated with incarceration and rehabilitation or counselling and psychotherapy. You will read more about the *'Mad or Bad?'* debate and its implications for therapeutic and forensic practice in Chapter 1 on 'Working therapeutically in forensic settings', and in other chapters throughout the book.

How to read and use the book?

To help you to get the most out of *Mad or Bad?*, we have asked the authors to write their texts in an accessible and engaging style. We have included activities in the chapters designed to encourage you as a reader to try things out yourself and reflect upon your own perceptions and beliefs in the process. 'Pauses for reflection' will encourage you to digest the material before moving on, and at the end of every chapter you will find signposts to relevant readings that will help you to further extend your understanding. We encourage you to engage with the material we present in *Mad or Bad?*, as the more you do, the more you will learn and the more beneficial it will be for your own studies and potentially also your practice – whether that is in counselling/psycho-therapy, forensic psychology or a related field.

Like with the phrase 'Mad or Bad?', you will find other terms in this book used with quotation marks around them. We have used this device, as common in social and human sciences discussion, for words needing further analysis or consideration, or sometimes when a term is being used which belongs to a particular viewpoint or approach. Quotation marks are also used if a term within a certain discussion does not have a clear, taken-for-granted meaning that, for example, we as writer and you as reader will definitely share. We've also used quo-tation marks if there are some issues to think about around what the word is used to mean in different contexts, or by different individuals and groups, or a different perspective.

While it can be debated whether it is possible to make a generally accepted distinction between counselling and psychotherapy, for the sake of convenience we have decided to use both terms interchangeably when talking about therapeutic work. So when you read about 'counselling' and 'counsellor' then this generally also includes 'psychotherapy' and 'psychotherapist' (and vice versa) – unless stated otherwise.

Finally, we hope that you will enjoy the artwork in this book. During the planning phase we decided that it would be interesting to invite Open University Psychology students and staff to contribute artistically to the look of the book, rather than to rely on stock images. This allowed us to explore what Open University students and staff thought about the topic 'Mad or Bad?', and importantly also allowed these groups to be co-creators of the book through this crowdsourcing initia-tive. Both students and staff members were contacted and asked if they were interested in submitting images for the book. We were delighted with the submissions and are very pleased that the students and staff members have added a creativity and energy to the book through the images they have created. You will see that each chapter has an image created by one student or staff member, and then selected by the editor team, and that the artists are all named in the book.

Outline of chapters

Browsing through the book you will see that *Mad or Bad? A Critical Approach to Counselling and Forensic Psychology* is organised in five parts, with four chapters in each part.

Part I (*Mad or Bad? – Setting the scene*) sets the scene for the rest of the book by exploring the predominant tensions between forensic and therapeutic agendas and settings (Chapter 1) and outlining how the perception of 'mad' and 'bad', and with it the provision of mental health and prison services, have changed over time (Chapter 2, 'Historical Overview'). This is followed by a chapter discussing how mental health/illness and crime are represented in the media (Chapter 3). This first part of the book finishes with a critical discussion of diagnosis and categorisation of behaviour as unlawful ('bad') or abnormal ('mad'), and how that relates to available treatment and support (Chapter 4).

The second part of the book (*Mad/bad identities*) considers the ways in which criminal and 'insane' identities may be considered gendered, classed, culturally and age-dependent experiences and be related to power and oppression. The four chapters in this part (Chapters 5–8) explore how race, gender, age and social class can shape beliefs and assumptions about crime and mental health/illness, and impact on the ways offenders and users of mental health services are criminalised and pathologised.

The third part of the book (*Sex and sexuality in mental health and crime*) examines issues around sex and sexuality in forensic and therapeutic settings. Chapter 9 considers different forms of sexual violence (especially rape and child sexual abuse), together with the processes leading to stigmatisation and secondary victimisation of victims when entering the criminal justice system. Chapter 10 focuses on the role of sex and sexuality in a therapeutic setting, exploring the dynamics of erotic transference in the therapeutic relationship and the case of sexual abuse of clients by therapists, as well as how practitioners can work affirmatively with sex in the therapy room. Chapter 11 considers 'paraphilias' – sexual behaviours which are psychiatrically considered to be 'abnormal' – and the problems with such diagnoses. It also explores the role of consent in delineating sexual practice, and how some have been considered 'mad' and others 'bad'. The concluding chapter of this part (Chapter 12) explores how sex work has been treated by both criminal and therapeutic approaches, and covers the importance of listening to the experiences of sex workers themselves, as wells as the territory between therapeutic work and sex work (e.g. somatic therapies, sexual surrogacy).

The fourth part (*Treatment*) introduces four approaches for working therapeutically with offenders and victims of crime. Chapter 13 introduces attachment-based therapeutic approaches, with their notion of different attachment styles dependent on early relationship experiences. Chapter 14 outlines the theoretical background and key principles of cognitive behavioural therapy (CBT) and the specific needs and challenges of implementing CBT interventions within forensic settings. Chapter 15 introduces key ideas and concepts of systemic approaches and how they are applied in two forensic settings – work with young offenders and their families in a community setting and with clients in a forensic mental-health inpatient context. The final chapter of this part (Chapter 16) discusses mindfulness and how ideas and concepts from this approach can be utilised in the therapeutic work taking place in prisons and with victims.

The last part of the book (*Dichotomies in forensic and therapeutic practice*) covers emerging areas of forensic and therapeutic practices, including examples where forensic and therapeutic approaches are integrated to treat and prevent both mental health issues and offending. It starts with a chapter on the distinction between forensic and therapeutic perspectives regarding memory (e.g. false versus recovered memories, Chapter 17). The next chapter explores the forensic and therapeutic perspective on self-harm and suicide (Chapter 18). Chapter 19 examines different contextual factors of psychotherapy in forensic settings, and the adaptations required of therapists and their methods for effective working in this context. The final chapter focuses on the prevention of mental health problems and offending behaviours, and discusses interventions designed to support people deemed to be at risk of developing either (Chapter 20).

In the conclusions at the end of the book we draw out some of the major themes and tensions that have emerged through the book and discuss their implications for therapeutic and forensic practice.

As you can see reading through this overview, inevitably we are covering some topics in this book which are emotive. Some touch on difficult experiences that many of us have come into contact with at some point in our lives (like self-harm or sexual violence). Some deal with subjects which are hotly debated, with feelings often running high on all 'sides' of the discussion (such as race and crime or sex work). Chapters on specific practices or theories can be challenging if they seem to contradict our own experiences of mental health struggles or criminal behaviour. While we won't go into graphic details about any crimes or forms of distress, there will be some descriptions and case-examples in all of the chapters. We'd suggest that before reading on you check in with yourself about which chapters you think might be challenging for you. That does not mean not engaging with those chapters at all, but perhaps thinking, before embarking on them, about the things they might bring up for you; reading them in a time and place where you can look after yourself if necessary; and considering what kind of support you might use if these chapters do leave you with anything that you need to process further. We've listed some resources that should be helpful at the end of the book in the conclusion section.

Pause for reflection

Looking at the book content, which chapters do you think will be particularly interesting for you and which are you unsure about? Are there chapters you think might be challenging for you? Is this all new for you or do you already have some knowledge and experience which it might be worth being aware of when you read the chapters?

We hope this introduction has helped to set up *Mad or Bad?* for you and sparked your interest to read on and find out more about the questions and debates at the intersection of counselling and forensic psychology.

The *Mad or Bad?* editor team

PART I

MAD OR BAD? – SETTING THE SCENE

1

WORKING THERAPEUTICALLY IN FORENSIC SETTINGS

ANDREAS VOSSLER, CATRIONA HAVARD, MEG-JOHN BARKER, GRAHAM PIKE, BIANCA RAABE AND ZOE WALKINGTON

Image 1   Mad or bad head. With permission, Sue Cheval

Introduction

The question of whether a person is 'mad' or 'bad' is not a new one and has concerned thinkers, policy-makers, judges and doctors throughout history. However, changes in mental health and the prison service since the nineteenth century have accentuated the 'mad or bad?' debate and led to a profound shift in the way people with mental health problems are treated legally and judicially (see Chapter 2 for an overview of historic developments). At the heart of this debate is the relationship between personal responsibility, accountability and criminal behaviour, culminating in the question: should someone with mental health problems be considered as fully responsible and culpable for their offences?

From a legal perspective, the issue might seem clear and straightforward at first sight. In the UK, and other Western countries, an offender's inability to distinguish between right and wrong and to form intent, due to a lack of mental facility, necessitates a verdict of diminished criminal responsibility, not guilt. Furthermore, under the 1983 Mental Health Act (amended in 2007) courts have the possibility, if there is the assumption of a diminished legal responsibility at conviction, to recommend detention and treatment in a secure hospital rather than a prison sentence (Davies & Doran, 2012). However, not only can it be very difficult to establish a clear relationship between the mental state at the time of the offence and the offence itself, research also suggests that the public are often not sympathetic to pleas of insanity in mitigation of commission of a crime as 'there is a perception that the insanity defense is morally questionable and exploits a legal loophole' (Gans-Boriskin & Wardle, 2005, p. 31).

In this chapter we take a closer look at how tensions related to the 'mad or bad?' debate surface in the practices at the interface of mental health and criminal justice – a working environment that has been described as among the most challenging for either set of professionals (Peay, 2010). The debates here are around the questions of whether a forensic setting is principally counter-therapeutic and if therapeutic and forensic agendas (promoting well-being vs. preventing re-offence) can be compatible. The chapter will set the scene for the book in comparing aims and agendas of therapeutic and forensic services and the ways in which issues such as risk, consent, disclosure and power are seen and dealt with in therapeutic and forensic settings.

Pause for reflection: Mad or Bad?

Reflect on your own position in the 'mad or bad?' debate: Should someone who has mental health problems be held fully responsible and accountable for their offences, or not, and how should they be treated?

Working in therapeutic and forensic settings

Before exploring the underlying differences and tensions in terms of the values, cultures and practices developed in the fields of counselling psychology and forensic psychology, it is useful to establish what exactly constitutes a 'therapeutic' and 'forensic setting'. This will perhaps not be as straightforward as you might expect as it can be difficult in practice to differentiate between a therapeutic and non-therapeutic setting and a forensic and a non-forensic setting (Rogers, Harvey & Law, 2015). For example, it is debatable whether preventative community programmes with young people who are considered as being at high risk of harming themselves or others constitutes a forensic setting.

Classic psychotherapeutic settings include private practices, where therapy is offered at a therapist's home or in private practice rooms, counselling agencies, and therapy services offered in the context of the National Health Service (NHS) in the UK (like 'Improving Access to Psychological Therapies' (IAPT) services). In other less traditional therapeutic settings, like for example counselling in schools or workplace 'employee assistance programmes', counsellors may work with people who do not always come of their own volition – an issue we will discuss further below. Technology-based services, like telephone and online counselling, are provided in settings beyond the classical face-to-face, one-to-one encounter between client and therapist.

There are a number of different types of forensic setting, the most obvious example being prisons. Prisons have different levels of security, depending on the level of risk the prisoner poses to public or national security, and range from Category A for prisoners deemed to pose the most risk to Category D 'open' prisons. In Scotland there are high, medium and low supervision categories and the Governor decides what category a prisoner will be. Women and young offenders are not assigned the same categories and are simply allocated either closed or open conditions in the UK. Offenders aged between 15 and 18 years are sentenced to Young Offender Institutes (YOI), which have regimes very similar to adult prisons.

There are also secure hospitals where individuals will be admitted and detained under the Mental Health Act. The decision to admit an individual to a secure hospital will be based on a comprehensive risk assessment and detailed consideration of how the risks identified can be safely managed while in hospital (NHS Commissioning Board, 2013). Many, but not all of those admitted to High Secure Services, will have been in contact with the criminal justice system and will have either been charged with, or convicted of, a violent criminal offence. High-security hospitals play a key role in assessing an individual's ability to participate in court proceedings and in providing advice to courts regarding disposal following sentencing.

Table 1.1　Brief institutional profile of a therapeutic and forensic service

Institution	Tavistock Relationships (TR) in London*	HMP Woodhill**
Description	TR was formed in 1948 and provides a range of counselling and psychotherapy services which support clients experiencing challenges in their relationships, their sexual lives and parenting. The services are offered on a sliding scale according to client income. TR also provides professional training and continuous professional development (CPD) for relationship therapists.	HMP Woodhill is a Category A male prison, which first opened in 1992 serving courts across the Thames Valley Region as well as Northamptonshire. It has a capacity of 819 and has both single and dual occupancy cells. In 1998 one wing was re-designated as a close supervision centre, which holds a small number of prisoners who are among the most difficult and disruptive in the prison system.
Main aims and objectives	– Increase the availability of relationship support so every couple can access help when they need it. – Provide affordable, accessible and evidence-based psychotherapy services in a safe, confidential and non-judgemental environment. – Help partners to understand each other better and work through their relationship problems.	– Incarcerate offenders whose escape would be highly dangerous to the public, the police or to the security of the State for the term of their sentence. – Provides a recovery focused treatment for substance misuse problems. – A minority of inmates might also receive courses in enhanced thinking skills, relationships and life skills.
Clients	Clients are from all types of background, age and culture. In 2015 nearly 3,500 people were seeking help at TR for relationship difficulties, parenting problems and issues around sex life. 71% of clients are suffering from mild, moderate or severe depression at their first visit (with 56% of clients 'recovering' from their depression by the end of therapy).	Category A male prisoners as well as foreign nationals awaiting deportation. Category A prisoners are the most dangerous prisoners and deemed to be the most at risk to the public. The types of offence inmates may have committed include murder, manslaughter, rape, indecent assault, firearms offences, class A drug offences and offences connected with terrorism.

*Source: TR Annual Review 2015 and www.tavistockrelationships.org; **Source: www.justice.gov.uk/contacts/prison-finder/woodhill

To illustrate the values, aims and agendas in therapeutic and forensic settings Table 1.1 provides you with the examples of two institutional profiles – one located in a traditional therapeutic context and the other one in a classical forensic setting.

Comparing these two institutional profiles helps to understand the differing and sometimes competing aims and agendas of services operating in the mental health and criminal justice system.

- In the mental health system, including therapeutic services, the central aim is to help clients/patients who are in distress and promote their individual well-being. Hence, the main focus of practitioners in therapeutic settings is the work with the psychological needs of individuals.
- In contrast, work in a forensic setting often seems dominated by the need to provide security and protection for the public. Punishment and rehabilitation of the offender, with the main purpose to prevent re-offending, are the central goals in the criminal justice system, especially in a secure prison context. Specifically helping individuals with their personal problems and mental health issues does not always seem a top priority in this context (Smedley, 2010).

The comparison illustrates how much the setting of a prison or medium secure hospital differs from the contexts in which most psychotherapy is conducted in the mental health system. The difference in values and agendas can be understood as a reflection of the 'mad or bad?' debate (mad – treatment, bad – punishment and protection of the public) and often lead to tensions for mental health practitioners working therapeutically in forensic settings. They can find themselves at odds with the prevailing institutional values and fundamental aims as well as the professional mindset of their forensic colleagues (e.g. prison officers). They might also find themselves in a dual professional position where they are expected to focus on both the specific needs of their clients as well as risk management and protection of the public – two aims that are not always easily compatible, as we will see in this book.

Before we explore the issues and challenges of working therapeutically in forensic settings in more depth you might want to know what kind of therapeutic practitioners and related professionals work with mental health issues in these settings. Information box 1.1 provides you with an overview of the main professional groups that are employed in forensic services to work with these issues.

Information box 1.1: Professionals working with mental health problems in forensic settings

Counsellors/Psychotherapists

These two professional groups are quite similar, although often psychotherapists are trained more extensively (and to postgraduate level) whereas counsellor training can include training courses at Diploma, Degree or Masters level. Both use therapeutic skills and techniques (which approach they follow depends on their training, see Chapters 13–16) to help clients with their problems. Currently counselling and psychotherapy are not regulated in the UK, meaning there are no minimum requirements to practice, and no laws preventing anyone calling themselves a counsellor/therapist. However, most reputable counsellors/therapists will be registered with a professional organisation and meet the relevant standards for registration regarding training and supervision. The psychological therapists' register of the British Association for Counselling and Psychotherapy (BACP) was the first to be accredited by the Professional Standards Authority (PSA) for Health and Social Care, an independent body accountable to the government in the UK. BACP registered practitioners must also abide by the ethical and professional standards of the professional body.

Practitioner Psychologists

Through first studying a British Psychological Society (BPS) accredited undergraduate psychology qualification, which provides Graduate Basis for Chartered membership (GBC), Practitioner Psychologists then complete a postgraduate training programme (usually taking three years) in one of seven areas of applied psychology. The following three areas are particularly relevant for therapeutic work in forensic settings:

* *Counselling and Clinical Psychologists*: These are both trained to doctoral postgraduate level and are the main professional groups providing psychological therapy in forensic settings. As a broad and general distinction, Clinical Psychologists will often be trained in cognitive behavioural therapy and work briefly with clients whereas Counselling Psychologists tend to work from a humanistic philosophy and integrate different therapeutic approaches dependent on the client's needs.
* *Forensic Psychologists*: While many Forensic Psychologists are employed by the UK Prison service, they can also be found working in probation services, secure hospitals and other forensic services (Lantz, 2011). They are trained to Masters level at a minimum and work, for example, on the development and provision of treatment programmes for offenders, advise parole boards, and give evidence in court processes.

Forensic Psychiatrists

These are medically qualified doctors who have specialised in forensic psychiatry. Their work includes the assessment and psychiatric treatment of offenders with mental health problems in prisons, secure hospitals and the community. They often work with more severe mental health problems, and as medical doctors they can prescribe drugs. They have a good understanding of criminal, civil and case law relating to patient care in forensic settings and are often involved in risk assessment (e.g. in cases of violent or self-harming patients).

A good starting point for our exploration of therapeutic work in forensic settings is the list of challenges in providing therapy in a custodial setting (like a prison) outlined by Smedley (2010). It includes practical problems that can make it impossible for prisoners to attend therapy sessions (e.g. because they are 'locked down' due to security concerns) or lead to a disruption or abrupt termination of the therapy process (e.g. if the prisoner is moved to another prison). The author also refers to the fact 'that demand for mental health assessment and interventions in the prison far outstrips supply' (p. 94). Other challenges are the lack of opportunities for practitioners to have team discussions and peer support and the lack of privacy for their clients, which may impede confidentiality. Confidentiality – the general principle in therapy that everything disclosed by the client will be treated as confidential and kept private – might also be impeded in situations when therapists, under prison rules, are obliged to disclose information related to security risks that emerge in therapy sessions to the prison authorities. In the following section we will take a closer look at four particularly important themes and challenges of working therapeutically in a forensic setting.

Common themes and challenges of therapeutic work in forensic settings

The issues in this section are relevant for counsellors and psychotherapists in general, not only when working in forensic settings. However, in a forensic setting they often appear in an aggravated form, posing specific challenges and dilemmas for therapeutic and forensic professionals to navigate. When discussing these issues in the following, we will first outline their general significance in the therapy world before considering how they play out specifically in a forensic setting.

Risk and security

Issues around risk and security can be seen as one of the elephants in the therapy room – although these themes are ever present and inherent to any therapeutic work, they don't often surface in the discourse around therapeutic practice. This might have to do with the fact that it is fortunately rare that therapeutic practitioners are physically or sexually attacked or harassed by their clients (Bond, 2010). Nonetheless, the specific set-up of the therapy situation – with both therapist and client previously unknown to each other – inevitably entails elements of risk and unpredictability for both sides. For example, clients can run the risk that their symptoms might worsen during the therapy process (5–10% deteriorate during counselling or psychotherapy; Cooper, 2008), and a small minority might also find themselves harmed and damaged by the sexual misconduct of their therapist (see Chapter 10). Therapists, particularly those seeing clients on their own in private practice and in their homes, are generally vulnerable to physical or sexual assault and offences by their clients.

Hence, for Bond (2010), part of the ethical responsibility to oneself as a practitioner is to take precautions and organise the therapeutic work in ways to reduce risks. Therapists should ensure they speak on the phone to the client before the first therapy session to make a preliminary assessment. In the therapy room they could install a telephone with an outside line, or an alarm or 'panic button'. Therapists can increase security by having colleagues or a receptionist in the same building when seeing clients (often the case when working for an agency or therapy centre). Many organisations have implemented policies and procedures for risk assessment and management (e.g. assessment tools to capture risk information; Johnstone & Gregory, 2015). However, there can be 'tensions between organisational perspectives on risk and the perspectives held by practitioners and clients' (Melville, 2012, p. 24) when adhering to organisational procedures threatens to restrict confidentiality and to impede the therapeutic relationships. Despite possible precautions, practitioners might still experience a sense of danger in certain situations (e.g. when affected by the client's sense of threat to themselves) which can impact on their ability to work creatively with this client. In cases where it is impossible to restore a sense of personal safety (e.g. through supervision) it is seen as good and ethically sound practice to refer the client to another practitioner or agency (Bond, 2010).

In forensic settings practitioners won't be able to escape the themes of risk and security as they are a dominating contextual factor in this working environment (Logan & Johnstone, 2013). Risk assessment and security considerations will inevitably influence treatment planning and interventions and will also have an impact on the therapeutic relationship between therapist and client (Davis, 2012; Harvey & Smedley, 2010). Within the prevailing risk discourse, offenders are to some extent considered as a continued security risk due to their violent and/or criminal history ('the past is the best predictor of the future') and diagnostic categorisations implying volatility and potential risks (Melville, 2012). Dependent on the client's individual security classification, therapists will need to follow certain security protocols when offering therapy sessions in secure settings. Being aware of the client's criminal record and offence, they may also have to deal with their anxiety levels about potential violence during therapy sessions, and seek support in supervision if they feel impaired by their fears. If they feel appalled by the offence committed by their client, it will be challenging to offer therapeutic intimacy and to develop an accepting stance towards the person – without accepting the offence (Davis, 2012). You will hear more about how the therapeutic relationship is affected by risk and security considerations, and the institutional environment in forensic services more generally, in the chapters in the 'Treatment' part of this book and in Chapter 19 on 'Contexts'.

Consent

In addition to safety, confidentiality, and the avoidance of exploitation, a key ethical principle across counselling, psychotherapy and counselling psychology is that therapy is a voluntary endeavour which clients freely choose to engage in (Bond, 2010). This is part of the ethical principle of autonomy or respect for the client's right to be self-governing (British Association for Counselling and Psychotherapy, 2016b). Another way of putting this would be to say that clients need to provide their consent to engage in therapy. Under UK law consent is defined as being present if a person agrees to something by choice and has the freedom and capacity to make that choice (see Chapter 9). Capacity means that they need to be in a mental state where they are capable of making a rational decision (e.g. not drunk or intellectually impaired), and also that they need enough information with which to make the decision (e.g. about what therapy will actually involve). Consent is highly related to power, which we will come to in a moment, because it is very hard to freely consent to something if you have far less power in the situation than the other person, for example if you feel like the therapist is pressuring you to attend.

Consent should be dealt with in therapy through the making of a contract between client and therapist (Bond, 2010). This usually happens in the first session but may be revisited through the sessions.

In the contract, the therapist should make it clear to the client what their form of therapy involves (so that they can make an informed choice about whether it is for them) and any boundaries around time, space etc. They should also stress that the client is at liberty to stop coming to therapy at any point. This is vital because the most important factor in determining the success of therapy is the therapeutic relationship (Cooper, 2008), so clients need to feel able to move to a different therapist if they do not feel a good rapport. In regular counselling and therapy there are actually many circumstances in which a client may not be able to give informed consent, for example if this counsellor or form of therapy is the only one available to them where they live, or for a price they can afford; if they are being pressured to attend therapy by an employer or teacher due to organisational or school policies; or if the client has been in therapy for a while and simply does not feel able to tell the therapist that it is not working for them anymore. In all of these situations it behoves the therapist to work with the client in order to reach a point where they are freely consenting to be there, and would feel able to stop coming if that was in their best interests.

Of course, consent is likely to be an even more complex issue within forensic contexts. Therapeutic work in such settings usually requires the consent of the service user – as with any therapy – but this may not always be possible, for example in situations where attending one-to-one or group therapy is part of the sentencing. Under such circumstances the service user is not freely consenting to therapy because they are forced to be there. There are also issues in situations where service users know – or believe – that attending therapy might get them time off their sentences, in which case they will feel under pressure to attend. Many authors stress the importance of therapeutic roles being kept very separate from forensic roles, for these kinds of reasons (Greenberg & Shuman, 1997). However, there will still be challenges for practitioners working with service users who are pressured or forced to attend therapy (see also Chapter 19).

Self-disclosure

Clients' self-disclosure is a central feature of counselling and psychotherapy processes, and human relationships more generally, with potentially positive effects on psychological health and well-being (Forrest, 2010). Therapeutic work is reliant on clients opening up and sharing their thoughts and feelings so that the therapist can develop an understanding of the client's situation and provide suitable interventions. In psychotherapy research, client engagement and involvement, including self-disclosure, have been identified as one of the factors clients contribute to a successful psychotherapy process and outcome (Bohart & Wade, 2013; Tyron & Winograd, 2011). Talking about previously unrevealed experiences and related feelings can increase trust and help to build a strong therapeutic relationship, provided the therapist responds adequately to the disclosures (Fitzpatrick, Janzen, Chamodraka & Park, 2006).

There are a number of individual factors that can influence a client's ability or willingness to self-disclose in therapy. For example, people might find it generally difficult to trust others and disclose their feelings if they had traumatic or abusive relationships in the past (Harvey & Endersby, 2015). Saypol and Fraber (2010) found that clients with a fearful attachment style (a general way of relating to other people; see Chapter 13) tend to disclose less and also feel less positive about the disclosure of unrevealed material in therapy. Mental health problems, like depression or anxiety, can affect both the level and content of client disclosure in therapy. Finally, and particularly with highly stigmatised material, if and how much a client is willing to share will also depend on the anticipated level of shame and vulnerability when disclosing (Farber, Berano & Capobianco, 2004).

Pause for reflection: Self-disclosing in a forensic setting

Imagine that you are an inmate in a high-security prison. How would you feel about disclosing your violent thoughts and fantasies (towards yourself and inmates) to your therapist, knowing that they are obliged to pass on information related to security risks to the prison authorities?

In forensic settings, like prisons or secure hospitals, disclosing is a much more complex process. In addition to the individual factors discussed above, the decision to share difficult material with the therapist is here affected by specific contextual factors. These are environments in which inmates learn for their own safety not to show weaknesses or vulnerabilities to peers and officers. This is often paired with a culture in which 'grassing' on other inmates is a taboo – both factors that can make it more difficult to open up and talk about experiences of, for example, bullying or violence (Crewe, 2009). Clients are also aware of the confidentiality limitations and the therapist's obligation to pass on risk-related information, which means that client's disclosure in therapy can have negative consequences for their own liberty (e.g. when monitored or their leave is cancelled due to safety considerations;

Harvey & Endersby, 2015). Hence, it would be short-sighted to always see it as a sign of lacking therapy motivation if clients are reluctant or unwilling to disclose. Rather, they have to make pragmatic decisions considering the potential short- and long-term costs and benefits of a disclosure in a forensic setting.

Power

An aspect often critically discussed in the counselling and psychotherapy literature is the unequal division of power between therapist and client in therapeutic practice (e.g. Barker, Vossler & Langdridge, 2010; Howard, 1996). It is the therapist who has the power to dictate the therapy setting and ground-rules. While they reveal hardly anything about themselves in the session, the client is expected to lay open sensitive thoughts and feelings in front of the therapist in a situation when they are particularly vulnerable (McLeod, 2003). Together with the expert knowledge and language used by practitioners, this creates a power imbalance between therapist and client – something that has the potential to disempower clients as it 'may mystify problems so that clients become dependent on therapists and lose trust in their own abilities' (Barker et al., 2010, p. 340).

How the power imbalance might impact on therapeutic practice depends on the therapist's awareness of the risk of dependency of vulnerable clients in the therapeutic relationship, and how the therapy is delivered. It is part of therapist's responsibility to respect their client's autonomy and strive to support clients' control over their lives (Bond, 2010). Brief therapy approaches have shown that it doesn't necessarily need long therapy processes to help and empower clients in difficult situations, and a therapist can encourage their clients to use self-help material and community support in their everyday life at home. Clients have generally more control over what they want to disclose and the course of each session if the therapy is delivered online or over the telephone. The fact that they are not in the same room with the therapist can make it easier for them to express criticism or opt out of the session if they don't feel understood (Vossler, 2010a).

In a forensic setting, the power differential between therapist and client is more visible and heightened in the awareness of both therapists and clients. For example, in a secure or prison setting, therapists can be associated with the prison regime as they move around freely in the prison and carry keys to lock and unlock the doors – which is in stark contrast to their clients, whose movements are restricted and who can only get access to therapy through prison officers (Harvey & Smedley, 2010). Therapists might be seen as powerful figures that play an important role for prisoners' chances and opportunities within the prison environment and beyond. All these factors will impact on the therapeutic relationship, and power imbalances in forensic settings can in some cases lead to boundary breaches and inappropriate relationships. Developing an awareness of these specific power issues and the feelings and attitudes towards clients is therefore a vital skill for a therapist working in these settings.

Some of the challenges of working therapeutically in a forensic setting that we have discussed in this section are interlinked in a recursive way. For example, a risk-dominated forensic practice can hamper the disclosure of sensitive material in therapy, and the lack of relevant information can make it more difficult for therapists to develop risk management strategies to support their client.

You will also see that these themes and challenges are running through this book and will surface in many of the following chapters, particularly in the chapters of Part III ('Sex and sexuality in mental health and crime') and Part IV ('Treatment').

Conclusion

This chapter has focused on the issues and challenges of working therapeutically in forensic settings. The aims of practitioners working in a therapeutic setting are to help individuals with life problems, while in forensic settings the aims are to manage risk and protect society. The differences between mental health and criminal justice systems are further accentuated by the fact that 'each system ... is underpinned by different funding streams, governed by different legislation and reporting to different governmental departments' (Rogers, Harvey, Law & Taylor, 2015, p. 6).

The differing aims of therapeutic and forensic settings underpin the systemic problems and challenges of working therapeutically in forensic settings. The need to simultaneously focus on the micro (helping clients with their specific needs, and managing risk to the client and practitioner themselves) and the macro (managing risk to others within the forensic setting, and to society) are at the heart of the challenges that forensic practitioners face. It could be argued that in forensic settings increased concern with risk and security, and greater power differences between practitioner and client coupled with the greater potential risk to clients regarding self-disclosure and potentially limited ability to give true consent, may make it less possible for *both practitioners and offenders* to engage willingly and fully with therapy. While this argument – that the forensic setting can be viewed as principally counter-therapeutic – can be usefully debated, it should not always be seen as an inevitable consequence of working in forensic settings. As will be shown in this book, there is much evidence that despite the recursive interlinking of these issues, there is much that can be achieved with therapy in forensic settings.

Suggestions for further reading

Harvey, J. & Smedley, K. (Eds.) (2010). *Psychological therapy in prisons and other secure settings*. Abingdon: Willan.
This book introduces a range of therapeutic approaches used in forensic settings and discusses the specific challenges of this kind of work.

Rogers, A., Harvey, J., & Law, H. (Eds.) (2015). *Young people in forensic mental health settings: psychological thinking and practice*. Basingstoke: Palgrave Macmillan.
A very useful book providing an up-to-date overview of psychologically informed services and mental health provision in the UK for young people who display high-risk behaviours.

2

HISTORICAL OVERVIEW

CATRIONA HAVARD AND KATHERINE D. WATSON

Image 2 Body at the old house. With permission, Julie Barber

Introduction

As you have read in Chapter 1, being labelled as 'mad or bad' can determine whether a person is sent to prison or a psychiatric hospital. Historically, what has been perceived as 'mad' or 'bad' has altered over time as society has changed and developed. Behaviours such as being homosexual or having a child outside marriage were in fairly recent history considered to be 'mad' and 'bad', but now in many cultures are considered to be perfectly acceptable. Conversely, while taking opium and cocaine was perfectly normal in the Victorian era, it would now be considered 'bad' and illegal.

This chapter provides an overview of the history of the treatment of people with mental health issues and how this has changed to the present day, including the creation of mental health institutions and the development of new therapies. The chapter will also look at the development of the prison service and how prisons have changed over the years, including the advent of the probation service and community sentencing. The final section summarises the historical development of medical intervention in the assessment and management of the mental health of offenders. Unlike many of the other chapters in this book, this chapter does not engage in contemporary debates or critical evaluation, but provides a brief history of how mental health and criminal offending have been treated over time, particularly in the UK and the USA.

A brief history of the treatment of mental health

'Madhouse' to asylum

The term 'mental health' was not commonly used until the 1900s; until then, 'mad', 'lunacy' and 'insanity' were the accepted terms. Throughout this chapter the term 'mental illness' will also be used, since it was common in the past; however, the preferred modern term, 'mental health issues' or 'mental health problems', will be employed throughout the rest of the book. These terms reduce the stigma previously associated with the old 'mental illness' label, which suggested that sufferers should be segregated from the rest of the population.

One of the first hospitals to open its doors to the mentally unwell was St Marys of Bethlehem Priory in London. It was originally founded in 1247 to heal sick paupers, but over the years it began to take in more people with mental illness. In 1403 the hospital was taken over by the Crown and turned into a 'madhouse' or shelter for the insane; from 1547 the City of London ran it as a hospital for the mentally ill until 1948 (Kent, 2003). The hospital's name changed from Bethlehem, to

Bethlem and then in turn to Bedlam, a term that is still used to refer to disorder, chaos and mayhem.

During the eighteenth century Bedlam was open to the public and visitors could pay a fee to come and gawk at the patients. In the early 1790s William Tuke, a devout Quaker, led an investigation into the English 'madhouses' and was horrified by what he found. Many of the patients were kept in awful conditions, chained to walls or beds in cramped conditions, sleeping on straw. The treatments given to the patients were often harsh, such as being starved, beaten and drenched in cold water, but Tuke believed that 'mad' people should be treated with kindness rather than cruelty. In 1796 he opened the York Retreat as an asylum to protect those with mental health problems from society, rather than to protect society from the 'mad' as had been the ethos of previous institutions. This heralded a new era in the treatment of mental health patients across Europe and the USA and initiated the age of the asylum (Kent, 2003).

Pause for reflection: Symptoms and causes of mental illness

In 1810 London physician William Blake created a table of the causes of insanity of those admitted to Bethlem, including grief, love, jealousy, pride, religion, study, drink and intoxication, childbed (giving birth or nursing), fevers, family and heredity, contusions and fractures of the skull, and venereal disease (Appignanesi, 2008).

How does this list differ from the way we currently think about mental health problems?

Would mental health professionals today recognise these as symptoms or causes of mental illness?

Blake's list is very different from that used in current diagnosis and descriptions of mental illness, and illustrates the contemporary lack of medical knowledge about mental health problems. Another difference is that the list focuses more on causes whereas mental health professionals today tend to concentrate on diagnosis and treatment. However, it could be argued that many of the issues in the list, such as jealousy (Kingham & Gordon, 2004), alcohol (Shivani, Goldsmith & Anthenelli, 2002) and grief (Ott, 2003), can have a profound effect upon mental health.

The York Retreat was set up as a charitable non-profit sanctuary, where treatment was not based upon medical knowledge but on

Christian morals and common sense. Patients were not punished for their behaviour, but treated with kindness and very seldom restrained, though they were occasionally placed in straightjackets if it seemed they might harm themselves. While the York Retreat followed a Quaker philosophy of moral, rather than medical therapy, in the early nineteenth century a number of other medical institutions were established, such as St Luke's hospital and Manchester Lunatic Asylum, with the aim of treating those with mental health problems (Jones, 1993). By 1914 there were over 100,000 patients in over 100 mental hospitals in the UK (The Timechamber, 2007).

The development of treatment

In the early mental health hospitals such as St Luke's, treatment still focused on cold water plunges, drugs to induce vomiting, bloodletting and rotation therapy (sitting in a suspended rotating chair). It wasn't until the early twentieth century and the publication of Sigmund Freud's psychoanalysis theory that the 'talking cure' was seen as a form of treatment. Freud believed that mental health problems came from suppressing unconscious desires, fears and childhood memories that could be uncovered by using techniques such as free association, where the patient is asked to relax and say the first thing that comes into their mind, and dream analysis. Once unconscious memories and fears were brought into consciousness the patient's symptoms would be alleviated (Parker, 2010). Psychoanalysis started the revolutionary Psychodynamic movement, which influenced not only psychiatry and the way patients were treated in mental health institutions, but has also had lasting influences on the field of psychology and counselling (Porter, 2003; see also Chapter 13). However, Freud did not envisage psychoanalysis as a treatment for those with severe mental illness, who filled asylums in large numbers (Kent, 2003).

In the 1920s and 1930s new techniques were developed to treat the mentally ill. One experimental technique thought to be effective for schizophrenia was insulin shock, or insulin coma therapy (ICT). The patient was given a series of insulin injections until their blood sugar dropped and they went into a coma. Once comatose the patient was given a glucose injection to revive them, a process repeated over a series of days or weeks. This therapy carried serious risks, including brain damage from the comas; one in every hundred patients died and many others were left feeling terrified or disorientated (Kent, 2003). ICT was used throughout the 1940s and 1950s in many psychiatric hospitals, but was replaced by the advent of new drugs.

Another new technique was the use of electro-shock or electrocon-vulsive therapy (ECT), whereby seizures were induced by passing an electrical current through the brain. This was repeated until the patient stopped showing symptoms. ECT was seen as a major breakthrough and was used to treat a number of illnesses, including schizophrenia, depression and bipolar disorder. It is a treatment that is still used today, as a last resort for those with major depression when other treatments have failed, although it can have adverse effects, such as loss of mem-ory and confusion (Dunne & McLoughlin, 2012).

The 1930s saw the advent of an operation called the prefrontal lobot-omy, in which a series of nerves at the front of the brain were severed. Although lobotomy did appear to reduce the anxiety or violent out-bursts of some patients, many others lost their ability to speak or think clearly due to brain damage, and some needed more care after the surgery than they had before (Kent, 2003). However, lobotomy was seen as being at the cutting edge of medicine, and was a popular treat-ment for patients with severe disturbances. By 1951, 12,000 patients in the UK had undergone lobotomy until growing doubts about its effec-tiveness, and the psychopharmacological revolution, reduced the number of operations so that by the 1970s only just over 100 were performed every year in the UK (Barraclough & Mitchell-Heggs, 1978).

In the 1950s and 1960s of number of new drugs, including largactil, thorazine and lithium, were developed to help treat conditions such as depression, schizophrenia and bipolar disorder. These anti-depressant and anti-psychotic drugs made it possible for many patients to leave psychiatric hospitals, although they often caused adverse physiological effects (e.g. uncontrollable facial twitches, tremors, dizziness and fatigue). Furthermore, Freudians argued that anti-psychotic drugs sim-ply masked the symptoms of sufferers, making it more difficult to get at the root of the problem (Kent, 2003).

Medication still remains a key treatment for mental health problems and an individual's diagnosis will determine the types of drug they are prescribed. In 1952 the American Psychiatric Society developed the Diagnostic and Statistical Manual (DSM) of Mental Disorders. The DSM contained a number of short descriptions of mental illnesses and was designed as a handbook to help doctors and other professionals make diagnoses. The DSM is still used today, although it has been criticised as pathologising everyday life and putting diagnostic labels on emo-tional reactions that fall within the normal range (Kent, 2003). Other critics claim that mental health problems cannot be measured or cate-gorised objectively (Szasz, 1961) – an issue explored further in Chapter 3, which takes a critical perspective on diagnosis and categorisation.

The growth of drug therapy to help people with mental health prob-lems manage their symptoms reduced the need for long stays in mental

Table 2.1   Mental health timeline

Legislation	Service/Treatment development
1700–1800	
1774 – Health of Prisoners Act authorised magistrates to appoint prison doctors	
1800–1900	
1800 – Criminal Lunatics Act authorised indefinite detention of someone who had committed a criminal act during a bout of insanity	**1863 – Broadmoor Criminal Lunatic Asylum** opened for the criminally insane
1840 – Insane Prisoners Act authorised the transfer of any insane prisoner to an asylum	**1896 – Psychoanalysis** or 'talking cure' developed by Sigmund Freud
1845 – County Asylums Act mandated every county and borough in England and Wales to provide asylum treatment for pauper lunatics	
1883 – Trial of Lunatics Act established a special verdict that the accused is guilty but insane, and is to be kept in custody as a criminal lunatic (until 1964)	
1891 – Lunacy Act under which all patients in asylums were detained, without options for voluntary admission	
1900–1950	
1930 – Mental Treatment Act introduced voluntary admission with the aim to provide treatment	**1927 – Insulin shock therapy** introduced by Manfred Sakel to treat psychosis/schizophrenia
1957 – Homicide Act (England and Wales) made it possible to consider diminished responsibility due to an abnormality of mental functioning as a defence, to reduce a conviction from murder to manslaughter	**1939 – Electroconvulsive therapy (ECT)** begins to be used in England, USA, the Netherlands, France and Switzerland for affective disorders such as depression.
1959 – Mental Health Act changed the way patients could be admitted to hospital against their will and shifted the power of admission from the judiciary to the medical profession. It also resulted in the deinstitutionalisation of many mental health patients to care in the community	**1940s/50s – Person-Centred Therapy** developed by Carl Rogers
	1950s – Rational Emotive Behaviour Therapy (REBT) developed by Albert Ellis
	1952 – Diagnostic Statistical Manual first edition published by the American Psychiatric Association

Legislation	Service/Treatment development
1950–2000	
1985 – Mental Health Act introduced additional safeguards for patients and listed four legal categories of mental disorder: mental illness; psychopathic disorder; mental impairment; severe mental impairment	**1960s – Cognitive Therapy** developed by Aaron Beck
	1962 – HMP Grendon opened as an experimental psychiatric prison providing treatment to prisoners with anti-social personality disorders
2000 to present	
2007 – Mental Health Act replaced the four categories of mental disorder with 'any disorder or disability of the mind'	
2009 – Coroners and Justice Act required murder defendants to provide medical evidence of diminished responsibility	

health institutions. This, coupled with the advent of government policy to support 'care in the community', eventually led to the closure of many British and American asylums. In the UK the asylum population dropped from 150,000 in the 1950s to 30,000 in the 1980s (Porter, 2003) however, not everyone thought care in the community worked. By the end of the twentieth century there was an increase in mental health problems recognised by the DSM, such as post-traumatic stress disorder (PTSD), and new forms of therapy to accompany them. But the DSM has been a source of controversy with some political implications: in 1974 gay and lesbian groups lobbied to have homosexuality removed from its list of mental illnesses; conversely, Vietnam veterans fought to have PSTD included, so anyone suffering from the condition could claim medical health insurance (Kent, 2003). There has also been a rise in the prescription of psychiatric drugs and it has been argued that this is associated with the increased influence of the pharmaceutical industry (Moncrieff, 2003).

Today people suffering from mental health problems may be offered drugs, group therapy, family therapy, behaviour modification, and cognitive behavioural therapy (CBT), as well as admission to psychiatric wards. Psychiatric drugs can help to alleviate symptoms, while talking therapies are employed to help people deal with the symptoms and underlying causes of their mental health issues. However, at the time of writing the mental health services in the UK are overstretched and waiting times for talking therapies can be up to a year (Mind, 2013).

The chapters in Part III on 'Treatment' will look in more detail at different types of therapy and the approaches they use. The next section examines the history of the prison and probation services.

A brief history of the prison service

The aim of the criminal justice system is to detect and prevent crime, to rehabilitate and punish offenders and to support victims and witnesses. It comprises a number of different agencies, such as the police, the Crown Prosecution Service (courts), and the National Offender Management Service (prisons and probation services), that all work together and are overseen by the Ministry of Justice, the Home Office and the Attorney General's Office (McMurran, Khalifa & Gibbon, 2009). This section looks at the development of the prison service and how sentencing developed from a form of punishment to involve rehabilitation.

For centuries prisons were used simply as a place to hold people until they faced trial or punishment, which often consisted of the death sentence or transportation, for example to the American colonies or Australia. It wasn't until the middle of the eighteenth century that a prison sentence, with hard labour, was seen as a suitable sentence for minor offences such as theft (The Howard League, 2016). From the late eighteenth to the middle of the nineteenth century prisons changed dramatically, from chaotic places that housed a mixture of prisoners to regulated institutions that were quiet, orderly and populated only by prisoners and prison staff.

In 1777 John Howard's *The state of the prisons in England and Wales* captured the public's attention about the awful conditions inside local prisons, where illness, gambling and drinking were rife, and many prisoners who were acquitted were unable to leave as they could not afford to pay the jailers to release them (McGowen, 1995). In 1779 the Penitentiary Act made it possible to sentence offenders to one of two planned state-run prisons in England. During their imprisonment offenders would be subjected to solitary confinement, religious instruction, a harsh diet, and would be required to work without payment and wear a uniform. Officials working in prisons would be paid a salary, with the costs being recovered from prison labour (Wilson, 2014). Although a change of government shelved plans for the penitentiaries, the Act paved the way for local prison reconstruction and reform, derived from an ethos that if prisoners were kept in clean, secure conditions and subject to hard labour, solitude and religion they could be rehabilitated into law-abiding citizens (Jewkes, 2011a).

By the nineteenth century many British prisons still operated with different local regimes and qualities. In 1877 the Prison Act was passed to bring local prisons under the control of the state in England and Wales, and then in Scotland in 1878. This Act paved the way for the current prison service, and saw the transfer of prison administration to the Home Secretary (Wilson, 2014). In 1895 a report to the government suggested that the aim of prisons should not only be to punish but also to reform, so that men and women left prison as better people, while younger prisoners should not be incarcerated in the same place as older offenders. This report led to a new Prison Act in 1898 which placed more emphasis on reducing recidivism (Parliament, 2016, www.parliment.uk).

Prison populations remained relatively stable until after the Second World War when numbers began to rise dramatically, from 15,000 in 1945 to 42,000 in 1978. Many prisons became overcrowded and the conditions inside were very poor due to lack of funding and the ageing Victorian prison infrastructure (McGowen, 1995). In January 2016 there were 85,461 prisoners in England and Wales and 7,887 prisoners in Scotland (www.offendersfamilieshelpline.org/index.php/prisoner-category). Today the UK prison population is the largest in Western Europe. Neither crime rates, the creation of new offences nor population have risen at comparable rates, suggesting that the twenty-first-century increase in the prison population is largely the result of longer custodial sentencing and release policies (Jewkes, 2011a).

A report by the Prison Reform Trust (2015) showed that prisons have been overcrowded every year since 1994, with fewer staff employed and ever higher death and assault rates. The report also stated that prisons have a very poor rate for reducing reoffending and that 45% of adults are reconvicted within a year of release. This was especially the case for those serving short prison sentences of less than 12 months, who were more likely to reoffend in comparison to those serving 12 month community sentences for similar offences. Prisons are not the only places in which offenders can be penalised; the information box looks at the issue of community sentences and the history of the probation service.

Pause for reflection: Do prisons work?

There are various roles for imprisonment, for example, as a punishment for crime, as a deterrent, for public protection, rehabilitation or simply because there is no other choice for the offender. Thinking about what you have read so far in this chapter, do you think prisons help to rehabilitate offenders or are they just a means of punishment? Why do you think that ex-prisoners reoffend so soon after being released?

Information box 2.1: National Probation Service

The National Probation Service, established in 1907, is responsible for supervising offenders in the community. Its origins can be traced back to 1876 when Frederick Rainer made a five shilling donation to the Church of England Temperance Society to help break the cycle of those who became repeat offenders through drunkenness. The National Probation Service works closely with the courts, preparing pre-sentence reports on risk assessment, offence and proposed sentencing. Probation officers can also work within prisons, looking at sentencing, treatments and working with the local probation service where the prisoner will be released.

Over the years the Probation Service has obtained more powers to take the lead on community sentences, including drug testing, electronic tagging and providing probation hostels. It also works with police, mental health services and the prison service under the Multi-Agency Public Protection Arrangements (MAPPA) to manage violent and sexual offenders (McMurran, Khalifa & Gibbon, 2009).

An historic overview of forensic mental health

Pause for reflection

Please compare the two statements below. What do they tell you about the ways in which mental health provision for prisoners has changed over time? What do you think some of the reasons for these changes might be? Is this simply a story of 'progress'?

Reading Gaol, 1897: 'Prison doctors have no knowledge of mental disease of any kind. They are as a class ignorant men. The pathology of the mind is unknown to them. When a man grows insane, they treat him as shamming. They have him punished again and again.' [Oscar Wilde, *Daily Chronicle*, 28 May 1897]

Bradley Report, 2009: 'Drug and alcohol issues are a major problem among the prison population and dual diagnosis (mental health problems combined with alcohol or drug misuse) is common. Mental health services and substance misuse services in prisons do not currently work well together ... dual diagnosis is used as a reason for exclusion from services rather than supporting access.' [p.107]

Forensic mental health care takes two forms: assessment of offenders for the courts, in which psychiatric experts have become increasingly important since the Victorian period; and treatment after conviction, in prison or a secure psychiatric facility. The underlying issues have been the same for the past two centuries: the difficulty of defining criminal responsibility – the 'mad or bad' debate; and the risk posed by mentally ill offenders to themselves or others.

Statutory provision for the medical care of prisoners began in the late eighteenth century, when the 1774 Health of Prisoners Act empowered county magistrates to appoint prison doctors paid from the local rates. This service remained localised until the 1877 Prison Act created a national prison service under central government control. By then it had long been evident to Prison Medical Officers (PMOs) that the prison population included a higher than average proportion of the insane (Guy, 1869), a fact that is still true today (McRae, 2015); thus, a significant proportion of their duties was taken up by mental health assessments of remand and convict prisoners who, under the terms of the 1840 Insane Prisoners Act, could be removed to an asylum. As a result of their experience, some PMOs became experts on forensic mental health (Eigen, 1995). Members of the new medical specialism of psychiatry also sought to establish themselves as experts on mental health and criminal responsibility.

Offenders could be acquitted on the grounds of insanity if the court was convinced that their free will had been undermined by disease. While such a decision was relatively straightforward in the case of the stereotypical 'raving lunatic', it was much more difficult in the absence of the classic symptoms of insanity, especially if the individual had apparently normal intelligence. As psychiatrists identified more varieties of insanity, the distinctions between them gained forensic importance, particularly in the case of partial insanity, when a person was insane in relation to one issue but appeared otherwise rational. Lawyers disputed the degree to which free will was lacking in such cases, and when Daniel McNaughtan was acquitted of murder on the grounds of insanity in 1843 the issue came to a head: public outcry led the government to appoint a judicial committee to review the decision. The resulting guidelines, known as the McNaughtan Rules, stated that to establish a defence on the grounds of insanity it must be clearly proved that the individual was suffering from a 'disease of the mind' so that he did not know what he was doing; or, if he did, that he did not know it was wrong. The McNaughtan Rules remained the only test of criminal responsibility in England and Wales until the 1957 Homicide Act introduced the concept of diminished responsibility, a partial defence to murder which reduces a conviction to manslaughter (more on the McNaughtan Rules in Chapter 3). The incidence of both pleas has been in decline since the 1990s, and the 2009 Coroners and Justice Act amended the law of diminished responsibility to require that the defendant suffer 'a recognised medical condition', giving medical evidence a central role. Although psychiatric evidence in insanity trials has been common since the nineteenth century, it was only mandated in all insanity trials by the 1991 Criminal Procedure (Insanity and Unfitness to Plead) Act (Loughnan & Ward, 2014).

There was no formal legal provision for mentally ill criminals, who were either acquitted and released or convicted and gaoled, until the 1800 Criminal Lunatics Act authorised the indefinite detention of individuals acquitted on the grounds of insanity. A new category of offender, the criminal lunatic, was now the object of forensic interest and by mid-century their growing numbers necessitated a special institution for their secure confinement. Broadmoor Criminal Lunatic Asylum, the nation's first secure psychiatric hospital, opened in 1863 to provide a therapeutic regime for a patient population largely comprised of violent offenders who could be released only when medical staff were convinced they would not reoffend. Today Broadmoor is one of only three such facilities, the others being Rampton (1912) and Ashworth (1990), both opened as Broadmoor overspill facilities. All three hospitals were administered by central government departments, and were thus outside the National Health Service, until 2001.

Mentally ill criminals can also be treated within prisons. In 1939 the East–Hubert Report recommended the creation of a special prison to provide psychological treatment designed to reduce the risk of reoffending. Special psychiatric wards were set up in prisons (Wormwood Scrubs 1946; Wakefield Prison 1947), and prison psychologists were introduced in 1950. In 1962 Grendon Prison opened for prisoners with mental disorders considered responsive to treatment; a significant proportion of its population is made up of prisoners with personality disorders. HMP Grendon will be discussed in more detail in Chapter 19.

Information box 2.2: Psychopathy

The concepts of psychopathy and personality disorder are linked to two long-standing areas of debate: (1) where the boundary between the bad and the mad is difficult to identify, who determines criminal responsibility? (2) since the nature of the psychopathy makes patients dangerous, should they be confined to safeguard the public? If so, where – in a prison or a hospital?

The maladaptive behaviour pattern now known as 'personality disorder' has a long history. Early nineteenth-century psychiatrists believed that mental illness resulted from a derangement of one of three essential faculties: reason (intellectual understanding), emotion (feeling or empathy), and will (the ability to control thoughts and feelings) (Colaizzi, 1989). Largely as a result of observed cases of violence, by the late 1820s there was a growing medical acceptance that a person might have normal intelligence but a warped personality which made it difficult or impossible to resist impulses. In 1835 the term 'moral insanity' was coined to describe an affective form of this disorder, in which an individual's emotions, but not their reason, were abnormal (Prichard, 1842).

By the twentieth century the emerging discipline of criminology had embedded the concept of moral insanity in the 'psychopathic personality', an illness identified by Victorian psychiatrists. Its symptoms of criminality, aggression, impulsivity and lack of remorse, compounded by intelligence, made patients dangerous. Interwar psychiatrists considered them responsible for their actions and psychopaths who committed crimes were imprisoned. Preventive detention became an option under the 1959 Mental Health Act, which gave psychopaths both medical and legal status: 'a persistent disorder or disability of mind ... which results in abnormally aggressive or seriously irresponsible conduct ... and requires or is susceptible to medical treatment' (Mental Health Act 1959, s.4). The Mental Health Act 1983 retained 'psychopathic disorder' but stipulated that treatment must be 'likely to alleviate or prevent deterioration'. This permitted detention of remand prisoners and those with untreatable mental disorders, heralding the 1990s shift towards public protection. The numbers detained under the legal category 'psychopathic disorder' were small, only 655 out of a total of 14,681 mental health detainees in England in 2006 (Forrester et al., 2008).

Policy debates about the care and disposition of mentally ill offenders were resolved in favour of preventive custody in the Mental Health Act 2007, which abolished the term 'psychopathic disorder' and excluded 'personality disorder', replacing them with a deliberately wide definition of mental disorder. Moreover, the Act permitted detention if 'appropriate medical treatment is available', with no stipulation that the patient must benefit from it. Thus, patients may now be detained for public safety even in the absence of effective treatment (Glover-Thomas, 2011; McRae, 2015). It remains to be seen whether the positive inferences of this change – improved access to assessment and appropriate treatment for personality disorder – will occur. Given the prevalence of personality disorders in prisons, approximately 63% of the population in 2007, it is clear that the development of personality disorder-specific services would significantly improve prison mental health services (Bradley Report, 2009).

Conclusion

This chapter has explored how mental health services have developed from 'madhouses' to care in the community and psychiatric wards, treating those with mental health problems in a more humane way.

Mental health treatments have developed from cold water plunges and lobotomies to psychotropic drugs and talking therapies. However, it should also be noted that there is still controversy over the diagnosis of mental health problems (Szasz, 1961) and the increase in prescription of psychiatric drugs (Moncrieff, 2003). Furthermore, those who suffer from mental health issues can still find it difficult to receive treatment and may still feel stigmatised due to being labelled as having a 'mental illness' (Corrigan, 2004). Many who have been prescribed medication can experience adverse effects that impair their quality of life (Haddad & Sharma, 2007).

Prisons have developed from places to hold prisoners to a means of punishment and have become regulated over the last couple of centuries to the present day. Although it appears on the whole conditions have improved for prisoners, the prison system is currently experiencing significant problems of overcrowding, stretched resources and a high rate of repeat offending. This seems to suggest that prisons are not always effective for rehabilitating offenders and reducing recidivism. In some cases it appears that community sentencing under the gaze of the Probation Service can be more effective than short prison sentences.

The final part of the chapter examined the legislative and medical approaches to the risks posed by mental health issues in offenders. While some degree of risk assessment has always existed in forensic mental health decision-making, late 1990s proposals linked mental health provision and preventive detention for the first time, as part of a state-led response to the notion of dangerousness which culminated in the 2007 Mental Health Act. Personality disorders are now recognised as among the most immediate challenges facing prison mental health services.

Suggestions for further reading

Forrester, A., Ozdural, S., Muthukumaraswamy, A., & Carroll, A. (2008). The evolution of mental disorder as a legal category in England and Wales. *Journal of Forensic Psychiatry and Psychology, 19,* 543–560.
Provides a critical historical summary from the eighteenth century to 2007.

Creese, R., Bynum, W. F., & Bearn, J. (Eds.) (1995). *The health of prisoners.* Amsterdam and Atlanta, GA: Rodopi.
Provides an overview of the development of medical care for English prisoners since the eighteenth century.

3

MEDIA REPRESENTATIONS

TROY COOPER AND SIMON CROSS

Image 3   Joker. With permission, Meg-John Barker

Introduction

In most modern media, whether fictional or news, the focus on portrayal and representation of crime is considerable and usually unquestioned. Crimes which dominate are murder and interpersonal violence with styles of depiction, description or reporting which are highly judgemental and make considerable use of stereotypes and assumptions (Philo, McLaughlin & Henderson, 1996). However, while murder is the criminal act that creates greatest apparent public anxiety about crime in Western societies, it is in fact the crime with the lowest risk of occurrence compared to other crimes (McIntyre, 1967; Office for National Statistics, 2015) and hence is hugely over-represented in media reporting. This focus therefore reflects concern not with actual but *perceived* risk or danger, and in this chapter we will discuss how that intersects with the moral and emotional significance of extreme and violent acts. In turn we will consider how this then drives the need for accountability and culpability, and that society appropriately punishes those who transgress in this way.

Drama focused on crime is dominated by police and crime shows and films which have proliferated hugely in UK and US television since the 1950s. These dramas are enormously popular and have always focused narrowly on violent offences, thereby over-representing them (Mayo Clinic, 2009), rather than the broader and more numerous array of other offences (Eschold, Mallard & Flyn, 2004). It is estimated that in 2013 in the United States two police and crime shows, *NCIS* (which stands for Naval Criminal Investigative Service) and *Criminal Minds*, averaged 33 million viewers per week (Patten, 2013) – about one in 10 of the US population. CSI (Criminal Scene Investigation) in the UK in 2015 had 4 million viewers (around one in 15 of the population), and in the US between 2010 and 2015 has run every week with around 25 million regular viewers. In Europe and the UK a particular genre called Scandinavian or Nordic Noir, concerning often extremely violent and bizarre killings rooted as much in complex and dark social and political problems as the mental health of the perpetrators, has recently become popular (Creeber, 2015). TV series *The Killing*, *The Bridge* and *Trapped* have cult followings and a considerable cultural commentary has developed about them. All these kinds of series hugely over-represent the probability of individuals with mental illness being violent and disordered (Parrott & Parrott, 2015), and one, *Criminal Minds*, is premised on the idea of profiling those involved in extreme and repeat violent offences in which mental illness or 'abnormality' is often a signature feature.

The intersection of mental state and crime in the way the judiciary has viewed culpability became significant throughout the nineteenth century as those identified as 'mad' by reason of mental state, illness or disorder – ongoing or temporary – came to be treated more leniently (or were perceived as such) in sentencing. The growing influence of the psychiatric profession in the nineteenth and twentieth centuries led to the medicalisation of evil acts (Smith, 1981) and eventually to the formal ability to plead or be judged guilty with diminished responsibility, or acquittal on the grounds of insanity – for a broader timeline and account of these developments look back again to Chapter 2.

Information box 3.1: The McNaughtan Rules

In 1843 Daniel McNaughtan tried to kill the British Prime Minister Robert Peel, but succeeded only in killing his secretary Edward Drummond. McNaughtan was acquitted of the crime after the trial was stopped because he was deemed insane, and he spent the rest of his life in Bethlem and then Broadmoor Criminal Asylum. The resulting public outcry led by newspapers over him 'getting off' led to the House of Lords issuing a ruling on the interpretation of a plea of insanity in mitigation of commission of a crime: the jurors ought to be told in all cases that every man is to be presumed to be sane, and to possess a sufficient degree of reason to be responsible for his crimes, until the contrary be proved to their satisfaction; and that to establish a defence on the ground of insanity, it must be clearly proved that, at the time of the committing of the act, the party accused was labouring under such a defect of reason, from disease of the mind, as not to know the nature and quality of the act he was doing; or, if he did know it, that he did not know he was doing what was wrong (8 ER 718, [1843] UKHL J16 para 28).

As mentioned in the previous chapter, this became known as the McNaughtan Rules and the basis for pleas of diminished responsibility or guilty but insane judgments. Although based on a British criminal case, McNaughtan Rules have been adopted in the US and many other English-speaking judicial systems. However, a critical decision for courts has become the implementation of the last two clauses, and in particular the question of whether the defendant knew what they were doing was wrong. It is this area which dominates media reporting of violent crime, and dramatic representations of it.

In this chapter we will explore and illustrate how in media portrayals or representations – in television and film fiction and news event reporting – the legal and medical construction of insanity as 'a defect of reason' which mitigates against punishment has created dynamic and compelling tensions in the space between 'mad' and 'bad', which are most often addressed by applying moral rules and understandings.

One highly significant source of tension is the threat that those who might have committed crime and are deemed 'mad' could be 'getting away with it', by lying or feigning the conditions that allow them not to be held responsible. This is a central issue in any media treatment (mediation) of exemption from punishment on these grounds. 'Getting away with it' in this context of course usually means being offered treatment in a psychiatric institution rather than a prison. Despite the considerable research and historical evidence of the frequently very poor and even cruel 'treatment' regimes used in those places (Appiganensi, 2008; Porter, 2003), in the media debate between 'bad' and 'mad' treatment is most often positioned and represented as the opposite of punishment – as pandering, cosseting and even luxury.

We shall also consider how moral judgements about those who transgress societal rules can equally apply to the victim. Issues concerning the responsibility and even culpability of victims of interpersonal violence for their own victimisation are often put at stake in news reporting and fictional representations – did the victims provoke the crime against them or even were they 'asking for it'? Key questions that media representations of crime and criminals seek to address is how perpetrators can be *shown and known* to be mad or bad, and what was the victim's role in their victimisation. Cross (2010) has explored how the signs and criteria of being mad or bad, innocent or guilty, provoked or provoking, are made visual in the popular press and how they then play into moral judgements of degree of culpability and responsibility. Many of the themes of this chapter will be relevant to Chapters 5–8 in Part II of this book, which reference in greater detail how attributes like gender, ethnicity, age and class intersect with crime and issues of mental health or illness, and are both reflected in and reproduced through media representations.

Fictional drama portrayals of the mad and the bad

We now turn to the representations of madness, badness and criminal acts in film and broadcast/webcast drama, and how these are focused on moral judgements of responsibility and the degree of accountability a perpetrator of violence or their victim should have within their particular socio-cultural and historical context. Otto Wahl (1992, 1995), Stephen Harper (2009) and Michael Birch (2012) have produced detailed and compendious analyses of research evidence on the depiction of madness in films and broadcast/webcast drama. Wahl (1995), in a chapter tellingly entitled 'Murder and Mayhem', documents over 150 films released between 1985 and 1995 which either had a major character with an identified mental problem in the plot description or had a title including a term connoting mental health problems. The chapter discusses how the majority of these films position those with mental problems at the centre of the violence, producing unpredictable and extreme behaviour which has dire consequences for the 'normal' people it is inflicted on. Birch (2012) carries this analysis forward to modern films, and discussed the development of the 'not quite right' personality who, rather than being the obviously maniacal and psychopathically homicidal protagonists of early films, poses more danger because abnormality can be concealed and danger is hidden.

Birch argues that Alfred Hitchcock's 1960 film *Psycho* began a whole sub-genre of this kind. In most of this film madness is viewed as illness, albeit an irretrievable and highly dangerous one, with a view of Norman Bates by the end of the movie as utterly transformed and deranged. Echoing nineteenth-century psychiatric ideas, Hitchcock also used a powerful 'contagion' view of this 'disease' of madness – that those who are sane and well can become infected by prolonged contact with the mad, and their own health and welfare is at risk from that very contact.

Activity 3.1

Think about a film you have seen which features a protagonist who commits murder, and who is eventually shown to be 'mad', but part of the tension is coming to know this. Rather than being obvious, there is the growing sense of unease about a character being 'not quite right'. Examples we have seen are *American Gothic* (1988), *Betty Blue* (1986), *Donnie Darko* (2001) or *I love You Phillip Morris* (2009).

Now think about:

* When as an audience you met the 'mad' character in your chosen film, what kinds of things show they are 'not quite right'?
* Did the 'mad' character have anything particular about their appearance, the way they spoke, what they were doing or how they looked compared to how other characters are portrayed? What about the lighting or the camera work around them – did that give you clues?

The horror crime genre which began in the 1970s focused in particular on one area where 'mad' and 'bad' were not seen as mutually exclusive – the notion of evil. Here is a state of madness which is extreme because the person concerned is neither normal nor rational, and they are focused on intentional malevolence to others with full knowledge of what they do. A good example is in one of the most popular and highest earning horror movies of recent years: the *Nightmare on Elm Street* series. These feature a protagonist Freddy Kruger who was a child murderer killed by the parents of his victims in the town where they all lived, and who comes back supernaturally to seek revenge for his death. There is no doubt in the films that Kruger is 'mad' in both life and death and, to underline how complete this is, it is part of the story that he is the offspring of a mental health nurse gang-raped by mentally ill patients. By this plot device Kruger's evil is actually rooted in his genesis by 'mad' men – and note how the 'treatment' context is positioned in this story device as one open to exploitation by the mentally ill, as Freddy's mother is a mental health nurse raped by her patients.

Risk, responsibility and retribution weave through this series of films and the genre to which they belong. So too does the proposition that particular forms of 'madness' must be at the heart of any crimes of enormous magnitude, any outrageous crime, because no one sane could contemplate doing them, whatever the provocation or reasons. This is a theme to which we will return when considering the news media representation of particularly violent real-life crimes, and how fictional mediations and the framing of real-life crimes intersect to produce particular moral judgements about the culpability of perpetrators.

The development of anti-psychiatric and sociological 'labelling theories' in the 1960s and 1970s contributed to some change in cinematic representations of mental health – one of the most famous is *One Flew Over the Cuckoo's Nest*, made in 1975. But Wahl (1995, p. 38) points out that even though it won five academy awards for its ground-breaking sympathetic depiction of mental illness, the film makers did not resist the push towards 'othering' – making clear that those with mental illness are very different in appearance from normal people as a sign for much deeper differences. The producers of the movie had wanted to use actual patients from Oregon State Hospital for a large number of walk-on parts needed in the movie, but this was rejected because 'real patients did not look distinct enough to depict mental patients on screen'. They had to recruit actors and spend a great deal of effort making them look unusual to make sure it was clear they were 'mad'.

The fear and othering of those with mental illness makes them far more likely to be represented as aggressors than victims in most media representations. For example, Birch (2012) cites a survey of day-time soap opera episodes which featured characters with mental health problems, finding that 83% had the character committing an act of violence and 13% had them as victims of acts of violence. Yet in the real world, where social injustices abound, these statistics should be reversed – those diagnosed with a mental illness are far more likely to be victims of violence than to commit it. This reversal of reality is grounded in the over-representation in dramas of 'mad' mental illness like psychosis or psychopathic conditions, rather than the 'sad' conditions of depressions, anxieties, phobias, addictions, obsessions and compulsions.

In *Media and Crime*, Yvonne Jewkes (2011b) notes: 'News reports about crime are replete with the language of otherness; people who offend do so because "they" are not like "us"'. We suggest that this is doubly so in the case of mentally disordered offenders because as Blackman and Walkerdine (2001) observe, 'the mad and the bad' occupy a symbolic space in the popular press because they threaten the 'boundaries by which the distinctions between good and evil, mad and bad, and rational and irrational are usually drawn'. Blackman and Walkerdine also point out that media portrayals about the 'mad and the bad' act as repositories for cultural fears about the capacity we all have to commit evil acts. At the same time, they also tend to offer reassuring distance by portrayal of them as the actions of pathological loners, individual and uniquely evil monsters, who will be taught the lessons of culpability.

Jewkes' (2011b) work on media and crime also points to a transition from a nineteenth-century view of culpability, as directly related to the gravity of a crime and the crime itself, to one in which the gravity and significance of crime is produced through mediated constructions of who the perpetrators 'are' and who the criminals 'are'. This might be graphically illustrated by the treatment of children when perpetrators (accounts of children who murder are most often focused on their pure evil or perversion), or when victims (where children are positioned as innocent, angelic and unwitting). When women are victims of crime they are innocent if conforming to norms for conventional femininity (mothers, wives or sexually inactive and domestically focused), or culpable in their own victimisation (for example, prostitutes or those active outside the home in ways, at times and in places considered unfeminine). In particular, Jewkes (2011b) examines the use of processes of stigmatisation and sentimentalisation in media portrayals of women, whether they are in the role of perpetrator or victim, as the result of social and judicial contexts which are profoundly patriarchal.

Pause for reflection

Consider your favourite crime or police broadcast/webcast shows and why you enjoy them so much. Try to make connections about what really appeals to you.

- Who are the victims and perpetrators in the crime shows? Are there any clear patterns you can see about who comes into each category?
- Have you seen any episodes featuring characters (crime investigators, victims or criminals) with mental health problems or illness? What kinds of health problem or illness were they?

News media representations of mad or bad in violent crime

News media, especially the hyper-moralistic British tabloids, speak to an imagined audience: addressed as known and understood to have shared understandings, experiences, social morals and values as the consumers of that source. Tabloids often promote themselves as the *vox populi* of their readers – try putting 'newspapers vox populi' in a search engine and see what you get. Newspapers and news media typically report and explain to their readers following the five journalistic 'W's that every trainee journalist is taught to be the basics of any story: who, when, where, what and why. However, extreme and violent crime often disrupts this cosy communication because the 'what' and the 'why' parts of a story are often contested and contradictory when issues of state of mind are involved.

A case in point concerns British serial killer Peter Sutcliffe, known as the Yorkshire Ripper, who was responsible for 13 murders and seven attempted murders of women. At his 1981 trial, which had saturation news media coverage, Sutcliffe was diagnosed as suffering from paranoid schizophrenia, which was rejected by the prosecution (after initially accepting it). Sutcliffe was found guilty and sentenced to multiple life terms in prison, before being sent to Broadmoor Hospital in 1983. In the court of public opinion, UK tabloids mounted a campaign to resist his 'cushy' imprisonment in Broadmoor on the grounds that he is evil, feigning mental illness, and deserving of a harsh penal regime and to be held morally accountable for his actions (Cross, 2014).

Moral judgement pursued by news media in these cases often employs the concept of 'evil', in much the same way as the scriptwriters of *Nightmare on Elm Street* characterised Freddy Kruger. It is used with acknowledgement or even support for the possibility of 'madness', but as an additional judgement about the 'badness' of the perpetrator which doesn't allow for mitigating circumstances for criminal or violent acts.

To begin to understand this more, consider the following case: in February 2012 in England, shortly after discharge from a psychiatric hospital, Hannah Bonser, a 26-year-old woman with a history of mental disorder, stabbed to death a 13-year-old girl. Bonser's diminished responsibility plea for the crime was rejected and she was found guilty of murder. Bonser's conviction was headlined in Britain's best-selling tabloid title *The Sun* where she was described as 'Twisted' and (quoting Bonser's brother) 'evil, like the Exorcist' (15 July 2012, p. 1). The paper's online version was accompanied by readers' letters applauding the verdict and admonishing the psychiatrists who had discharged 'evil Bonser' from hospital.

Activity 3.2

Consider how Bonser was portrayed by the news media in that one key description 'Twisted'. That word describes a normal form – a normal woman – distorted or bent out of her usual shape (twisted) to perform an outrageous act. Her brother apparently references the film *The Exorcist* – one of the earliest and most well-known horror films from the 1970s which began a genre of demonic, child possession horror movies like *Rosemary's Baby* and *The Omen*. By putting that film reference alongside 'Twisted' the implication is clearly that Bonser was bent out of shape by forces external to her – evil forces with supernatural powers.

Now let's think through some of the possible effects of 'othering' Bonser by suggesting possession by demons. For example, we would suggest that by using this description her brother clearly disowns her, and is saying of her relationship to him and the rest of her family 'she's not one of us'. By distancing her from himself and the family in this way, we think the brother is also saying that the family is not involved in or accountable for what she has done. What do you think?

Try taking our approach further to think about Bonser as a young woman living in the UK, and what the usual social expectations are of young women in relation to violent acts. We propose that the 'Twisted' headline plays into a *gendered* perception of 'madness and badness' – for example, femininity, unlike masculinity, is seen as gentle, nurturing and (specifically) non-violent – and situates the act of murder as *even more* abnormal and *more* abhorrent than usual, specifically because it was performed by a young woman.

What do you think?

By both influencing and responding to public feeling, media representations can have considerable effects on social, political and
judicial attitudes and responses. In 1996 an Australian Martin Bryant
massacred 35 people in Tasmania. The story of the mass killing was
headline news around the world, including in the British tabloid *Daily
Mirror* where his courtroom admission of guilt was headlined: 'I'm
guilty ... ha ha ha' (12 November 1996, p. 4). The paper described
Bryant as a 'psycho who never stopped smiling', the significance of
which was reinforced by showing five family photos showing Bryant
from baby to adult 'still smiling'. The use of the pictures made clear
that his smile had deeper, sinister, meaning and the focal image on the
page was of the adult Martin Bryant looking unmistakably 'mad'.
Readers uncertain as to what the image meant could rely on the cap-
tion: 'The mad staring eyes of Martin Bryant who finally confessed
yesterday'. This visual mediation of Bryant's insanity has since been
shown to be a manipulation by the newspaper in order to demonstrate
his 'madness'. In fact the photograph showing Bryant's 'mad staring
eyes' was later found to have been 'manipulated to lighten the eye area
[and] left Bryant looking quite deranged' (Turner, 1996, p. 269). The
source of the manipulation proved to be Rupert Murdoch's newspaper
The Australian.

However, this case is highly instructive because while initially press
reports 'othered' Bryant as described, and 'diagnosed' the killer a 'nut',
they later changed their representation of him to emphasise his guilt
and moral accountability. McCarthy and Rapley (2001) explore how
during the trial argument and evidence went back and forth on whether
he was mentally ill despite uncontested evidence of severe intellectual
disability by which, when he left school four years before the attack,
he was given a disability pension. This disability co-existed with a long
developmental history of violent behaviour and poor impulse control,
anti-social behaviour and social isolation, which on its own brought
into question whether Bryant was aware that he was doing wrong at
the time of his crime (defined by the Lord Chief Justice in 1960 as
requiring not only reasoning like a person of normal mind, but also
having the ability to control action and exercise willpower in line with
this rational reasoning). They show how broadsheet newspapers followed this by constructing and deconstructing the 'psychiatric case' of
the mass killer so that after presenting him as 'mad' initially, 'badness'
and culpability were gradually re-established, forming the basis of calls
on behalf of the public from the media for appropriate punishment.
The result was that Martin Bryant was eventually sentenced to 35 life
sentences, and 1035 years without parole in prison.

Finally, consider a case study where the perpetrator of an extraordi-
narily violent set of murders repudiated any argument put for mitigation

due to mental illness, and proclaimed himself completely aware of what he did at the time he murdered, but refusing to accept it was the wrong thing to do. He argued that a set of compelling social and political reasons justified his criminal killing, and hence made them not criminal. The ensuing court case hinged on definitions of rationality and rational thinking to determine whether he did know what he was doing, and on whether to be irrational was always to be understood as 'mad' or could simply be 'bad'. Media reporting and public debate across Europe on these issues and the case were considerable throughout the trial.

Case example: Repudiation of mental illness as mitigation in criminal cases

On 22 July 2011 in Norway, Anders Behring Breivik exploded a bomb outside the Norwegian prime minister's office in Oslo that killed eight and injured scores of people. A few hours later Breivik arrived at Utoya Island, the site of a Labour Party youth camp, where he methodically shot and killed 69 people, mainly teenagers. It was a deeply disturbing incident, the shock of which was compounded by Breivik's statement that his actions were 'necessary' to awaken Norway to the threat posed by Islam. Breivik's appointed lawyer initially responded by telling reporters his client was insane. Four months after the attacks psychiatric thinking apparently endorsed the lawyer's proposal, and forensic psychiatrists diagnosed Breivik to be a paranoid schizophrenic living in his own delusional world and not responsible for his actions.

The diagnosis angered survivors and bereaved families and news and commentary media because a future trial could find Breivik to be of diminished responsibility and order him to be sent to a psychiatric hospital for treatment rather than to a prison for punishment. Breivik himself was aware of the implication of the schizophrenia diagnosis, describing it as 'insulting' because it undermined his claim to political (though *not* criminal) responsibility for the massacre. A second forensic psychiatric assessment concluded one week before the trial found that Breivik had a 'narcissistic personality disorder' but not a mental illness. He was therefore judged in this second evaluation to be sane within the McNaughtan formulation.

Breivik's trial hinged on prosecution attempts to declare Breivik insane while his defence argued his actions were those of a politically motivated sane individual. In the end, the District Court of Oslo trying him found him to be sane and to be guilty, and declared Breivik's views on multiculturalism, immigration and Islam to be absurd but not delusional. His claim to be part

(Continued)

(Continued)

of a modern-day Knights Templar movement was judged to be nonsense rather than the deluded rambling of a paranoid schizophrenic.

Commentary

While news coverage shows the public and forensic psychiatry united in rejecting the validity of Breivik's arguments, they diverged completely on the source of them. Forensic psychiatry in two separate assessments deemed him 'mad', suggesting that the arguments and evidence of his apparent rationale were in fact irrational, delusional and 'labouring under a defect of reason', as the McNaughtan Rules stipulate. Public opinion, the newspapers and the jury decided that Brevik's arguments and the evidence he offered to justify his actions were simply wrong – absurd and nonsensical, but not caused by a 'defect of reasoning' which compelled him to action. In consequence, Brevik got the verdict he wanted and was sentenced to 21 years in prison with a minimum of 10 (the maximum sentence possible in Norway), with the possibility of extension were he considered a continuing danger to society.

The Bryant and Breivik cases show both the highly subjective and complex nature of judgements which are made about 'madness' in psychiatric and legal procedures, and the symbiosis between media representations and public expressions of belief and reaction which create the frame in which those decisions are made. These cases are not only complex illustrations of the interactions and tensions in media representations of the 'mad' and 'bad' and how the space between those two constructs is negotiated, but also of their dynamic and emergent nature in relation to the feedback from audiences.

Conclusion

Since the 1990s, when Victorian-built asylums were finally closed in favour of care in the community policies (see Chapter 2 for a more detailed description), popular fear of madness and violence has been a driving force for media portrayals of the 'mad and bad'. Criminologist Hershel Prins (1995) noted that while cinematic portrayals of the 'mad and bad' are often laughably (if insultingly) stereotypical, tabloid press portrayals are worse in their crudity and real-world influence. They have been shown to have a real-world impact on politicians' policy responses for protection of the public from dangerous psychiatric patients – despite clear evidence that there has been no increase in killings perpetrated by psychiatric patients in the era of community care (Wahl, 2003). Popular understanding of, and reaction to, serious mental illness has been dominated by a *perception* of dangerousness fostered and developed by media representations.

Sociologist Nikolas Rose has noted how psychiatric governance is now dominated by 'risk-thinking', which until the 1990s was the concern of only a small number of forensic psychiatrists. In his work on psychiatry and risk, Rose (2002) has pointed out how the equation of madness with risk is not new, but that the 'mad and bad' are now centre stage in public debate, transfixed by news headlines about madmen discharged from hospital and poised to kill members of the public. Rose describes how the tenor of public debate about psychiatric policy has mutated from seeing patients as victims of institutionalised asylum-based policies to seeing the public as victims of new community-based mental health policies. Rose pithily sums up change in the tenor of the debate as 'from care in the community to scare in the community' (2002, p. 182).

In this chapter we have explored how it is not facts but socially constructed judgements, values and ethics which largely determine who and what is assigned as 'mad' or 'bad' (Busfield, 1994), and how these judgements are served up daily for media audiences as entertainment and spectacle whether in fictional or news form. Within these mediations is a general denial of complexity and of how cultural, social, demographic and historic factors intersect in the construction of crime and mental illness, and who is positioned as 'mad', 'bad' or an evil combination of both. Finally, while in recent years stigmatisation of mental illness has become somewhat more nuanced and less monolithic in some media representations (Sieff, 2003; Signoriella, 1989), there is continuing evidence of its significant and problematic effects on public expression of attitude, self-stigmatisation of those with mental health issues, and the enactment of social policy and legal decisions (Dowler, Fleming & Muzzato, 2006; Scrambler, 2011; Sieff, 2003; Tyler, 2006; Wahl, 2003).

Suggestions for further reading

Birch, M. (2012). *Mediating mental health: contexts, debates and analysis.* Farnham and Burlington: Ashgate.
This is a broad introduction to current theory and research of media representations of mental health, including an excellent overview of methodological issues in researching this area.

(Continued)

(Continued)

Cross, S. (2010). *Mediating madness: mental distress and cultural representa-tion*. Basingstoke: Palgrave Macmillan.
Provides an understanding of points of change and continuity in cultural images and representations of madness, and of how this relates to the cultural politics around mental distress.

Jewkes, Y. (2011). *Media and crime* (2nd ed.). London: Sage.
Explores processes of othering of both criminals and victims in crime report-ing and other types of mediation, and 'insider' and 'outsider' processes of inclusion and exclusion grounded in social values and moral judgements.

4

DIAGNOSIS AND CATEGORISATION

DAVID PILGRIM

Image 4   How deep does it go? With permission, Andreas Vossler

Introduction

This use of medical labels to categorise psychological states is both common and contentious. In principle, medical practitioners are trained to discern what is wrong with someone ('diagnosis') in order to estimate, with good reason, what originally caused the problem ('aetiology'), how it then developed in their body ('pathogenesis') and what will happen to the problem with and without treatment ('prognosis'). This logic, heavily instilled in medical students as a form of professional authority and responsibility, tends to work best in relation to acute infections and sudden or gradual loss of physical and sensory functioning. Its particular advantage is that it guides good treatment for the problem specified (called 'treatment specificity').

As will be clear below, there has been much criticism of the application of this logic to psychological functioning. Some early critics of psychiatric diagnosis (Szasz, 1961) emphasised that it has no objective basis, such as a blood test or visible and measurable bodily signs. Accordingly, these critics argued that a symptom-only basis for diagnosis (i.e. what the patient says and does) rendered a medical approach to psychological difference in society illegitimate.

Szasz talked of the 'myth of mental illness'. He was a psychiatrist and psychoanalyst and so emphasised that people had undeniable problems, i.e. conduct affecting themselves and others. However, for Szasz these were 'problems in living', not illnesses or a function of a putative disease process inside the body of the identified patient. For Szasz the application of medical labels to psychological deviance was simply a form of mystifying and disparaging name calling. For him, diagnostic psychiatrists were like the witch-finders of medieval Europe and so psychiatric patients were like modern-day witches. This critique led Szasz to argue that there were true illnesses, discerned by bodily signs and laboratory measures, and there were problems in living, which were then wrongly classified by psychiatry.

A difficulty with this dichotomisation from Szasz is that *physical diagnoses* can be imperfect too. For example, the diagnosis of Type 1 diabetes seems to be a clear-cut and successful case of the medical logic noted above. However, while we understand the pathogenesis of diabetes, its aetiology remains uncertain. Take another example of muscular-skeletal problems. They too are often of uncertain aetiology, their untreated prognosis varies and they lack treatment specificity; a range of treatments may be tried, even including anti-cancer agents. Thus Szasz was correct to draw attention to the scientific weakness of psychiatric labelling but he was wrong to assume that physical medicine is scientifically precise and coherent in all cases (Pilgrim, 2008).

Activity 4.1: Naming

One of the routine purposes of language is to name the world. Words have an inevitable and useful 'indexical' function – they point to some aspect of our shared experience to provide us with both confidence in our lives and a basis for communication with others. What is the difference between naming people and naming objects in the world? Are some forms of naming of people validating and others invalidating (and maybe are some neither or both)? Are different emotions and assumptions attached to some of our labels and not others? Do some groups have more power than others to offer their preferred form of naming? What happens if names are offensive? *Write down your thoughts on the naming of our world in different settings, when answering these questions.*

When you have done this, think of a person you know with a mental health problem and make some notes for yourself about the role of diagnosis in his or her life. *Did the diagnosis help them or others? What consequences have there been for the person of receiving a diagnosis? Have third parties been helped by the diagnosis?*

When looking at your responses you may have noted that labelling is sometimes anxiously sought and gratefully received and sometimes it is unhelpful and experienced as stigmatising (Angermeyer & Matschinger, 2003). Also, the identified patient may resent a diagnosis but others may find it useful (Frese, 2010).

Diagnostic systems

Currently there are two international classification systems that rely upon the legitimacy of the medical labelling of psychological states. The first is produced by the World Health Organisation (the International Classification of Diseases or ICD) and the second by the American Psychiatric Association (the Diagnostic and Statistical Manual or DSM). They are not identical but very similar. As they have been revised in different editions every few years since the Second World War, they have influenced each other.

An indication of the dubious scientific status of psychiatric knowledge is that psychiatric diagnoses were not included in the International Classification of Diseases (ICD) until 1949. The system had been operating for 50 years before that and had focused primarily on causes of death and the epidemiology of infectious diseases. The flexible and shifting subjective judgements of psychiatry compared poorly with this type of hard data. For this reason, psychiatric knowledge has often been considered to be dubious within medicine itself; this is not simply a matter of anti-medical criticisms from outside the profession.

The medical logic for the diagnosis of individuals was noted above. One consequence (and this is important for our purposes here) of that logic is that the world is divided into those who have pathology and those who do not. Medicine works on a *digital* logic (present/absent). By contrast, psychological models tend to assume continuous distributions of emotional states, such as being anxious. This is then an *analog* logic of 'more or less'. You might have spotted that the first of these creates a neat administrative picture but the second does not. If cases are categorised and distinguished from non-cases (in medical terms 'no abnormality detected') then healthcare systems can plan around quantifiable 'diagnostically related groups' or 'DRGs'.

A good example of a form of analog psychological assessment, competing with psychiatric diagnosis, in forensic settings is the work of Robert Hare, the Canadian psychologist who developed the Psychopathy Checklist (Hare & Neumann, 2008). Hare uses the term 'psychopathic' to refer to an exaggerated combination of anti-social, narcissistic and histrionic personality functioning. For this reason it does not fit with the singular description of those forms of personality disorder in DSM ('narcissistic personality disorder' is absent from ICD). Hare points to elements of the three categories being present in incorrigible, self-centred individuals. We are all more or less psychopathic but offenders score higher than average citizens on Hare's psychometric device and some offenders score very highly and are thus very high risk in society.

Hare's view of us all being on a spectrum from possessing no psychopathic to extensive psychopathic features is much the same as ordinary descriptions of being very virtuous or very evil. Basically it is a psychological framing of everyday *moral* description of good and evil, with the assumption that we vary in that balance in our dealings with others. His concept is popular and makes sense psychologically because it is a continuum (though it is not a concept embraced by all clinical psychologists and psychiatrists). Until 2007 in Britain the term 'Psychopathic Disorder' was a legal category of mentally disordered offenders under the Mental Health Act. Thus, 'psychopathy' has been a clinical concept that has survived being rejected by the classification systems of ICD and DSM (there is more on psychopathy in information box 2.2, Chapter 2).

Note that analog assessments still require decisions about cut-offs, which ultimately are arbitrary judgements (the same point applies to judgements about what constitutes hypertension). Hare also has made the fair point that psychopathic tendencies can aid and abet non-criminal success, with business leaders and politicians having higher than average scores on his checklist (Babiak & Hare, 2006). This reminds us to be aware of psychological processes common to criminal and non-criminal populations.

By contrast to analog assessments and the challenge of cut-offs, the administrative advantage of psychiatric diagnoses is that they are aligned with the digital logic of the criminal justice system. Judges and juries, like medical doctors, work within a world of present/absent but in their case it is about guilt and innocence. The relevance for us is that in cases of judgments about criminal responsibility, the logic of ill/not ill offers more clear-cut answers that fit with court logic. For example, judgments about 'diminished responsibility' or 'not guilty due to insanity' can be made with the digital logic of 'mentally disordered/not mentally disordered'.

Note here as well that by the mid-twentieth century, the latter terms had displaced ones of 'mental illness' alone in the world of medicine. This is because ICD and DSM now included forms of mental abnormality, such as 'personality disorder', 'mental handicap' and 'substance misuse'. These diagnoses were added to those of 'mental illness' to create the wider notion of 'mental disorder'.

Legal aspects of the use of diagnosis

The above description, with its allusion to doubts about the scientific coherence of psychiatric knowledge, sets many hares running when we think about the criminal justice system.

First, psychologists argue that in reality we are all more or less responsible for our actions (the matter of 'insight') over time and place. However, black and white definitive judgements about our psychological competence are forced onto us all culturally by legal decision-making. And notwithstanding the flaws in medical reasoning noted above, psychiatry provides more convenient *digital judgements* of present/absent than do psychological reports for the courts. More complex multifactorial psychological formulations are more scientifically persuasive and biographically sensitive than psychiatric categorisation. However, that biographically-nuanced and socially-situated complexity offered by psychologists may not fit well with court decision-making about 'disposal'. Complexity implies messiness, whereas administrative systems like the courts and healthcare prefer to operate with clear and fixed categories.

Second, and following from this convergence of medical and legal digital logic, the judicial system has a cultural history, which limits itself to the clear-cut assumption of *moral autonomy*. That is, in the absence of evidence to the contrary (in this case the mitigation of the presence of 'mental disorder') all adults are assumed to be individually responsible for their specifiable actions all of the time. Following from this assumption, judgments about criminal responsibility are individually focused and, by and large, ignore the complicit and supportive interpersonal field of the offending (Reeves, 2014). The specific exception to this is when a third party is found guilty of aiding and abetting a crime. But more generally the matter of third-party complicity is ignored.

Take the example of sex offending against children. Case studies of sexual exploitation on the streets of England showed that the activity of criminal gangs entailed the supportive actions of others who were not directly offending (such as local authority employees fearful of being accused of racism) and the inaction of the police who disbelieved child witnesses (Jay, 2014). Similarly, in the case of Jimmy Savile and his offending in the BBC and the NHS (among other places) after his death it became evident that his peers were aware of his offending, his managers ignored strong signals about it and police action was absent and ineffectual over a number of years (Smith, 2016). Further, one problem with the moral autonomy assumption is that it crudely ignores social psychological complexity in open systems and how our social networks often unconsciously shape who we are and how we act (Christakis & Fowler, 2010).

Third, those classified as being mentally abnormal in the criminal justice system may end up in the prison system or in the healthcare system. In the first case they are less likely to receive a therapeutic regime to support them. This might imply that a *'therapeutic disposal' is more humane* but not necessarily. For example, some prison regimes have dedicated sex offender and drug treatment services, whereas much of high and medium secure psychiatric facilities lack these and focus more on the biomedical treatment of mental illness.

Fourth, a more important tension than the one about treatment availability in the two systems is that of *open-ended detention* and decision-making affecting it. In the penal system a sentence is typically defined and duly served. In the case of secure psychiatric provision, mental health legislation allows for open-ended detention. Thus the mentally disordered offender put in a healthcare facility may be disadvantaged compared to the right to eventual liberty of the prisoners, having served their agreed detention for an identical crime. The rationale of judging dangerousness is then different in the two systems.

In the case of the penal system, offender patients have a defined period of preventative detention linked to a punishment tradition (a culturally agreed approximate 'tariff' of years served for a particular offence). This is based on *retrospective* decision-making about an agreed crime committed. Psychiatric detention (and this is true too of non-offenders under 'civil sections' of our mental health legislation) is guided by *prospective* judgements about risk to others. Past conduct is certainly a guide but it is a consideration of future action that is important for mental health professionals. They have an understandable tendency to make cautious judgements about discharge (leading to an inflation of false positive decision-making). In the case of the prisoner who has served his time, he is free to go. This is the case even in the case of high recidivism risks (sex offenders are an example here, see below).

Fifth, in either system there is a challenge for those attempting psychological interventions. So much of the general rationale of the latter traditionally has emphasised *voluntarism*. The ideal form of counselling or psychological therapy involves a client attending sessions voluntarily and then experimenting with change in their lives in open society. By contrast, such interventions with offender patients entail the intervention being imposed or at least agreed upon as a condition of detention, thereby making it a constrained choice. As explained in Chapter 1, in such circumstances the degree of authentic motivation of the client is difficult to ascertain. In simple terms, if we are to break any habit (in the case of offenders 'bad habits') then we have to desist from it now and in the future. And we all know that old habits die hard and so this matter of desistance is an important psychological consideration when thinking about change. Diagnosis is linked to deterministic logic (the patient is set on tramlines created by their mental disorder), whereas formulations work in part at least with contract formations about the offender's own view of their life and attempts to take responsibility about it.

Sixth, risk assessments in closed systems (i.e. courts, prisons and secure psychiatric provision) are without reference to the *ecology of risk* in open systems (Hiday, 1995; Silver, Mulvey & Monahan, 1999). I noted above that in open society (an open system) life is different from the closed world of prison or secure psychiatric provision. A point diagnosis offers little in assessing likely outcomes for offenders when they move from the latter to the former. By contrast, a formulation would take into consideration the different contingencies operating in each, case by case.

For example, a person detained may remain clean of substances but when returning to their neighborhood and preferred social networks they will be exposed to old contingencies and triggers about their drug and alcohol use (Soyka, 2000; Swartz et al., 1998). This is important because acute intoxication is a better predictor of risky conduct than a psychiatric diagnosis; most of the late night chaos on the streets of our cities at the weekend is created by those who are considered to be 'psychologically normal'. This also raises the question about when intoxication is a symptom of a mental disorder and when it is an aspect of normal conduct. This point is especially pertinent in relation to young adults in some cultures, such as in Britain at present.

Take another example of 'stalking'. Only a minority of those committing this offence fulfil criteria for a diagnosis of a mental disorder. Most
of it is predicted by specific dysfunctional attachments in specific relational settings; most stalkers are lonely and socially incompetent or are
grudge bearing about their past relationships. Only a minority are
deluded (Mullen et al., 1999; Zona, Palarea & Lane, 1998). Whatever
their diagnosis and motivation, if stalkers are detained, then temporar-
ily they are segregated from their targets. However, on returning home,
their ecology of risk changes back to the context of their original
offending and alters its probability. Thus where people are not just who
they are is part of the picture of risk: a cue for the next point: context
and contingency in life are always important. Psychiatric diagnoses are
de-contextualised descriptions of abnormal human functioning.

Seventh, while the digital logic noted above shared by medical and
legal traditions works at the 'disposal' stage of decision-making, it helps
very little in terms of *risk assessment* and *risk management*. The latter
require multi-factorial formulations, which attend to both individual
and ecological factors (Silver et al., 1999). Simply arguing that a person
'has schizophrenia' has no predictive value in conditions of security (or
for that matter anywhere else) (Steadman et al., 1998). The question
begged is what risk does this particular person with that (or any other)
diagnosis pose given their particular history of offending, their particular resources for desistance ('impulse control'), the role of their social
networks in their level and type of risk and the specific ecological factors obtaining in the neighbourhood they might be released into (Estroff
& Zimmer, 1994)? These important intersecting factors are nothing to
do with diagnostically related groups at all, though sometimes specific
symptoms (such as command hallucinations and delusions with violent
content) do seem to increase the risk of reoffending for some individuals (Junginger, 1995; Taylor, 1985).

Eighth, a problem with the digital logic of medical and legal traditions is that the latter assume the simple presence or absence of moral
capacity and culpability. For example, a history of mental disorder
means that the attributed loss of reason might discredit a personal
account unfairly. It has been estimated that as many as 80% of
women with a diagnosis of 'borderline personality disorder' have
been sexually abused in childhood (Herman, Perry & Van der Kolk,
1989; Ogata et al., 1990). Supposing such an identified patient pursued a claim about the past crimes of others, their credibility might
be queried in the light of their diagnosis, affecting their capacity to
provide a credible witness account.

With regard to culpability, the intersection of medical and legal digital logic leads to another tension. Take the example of intoxication.
On the one hand, substance misuse is deemed to be a form of mental

disorder under both DSM and ICD. On the other hand, a dangerous drunken driver is deemed to be highly culpable (indeed more culpable than normal) in their recklessness and so is punished accordingly when detected. In other words, rather than the 'condition of substance abuse' being grounds for exculpation, it has the opposite implication in legal decision-making; it raises rather than diminishes the role of personal responsibility for the crime.

A similar argument could be made in relation to this point if we think about paedophilia and its impact on offending (noting here that not all child sexual offenders are paedophiles and not all paedophiles act on their desires). But if we do designate a singular and persistent sexual interest in children as a form of mental disorder, then should that be grounds for a defence, in relation to criminal responsibility, and if not why not? The ambiguity about this question is evident when we see child sexual offenders in *both* prisons *and* high secure psychiatric facilities. This mirrors a wider societal ambivalence about how to understand and respond to sexual offences against children. And that ambivalence has not been resolved. Indeed, it has been mirrored in the mixed response when the criminal justice and healthcare systems intersect.

Case example: How might a diagnosis influence sentencing?

Gerry was a serviceman in the armed forces and a happily married man with two children. However, since returning from service in Afghanistan and Iraq, he had terrible nightmares, waking up covered in sweat and feeling nauseous. To help him sleep he began drinking heavily in the hope it would 'knock him out' for a few hours, and as a result of his drinking he didn't seem to be getting on too well with his wife and children. Recently Gerry was arrested for serious assault after getting into a fight in a bar while intoxicated, and the other man involved in the fight died later in hospital due to head injuries. This was not the first time Gerry had been involved in a fight and he is considered to be overly aggressive, especially when he has been drinking. However, this is the first time someone has died as a result and therefore he is being tried with manslaughter. At the trial his lawyer says that Gerry has been diagnosed with PTSD, which results from his military service in Afghanistan and Iraq. His lawyer claims that the PTSD was a mitigating factor in Gerry's behaviour and the reason for his aggressive behaviour is that he misconstrues situations as being a threat to his personal safety, which is a direct result of his military service.

(Continued)

(Continued)

- Do you think that Gerry should have his PTSD diagnosis taken into consideration when considering his sentence?
- Should he be sent to prison to serve his sentence or to a secure hospital to be treated for his mental health problem?

Complexity and open systems

Taking all of the above into consideration, life and people are complicated and the eight points highlight a range of problems with digital logic, whether the latter is medical or legal in kind. The points pose an aggregating overall challenge for psychologists. In the criminal justice system, psychologists operate in a culture in which both medical and legal digital reasoning are common, and they do work, after a fashion, within *closed systems*, where moral responsibility is assumed to be an all or nothing matter.

And yet, we all conduct ourselves with varying degrees of insight about our actions in ever shifting *open systems over time and place*. In those changing and varied circumstances we are both determined and determining beings and the ratio between those components of being human varies over settings and across time for the individual being considered (Archer, 2000). It is only by 'othering' a sub-group of humanity (in this case mentally disordered offenders) that an illusion is created of a different set of psychological processes applying to them rather than those who are sane by common consent. But we have no evidence that this dichotimisation is either morally fair or scientifically valid. All the evidence is that psychological processes are common to us all, including those who commit offences and even those we deem to be criminally insane.

Holding on to an emphasis on psychological formulation, rather than diagnosis, is challenging but also important and fruitful if pursued consistently and in good faith in practice. For psychiatrists, as medical practitioners their training emphasises finding out what is wrong with people and how to treat that pathology. Psychologists are concerned instead with the interplay of causes and meanings in the lives of people. They ask overlapping questions. What has happened to this person in their life? What sense do we make of that? How have they coped and survived? What strengths do they have to change for the better? (See Johnstone and Dallos (2013) for more of these questions. Also the Division of Clinical Psychology in the British Psychological Society provides advice about how this stance is maintained (Division of Clinical Psychology, 2011 and 2013).)

Conclusion

Psychologists working in forensic settings are surrounded by the consequences of digital decision-making. The legal process has separated the criminal from the non-criminal and the psychiatric profession has separated the mentally abnormal from those who are not. Above, an eight-point checklist was offered that teased out the consequences of that digital regime. It is challenging, then, for those who operate analog reasoning, for example when providing psycho-social formulations of those detained in penal and secure psychiatric settings.

However, the shortcomings of psychiatric diagnosis and classification have now been well rehearsed and advice offered by, for example, the BPS about how to think and act in ways that respect causes and meanings, biographical nuances and the social context of people who are detained or then released. Moreover, as was noted above, although the digital logic of the law and medicine provides much social administrative neatness, it brings with it contradictions and challenges. Both medicine and the law might use digital logic but not always of the same kind. For example, substance misuse is a psychiatric diagnosis and the latter is used at times to excuse and explain ('exculpate') the offender's action. However, that medical view can be contrasted with police evidence about intoxication. Being drunk while driving does not exculpate the offender but makes them *more* guilty of anti-social conduct. Thus both medicine and the courts operated a digital logic (mentally disordered/not mentally disordered by the former and guilty/not guilty) but they are not equivalent in their logic or outcome. Here is another example of this lack of administrative fit between medicine and the law: why are some sex offenders in prison and some in secure psychiatric facilities?

The irony is that although complex psycho-social formulations are administratively inconvenient when people enter forensic settings, they become highly pertinent to decision-making about release or discharge. At that point, diagnosis *per se* offers little or no guidance to risk assessment and risk prediction. The nuances of the offender's history, their social networks and the ecological features of their home environment all become highly important to consider by professionals in their decision-making.

Finally, particular dilemmas about duty of care and defining the client arise in forensic settings. Psychological assessments and interventions in the latter always take into consideration third-party interests, especially the potential victims of crime. Whereas in voluntary settings the focus is on reducing distress and enabling confident social functioning, in forensic settings the needs of others are also relevant to consider. At times they may be privileged over that of the client.

Suggestions for further reading

Division of Clinical Psychology (2011). *Good practice guidelines on the use of psychological formulation.* Leicester: British Psychological Society.
This guide outlines best practice for Clinical Psychology diagnosis.

Division of Clinical Psychology (2013). *Classification of behaviour and experience in relation to functional psychiatric diagnosis: time for a paradigm shift.* Leicester: British Psychological Society.
This text discusses the limitations of diagnosis using DSM and ICD.

PART II
MAD/BAD IDENTITIES

5

RACE

HÁRI SEWELL

Image 5   BPD – depression and split personality. With permission, Robert Barton

Introduction

In 2016 reggae artist Gappy Ranks released a song called 'Red blood' in which he sang that whether you are Black, Indian or White ... red blood is still beating through your organs. He went on to juxtapose the concept that we are all the same as humans with the reality that racism still exists and that 'most men in jail is the Black man'. A similar tension has been present in the '#BlackLivesMatter' campaign, where some individuals replaced the slogan with '#AllLivesMatter', and totally misunderstood the meaning of the original campaigners that Black people are disproportionately being shot by the police, in addition to being disproportionately stopped and searched, convicted of crimes, and incarcerated.

Are we all the same really? Why do people of some races end up in prison in disproportionately high numbers? This chapter explores race in the context of mental health and the criminal justice system. People generally refer to race without thinking about what it really means. Race is presented in the media and in everyday conversations as a physical difference between people, but at the same time there is an overt or, more commonly, a covert or unconscious linking of race with particular attributes. This is called stereotyping. Some of the consequences of stereotyping include the fact that the attributes that are associated with groups who are in minority or who have historically been marginalised, tend to be negative. Further, when individuals from such a group are seen or interacted with, the stereotypes of the whole group are applied to the individual.

This chapter explores how popular notions of race are manifested in inequalities in society and in forensic mental health and counselling, as well as considering possibilities for addressing racial and ethnic inequalities.

Definitions and terminology

The Equality Act 2010 provides legal protections for people based on their race. The definition of race used in section 9 of the Equality Act includes colour, nationality and ethnic or national origins (Honigmann, 2013). Ethnicity has at its core a sense of shared identity and belonging for a group of people who usually share common cultures, faith, language, geographical origins and race (Fernando, 2010). The term Black, Asian and Minority Ethnic (BAME) groups is sometimes used as an alternative when discussing racial minorities. This is in recognition that not only do Black people face discrimination and inequality because of how they look or act or speak, but that other minority or marginalised groups face similar challenges on the basis of their ethnicity.

In academic or policy research race is usually understood as a characteristic of identity. The starting point for this is twofold: (1) the idea that there is general agreement that human beings fall into different racial groups, and (2) the idea that there is consensus about what those groups are. In reality, examination of both these aspects reveals less certainty than might be assumed. Let us consider this in more detail.

Underpinning the idea that people fit into known racial groups is a belief that race refers to well-defined genetic clusters discernible by the phenotype (the observable characteristics arising from an interaction between the genes and the environment). Notwithstanding the reality that some genetic differences in race are detectable, the variation between humans across so-called races is extremely small (Bamshad, Wooding, Salisbury & Stephens, 2004). Furthermore, there is also so much bi-racial parenting that people are often mixed, whether obviously so or not. For example, Scott Plous (2003) reports that 75% of African Americans have white ancestry. A further complication about race is that there is no international consensus about which races exist. For example, in the United States of America, Latinos and Hispanics are considered as races, and in South Africa 'Coloured people' are considered to be a different race from 'Black people' (Plous, 2003). 'Coloured people' refer to those who have mixed ancestry from Europe, Asia, and various Khoisan and Bantu ethnic groups of southern Africa. However, in the United Kingdom, neither Latinos, Hispanics nor 'Coloured people' are thought of as discrete races.

What this tells us so far is that in day-to-day life the reality of race rests more on social interpretations rather than on any physical differences between people.

Racialisation

Racialisation is the process by which White people have applied the notion of race to others, for example in the deeply problematic late nineteenth- and early twentieth-century scientific project of categorising different racial groups and determining how they differed from the presumed 'norm' of White people, in terms of intelligence, personality, etc. It is worthy of attention not least because the process of racialisation is not neutral (Garner, 2010). Racialisation serves to promote a sense of people being different (i.e. the 'other'), and usually it involves creating associations that are considered to be characteristics of the racialised group. Racialised groups can come to accept, and even internalise, that identity (Fernando, 2003).

Pause for reflection

Think about a time recently when the race or ethnicity of someone you had not met was referred to in a conversation with you. Consider what, if anything, you inferred about the person being spoken about, based on their race or ethnicity. What do you think the person who made the reference was trying to communicate by referring to race or ethnicity?

Social scientists study the difference that race makes to interpersonal relationships and experiences from birth all the way through to death. When researchers consider the differences based on race they have to be mindful that other aspects of identity may be a contributing factor to these variations and in some cases may even be more pertinent. A good example is social class (Marmot et al., 2010). Nazroo and Williams (2006) found that racism in its various forms also led to socio-economic inequalities. As you will see in Chapter 8, there is a relationship between many social inequalities and the increased likelihood of mental health struggles, as well as being involved in crime and being dealt with more harshly by the criminal justice system. The correlation between ethnicity and class has been illustrated by a resource called 'Lives on the Line' (life expectancy at birth and child poverty as a tube map; Cheshire, 2012), suggesting an incremental decreased life expectancy travelling from west to east on the London Underground and rail lines. It also shows an increased representation of people from BAME groups in the London population following the same pattern going west to east.

People sometimes use the term 'BAME' as if it refers to a single group. There is, however, significant heterogeneity across racial or ethnic groups and their experiences of social, economic and political aspects of life differ. It is not possible, therefore, to describe here how inequalities affect each individual minority ethnic group. It is helpful, though, to appreciate that, overwhelmingly, people from the various BAME groups have poorer experiences and outcomes in life. A typical pattern is that Black groups and Irish, Bangladeshi and Pakistani groups are usually represented among those with the poorer experiences and outcomes. Groups such as the Chinese do better in most aspects of life, including outperforming White populations in areas such as education and employment (EHRC, 2015). For example, Chinese children in England achieve on average two grades higher in every subject at GCSE compared with their White peers (Centre Forum, 2016).

What you see in general terms is that proportionately more people from BAME face more disadvantage and that aspects of inequality interact with each other and compound situations. The following sections demonstrate the links between disadvantage and use of the mental health system and experience of the criminal justice system.

Race and mental health

Research and data analysis in the field of mental health is becoming increasingly more detailed, taking account of population changes (Glover & Evison, 2009; Wilson, 2010). The ethnic composition of adult populations in the UK is changing as a result of migration, the maturing of ethnic communities with a younger age distribution and inter-ethnic relationships. Policy imperatives have required public bodies to collect ethnic data from the 1990s and improved population data on ethnicity has been available since the 1991 Population Census. Because of the wide availability of data, it is even less acceptable to make sweeping generalisations about access, experience and outcomes of BAME groups in the mental health system.

Pause for reflection

'A consultant psychiatrist was showing a student around a brand new mental health hospital that was soon going to be opened in their area. The consultant psychiatrist stated that the design of the unit did not meet the needs of the local community as it included a lot of small rooms for one-to-one meetings with the patients. He said that there was a large Black community who would be using the services and they were not interested in sitting and talking.' (Based on a personal experience of the author.)

- If mental health services believe that Black people are not interested in talking treatments, what other treatments do you think they might offer?
- How do you think this approach would affect the experience that Black people have of mental health services?

Rather than focusing on different ethnic groups I have presented an analysis of five different domains in which inequalities occur in mental health (Sewell, 2012), namely:

- Disproportionate experience of factors that are linked to poor mental health
- Higher rates than average for utilisation of services or for particular diagnoses
- Lower rates than average for utilisation of services
- Poorer outcomes derived from the treatments and interventions in mental health services
- Poorer experience of relationships with mental health services and professionals.

An advantage of adopting this line of analysis is that it will have utility in any mental health service regardless of which BAME groups are represented in the area. It will retain its usefulness as an approach over time, as communities change.

Disproportionate experience of factors that are linked to poor mental health

There are many experiences that are known to be linked to poor mental health, such as the trauma of experiencing racism (Fernando, 2010: Van der Kolk, 2014), poor housing, unemployment, poor education (Marmot et al., 2010); economic hardship (Barr, Kinderman & Whitehead, 2015) and living in an urban environment (Morgan, McKenzie & Fearon, 2008). Most BAME groups will at some level experience factors that contribute to poor mental health (see Table 5.1). For some BAME groups, experience of current and historical discrimination, conflict and migration accentuate the impact on mental health.

Table 5.1 Disproportionate experience of factors linked to poor mental health

Factors	BAME groups affected
• Higher than average levels of social inequalities • Migration (positive correlation between migration and raised levels of mental health problems) (Cantor-Graae & Selton, 2005)	African, Caribbean, Bangladeshi, Black African, Irish, Pakistani, Roma, Gypsies and Travellers (Cemlyn et al., 2009; Cooper et al., 2008; Fung, Bhugra & Jones, 2009; Veling et al., 2007)

Higher rates than average for utilisation of services or for particular diagnoses

'Higher rates than average' use of a service is often referred to as 'over-representation'. Over-representation can be understood in different ways.

If 10% of the local adult population was from a BAME group and 20% of the psychiatric inpatient population was from that group, this could be considered to be over-representation. However, some researchers argue that rather than using numbers in the adult population as the baseline against which over-representation is measured, the baseline should be 'people with a mental health problem' (see Gajwani et al., 2016; Glover & Evison, 2009; Singh et al., 2013). If 10% of the local population is from a BAME group but 20% of the people from the local population who have a mental health problem is from that BAME group, then, some researchers argue, a 20% admission rate would reflect a responsiveness to need rather than over-representation. However, Fernando (2003, 2010) and Bhui (2002) suggest that *over-representation* is an appropriate term because the need is driven by racism and inequality in wider society and within psychiatry and mental health services.

The ethos of the Mental Health Act 1983 (revised 2007) is that people should be treated within the least restrictive setting possible and mental services strive to reflect this in their provision (Tang, 2012). Over-representation in more restrictive services, as shown in Table 5.2, is therefore seen negatively by individuals and by communities that are over-represented and a consequence is that these groups begin to treat services with suspicion, and relationships are poorer than for White populations (Fountain & Hicks, 2010; SCMH, 2002).

Table 5.2   Over-representation in services or for certain diagnosis

Type of over-representation	BAME groups affected
1. Higher than average detention rates in psychiatric hospital	African Caribbean, Bangladeshi, Black African (Mann et al., 2014). Black other, Irish, Pakistani, Roma, Gypsies and Travellers groups (Care Quality Commission, 2015)
2. Referral by courts to mental health services and secure services	African Caribbean, Black African and mixed White/Black groups (Mann et al., 2014; Prins, 2010)
3. Diagnosis of psychosis	African Caribbean, Bangladeshi, Black African, Black other, Indian, Irish, Pakistan (Cooper et al., 2008; Kirkbride et al., 2008; Mann et al., 2014)
4. Community Treatment Orders (CTOs)	All BAME groups apart from Chinese, Irish and White/Black Caribbean mixed are subject to proportionately higher numbers of CTOs (Care Quality Commission, 2010)

Lower rates than average for utilisation of services

One domain of inequality is where BAME groups have lower rates than average for utilisation of services at the most therapeutic end of the spectrum. In current mental health services, the most frequently accessed counselling services are IAPT services (Improving Access to Psychological Services). IAPT are usually community-based or primary care-based services and provide talking treatments. The most frequent modality of therapy is cognitive behavioural therapy (CBT) (see Chapter 14) but national guidelines do not make this mandatory. The government-sponsored research by Glover and Evison (2009) high-lighted that women from Bangladeshi, Chinese, Indian and Pakistani backgrounds and men from Chinese, Indian, Mixed White and Black Caribbean backgrounds were less likely to enter IAPT services.

Poorer outcomes derived from the treatments and interventions in mental health services

Mainstream mental health services are provided to all communities with the intention that they are equally helpful for people irrespective of their race. However, there is evidence that there are ethnic inequalities in the outcomes derived from treatments within mental health services, as Table 5.3 shows.

Let's look a bit closer at two examples from Table 5.3 – the number of repeat admissions and the drop-out rates from CBT. Repeat admissions indicate that someone who is known to services and most probably being supported by a community team has a relapse. When certain groups experience higher than average rates of repeat admissions it is an indicator that community services are less effective in

Table 5.3   Poorer treatment and intervention outcomes

Area service with BAME have poorer outcomes	BAME groups affected
1. Psychiatric repeat admissions	Asian and Black groups have more repeat admissions (Singh et al., 2007)
2. Length of stay on psychiatric wards	Black Caribbean and White/Black Caribbean mixed have the longest length of stay (Care Quality Commission, 2010)
3. Talking therapies	African Caribbean and Black African people have higher drop-out rates for cognitive behaviour therapy for schizophrenia (Rathod et al., 2012)

supporting them to avoid admissions. With regard to drop-out rates from CBT, this possibly indicates that either the relationship between the person and the therapist broke down or that the person felt that the therapy was not working for them, or both of these things.

Poorer experience of relationships with mental health services and professionals

The fifth domain to be considered is the comparative experience of BAME groups in mental health. Many studies show significant problems in relationships between BAME communities and their levels of satisfaction with services. Such research is usually qualitative. The *Breaking the circles of fear* (SCMH, 2002) research is such an example but still provides rich information on the low levels of satisfaction that African Caribbean communities have with mental health services. Raleigh et al. (2007) found lower satisfaction rates for community mental health services reported by Asian groups whereas disparities for other BAME groups were statistically insignificant. This is in contrast to the body of research that shows a cumulative picture of high levels of dissatisfaction for other BAME groups as well (e.g. Bowl, 2007a, 2007b; Mohan et al., 2006; Parkman et al., 1997). A qualitative study of adult mental health inpatient services reported that Black and Mixed groups had higher rates of dissatisfaction for inpatient stays (Mental Health Act Commission, 2006).

In many research papers hypotheses were developed about the causes for ethnic inequalities in mental health. A literature review (Grey et al., 2013) identified the themes that are evident in explanations given for the ethnic inequalities in the experiences of mental health services, such as:

- The fact that psychiatry was developed based on Western ways of viewing the world and that this makes its transferability to other cultures difficult;
- Communication barriers arising from cultural and linguistic differences;
- Racial discrimination (racism) and social disadvantage.

While genetic predisposition as an explanation has been discredited (Fernando, 2014), it can now be considered as widely accepted that ethnic inequalities in mental health are related to the experiences of racialisation and discrimination that BAME people face, as explained in this chapter (see also Wallace, Nazroo & Becares, 2016).

Race and the criminal justice system

The association between race and criminality has been strong and repeatedly reinforced since the post-Darwin White supremacist essays of the nineteenth century, which explicitly made that association (Phillips & Webster, 2014). Not only is there a stereotyped link in people's minds, data in criminal justice consistently show variations, usually inequalities. Section 95 of the Criminal Justice Act 1991 requires the Secretary of State to publish data on ethnicity and race.

Information box 5.1: Key statistics in England and Wales 2013/14

* People from Mixed, Black, Asian and Chinese groups are at higher risk of being a victim of crime compared with White people.
* 25% of stops and searches were on BAME people despite being 13% of the population.
* Black people were more likely to be stopped and searched by the police than any other group.
* Black people were three times more likely than White and Chinese/ other groups to be arrested.
* Mixed ethnic groups were twice more likely than White and Chinese/ other groups to be arrested.
* Black people were three times more likely than White people to be prosecuted.
* Mixed ethnic groups were twice more likely than White ethnicity to be prosecuted.
* Black people accounted for 3% of the population but 13% of those remanded in custody.
* BAME defendants remanded in custody were more likely to be acquitted or not tried.
* People from Black and Mixed groups had rates of custodial sentences 3% and 5% higher than White people.
* People from Chinese and other ethnicities had the highest rate of custodial sentences.
Source: Ministry of Justice (2015c)

The high custodial rates for Black people seen in England and Wales are mirrored in the United States. Sakala (2014) highlighted that whereas Black people made up 13% of the population, they accounted for 40% of those incarcerated. This compares with Whites (non-Hispanic) making up 64% of the population, but only 39% of those incarcerated. The US Bureau of Justice Statistics reported that Black people (African Americans) were more likely to receive a custodial sentence and that sentences were longer than the average (Rhodes, Kling, Luallen & Dyous, 2015).

In broad terms, mental health and the criminal justice sectors have similar patterns in so far as Black people are over-represented within them. Literature that considers ethnic inequalities in the criminal justice system often suggest that racism plays a part at all stages, primarily arising from stereotyping. Social inequality is linked to crime (see Chapter 8) and the fact that higher proportions of people from BAME come from poorer backgrounds means that they are more likely to be involved in criminal behaviour (Maguire, Morgan & Reiner, 2012). Additionally, racist stereotypes are clearly involved in the targeting of BAME groups by the police and the ways in which BAME people are treated within the criminal justice system.

When considering criminal behaviour, it is helpful to hold in mind that the criteria for a crime is defined in a particular law. Society and politicians make choices about the actions are to be deemed as crimes (e.g. in regard to drug use). The extent to which a crime is policed, enforced and punished is influenced by the feasibility of detecting the crime in the first place; culture and public attitudes; resources available and discriminatory policies and practice. Criminality can therefore be understood not purely as behaviours of individuals who are 'bad' or who have done bad things, but rather as a set of relationships and choices with powerful and influential classes in the role of legislators, policy-makers and media outlets (influencing culture and public attitudes). This critique is based on what is referred to as the social construction of criminality (Gregoriou, 2012).

Unconscious bias

In all relationship-based activity the possibility of unconscious bias, also known as *implicit bias*, exists.

Pause for reflection

How many times in the last week have you rolled your eyes or tutted at something someone has done? Have you ever had a reaction to something someone has done and then hoped that it wasn't noticed (e.g. a frown in disgust)?

Sometimes we react to things without thinking. The idea of what is 'normal' is so much part of how we live that when someone acts in a way that seems 'abnormal' our responses are played out without us even thinking about it (see also Chapter 11). This reflects unconscious bias which Greenwald and Krieger (2006) explain as mental processes (for example, memory, stereotyping, attitudes) which are outside people's consciousness. The consideration for professionals in mental health or criminal justice settings is not *whether* they hold biases, but the extent to which they are *aware* of them, and seek to mitigate against them having a negative impact in their work. Prejudice arises from both conscious and unconscious bias.

Inequalities arise from individual and collective behaviours and attitudes that lead to unfair outcomes. Unconscious bias is therefore linked to institutional discrimination where shared and undetected biases become enshrined in policies and processes. A detailed and analytical comparative study of the use of stop and search powers in relation to White and Black people in England identified that Black people were more likely to be stopped (Bowling & Phillips, 2007). In explaining these findings, the authors point to overt prejudice and stereotyping and also unconscious bias.

One form of unconscious bias is White privilege (Kendall, 2012). A telling example emerged in the aftermath of street protests in Ferguson, Missouri, in the United States following the fatal shooting of a young African-American man by a White police officer. At the time a White male political commentator explained that to avoid the charge of having a concealed weapon, he would immediately announce that he had a (licensed) gun and would open his jacket or lift his shirt to expose the weapon. He said this in all seriousness without insight into his privilege. Sadly, in July 2016 when an African-American man, Philando Castile, was stopped by the police while he was driving, Castile announced to the police officer that he had a gun in the vehicle. He was asked for his driving licence and insurance papers and upon reaching for these Castile was shot dead by the police officer.

Race and ethnicity in counselling in a forensic setting

You will learn throughout this book that the quality of the relationship between the service user and counsellor in forensic services is critical to facilitating positive experiences and outcomes from treatment. Once a therapeutic relationship is formed between the counsellor and the service user, all of the qualities that contribute to good engagement in any setting will be applicable. However, Zach Eleftheriadou (2010), in his chapter 'Cross-cultural counselling psychology', reports that service providers often hold stereotypes that Black people are not suited to counselling.

Factors that will affect the quality and nature of relationships between a Black service user and a psychologist in a forensic context are:

- the impact of the restriction of liberty and compulsion;
- the perspective of the service user about the impact of racism in their lives so far and how they integrate this into their current situation;
- the impact of the visual representations of BAME people on both the service user and clinicians.

Pause for reflection

In what ways might your thinking about Black people be influenced if every day you see a significant over-representation of Black people treated for mental health problems and/or referred to the criminal justice systems?

Towl (2011) illustrated that incarceration, with the inherent explicit power relationships and institutionalised practices, has an impact on the counselling process (see Chapters 1 and 19). A White counsellor working with a client from a BAME background may experience greater challenges in building a trusting relationship because they may be perceived as representing the very systems of power by which the person feels attacked. Even where there is ethnic matching between a practitioner and client, the role of the professional as an agent of the system affects the relationship (see Liggan & Kay, 2006).

Case example: Calvin

Calvin is a patient in a high-security hospital on a section 37/41 of the Mental Health Act, which means that risk to the public was considered to be so great that a Crown Court made an order, with restrictions, which means that Calvin cannot be released without prior approval of the Secretary of State for Justice. He is of Caribbean background, is 1.9 metres tall and very thin. After four sessions of counselling, Jenny, the White

(Continued)

(Continued)

psychologist, reported in a multidisciplinary meeting that Calvin appeared to find it difficult to engage with the sessions. She described that he spent most of the session responding in freestyle (improvised) rap which made no sense to her. After some input from other clinicians she was encouraged to try to engage with the content of the raps to gain more understanding and to improve engagement. This strategy worked and delivered fresh insights.

• Why might the counsellor have been so ready to label Calvin as not engaging with counselling?

Psychological possibilities for change and improvement

The case example above illustrates cultural difference as well as possible unconscious bias. Though it is not possible to know everything about every culture and subculture, clinicians need to proactively engage with the individual in the context of their culture (Fernando, 2010). Unfortunately, training on race and cultural diversity is often very slim on counselling and psychotherapy courses, and social inequalities also have a major impact on the kinds of people who can afford to undertake such trainings.

When working within an ethnically diverse setting it may benefit a counsellor or psychotherapist to have access to, and be capable of using, adapted versions of therapeutic techniques. For example, Rathod et al. (2012) explore how CBT can be adapted to meet the needs of people from BAME groups in Britain. Miranda et al. (2005) also presents adaptations of CBT for minority ethnic women in America.

Activity 5.1: Intersectionality

Think of the different ways you could identify yourself, for example, your age, your race, gender, nationality, faith/religion or sexuality.

• Consider situations where different aspects of your identity have been more at the front of your mind.
• How do these different elements intersect? For example, is your experience of being the gender you are impacted by your religion, cultural background or generation? Is your experience of your sexuality impacted by your age, gender or class?

Focusing on race and ethnicity poses a risk that other aspects of identity become overshadowed or even overlooked. A woman of a BAME background may be a member of a sexual minority. This latter aspect of identity could be more to the fore for her, possibly as a result of the kind of discrimination she faces. Often discrimination stems from the combination of different aspects of identity. For example, the discrimination faced by a Black bisexual woman will be different from that experienced by a White gay man. The study of intersectionality (a term coined by Kimberlie Crenshaw, 1994) is concerned with understanding the nature of multiple aspects of identity and discrimination (Walby, Armstrong & Strid, 2012). In counselling it is vital for a psychologist to be mindful that someone may bring up experiences that relate to discrimination in relation to hitherto unexplored aspects of identity, and that different aspects of identity and experience interact and intersect.

Conclusion

We have seen in this chapter that BAME people face inequality and discrimination in virtually all aspects of social, economic and political life. This includes their experiences within the criminal justice system, within mental health, and within the sub-speciality of forensic mental health.

Professions in all of these areas need to incorporate into their work an awareness of the particular context of people's lives. Counsellors must take steps to detect their unconscious biases and engage in activities to challenge their own prejudices.

Suggestions for further reading

Fernando, S. (2010). *Mental health, race and culture* (3rd ed.). London: Palgrave Macmillan.
Updated twice since its first publication in 1991, this text provides helpful definitions of terminology relating to ethnicity, race and culture. It explores the negative impact on mental health of BAME groups and their experience in services as a result of both cultural differences and racism enshrined in psychiatry.

Phillips, C. & Webster, C. (Eds.) (2014). *New directions in race, ethnicity and crime*. Abingdon: Routledge.
Provides information on racial inequalities in the criminal justice system as well as a good critique of the factors that lead to disparities. Provides insight into issues of inequality and the criminal justice system facing a range of ethnic groups.

6

GENDER

JANE E.M. CALLAGHAN AND JOANNE H. ALEXANDER

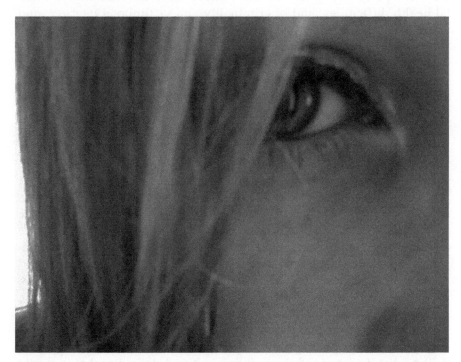

Image 6 Do you see me? With permission, Rebecca Jackson

Introduction

Does gender *matter* when we are working with those society designates as 'the mad' and 'the bad'? This chapter explores the importance of gender in understanding and intervening as mental health professionals, working in criminal justice contexts. To do this, we will explore how gender intersects with mental health, and how it intersects with criminality. In other words, we will think about how being a man or a woman (or being cis or transgender, or non-binary) might shape involvement in criminality, and whether gender, and our perceptions of masculinity and femininity might play a role in reporting patterns, and the way that we see victims and perpetrators. We will also consider the role gender plays in mental health, considering why men or women might be over-represented in particular mental health diagnoses, and how the mental health of men and women is 'read' differently. Finally, we will explore how gendered experiences and understandings of mental health difficulties, and of criminality and victimhood *intersect*, and what the implications of this might be when counselling men and women in forensic mental health settings.

But what is gender? While *sex* refers to the biological qualities of being male or female (e.g. our external genitalia, having breasts, amount of body hair, etc.), gender 'refers to our culturally and socially constituted experiences and attitudes associated with "masculinity", "femininity" or non-binary gender identities' (American Psychiatric Association, 2012, p. 11). In other words, gender is not so much about the bodies we inhabit, our chromosomes or our hormones, and more about our identity, and how we understand (and act on) culturally what it means to be a man or a woman, masculine or feminine. Gender is often understood as a binary construction – you are either masculine or feminine, one thing or the other. However, in recent years, this dichotomous understanding of gender has been increasingly challenged, as we have begun to recognise that gender is more complex and multifaceted than this simplistic binary model allows (Barker & Richards, 2015). This has enabled an acknowledgement, for instance, of transgender and non-binary gender identities.

Like gender, ideas about deviance and normalcy are constituted as a binary, and they are mutually dependent categories. It is difficult to define what it means to be masculine, without defining what it means to be feminine. Similarly, it is difficult to define 'normal' without a concept of 'deviance'. 'Deviance' and 'normality' are socially agreed concepts – taken-for-granted, common-sense ideas that function to draw boundaries around our sense of what is acceptable and what is not, what is the norm and what is 'other'. Complex classification systems were set up that categorise, 'diagnose' and medicalise experiences of distress (Bentall, 2004). These increasingly sophisticated labelling practices intersect with legal practices (like the Mental Health Act in the UK) to position those with mental health difficulties as different, deviant and in need of control – through medication (Bentall, 2004), through processes like sectioning (Buckland, 2016) and confinement (Foucault, 1977).

If we see a person as a member of a group (man or woman; mentally 'ill' or 'normal'), we tend to stop seeing them as individuals, judging them instead by our perception of the group. Stereotyped representations draw on fixed ideas about gender (e.g. women are emotional, nurturing, men are aggressive, rational) and of normality (e.g. handwashing is 'normal', but handwashing 30 times a day is 'abnormal'), and have the power to change the way we see people. Stereotypes emphasise homogeneity, rather than diversity, as we tend to see individuals as a 'type' or category of person – as representatives of a particular group.

Representations of gender and criminality

There appears to be a strong relationship between gender and criminality. Men are reported to commit more crime than women (Heimer, Lauritsen & Lynch, 2009). In the UK, 85% of arrests are of men, men account for 75% of criminal sentences, and 95% of the prison population (Ministry of Justice, 2014). How might we make sense of this gendered pattern of criminality? The 'common-sense' explanation of the apparent link between gender and offending behaviour suggested that this was a consequence of biological sex. This kind of account would suggest that male biology makes men more vulnerable to involvement in crime. For example, it has been suggested that men are more frequently involved in violent crime than women, because their higher testosterone levels predispose them to aggression. Reviewing literature on the relationship between testosterone and aggression, Batrinos (2012) notes that testosterone activates the amygdala, the brain structure associated with emotional regulation, and that in this way it raises emotional reactivity and impulsivity, making an aggressive outburst more likely.

While testosterone and other aspects of male biology may explain some of the gendered patterning observed in offending behaviour, it is not a sufficient explanation for all differences. For instance, the gap between men's and women's offending is narrowing (Kruttschnitt, 2013). This suggests that we must also consider the role of the cultural construction of masculinity and femininity in producing the gap. Kruttschnitt suggests that the narrowing of the gap is not attributable to an actual change in male and female offending behaviour, but rather that it is a consequence of changes in sentencing practices. Women are more likely to be prosecuted for particular crimes than they were previously.

The ideology of gender naturalises criminality (and particularly violent criminality) for men. Men who commit crime are seen as simply living up to culturally agreed concepts of masculinity – aggression, impulsivity, competitiveness, etc. (Mcfarlane, 2013). Men are seen as more 'dangerous' and more of a social threat than women. For instance, consider why it might be that men account for 75% of criminal sentences, but that they make up 95% of the prison population. How do we make sense of that disparity between sentencing rates and the form of punishment given? And how does this naturalisation of crime as 'masculine' sit with the reality that men are *also* the most common victims of crime (Office for National Statistics, 2014)?

Women who offend are often understood with reference to either deviant femininity or mental illness. Female violence in particular is typically described in media representations as the action of 'deviant' women – women who are either unwell or are evil (Evans, 2012). Even in extreme cases of women who have been abused by partners over a long period of time, and then ended that abuse by killing their partners, violence is not represented as a *reasonable* or *natural* choice for women, rather it is positioned as always either unnatural and deviant or as a product of mental illness. For example, Noh, Lee and Feltey (2010), in a study of newspaper accounts of women who killed abusive husbands, 'found that leading explanations for why battered women kill medicalised then criminalised their actions; they were mad then bad' (p. 110).

Case example: The Moors Murders

Between July 1963 and October 1965, Ian Brady and Myra Hindley murdered five children, aged 10–17, after having sexually assaulted at least four of them. Hindley and Brady buried their victims in shallow graves on Saddleworth Moor.

In most of the cases, Brady asked Hindley to make first contact with the potential child victim, for instance offering them a lift in her van. Brady and Hindley had different accounts of the murders – with Hindley claiming that Brady committed most of the murders out of her sight, while Brady suggested she was present, and in some cases was actively involved in the murders.

Throughout the trial, Myra Hindley was often referred to in the press as 'the most hated woman in Britain'. Even today, in 2016, a google search for 'Hindley' and 'most evil woman' returns thousands of hits. In contrast, a search for 'Brady' and 'most evil man' returns none.

Hindley appealed against her life sentence several times, describing herself as reformed, and no longer a danger to society. The *Daily Mail* (Williams, 2013) quoted her as saying 'although by the end I had become as corrupt as Ian was, there is a distinction ... I did not instigate ... but I knew the difference between right and wrong. ... I didn't have a compulsion to kill ... I wasn't in charge ... but in some ways I was more culpable because I knew better.' The article goes on to note: 'She even spoke of her "love" for children and desire to work with old people if she was ever released. ... [She] was "extremely tearful" as she stated "I've affected so many people".'

In contrast, Brady has campaigned for his right to die. Consider this extract from a newspaper report on his appearance at a mental health tribunal in 2013:

> Moors murderer Ian Brady denied he was insane as he recalled cooking steaks with Ronnie Kray whilst mingling with some of Britain's most notorious criminals during his half century of incarceration. In an extraordinary four-hour display which veered between vaunting self-aggrandisement and breath-taking callousness towards his victims and their relatives who were watching via video-link, the child killer failed to express any remorse for his crimes. ... Brady repeatedly stonewalled at suggestions he had a personality disorder or that his five murders were evidence that he was 'abnormal'.

- What role do you think gender and mental health play in the crime, in media descriptions of the crime, and in the descriptions of Hindley and Brady?

Gender and mental health

In this section we will consider how gender and mental health intersect, paying attention to the role of stereotypes, stigma and gender norms in perceptions and experiences of mental health. Mental health is still highly stigmatised (Gale, 2007; Hinshaw, 2006), but some mental health conditions (like schizophrenia and personality disorder) are more stigmatised than others (like depression) (Bentall, 2004). Mental health labels and the associated stigma can mean that people who have mental health issues and who offend may be seen differently from offenders who are seen as having 'normal' mental health functioning. This does not just have consequences for how we see people, though – it also impacts how people feel about and see themselves, and how they are treated by others (Ringer & Holen, 2015; Smith & Tucker, 2015).

Like offending, there are also gender patterns in the experience of psychological distress and mental health difficulty, and the way that mental health is seen socially, and how it is stigmatised. This can be seen, for instance, in the way that depression is both expressed and detected in gendered ways. Women are more likely to be diagnosed and treated for depression than men (Mental Health Foundation, 2015). Some research has pointed to women's apparent biological vulnerability to depression, suggesting that their varying hormonal patterns (as a consequence of menstruation, childbirth and menopause) is linked to mood variation that might underpin depression (e.g. see Altemus, Sarvaiya & Neill Epperson, 2014). However, it is important to note too that there may be cultural factors at play. For instance, balancing social expectations around childcare, domestic and paid work can be very stressful, while appearance pressure for women can also place a strain on women's self-esteem (Nolen-Hoeksema, 2001). However, Kendler and Gardner (2014) suggest that it might be more useful to focus on gendered pathways and risks of experiencing major depression, rather than sex differences in rates of depression. They found that experiences of childhood sexual abuse, early anti-social behaviour and drug abuse, and stressful life events (financial, occupational and legal) had a stronger impact in terms of men's risk of depression, while experiences of parental warmth/coldness, divorce, level of social support and extent of marital satisfaction had a stronger impact on women's risk. This suggests that men's and women's differential life experiences and pressures may have considerable influence. Further, doctors are more likely to diagnose and treat depression in women than in men, even when they present with identical symptoms (WHO, 2000), while men are more likely to receive support for substance misuse (Annsseau et al., 2008).

Another example of gender-based variation in mental health diagnoses is in the area of personality disorder. While narcissistic and borderline personality are assumed to have common histories (most typically associated with abusive and neglectful care in childhood), their expression and rate of diagnosis are highly gendered, with men being far more likely to be diagnosed as 'narcissistic' and women as 'borderline' (American Psychiatric Association, 2013). Women diagnosed with borderline personality are often highly stigmatised, as 'vulnerable', 'mad', 'unpredictable', 'irrational' and 'overly emotional' (Reavey & Warner, 2006). Looking at the rates of hospitalisation and institutionalisation for men and women, the 'borderline' diagnosis is one of the most frequent reasons that women are treated in inpatient units. Because the symptomatology of personality disorder could equally be interpreted as the effects of particular types of trauma, Reavey and Warner (2006) suggest that borderline personality disorder as a label functions as a warrant to institutionalise and further victimise female victims of child abuse and sexual violence.

When looking at incidence of psychosis, a gendered pattern is also in evidence. The incidence of psychosis is higher in men than women (Aleman, Kahn & Selten, 2003), and the pattern of symptoms is different, with men more likely to experience incongruous or absent mood, very low motivation, reduced speech, and women more likely to experience hallucinations and delusions, and confusion. Men are more likely to have comorbid substance abuse than women, and women have better recovery rates and are less likely to experience relapse. These variations suggest that some of the 'content' of our psychological distress is shaped by cultural expectations of gender – for example, that men 'act out' more and express their distress in overt behaviours, like aggression, alcohol use, etc., but that women *internalise* their problems (Rice et al., 2015).

Gender, mental health and 'victimhood' in the criminal justice system

In providing support for victims of crime, it is important to always take into account the role that gender might play in their lived experience. For instance, victims of house breaking may find that their traditional gender roles – as protector or as home maker – introduce specific challenges in recovery from the crime. While in this section, we will predominantly focus on women as victims of gender-based violence, it is important to note that men are the most typical victims of reported crime, and that young and black men are particularly over-represented among victims (Newburn & Stanko, 2013).

Gender does take on a particular significance in addressing the needs of victims of gender-based violence, like rape and sexual assault, domestic violence (or intimate partner violence) and child sexual abuse (see Chapter 9 on 'Sexual Assault and Abuse'). For example, women victims of these kinds of crimes are often subject to expectations about how they should behave as victims. In court cases, their credibility is evaluated against their performance of what is socially agreed to be the acceptable behaviour of 'good' victims, which typically means that they should conform to socially accepted notions of femininity (Anderson & Doherty, 2007). For example, consider the recent case in the US of the rapist Brock Turner. The attorneys in this case portrayed the victim as a 'party girl', placing an emphasis on her behaviours (e.g. drinking and dancing) prior to the attack. In this sense, she violated dominant ideas of appropriate feminine behaviour. Both the judge and the attorney were more concerned about the impact of the rape on the rapist, and he was awarded a lenient sentence based on concern about his blighted future. There was an emphasis on his privileged social position, as a college student and sportsman from a 'good family', and on her prior sexual availability and drunkenness. In this sense, he is represented as a socially appropriate man, whose behaviour is understood as an error of judgement, and an extension of his natural masculinity, rather than a serious crime. In contrast, she is effectively balanced for the incident, because of her supposed violation of the ideals of 'good femininity'.

The intersections of gender and good victimhood can be complex for women victims. For instance, to be a credible 'good victim', a woman must fight back, enough to show her resistance, but eventually must be 'overpowered'. To be 'feminine' and a victim means resisting enough, but not violating constraining notions of good feminine embodiment, with its associations of weakness and physical incompetence (Anderson & Doherty, 2007; Callaghan & Clark, 2007). Male survivors of sexual violence, domestic violence, child sexual abuse and sexual exploitation face a different, but equally gendered, set of challenges. They often find it difficult to have their voices heard. For instance, in a study of how lay people understood male sexual abuse victimisation, Esnard and Dumas (2013) found that participants drew on stereotypes that male children are more able to defend themselves, and that boys are sexually proactive. Consequently, boys were more likely to be blamed for their own victimisation.

In domestic violence, gender has historically been understood to shape the dynamics of abusive relationships (Dobash & Dobash, 1992). Feminist models of domestic violence suggest that domestic violence is not just about physical violence, but is part of a broader pattern of coercive control, abuse and harassment of women; it is one instance of a broader pattern of gender oppression of women. In contrast, proponents of a family violence model of domestic violence (e.g. Straus, 2012) argue that men are almost as likely to be victims of domestic violence as women, and that domestic violence is therefore not best understood as 'gender based', but rather needs to be understood as a product of dysfunctional styles of relating. This approach suggests that domestic violence is part of a broader pattern of interpersonal hostility and aggression that is related to familial difficulties, not to gender oppression.

One claim that has received a lot of publicity in recent years is the idea that men and women are equally violent in intimate relationships. Is this true? The answer to this question is not simple. Johnson (2005, 2006) suggests that men and women are roughly equally involved in the kind of aggression that is associated with 'fights' in intimate relationships (e.g. hitting or pushing a partner in the heat of the moment in an argument, as an isolated incident). Some relationships are high conflict, characterised by mutual aggression, and in these kinds of relationships there is also gender symmetry. However, Johnson suggests that some relationships are characterised by 'intimate terrorism' – coercive behaviour, ongoing emotional and psychological abuse, and violence. In these kinds of relationships, men are far more typically abusers, and women are more commonly the victims.

Regardless of the gender of the perpetrator and victim, it is important to work with clients in a way that honours the gendered nature of their experiences. Gender plays a role in the experience of violence in intimate relationships. Consider the following extracts from interviews with people who have experienced domestic violence – the first from an interview with a male perpetrator, the second narrating the experiences of a male victim:

> 'She was a slut, never allowing me to come close to her unless she wanted something for herself or for the kids, all a man needs from his wife is a smile, some good gentle words ... she is tough, she never gives a thing.' (Borochowitz, 2008, p. 1177)

> 'She now has him in the corner and is scratching his head on both sides with her nails. "Playful tickling" she calls it. It stings, oh how it stings. His anger with this treatment makes him feel physically sick. She insists that she is not hurting him: this is only affection. Affection that leads to a number of scratches on his face.' (Allen-Collinson, 2009, p. 29)

In both cases, ideas of masculinity and femininity play a role in the way that the violence is implemented and understood. Male victims of domestic violence must still wrestle with complex issues relating to masculinities and femininities. Gender does not disappear from relationships of power and abuse when the violence involves a female perpetrator. Winstok and Straus (2014) suggest that when there is a gap between gender roles and expectations in relationships and individuals' perception of their current relationships, this sets up conditions for stress and depression, and that this mediates depressive responses to relational violence for male and female victims. They suggest that male victims experience higher levels of depression, because in addition to the impact of the violence itself, their violent female partners violate gender role expectations and their sense of what is desirable in an intimate relationship.

Gender also remains a factor in the experience of violence in same-sex relationships (McClennen, 2005). For instance, gender impacts on perceptions of domestic violence in same-sex couples, and stereotypes impact the way people are viewed and supported, with women victims being less likely to be believed, but male victims experiencing high levels of victim blaming and challenges around why they did not resist or fight back (Wasarhaley et al., 2015). Stereotypes about men being more likely to be perpetrators, and also about the roles of masculinity and femininity in same-sex couples influence the likelihood of being seen as either victim or perpetrator (Seelau & Seelau, 2005), and shape the form and experience of the violence itself (Waldner-Haugrud, Gratch & Magruder, 1997).

Activity 6.1

Sam and Robin were married for 10 years – a marriage that was character-ised by a lot of volatility. Robin had repeated extra-marital affairs, but jealously guarded Sam's time, controlling their access to friends and family. While Robin was not routinely violent, when Sam did not do as they wanted, Robin would explode with rage, breaking furniture, punching, hitting and kicking. Sam would conform to what Robin wanted to keep the peace. When they separated, two years ago, Robin sent a deluge of emails, text mes-sages and phone messages, begging Sam to return, threatening to hurt themselves. At the same time, Sam would carefully watch Robin's social media accounts, monitoring them for emotional tone, and occasionally sending jealous messages if they noticed that Robin seemed interested in a new potential partner.

   Six months ago, Robin allegedly broke into Sam's flat. Sam claims that Robin sexually assaulted them. Sam then stabbed Robin, apparently in self-defence. Robin denies this, claiming that Sam invited them over to discuss Robin's new partner, and that Sam stabbed them in a fit of jealousy.

* What are your own reactions to the report? What thoughts and feelings did you have as your read about this case?
* How would you attribute 'blame' in the interaction?
* What gender do you think Robin and Sam are? Why?
* Flip the gender (or assign gender if you did not on first reading). Does this change the way that you read the case?
* Did the case challenge some of your taken-for-granted assumptions about violence and victimhood? Did gender play a role in your reactions?

Trans individuals, criminality, victimhood and mental health

So far in the chapter, we have considered gender in relation to domi-nant binary constructions of masculinity and femininity. It is also useful to think about gender, mental health and ideas about criminal-ity in relation to transgender or non-binary gender individuals. Transgender individuals are people whose gender identity is different from that which they are assigned at birth, while non-binary gender refers to a sense of gender identity that is not fixed as either mascu-line or feminine. In this section, we will focus particularly on trans issues, and explore how transgender people are considered in rep-resentations of both mental illness and crime and 'deviance', and what the implications of this are for counselling in a gender-sensitive way in forensic contexts.

Historically, trans men and trans women have been subject to erasure, hidden under mislabels like 'drag queens' or 'transvestites' (Namaste, 2000). However, in the past decade, there has been far more visibility for transgender individuals, often seen as facilitated by the emergence of supportive online communities and activism (Fink & Miller, 2013). As transgender identities have become increasingly culturally recognised in the West, new debates have emerged that reposition trans identities as a site of legal contention. For example, debates have emerged around the rights of women to be recognised as women, and particularly to have access to women-only spaces (Tosh, 2016). A particularly visible public debate has focused on a moral panic around the access of trans women to women's toilet facilities. There have also been debates about whether trans women should have access to women-only services for victims of crime (like domestic violence shelters, rape crisis services, etc.), and whether trans women who are convicted of crime should be housed in women's prisons. Those who have undergone or are undergoing 'gender reassignment' are protected under the Equality Act 2010, but this legal protection does not yet extend to individuals who are gender neutral, non-binary or gender-queer, and who consequently do not desire gender alignment. Trans women who have transitioned (or are transitioning) have the right to be recognised as women, and have a legal right to access the same services and facilities as other women. However, some radical feminists have refused to acknowledge trans women as women, and have argued that such laws further privilege the needs of 'men' over the needs of vulnerable women (Jeffreys, 2014a). This debate has had significant implications for trans individuals in forensic contexts, where, for instance, trans women who have not legally started the process of transitioning, but who have lived as trans women for some time, have nonetheless been denied access to women-only prisons, resulting in risks to both physical and emotional health (Lees, 2016). As mental health practitioners working in forensic settings, it is important to consider and respond to these issues, and to understand how mental health, gender and being an offender or a victim intersect.

Gender-sensitive approaches to working with offenders – two case studies

Working with mental health and offending behaviour, we should always be sensitive to the interface of these issues with gender and inequality. We present two case studies to illustrate the importance of understanding this interface. The first is an individual case study, focused on one woman's experience of violence, criminality and mental health. The second is an example of a gender-sensitive approach to working with mental health and offending.

Case example: Beth

Beth is 26 years old, and has been in and out of the criminal justice system since she was 13, when she was sent to a Young Offender Institute (YOI) following an incident of TWOCKING (stealing a car). She describes her father as 'a professional car thief', and seems quite proud of him, joking about his prowess and his ability to steal 'anything on wheels'. Her stepfather was addicted to alcohol, and he abused her sexually and physically, from the time he moved in with her mother when she was eight, until a year after her first detention. She feels her mother knew about this abuse, but did not act because she was infatuated with her stepfather. In the YOI, Beth was subject to significant bullying, and soon after leaving she became involved in a coercive relationship. At 16 she gave birth to her first of three children. Having worked for several years as a sex worker, Beth was arrested several times, and eventually was detained under the Mental Health Act, after she was picked up behaving in a way that was endangering herself and others, in a local shopping mall. She is currently being held in a secure mental health ward. She is very seductive in her interactions with staff and with fellow patients, and has been framed as a management problem by staff because of her promiscuous behaviour. She has terrible nightmares, and disturbs others on the ward, waking up screaming. She is reluctant to eat, and alternates between being quite aggressive with others and seeming both vulnerable and frightened.

- What are your initial reactions to this case?
- As a counsellor in this context, what would you see as the main work that needs to be done?
- What questions would you want to ask before starting to work with her?
- Consider whether gender stereotypes might play a role in how you are making sense of the case study.
- How would you take gender issues into account in working with Beth?

It is quite common that girls who become criminalised have histories of violence and trauma. In Beth's case, repeated experiences of gender-based violence is an obvious component of her criminal involvement. In addition, sexualisation is one possible response to histories of violence and trauma. When hospitalised as a result of her mental health vulnerabilities, her sexual acting out is reframed a 'behavioural problem' to be managed. For women survivors of gender-based violence, this kind of experience is often highly problematised, perhaps because of cultural stereotypes that 'nice girls' should be monogamous (Hollway, 1984) and 'slut shaming' is common (Armstrong et al., 2014), and can be a source of both conflict and shame. However, as a counsellor it is important to locate this 'problem' both in her history of violence and trauma and in relation to dominant stereotypes about female sexuality.

Case example: The Good Loaf Bakery

The Good Loaf Bakery is one of a number of community-based interventions and projects aimed at supporting and rehabilitating offenders in Northamptonshire. This not-for-profit social business works specifically with women who have been involved with criminal justice, women deemed vulnerable and economically disadvantaged who have offended or are at risk of doing so. The project recognises that women who offend are often disadvantaged in multiple ways, economically, materially, and having complex personal histories and subject to broader social inequalities that trap them in cycles of poverty. Support takes a multi-layered and holistic approach, and provides opportunities that reduce recidivism and improve women's immediate and future employment prospects, and their mental health.

   Note that, while The Good Loaf has a therapeutic and rehabilitative intention, this is achieved through an active model of work and community that enables participants to develop confidence in themselves and trust in others.

The two case examples offer important insights into the way that histories of violence, disadvantage, mental health challenge and gender intersect to produce increasingly complex patterns of both offending and of mental health difficulty.

Conclusion

In this chapter, we have explored the importance of gender in our understanding of mental health, offending and victimisation. Gender plays a role in mental health issues that individuals present with, crimes people become involved with, and the way that mental health, criminality and victim status are represented and treated. Gender also intersects with culture and race in experiences of mental health and of offending. When doing counselling work in forensic settings, it is therefore vital that we take into account the role of gender and practise in gender-sensitive ways.

Suggestions for further reading

Renzetti, C. M., Miller, S. L., & Gover, A. L. (2013). *Routledge international handbook of crime and gender studies*. London: Routledge.
This book offers an authoritative overview of the intersections of gender and crime.

Davies, P. (2010). *Gender, crime and victimisation*. London: Sage.
This book provides an overview of current literature on gender and crime, with a strong focus on victimisation.

7
AGE

EMILY GLORNEY

Image 7 Tearful. With permission, Sarah Shipley

Introduction

Social and personal experiences throughout the lifespan influence how we think about ourselves in the context of other people (e.g. Young, Klosko & Weishaar, 2003). Ideas about the development of a fundamental sense of self developed during early adulthood are important to keep in mind when considering arguments around the labels of 'mad or bad?'. For example, to what extent might we expect movement towards or away from a criminal identity throughout the lifespan? At what points in our lives might we be more or less vulnerable to problems with our mental health that might influence our identity? How might others' perceptions of us influence how we think about ourselves and shape our behaviour at varying points throughout the lifespan? The first question raises issues around whether people are more or less likely to engage in offending behaviour at differing ages and the extent to which we might expect good outcomes in efforts to reduce risk of reoffending at different points in the lifespan. The second question raises issues around age-related vulnerabilities to mental health problems and the impact that the emergence of these might have on behaviour and self-concept. The third question raises issues around social expectations on age-related behaviour and the consequences of operating within or without such constructs. It is these issues that are discussed throughout this chapter.

Activity 7.1

Read the following cases and think about the role of age. What sort of age do you think each person might be and how do you think that age might have influenced their circumstances?

Joanna is struggling to manage her feelings of low mood. She is not going out much and no longer talks to people. She is not eating or sleeping properly and she has started to think that life is not worth living.

John has recently served a custodial sentence for a sexual offence. He engaged well in treatment and his supervision team assessed him as being at low risk of committing another sexual offence, although he will continue to be monitored in the community.

Representation of age groups in popular culture and the media

Debates about childhood in the context of innocence or malevolence have continued for centuries, with the dominant Western cultural narrative for the past 100 years or so being one of children as innocent (Valentine, 1996). Investment in the protection of the innocence of childhood is evident in debates around television programming and film and game classifications, as well as restrictions on internet usage. Cultural concepts of childhood innocence were challenged when, in 1993, two ten-year-old boys killed a two-year-old boy, Jamie Bulger. The perpetrators were portrayed in the media as monstrous and, indeed, were the subject of a Niklas Rådström play entitled *Monsters* in 2009. The actions of the boys who killed Jamie Bulger were so beyond the social expectations of the behaviour of children that a collective irrational belief set took hold and was perpetuated through the media. The unthinkable actions of Jamie Bulger's killers were not at all in line with the idealised notions of childhood prevalent at the time. By way of reconciling the idealised with the real, the two boys were jettisoned from childhood and portrayed as evil. As a result, the media reflected a panic about the poor moral health of society (Jewkes, 2015) and there were calls for tougher legal action to be taken against children and young people who committed offences (Valentine, 1996). These narratives bore a strong influence on public perceptions of children and young people and contributed to ideas around one's own children as being innocent and other children as being demons (Valentine, 1996).

As with the notion of childhood, dichotomies exist within that of adulthood. Children rely on adults for the meeting of basic needs such as love and safety and their learning of the navigation of the social world; adults are responsible, wise and safe. Children experience contrasting messages about the concept of adulthood through stranger danger campaigns (e.g. 'Charley Says' in the 1970s and 1980s; the Child Exploitation and Online Protection Centre's Thinkuknow campaign for online safety since 2003) and rehearse messages that children should not talk to or go along with strangers because there is an inherent danger in adulthood. These campaigns originate from a position of perceiving children as vulnerable to exploitation by other people, typically adults. However, across all ages, many offences involve someone known to the victim (e.g. Home Office, 2010a; Ministry of Justice, 2013) but a sense of vulnerability to strangers persists alongside a fundamental need to feel safe.

The media stereotypes older adults as being vulnerable. For example, television and film characters might represent a grumpy old man, a sweet old lady, or a lonely, weak and vulnerable person. In such portrayals, the characters typically embody physical and cognitive ineptitude and low social status, consistent with social constructions of older adulthood (Cuddy & Fiske, 2004). Media reports of crimes against older adults often emphasise vulnerability and provoke a sense of pity in the reader. Whatever your media preference, there are sure to be examples that come to mind when thinking about stereotypes of people across different ages.

Age-related vulnerabilities to developing mental health problems

Late childhood and adolescence are thought to be critical risk periods for the development and emergence of difficulties with impulse control and anxiety (Kessler et al., 2007). Adversity or difficulties across multiple life domains can contribute to the emergence of a mental health problem. For example, children and young people with a diagnosis of conduct disorder are more likely than their non-diagnosed counterparts to: be boys aged 11–16; live in a large family with poor functioning, have parents with mental health difficulties, police contact, no educational qualifications, be raised in a low-income family and have one or both parents unemployed; be living in social rented sector accommodation; have poorer general and physical health and additional mental health problems such as emotional or anxiety disorders; have difficulties with basic educational attainment such as reading and writing, special educational needs, disruptions to schooling such as long periods of absence, expulsions and changes of schools; have difficulties in the negotiation of social relationships; be lacking in social and personal support; be tobacco, alcohol and drug users; be likely to self-harm or try to kill themselves (Office for National Statistics, 2005). Considerations for assessment, formulation and treatment are offered later in this chapter.

The period between late adolescence and 25 years of age is thought to be critical for the emergence of schizophrenia and substance use disorders (e.g. Jones, 2013). Mental health must be a key consideration in the assessment and treatment of adolescents and young adults because stress and associated difficulties with coping (for example, being in contact with the criminal justice system or being in prison) might trigger existing vulnerabilities into the emergence of mental health problems.

Between early adulthood and up to the mid-50s, the most common mental health problems tend to be related to depression and anxiety for both men and women (McManus et al., 2009; refer to Chapter 6 for a more detailed discussion on gender and mental health). The highest rates of suicidality and self-harming behaviours also occur during this age period (McManus et al., 2009). The role of socio-demographic factors is evident here and demonstrates the dynamic nature of mental health across the lifespan. For example, relationship status influenced rates of mental health problems, suicidality and self-harm for both men and women (McManus et al., 2009). The influence of the environment and our sense of self and identity as we age is also evident among the mental health of older adults. For example, as we experience increasing numbers of bereavements and physical health problems there is a risk of reduced social interaction and increased loneliness, which relates to poor physical and mental health (e.g. Holwerda et al., 2016). Consideration of problems related to cognitive decline (e.g. difficulties with problem solving) and degenerative brain disease (e.g. dementia) might also be important in the context of assessment and formulation of older adults in counselling and forensic practice.

Case example: Age and cognitive decline

In 2015, Greville Ewan Janner, The Lord Janner of Braunstone QC and former Labour MP, was charged with multiple counts of sexual assault perpetrated against boys spanning decades. At the time when Lord Janner faced court proceedings he was in the advanced stages of Alzheimer's, a form of degenerative brain disease that affects cognitive processes. As a consequence of his mental disorder, the court ruled that Lord Janner would not be able to participate meaningfully in the trial because he would be unable to understand and follow trial proceedings, which is one of the legal requirements for being mentally fit to take part in a trial. When an accused person is found unfit to plead, then a trial of the facts to determine the truth of the allegations can take place. Lord Janner died in December 2015 before the trial of the facts took place (source: Henriques, 2016).

- Can you think of other issues or problems among people of different ages that might have an impact on someone's ability to take part meaningfully in a court trial?

Age and the legal and criminal justice system

Criminal law in England and Wales states that children under the age of ten years have not reached a point in cognitive and moral development to know what is right and wrong (*mens rea*) and, therefore, children under the age of ten years cannot be tried for a criminal offence. You might be wondering how a child could not have criminal responsibility on the day before their tenth birthday but are deemed to have the capacity to hold criminal responsibility the following day? This is a good question, related to individual differences, and one that has attracted international debate (for an example in the UK, you could read about the case of the murder of Jamie Bulger and the legal debates during and after the trial). There are variations in how different jurisdictions manage children and young people who engage in harmful behaviour and the age of criminal responsibility varies from six years (e.g. North Carolina, USA) to 18 years (e.g. Brazil). It is likely that the differences in the ages of criminal responsibility are influenced by how people in different societies and cultures think about children and young people. For example, in Scandinavian countries – where the age of criminal responsibility is 15 years – problematic behaviour in childhood and early adolescence is conceptualised as part of the developmental process and structural responses include care and support in the community to address behaviour rather than labelling as 'bad' and effecting social exclusion through imprisonment.

In 1998, the UK government introduced Anti-Social Behaviour Orders (ASBOs) as a means of tackling low-level behaviour that was problematic for communities but which would be unlikely to receive a criminal prosecution. Examples of such behaviour include rowdy or noisy behaviour in otherwise quiet neighbourhoods, loitering, spitting, swearing, graffiti, and dealing or buying drugs on the street, and people given an ASBO might be subject to restrictions on movement in place and time and enhanced surveillance. Breach of an ASBO was a criminal offence and attracted penalties ranging from a fine to a custodial sentence. ASBOs could be applied for two years to anyone ten years of age and above and were controversial (they were replaced with a civil offence in 2014). For example, there were debates around whether ASBOs were creating further tensions in society by emphasising the divide between people engaging in nuisance behaviour and people engaging in conforming behaviour (e.g. Squires, 2008). There were also debates about the extent to which young people were being criminalised for behaviour that otherwise might be conceptualised as part of the emergence of, or transition to, adulthood (e.g. Arnett, 2007; Brown, 2011).

Pause for reflection

How much emphasis do you think should be placed on someone's age when deciding whether behaviour is appropriate or anti-social? For example, if someone were loitering in a park would it feel differently to you if someone were a child, an adolescent, in their 20s, in their 50s, or an older adult? Might you respond differently to someone's behaviour, depending on their age?

From the perspective of labelling theory (see Chapter 3), when young people were given an ASBO they were labelled as anti-social, they were responded to by systems (e.g. the police) and society as being anti-social and, in turn, the young person's self-concept aligned with the structural responses to them and they then behaved in ways that were consistent with their revised self-concept, i.e. anti-social and criminal behaviour. It might be that you could account for the ASBO statistics with reference to labelling theory. For example, in the period between April 1999 and December 2013 the majority of ASBOs were accounted for by adult men, but with a disproportionately high number at 36% being applied to young people aged 10–17 years (Home Office and Ministry of Justice, 2014), relative to the population of around 10.5% (Youth Justice Board and Ministry of Justice, 2015).

Furthermore, young people aged 15–17 years were one of the age groups most likely to breach an ASBO (Home Office and Ministry of Justice, 2014). This indicates that young people in mid-late adolescence in particular were vulnerable to criminalisation and possibly received criminal convictions as a consequence of a panic about the poor moral health of society at the point of introduction of the ASBOs (you will recall that this was six years after the murder of Jamie Bulger) rather than because of an inherent badness about young people.

Debates around the use of ASBOs influenced practice and, after the peak in 2005, there was a year-on-year decrease in the number of ASBOs applied until they were replaced in 2014 (Home Office and Ministry of Justice, 2014). At the same time, there was also a decrease in the numbers of young people (aged 10–17 years) having contact with or entering the criminal justice system (Youth Justice Board and Ministry of Justice, 2015). For example, in 2009/10 young people accounted for about 23% of all police recorded crime (Cooper & Roe, 2012) whereas in 2012/13 this figure fell to 11.8% (Youth Justice Board and Ministry of Justice, 2015).

The reduction in the prevalence of police recorded crime by young people probably reflects changes in police practice (e.g. a shift in emphasis on targets) as well as a focus on the needs of young people in the criminal justice system and as addressed through the Youth Justice Board. However, young people continue to be over-represented in the criminal justice system and reoffending rates by young people (36.1% in 2012/13) are higher than for adults aged 21 and over (24.2%) (Youth Justice Board and Ministry of Justice, 2015). This suggests that there is still work to be done to prevent young people getting involved in crime and supporting young people in moving away from crime.

Crime statistics in England and Wales are collated as relevant to the criminal justice system and differing age-related practices in sentencing and disposal; for example, 10–17 years, 18–20 years, and 21 years and above. As such, there is very limited age-related information about adult perpetrators of police recorded crime. However, the Office for National Statistics' annual Crime Survey England and Wales (which interviews a sample of the population of England and Wales on their experience of crime) provides some insight into the relevance of age in crime victimisation. You will recall the media stereotypes of older adults as being vulnerable to victimisation and harm. However, the chance of being a victim is generally thought to decrease with age. For example, around 0.2% of people aged 75 and over were thought to have been a victim of a violent offence in 2011/12, in comparison to 8.4% of young people aged 16–24 years (the age group most likely to experience violence victimisation) (Office for National Statistics, 2013). Of course, it might be that some younger people have more exposure than older adults to situations where they might encounter violence (e.g. such as with people using drugs and alcohol, which can increase risk of violence). Nonetheless, the portrayal of older adults being vulnerable to crime is not fully supported by crime victimisation data.

Age is a relevant consideration not just in terms of vulnerability to commit offences or experience victimisation but also in terms of reducing and assessing the risk of reoffending by people leaving custody. In line with a reduction in young people entering the criminal justice system, the numbers of young people in prisons has been steadily decreasing since a peak in 2009 (Youth Justice Board and Ministry of Justice, 2015). Most prisoners are aged between 30 and 39 years but there has been a steady increase in prisoners over the age of 50 years (Ministry of Justice, 2015b). As of June 2015, one in seven prisoners were over the age of 50, the highest prevalence ever recorded in UK prisons (Ministry of Justice, 2015b).

Age-related vulnerabilities to committing crime

Ascertaining a critical risk age period for engaging in criminal behaviour is problematic because of differing approaches to the measurement of age-crime onset. Using an index such as the first criminal conviction requires acknowledgement of the time elapsed between committing the offence, apprehension, police and trial proceedings and prosecution; this sometimes occurs years after an offence occurred. You can probably think of examples of cases where this is an issue, such as lengthy murder investigations or historical sexual abuse. You might be thinking that you could ask someone when they first engaged in problematic or anti-social behaviour and this can indeed be useful when thinking about risk and treatment needs. However, using an index such as self-reported offence-related behaviour requires acknowledgement of data quality (such as fallibility of memory, motivation for self-disclosure) and ethics of managing a previously unreported disclosure. With either index, implications for research include potential over-estimations of the age of offending onset and the reliability of the conclusions that can be drawn from the findings, both of which have implications for how we understand patterns of offending behaviour.

Regardless of the approach to exploring crime onset, patterns reflecting a general age-crime curve are evident with a peak in frequency of offending in mid-adolescence to the early 20s, then a rapid decline, evident for both males and females (Liu, 2015). The age-crime curve is commonly attributable to developmental factors (Shulman, Steinberg & Piquero, 2013) such as a biological vulnerability to risk-taking behaviours (e.g. Steinberg, 2007), but the high prevalence of poverty among young people has also been suggested to account for this phenomenon (e.g. Brown & Males, 2011).

There are well-established differences in patterns of offending behaviour across adolescent-limited and life-course persistent offenders (Moffitt, 1993). Moffitt proposed that adolescents whose offending behaviour was limited to their point in maturation had no clear engagement with problematic or anti-social behaviour in childhood but were influenced by models in their environment that effected their anti-social behaviour or desistance. Conversely, people who transgressed legal boundaries throughout the lifespan experienced specific bio-psycho-social vulnerabilities to offending behaviour. The interaction between the person and the environment shaped the self-, other- and world view and led to the development of a personality structure that supported criminal behaviour throughout the lifespan (Moffitt, 1993). However, if it is established that young people can start offending and then stop, might it also be the case that older people can start to commit offences during adulthood?

This is not a straightforward question to answer. When looking at conviction data alone, Beckley et al. (2016) suggested that it looks like there are some people who embark on criminality in their early-mid adulthood. However, when a combination of conviction and self-report data are used it is found that most people with a first conviction in adulthood had experienced problematic or anti-social behaviour at some point in their childhood or adolescence. So, if you asked yourself earlier 'why not just ask people about their behaviour?', then you were right to do so; the behaviour of these people just might not have attracted police attention before they reached adulthood.

However, there is some support for clear adult-onset offending behaviour. In the study by Beckley et al. (2016), people who did not have a history of offence-related behaviour earlier in life and committed a first offence in adulthood were likely to have a serious mental health problem such as schizophrenia, bipolar disorder or depression. Consistent with research looking at the additive effects of substance and alcohol use in combination with schizophrenia on vulnerability to violence perpetration (e.g. Arseneault et al., 2000) and crime in general (e.g. Hodgins & Janson, 2002), this suggests that some specific mental health problems might combine with other internal or external factors to increase risk for adult-onset offending behaviour. Adult-onset offenders seem to have a specific set of experiences different from the majority of offenders who typically engage in problematic and anti-social behaviour through childhood and adolescence and, sometimes, into adulthood. It is important to keep in mind that people with mental health problems are much more likely to be victims rather than perpetrators of crime (e.g. Walsh et al., 2003).

The relationship between mental health and crime is not straightforward, not least because there are similarities between the psycho-social vulnerabilities to offending behaviour and the development of mental health problems (e.g. poverty, stress, inconsistent parenting, attachment difficulties, abuse victimisation), and the heterogeneity of presentation and experience of difficulties. However, age of onset of criminal behaviour and mental health problems are important to explore in both counselling and forensic practice because such histories might inform an approach to treatment and management. For example, there is some suggestion that people who offend during adolescence and subsequently develop a mental health problem (the early starters) – who might share similarities with Moffitt's life-course persistent offenders – might present with a range of barriers to treatment, such as anti-social attitudes, reluctance to comply with authority and manipulative behaviour (Tengström, Hodgins & Kullgren, 2001) and treatment providers would need to have a clear formulation from which to make sense of and work with therapy-interfering behaviours. People who develop a mental health problem in adulthood and then commit crime (the late starters) might not present with these challenges to engagement in treatment (Tengström et al., 2001) because they might have a self-concept and mental maps that support more pro-social rather than anti-social behaviour. The late starters might require support in making sense of their acquired identity as an offender, particularly when they have had a catastrophic impact on other people, such as having taken someone's life (Ferrito et al., 2012).

An individualised understanding of risk and treatment needs is critical for prioritising and addressing factors that contributed to offending and enhancing individual strengths to support the process of rehabilitation or movement towards a healthier sense of self. Age plays an important (but sometimes overlooked) role in an understanding of risk assessment and management. For example, a life-course persistent offender might present differing levels of risk through the lifespan. This risk might depend on their sense of self-efficacy in committing offences, which could be influenced by physical strength and health, as well as greater levels of self-control and, in the case of sexual offending, reduced sexual drive (Hanson, 2002). There is some consensus that risk of reoffending declines with age, with substantial changes in risk reduction around the ages of 50–60 years (e.g. Fazel, Sjöstedt, Längström & Grann, 2006; Hanson, 2002; Thornton, 2006). Age is not a sufficient predictor of risk of offending as a single variable but is important to consider in the context of a formulation of risk and treatment needs in counselling and forensic practice.

Pause for reflection

What sources of information do you think would be relevant to access so that you can gain information about when someone's problematic, anti-social or offending behaviour started and what pattern this followed over time? How would you gain information about the onset and experience of someone's mental health problems? Might sources of information differ depending on the age of the client? How would you start to understand the relationship, if any, between someone's mental health problems and their offending behaviour?

Tip

Mapping out a chronological life history is a useful way of starting to explore the potential relationships between life events and experiences, including mental health problems and offending behaviour.

Age-related considerations for assessment, formulation and treatment

The vulnerabilities to mental health problems and offending behaviour with which children and young people present span multiple domains of bio-psycho-social development and there seems to be a clear dynamic relationship between the individual and environment. Therefore, a comprehensive assessment of the needs with which a child or young person presents across multiple domains of their life would be critical to a formulation of mental health problems and offending behaviour and prioritisation for interventions. For example, in the context of the treatment of conduct disorder, multi-modal interventions that address needs relating to emotional and psychological support, education, family, environment and life and occupational skills are recommended (National Institute for Health and Care Excellence, 2013). Multisystemic therapy is an example of such an intervention and is described and evaluated in Chapter 15.

Given that most offenders engage in problematic, anti-social or criminal behaviour as a young person, it follows that adult offenders might also present with needs across multiple domains. These problems and needs might be long-standing and could be reflected in the high prevalence in prisons of difficulties with interpersonal functioning and mental health (see Stewart, 2008, for an overview of mental health problems and needs among male UK prisoners, and Fazel & Seewald, 2012, for an international systematic review of mental health problems in prisons). For example, attitudes are not impervious to change but the function of anti-social attitudes and the strength with which they are held are important considerations in treatment and management. Age is important in this regard; anti-social attitudes held for decades and which might be important to an individual's identity are likely to be held strongly and are unlikely to be relinquished readily.

Think for a moment about a man in his 50s who had limited opportunities for education and occupational and life skills development because he spent most of his adolescent and adult life in institutions or prisons. Would you be surprised if he continued to use well-rehearsed strategies for survival in the community, such as breaking and entering derelict buildings for shelter and shoplifting to gain food? Indeed, this man might commit offences so that he can return to prison where basic needs for food and shelter can be met. Unless there are a series of sequenced interventions to build skills and confidence across life domains, then it is unlikely that offence-related needs will be addressed fully. Across all ages, motivation for movement away from an offender identity and towards a healthier, non-offending life, as well as interpersonal and behavioural challenges to the process of change, should be assessed and monitored. Structural challenges to the process and maintenance of change, such as resource limits in prisons and community services, should also be acknowledged.

Alongside the growing population of prisoners aged 50 years or over is an increase in demand for interventions to address physical and mental health and social and community support needs. There seems to be a group of older prisoners who enter prison with a high level of presenting need relating to health, social care and activities of daily living

(O'Hara et al., 2016), and there are other prisoners who age through a lengthy sentence and whose resettlement needs change over time in line with age.

In a systematic review of experiences of older adults in prisons, Maschi et al. (2011) reported that older adults feared physical and sexual victimisation in prisons usually perpetrated by young prisoners. Older prisoners also presented with specific anxieties related to dying in prison, access to social care on release from prison and access to services for age-related physical and mental health (Maschi et al., 2011). Services available to older adults in prison and on resettlement to the community are a neglected area and the Prison Reform Trust (2008) has called for staff training in prisons and probation services to support the assessment, treatment and management of older adults in the criminal justice system, as well as a more integrated approach across services. The impact of health-related met and unmet needs on an older prisoner's capacity to engage in interventions to address risk should be considered in the context of responsivity.

Conclusions

Age is an important but sometimes overlooked factor for consideration in assessment and formulation of mental health and offending behaviour needs of people across the lifespan. Within society, transgressions of expected age-related behaviours have led to changes in criminal justice policy that sparked debates about the criminalisation of young people. In turn, such debates have highlighted the relationship between criminality and identity. There are critical age risk periods for the development of some mental health problems and there are age-related patterns for offending behaviour onset and desistance, both of which are influenced by an interaction between an individual and their environment. Age is an important consideration in assessment and formulation. Here are some suggestions for practice:

- Give consideration in assessment to age-related vulnerabilities to developing mental health problems.
- Explore age of onset of offending behaviour and/or mental health problems to inform individualised formulation and treatment.
- Map out a chronological life history to explore relationships between life events and age of onset of mental health problems and offending behaviour.
- Consider how age-related needs might influence capacity to engage in interventions.

Suggestions for further reading

National Institute for Health and Care Excellence (2013). *Antisocial behaviour and conduct disorders in children and young people: recognition and management.* NICE Clinical guideline. London: NICE. Available at http://nice.org.uk/guidance/cg158.

Department of Health (2007). *A pathway to care for older offenders: a toolkit for good practice.* London: DH. Published on the Department of Health website in pdf format only. Available from www.dh.gov.uk/publications.

These two reading recommendations are best practice guidelines in working with children and young people (NICE) and older adults (Department of Health) in the criminal justice system in England and Wales. At the time of publication these are the two most recent documents but, as new research and evidence emerges, revised documents might be available on the respective websites and would supersede these documents.

8
CLASS

DANIEL HOLMAN

Image 8 On my way? With permission, Jhoanna Gonzalez

Introduction

As this chapter aims to demonstrate, and a number of classic studies have shown, social class is highly relevant to both counselling and forensic psychology, and crime and mental health more generally. We begin with the enduring idea that the working classes constitute a 'dangerous class', beset by social problems such as poverty and the breakdown of the family, and engaging in morally dubious or outright criminal behaviour. Various explanations are considered – the visibility of working-class crime, the role of labelling and the media, and the power of the criminal justice system. The chapter then moves onto issues of mental health, considering how rates vary by class. It suggests that since both mental health problems and crime are types of deviance, explanations of links with class are broadly similar, focusing on social causes and labelling. Finally, suggestions are offered for how the mental health treatment systems might more usefully incorporate issues of class into practice.

What is social class?

It is first necessary to explore what is meant by social class since it is a much-contested concept, both within academia and among the general population. Nonetheless, objectively it is clear that, as a starting point, there exists some kind of socio-economic structure or hierarchy, e.g. different people have different occupations and have different levels of income and education. The concept of social class takes this one step further and argues that this structure is grouped into a number of classes (though exactly how this classing occurs, and how many different classes there are, is open to debate; see Savage, 2015). It is useful to bear in mind that the concept of class refers specifically to this grouping, but there are of course overlaps with related terms and issues, such as poverty, socio-economic status, deprivation, and marginalisation, besides many others.

In recent years a very influential idea about class, associated with the sociologist Pierre Bourdieu, is that different classes not only have different levels of economic resources (*economic capital*), but other types of resources too (Bourdieu, 2002). Classes vary in terms of the social connections they have (*social capital*, or 'who you know'), and also their cultural knowledge and understanding (*cultural capital*). According to this perspective, a central idea underlying class is that different groups in the social hierarchy have differential power and access to resources – whether these resources are economic, social, or cultural – and that this grouping also influences the identities that people have. As will be shown in this chapter, class-related power and resources, as well as identities, influence whether people enact certain behaviours, whether these behaviours are classified as normal, deviant, or due to mental health problems, and how society responds to them. We have seen in the previous chapters that the same is true of gender-, age- and ethnicity-related power, resources and identities (as well as other axes of inequality). To give an example, judges generally have more power than defendants, but especially so when the defendant has a certain social position and identity associated with a lack of power and resources, such as money, social relations (e.g. a good lawyer, support of family), or knowledge of the criminal justice system, which all influence court outcomes.

Pause for reflection

What is your reaction to the concept of social class? Some people feel an affinity with class, and might have a strong class identity (e.g. traditional working class). Others feel that class has no relevance to their lives, perhaps instead seeing themselves as self-determined or unable to be classified.

Think about your own social class position and identity based on the discussion of what class is in the text.

- How have the different aspects of class influenced your experiences in life so far?
- How might these experiences influence you either as a client/patient in the mental health treatment system or prisoner/offender in the criminal justice system?
- How might your class background influence you as a psychotherapist or criminal justice system professional?

The dangerous classes

In August 2011 UK newspapers were replete with headlines such as 'YOB RULE', 'ANARCHY IN THE UK', and 'LONDON'S BURNING'. That the English riots received sensationalist media attention is unsurprising; these were highly visible events with fire, looting and violence. The cost of the riots was estimated to be around £200–300 million. In 2012 HSBC were fined £1.2 billion in a money laundering case, and since then, Britain's four big banks have been fined over £50 billion as a result of criminal wrong-doing. Following the riots, harsh sentences were handed out to make examples to others but not a single banker has been arrested. Although the HSBC scandal did receive media coverage, it was not nearly as extensive as that of the riots.

These disparities are stark, but are just one recent example of a long trend in working-class criminalisation, which noted criminologist Stuart Hall defined as 'the attachment of the criminal label, to the activities of groups which the authorities deem it necessary to control' (Hall et al., 1978, p. 189). Not many people would argue that riots did not need to be controlled, but the question remains as to why the crimes of the relatively powerless are much more criminalised than those of the relatively powerful. One possible explanation is that the crimes of the former tend to be much more visible, such as street crime, violent crime, or theft from property, while the crimes of the latter, such as fraud, tax avoidance or insider trading, take place away from the public eye. Indeed, visibility is one criterion used to distinguish 'white collar' (middle-class) crime from 'blue collar' (working-class) crime (Horsley, 2014). Reiman (2001) notes that white collar criminals are rarely arrested or charged, and when they are prosecuted and convicted, the sentences are very light relative to the costs for society. Similarly, Tombs and Whyte (2015) contrast the huge (and growing) scale of corporate crime against the lack of investigations and prosecutions. The theme of visibility is also evident in historical accounts of working-class criminality. One idea that has stuck is the notion of the 'dangerous classes'. In 1851 Victorian social reformer Mary Carpenter used this phrase to describe children who grew up in poverty and learnt criminal behaviour at a young age. Similarly, in 1872 social reformer Charles Loring Brace wrote about the dangerous classes of New York, who he argued were a separate criminal class beset by social problems such as poverty, cramped housing and the breakdown of the family. As Maffi (1995) argues, essentially the implied equation was 'proletarians = criminals'. Such ideas persist today. In recent years the term 'chav' has become popular, used to describe people from the so-called underclass (Jones, 2012). Similar terms may be 'pikey', 'townie', or 'scally'. Arguably, the function of such words is to 'other' certain sections of the population and associate them with morally questionable behaviour so that they become scapegoats for wider, deeper-rooted social problems.

Social class and mental health

As this book has set out to demonstrate, the way that behaviour is categorised as deviant is not just limited to crime. Mental health problems are also a type of deviance in the sense that they involve the infraction of social norms and rules. Many early studies demonstrated a link between social class and mental health problems. One of the first was by Faris and Dunham (1939), who found that the poorest parts of

Chicago had higher rates of treated schizophrenia and substance abuse disorder as measured by admission data. A classic US study by Hollingshead and Redlich (1958) found that those in lower class positions were over-represented in treatment, and were more likely to enter treatment via referral by official agencies such as the courts as opposed to choosing to enter treatment themselves. They were also more likely to have physical treatments such as shock therapy rather than organic treatments such as psychotherapy. More recent evidence from the *Adult psychiatric morbidity in England, 2007* survey shows that those with the highest household income were less likely to have common classified mental health problems than those with the lowest household income (McManus et al., 2009). For psychosis, prevalence rates were 0.1% among those in the highest income quintile compared with 0.9% in the lowest quintile.

How might social class differences in rates of mental health problems be explained? There are three main theories. The first is that it is something about lower social class circumstances that leads to poor mental health (social causation). For example, in their classic study, Faris and Dunham (1939) proposed that the poorest parts of Chicago had higher rates of classified mental health problems due to social isolation and loneliness, while Hollingshead and Redlich accounted for the association between class and mental health problems by reference to both adverse childhood experiences and differing levels of stress (Busfield, 2011). Nowadays research would recognise a range of social causes (or 'social determinants' as it is now often framed) as influencing mental health across the life course, including childhood experience (and even pre-natal experience), work and family life, and older age (Marmot et al., 2010). These include material deprivation (e.g. damp housing; Clark et al., 2012), poor working conditions (e.g. little control or autonomy and low pay; Siegrist et al., 2009), neighbourhood conditions (O'Campo, Salmon & Burke, 2009) and wider socio-political factors (Mattheys et al., 2016). A comprehensive list of social determinants can be found in the report by the World Health Organisation (WHO, 2014).

The second explanation suggests that it is not that lower class circumstances lead to mental health problems, but that mental health problems lead to lower social class circumstances. Those who develop mental health problems 'drift' down the social hierarchy (social drift hypothesis). According to Eaton (who was referring to schizophrenia in particular): 'Drift is the process whereby schizophrenics undergo downward class mobility after the onset of schizophrenia due to disability in the competition for employment' (1980, p. 149). Recent evidence suggests that social drift only explains a small part of the association between class and mental health problems (Hudson, 2005).

The third main type of explanation is that those in lower class positions are more likely to have their behaviours and actions labelled as mental health problems (labelling theory – see also Chapters 3 and 7), or in other words, pathologised. Hollingshead and Redlich (1958) found that the lower social classes were more likely to receive a diagnosis of psychosis (typically schizophrenia or bipolar disorder) whereas the higher social classes were more likely to receive a diagnosis of neurosis (typically depression or anxiety). Once behaviour is viewed as a mental health problem it comes under the auspices of medical intervention and control, which in some cases can have more damaging effects than the behaviour/problem itself (so-called 'iatrogenic' effects). The starkest historic example of this was the institutionalisation of the 'mentally ill' in asylums, where they were often subject to all kinds of bizarre and often inhumane treatments (see Chapter 2), including hydrotherapy, sterilisation, malaria fever therapy, shock therapies, and lobotomy (Braslow, 1999). In a well-known experiment, Rosenhan (1973) sent pseudo-patients to psychiatric hospitals to show how psychiatrists often mis-diagnosed them as having mental illnesses, and were therefore far from accurate in their diagnoses. Combined with Hollingshead and Redlich's finding concerning the more likely diagnosis of schizophrenia among people the lower social classes, this suggests that people from such classes have suffered injustices in the mental health treatment system, and not necessarily due to the conscious or deliberate intentions of particular individuals.

Although asylums are now more or less a relic of history, critics of the psychiatry profession argue that it essentially remains a means of social control. For example, Hurvitz argued that psychotherapy has a latent purpose 'in accord with the values of American capitalist society' (1973, p. 232). In other words, its purpose is to control people and bring them in line with the (usually white and middle-class) status quo, quelling defiance, rebellion or cultural diversity. Psychotherapy espouses values such as autonomy, individuality, self-sufficiency, self-realisation, and so on. However working-class values have traditionally been firmly centred around the idea of community, which is part of the reason why Freud (1919) argued that the poor are not well-suited to psychotherapy. Freud suggested a watered-down version of psychoanalysis for the poor: a large-scale, state-sponsored treatment involving direct suggestion and hypnosis (Winter, 1999). There are some echoes here with the recent Improving Access to Psychological Therapies (IAPT) programme, a large-scale NHS initiative to provide short courses of cognitive behavioural therapy to help tackle widespread depression and anxiety disorders.

Social class and crime

Although framed slightly differently, similar explanations exist for the link between social class and crime. This is unsurprising if we accept that crime and mental health problems are different types of social deviance. Thus similar types of social forces influence whether or not behaviour is categorised as criminal (and therefore in need of criminal justice intervention) or indicating mental health problems (and therefore in need of medical intervention), and indeed Chapter 2 explores how the boundary between these two categories is 'fuzzy' and changes over time. Merton's (1968) theory of structural strain suggests that deviance occurs where there is limited opportunity for advancement in formal legal structures such as employment. One issue with this theory, however, is that it predicts more lower-class criminality than there actually is, and less higher-class criminality. Yet we know that those further up the social hierarchy commit their fair share of crime, even if they already have relatively greater opportunity for advancement, for example in their careers, than their lower-class counterparts.

The media has long been a strong focus in criminology for the role it plays in emphasising certain deviant behaviours over others (more on this in Chapter 3). Hall et al. (1978) give the example of the 1862 'garrotting panic', garrotting being an attempt to strangle or choke someone during a robbery. As noted by Smallwood (2015), garrotting was not actually common, but the media loved to report it, and in an effort to make it appear as if they were tackling the problem, the police started to record crimes that would previously be reported as robberies or drunken brawls instead as instances of garrotting. In this sense, garrotting could be said to be *socially constructed* in that its purported existence was closely tied in with how the police and media dealt with the phenomenon. Examples of modern moral panics include paedophilia, gun crime, binge drinking, recreational drug taking, media violence, immigration and dangerous dogs (Critcher, 2008). Social construction also occurs in the way crimes are processed in official statistics (see also Chapter 5). Sometimes the same crime is treated differently depending on who commits it. Brookman (2005) argues that if homicide statistics included deaths from negligence and corporate manslaughter, the perception that homicide is a working-class crime would change. Tombs and Whyte (2007) estimated 1,600 people in the UK were killed as a result of work compared with just around 700 murder cases for the same year (Office for National Statistics, 2016). More recently, Tombs (2016) estimates that around 50,000 people die each year due to injuries or health problems associated with the workplace. Furthermore, there is a strong class patterning to those killed at work. Tombs and Whyte note: 'process, plant and machinery operators' are about ten times more likely to die or suffer a serious injury at work as 'managers and senior officials' (2007, p. xiv).

Given that powerful individuals and corporations own and control the media, it is not a coincidence that it emphasises the crimes of the relatively powerless. Similarly, there is a strong argument that the over-representation of working-class crime in the criminal justice system is a result of the way policing is organised, class bias in the courts, and the cost of legal defence (Taylor, Walton & Young, 1973). Reiman (2001) talks of this as a 'weeding out' process of the well-to-do from the criminal justice system at each of its stages: arrest, charging, convicting, and sentencing. Even though those in lower-class positions do commit more than their share of crimes, they are vastly over-represented in prison. In fact, this weeding out process starts with instances of individual deviant behaviour: to be recorded as a crime, such behaviour must first occur, be observed, be reported, and then be recorded. At each stage different social processes are in play that in effect act like a giant filter from the point at which deviant behaviour could be said to have occurred right through to conviction and sentencing (only a small minority of instances of deviant behaviour ultimately result in conviction). Class is highly relevant to this filtering process, shaping the behaviours people engage in and how they are seen by society, through to interactions with police – often seen as adversarial – and experiences with the criminal justice system. Reiman (2001) gives the example of fraud, typically a more affluent crime, where 63% of the convicted are sentenced to prison serving an average of 16 months, whereas for robbery these figures are 99% and 60 months. Navigating this system requires class-based resources: economic capital (being able to afford the best lawyers), social capital (having the right connections to the right people – again, lawyers are the obvious example), and cultural capital (knowing the system, understanding forms and formal procedures, how to talk and act to give oneself the best chance of those best outcome). This is not to say that class wholly determines legal outcomes, but that it has an influence. Societies tend to recognise this to some extent by providing a basic level of legal aid for those unable to pay (though this has been cut in England and Wales in recent years – see, for example, Smith and Cape (2017)).

Intersectionality

An increasingly influential theory in recent years is intersectionality – the idea that class cannot be separated from other aspects of social position and identity, such as ethnicity, gender and age (Crenshaw, 1991). We must therefore try to think of how class interacts with these other factors, so that a working-class person, for example, also has a certain gender, a certain age, a certain ethnicity, and so on, and that all these factors work together to shape who they are (see also Activity 5.1 in Chapter 5). Each intersection, i.e. combination of these factors, represents a certain *position* in the social structure, and is associated with a certain *identity*. As we have seen, both position and identity are important in explaining class differentials in crime and mental health problems.

Acknowledging intersectionality avoids the fallacy of assuming that all people from a certain social class are the same. This is an emerging field of research and so there are few studies. Using US data, Rosenfield (2012) looked at the interaction between gender, ethnicity and class in leading to differences in mental health (the so-called 'triple jeopardy' hypothesis), and found that black women, especially in higher-class positions, had lower rates of depressive symptoms compared with white females. She found some evidence suggesting that these low rates are due to black women in higher-class positions attaching greater importance to the self. Green and Benzeval (2011) found that social class differences in anxiety and depression widen with age in the West of Scotland, while Mangalore and Knapp (2012) found that lower income had a particularly strong effect on the prevalence of common mental health problems for African Caribbean, Pakistani and Bangladeshi people. These findings suggest future research in this area would benefit from a nuanced consideration of how socio-demographic factors work together to lead to mental health outcomes. Arguably, the intersection of class and ethnicity is especially important since ethnic minorities are more likely to come from working-class backgrounds, especially in the US (Crimmins, Hayward & Seeman 2004), which in part helps to explain why ethnicity is a more prominent concept when discussing social disadvantage there than class.

Pause for reflection

Think of someone you know quite well and how their various attributes influence who they are. You might consider their ethnicity, gender, age, class, religious status, relationship status, or other factors. Reflect on how the combination of these multiple different factors working together influences their social position and social identity. It is useful to bear in mind that intersectionality theory suggests that we cannot simply add up different aspects of social position and identity because they interact with each

(Continued)

(Continued)

other; to put it another way, multiple forms of (dis)advantage are mutually reinforcing. To give a concrete (hypothetical) example, a black person may earn on average £2,000 a year less than a white person, a woman £2,000 a year less, yet a black woman may earn £5,000 a year less because of the way racism and sexism combine (i.e. they do not simply add together).

Social class and mental health treatment

The last section of this chapter will focus on class in relation to mental health treatment. Mental health treatment cannot solve all of society's problems, yet it is sometimes able to help those who are in distress and suffering. The relevant question for this section is therefore 'what is the best way to organise mental health treatment to help those from lower-class backgrounds with emotional distress?'

With respect to mental health problems, the social determinants framework suggests that there is a very real and direct connection between the social problems of our times and people's mental health and well-being (WHO, 2014). This has become especially apparent in recent years with the financial crisis, which has led to an increase in bankruptcies, homelessness, unsecure employment and unemployment. For example, evidence suggests that the recent recession affecting Europe and North America has been linked to an increase in at least 10,000 suicides (Reeves, McKee & Stuckler, 2014). Promisingly, a group of psychologists have formed the *Psychologists against Austerity* movement in 2014, recognising the need for mental health practitioners to be aware of the wider social context of people's personal problems.

One recent useful model is the Social Class Worldview Model (revised) (SCWM-R), which is an 'approach to understanding the ways in which people understand themselves as social class beings and how individuals interpret and act on their social class environment' (Liu, 2011, p. 98). An essential aspect of the approach is a recognition that different people have different levels of awareness about their own and others' class position, and to work with this fact in clinical practice. A number of tangible suggestions are offered for professionals (see Information box 8.1). It is also important to acknowledge the variety in types of therapy. Specialist techniques such as psychoanalysis, and psychodynamic therapy more generally, are difficult to access through the public health system and are held to require a reasonable level of education (Busfield, 2011), whereas focused approaches such as CBT (see Chapter 14) are more widely accessible (though the debate on the effectiveness of different therapeutic approaches continues).

Information box 8.1: Social Class Worldview Model

Liu (2011) reminds us that it is important to try not to make assumptions regarding how clients make sense of social class due to their class background or outward class markers, e.g. style of dress. Instead, he suggests exploring this with clients by asking a number of questions:

- What was it like to grow up in your family?
- Who are the people that are important for you in determining your social class?
- If you were to describe your social class economic culture (the neighbourhood, programme, department, work site) that is important for you in evaluating your own social class status, what would that look like?
- What were you told about being rich or poor?
- Have you ever experienced discrimination because of your social class?
- How does it feel when you are not able to maintain your social class position?
- What were your first memories of being different from others with respect to social class?
- How have you experienced pressure to be like others with respect to social class?

Liu also suggests that helping professionals should be 'sensitive and aware of their own biases, worldviews, and perspectives on social class, classism, meritocracy, and inequality' (2011, p. 98), which is especially important with clients who have a different class worldview. Lastly, professionals should acknowledge that class is more relevant and important for some clients than others. The SCWM-R can provide a basis for how to ask questions about the role of social class in the client's life.

In my own work, I considered the importance of the cultural aspects of class for how people 'fit' with the process of talking treatments (Holman, 2014). Since talking treatments involve a deeply personal relationship between therapist and client, it follows that the quality of this relationship is fundamental to their effectiveness (Lambert & Barley, 2001). Moreover, the nature of this relationship is classed in the sense that therapists are professionals based in institutional settings. There are a number of aspects to working-class culture that are potentially mismatched with this arrangement. Based on semi-structured interviews with clients or potential clients, and building upon previous arguments in the literature, I uncovered four working-class 'cultural dispositions' (cf. Bourdieu) that might help to explain this cultural mismatch. First, the working classes have less of a tendency to reflect on their inner psychological state and verbalise it to others (sometimes referred to as 'psychological mindedness'; Beitel, Ferrer & Cecero, 2004)). Second, the working classes have less of an inclination to focus on emotional health; instead, mental health problems tend to be expressed in physical terms. Third, there is a tendency for working-class deference to medical authority; doctors are seen as having the answers and being responsible for applying the correct treatment. Lastly, working-class people are more likely to be focused on the practical 'here and now', and what can tangibly be done, or what concrete actions can be taken, about personal problems. The case study below is taken from this research.

Case example: Jane

Jane is a 57-year-old retired foster carer who lives on a council estate. She has a talkative and chatty personality. One might therefore suppose she would be suited for therapy. However, although Jane was talkative, she did not refer much to her own feelings. Rather, she seemed much more comfortable talking about the experiences of others or those in the community, with which she had extensive contact due to her role as a foster carer. When asked what she thought about the idea of therapy, she thought that community counselling in the home with other women would be a good idea, where the women could catch up and 'gossip all day'. This is the opposite to therapy in its purest sense, a form of individual psychological introspection. She also said how her family did not talk about emotions, which may have made her less able to benefit from therapy if she did indeed have it.

- Do you think therapy is a suitable treatment for Jane? If so, how can it be culturally tailored to her experiences? If not, is the problem with Jane and her class background or therapy itself?

The activity below encourages you to further think about the relationship between working-class circumstances, types of deviance, and the possibility of mental health treatment.

Activity 8.1: Work environments

It is possible to trace cultural dispositions to the material, health, occupational and educational characteristics of working-class circumstances. Thinking about the occupational lives of those in working-class versus middle-class positions is a sound starting point when reflecting on the implications of class for pathologisation, criminalisation and treatment/justice, since work constitutes a central part of most people's lives. Imagine a more typically working-class work environment (such as a warehouse), and a more typically middle-class work environment (such as an office).

How might these two different work environments:

- Provide different opportunities and incentives for criminal behaviour?
- Give rise to different levels and types of emotional distress?
- Result in therapy feeling like a comfortable or natural situation, or an uncomfortable and 'alien' situation?

Another layer to consider on top of work environments is employment conditions, encompassing such things as contracts, security, benefits and working hours. It has recently been argued that a new 'precariat' class has emerged, whose work is characterised by zero hours, part-time hours, short-term contracts and self-employment. Standing (2011) has argued that the precariat class is 'dominated by insecurity, uncertainty, debt and humiliation' (p. vii). It is easy to imagine how these working conditions might lead to rises in mental health problems, and recent evidence suggests that this is indeed the case (Vives et al., 2013).

Conclusion

This chapter has explored some of the key issues in relation to class-based pathologisation and criminalisation. It has suggested that working-class criminality has been disproportionately emphasised by both the media and the criminal justice system, partly owing to its visibility, but also because these institutions are owned and controlled by those with a great deal of power, which facilitates their control of the relatively powerless. Working-class *vis-à-vis* middle-class crimes can partly be explained by the opportunities for crime that working-class and middle-class occupations afford (e.g. property crime versus tax fraud). In relation to mental health problems, the chapter has suggested that higher working-class rates are chiefly due to either working-class circumstances (e.g. greater severity of childhood stressors) or because working-class deviance is more likely to be labelled as mental health problems (specifically as psychotic disorder). Certainly, the issues covered here are complex and multifaceted, and require a great deal of thought and reflection to fully understand. However, existing explanations provide at least a starting point for the conscientious practising professional to take up the challenge; that they attempt to do so is important for the sake of social justice and fairness.

Suggestion for further reading

Liu, W. M. (2011). *Social class and classism in the helping professions: research, theory, and practice*. London: Sage.
Although written for a North American audience, this book directly addresses the topic of this chapter for those who research and practise in the area of the helping professions.

Savage, M. (2015). *Social class in the 21st century*. Harmondsworth: Penguin.
An up-to-date exploration of social class in modern Britain.

Reiman, J. H. (2001). *The rich get richer and the poor get prison* (6th ed.). Boston, MA: Allyn and Bacon.
Again, a North American-based book, but this is a well-written, best-selling text on how the criminal justice system is biased against the poor. There are now 11 editions of this book; the 6th edition is referenced in this chapter.

PART III

SEX AND SEXUALITY IN MENTAL HEALTH AND CRIME

9

SEXUAL ASSAULT AND ABUSE

TARA N. RICHARDS AND JOAN A. REID

Image 9 Are you hurt? With permission, Jhoanna Gonzalez

Introduction

The next few chapters in this book include discussion of sexual situations where questions are sometimes raised about whether consent can or cannot be obtained (e.g. sex between a therapist or sex worker and their client, and sex in certain sexual contexts). In this chapter, you will explore explicitly non-consensual forms of sex: situations where people are coerced or forced into sex, where they are incapacitated and cannot consent, and where child sexual abuse (CSA) is involved.

The chapter is divided into two sections: CSA and adult sexual assault. Each section provides an overview of key research on the experience, including how *prevalent* victimisation and perpetration are, and the relationship between being a perpetrator or survivor and other factors. We also include discussions of the consequences for victims, key intervention strategies, and the research regarding the efficacy of these strategies, in each of these sections. After that, we outline treatment strategies for perpetrators of sexual assault and the research on their effectiveness. We then cover issues relating to the reporting of CSA and adult sexual assault to the criminal justice system, and issues relating to self-care for professionals.

Child sexual abuse

Child sexual abuse (CSA) refers to the sexual victimisation of children and adolescents perpetrated by caregivers, other adults, or peers (Finkelhor et al., 2014). CSA encompasses a continuum of sexually abusive experiences ranging from voyeurism (people watching children for sexual gratification) to rape occurring during childhood or adolescence. Estimates of the extent of CSA vary widely due to differences in factors like how studies define sexual abuse, the age group of children included in the study, and whether victimisation is examined over the lifetime (i.e. whether it ever happened) or during a period in time (e.g. whether it happened during the previous year). Two meta-analyses reviewing hundreds of studies from Australia, Europe, North America, Africa, Asia, and South America provide global estimates of CSA ranging from 18% to 19.7% for girls and 7.6% to 7.9% of boys (Pereda et al., 2009; Stoltenborgh et al., 2011).

Risk factors for CSA

Multiple risk factors for CSA have been identified and are important for counselling and forensic psychologists – and related professionals – to recognise. Collectively, research finds that girls report higher rates of sexual abuse than boys; however, it is unclear as to whether girls actually *experience* higher rates of sexual victimisation or if they are just more willing to disclose this victimisation (Stoltenborgh et al., 2011). Global research also indicates that the highest prevalence of reported CSA among girls is in Australia, while for boys it is in Africa, with the lowest rate across genders being in Asia (Stoltenborgh et al., 2011).

Pause for reflection

Think about the reporting and experiencing issues raised in the previous paragraph. What reasons can you think of why the rates of reporting CSA – or indeed adult sexual assault – might be less than the rates of people who experience it? Do you agree with the idea here that there might be gender differences in how many of those who experience CSA end up reporting it? If so, what reasons might there be for the under-reporting of sexual abuse by boys or men (think back of what you have read in Chapter 6 about gender differences)?

The risk of CSA also seems to increase with age (Finkelhor et al., 2015), particularly for girls (Putnam, 2003). Several studies also suggest that a child who lives without one or both of their biological parents is at higher risk of being sexually abused (Vogeltanz et al., 1999). Parental substance abuse has also been recognised as a risk factor for CSA (Vogeltanz et al., 1999). Finally, an increased risk of sexual abuse has been associated with disabilities, especially those that impair a child's perceived credibility, such as blindness, deafness, and intellectual disability (Westcott & Jones, 1999). In their research review, Wissink et al. (2015) found that the 'relative risk for sexual abuse was an estimated 4–8 times higher for children with intellectual disability compared to children with average intelligence' (p. 32).

The impact of CSA

CSA has been associated with a range of negative health consequences that might serve as targets for therapeutic interventions (Nelson, Baldwin & Taylor, 2012). For example, higher rates of mental health difficulties are reported among survivors of CSA compared to the general population (Martin et al., 2004). Common problems include depression (Mullers & Dowling, 2008), suicidal ideation (Dube et al., 2001), substance abuse (Bensley, Eenwyk & Simmons, 2000), and post-traumatic stress disorder (PTSD) (Putnam, 2003). Negative consequences of CSA have also been shown to be gendered in the kinds of ways you read about in Chapter 6 (girls internalising and boys externalising their distress).

Several studies have shown that younger victims of CSA are more likely to experience subsequent mental health difficulties than older victims (Cicchetti et al., 2010). In contrast, other studies have found that adolescents experience more self-blame for being abused than those victimised as younger children (Hunter, Goodwin & Wilson, 1992). Adolescent survivors of sexual abuse are also at greater risk for sexual revictimisation in adulthood than those who experienced sexual abuse during childhood (Classen, Palesh & Aggarwal, 2005; Humphrey & White, 2000).

Evidence also suggests a strong relationship between CSA and other forms of violence and abuse. The Adverse Childhood Experiences Survey, a retrospective study of more than 17,000 adults between 1995 and 1997, found that participants reporting CSA often also reported emotional abuse, physical abuse, emotional neglect, and/or physical neglect as well as a range of problems in their household, such as domestic violence, substance abuse, mental health problems, criminality, and/or parental separation/divorce (Dong et al., 2003). The strongest relationships for *polyvictimisation* (experiencing multiple forms of victimisation) have been found between CSA and emotional abuse, physical abuse, and physical neglect as well as CSA and household domestic violence (Dong et al., 2003).

The strong relationship between domestic violence and child maltreatment, including CSA, has been explained in the context of the intergenerational transmission of violence or 'cycle of violence' (Colman & Widom, 2004; Daigneault, Hébert & McDuff, 2009; Jennings et al., 2013). This explanation contends that children who witness and/or experience violence in their family of origin are more likely to learn to use violence in their own relationships than children who grow up in violence-free homes (Widom, 1989). This stems from social learning theory, which posits that individuals learn through observation and operant conditioning. Specifically, people are reinforced for behaviours which are rewarded in some way, but not reinforced for those that are not rewarded (Bandura, 1977). Research has found links between family of origin violence and risk of later domestic violence involvement as a victim and/or offender (e.g. Stith et al., 2000, 2004; Widom, Czaja & DuMont, 2015).

Despite this evidence for the intergenerational transmission of violence, it is vital to note that the majority of abused children do *not* abuse their own children or partners. Further, while parents are responsible for the overwhelming majority of physical and emotional child abuse and maltreatment, someone other than a parent is often responsible for perpetrating CSA (Sedlak et al., 2010). Research also indicates that approximately one-third of CSA cases include perpetrators under the age of 17 years old (Finkelhor, Hammer & Sedlak, 2008).

Therapy for survivors of CSA

Regarding CSA victims who experience negative mental health symptoms, research suggests that survivors benefit from specialised mental health care evaluations and associated therapy (Honor, 2010). Numerous empirically-supported therapy options for treating psychological trauma and PTSD exist (see SAMSHA's National Registry of Evidence-Based Practices, 2016). However, Trauma-Focused Cognitive Behavioural Therapy (TF-CBT) (Cohen, Mannarino & Deblinger, 2006) and Eye-Movement Desensitisation and Reprocessing (EMDR) (Shapiro, 2001) are the two psychotherapies recommended by the World Health Organisation for the treatment of PTSD (WHO, 2013).

TF-CBT involves the delivery of individual sessions to both the child and a non-perpetrating parent or guardian, as well as dual caregiver/ child sessions. The tenets of TF-CBT are represented by the acronym PPRACTICE which mean that they include: Psycho-education; Parenting skills; Relaxation; Affective (emotional) modulation; Cognitive coping and processing; Trauma narrative; In vivo mastery of trauma reminders; Conjoint child–parent sessions; and Enhancing future safety and development (Cohen et al., 2006). The approach used for the more therapeutic aspects of the sessions is CBT, which you will read more about in Chapter 14. Multiple randomised controlled trials have demonstrated the efficacy of TF-CBT in reducing PTSD symptoms (Cohen et al., 2006) even among children as young as 3–6 years (Scheeringa et al., 2011).

EMDR is an integrated psychotherapy that helps people to access and process disturbing past life events and present triggers (things like sounds or sights that bring back memories of the trauma and cause intense emotional and physical reactions) (Shapiro, 2001). EMDR involves clients recalling a distressing image while receiving sensory inputs, such as side-to-side eye movements. It has been supported by many empirical and case studies testing its effectiveness with children with PTSD (Rodenburg et al., 2009) as well as the treatment of those with intellectual disabilities and limited verbal capacities (Mevissen, Lievegoed & de Jongh, 2011). We will finish this section by considering a case example to demonstrate how EMDR works in practice.

Case example: Shawna

At 17 years old Shawna was facing criminal charges including assault. She resided in a juvenile justice programme designed for delinquent young people with mental health diagnoses. Shawna's outbursts continued to occur on a daily basis or even several times during a 24-hour period. Her therapist observed that Shawna had limited verbal abilities and little to no insight or explanation for her aggressive behaviour. Postulating that it may be linked to previous trauma, the therapist utilised EMDR with Shawna during two individual sessions to address this. Importantly, EMDR does not require that the client have insight into their trauma experience or its link to aggression (Worthington, 2012).

When asked about past trauma to determine the focus of EMDR treatment, Shawna revealed that she had been raped at gunpoint and was also forced to watch the rape of another girl. A secondary trauma resulted from the gang rape: Shawna became pregnant and suffered a miscarriage. She was distraught over this loss and believed that her drug use during the pregnancy caused the miscarriage, stating 'I killed my baby'.

When reprocessing these disturbing memories Shawna identified an image, belief, emotion, and bodily sensations associated with them. For each trauma, she described the image and identified a negative cognition, which was phrased in the present tense (e.g. 'I am going to die') to emphasise the incongruity (i.e. although she is not in current danger, she feels she is going to die now). Shawna also identified a preferred more adaptive, positive cognition (e.g. 'I survived and I am safe'). Her level of belief in that positive cognition was measured by the Validity of Cognition Scale (Shapiro, 2001). The emotion associated with each event was also identified (e.g. fear, shame, sadness), and the level of disturbance was measured using the Subjective Units of Distress/Disturbance Scale (SUDS). The bodily sensations associated with the disturbance were also identified by Shawna.

Related to the gang rape, as she recalled these events, Shawna experienced feelings of anxiety and intense fear accompanied by rapid breathing and a tightening in her chest. Her negative cognition was 'I am going to die'. After reprocessing this experience, using EMDR, her SUD level decreased from a 10 to a 0, and she fully believed that she was now safe (her preferred positive cognition). This event was clearly related to the safety issues that had come up. In retrospect, her aggressive reactions to facility staff and peers were driven by hypersensitivity to threats. Research has found that victims of interpersonal conflicts can become aggressive due to hypersensitivity and misperceptions, with even minor slights interpreted as hostile threats (Worthington, 2012).

Related to her miscarriage, Shawna recalled memories of being at the hospital, experiencing the miscarriage, and being told that it was her fault. These memories elicited feelings of sadness, guilt, and fear, along with an associated discomfort in her stomach. She believed that she was 'a bad person/mother'. Reprocessing these memories resulted in a considerable decrease in her SUD level (from 9 to 0/1) and allowed Shawna to believe that she was kind and caring. After reprocessing these two traumatic events, Shawna improved remarkably with only one incident of emotional distress requiring staff intervention in the following four months.

CSA survivors who do not show symptoms may also benefit from therapeutic intervention and education designed to prevent repeated sexual abuse, to normalise and clarify their feelings and to educate them regarding healthy sexual behaviours and personal boundaries (Honor, 2010). Recovery for all CSA victims who remain in the home with their families may be facilitated by emphasising families' strengths and identifying and addressing their weaknesses (Honor, 2010). Whole-family approaches are discussed in more detail in Chapter 15.

Adult rape and sexual assault

Studies estimate that one in five women in England and Wales aged 16–59 have experienced some form of sexual violence since the age of 16 (Ministry of Justice, 2013). Similarly, the National Intimate Partner and Sexual Violence Survey (NISVS) (Black et al., 2011), a nationally representative survey of adults in the United States, estimates that one in five women and one in 71 men report rape at some point in their lives. Further, almost 45% of women and 25% of men report sexual violence or victimisation other than rape during their lifetime. US research also indicates that people of colour are at a disproportionate risk for sexual assault compared to their white counterparts, with American Indian and/or Alaskan Native women and black men experiencing the highest rates of sexual victimisation (Black et al., 2011). See Chapters 5 and 6 for more on the involvement of race and gender in crime, including sexual abuse and assault.

Perpetrators of adult sexual assault often know their victims. Female victims are most likely to be sexually assaulted by a current or former intimate partner (51%) or an acquaintance (41%) (Black et al., 2011). Thus, when a woman is sexually assaulted she is most often victimised by the same person who says 'I love you'. Further, intimate partner sexual violence is often repetitive, such that it occurs multiple times over the course the relationship and often co-occurs alongside other types of intimate partner violence, such as physical and emotional abuse.

Pause for reflection

Think about how the therapeutic process might need to be different for survivors of intimate partner sexual assault compared to people who are assaulted by strangers. How might feelings of self-blame or personal culpability for the assault be similar or different? How might the added 'betrayal' of intimate partner sexual assault impact upon a survivor's healing process?

The impact of adult sexual assault

As with CSA, adult victims of sexual assault are at an increased risk of a wide range of negative consequences. Research has demonstrated that sexual assault is associated with substance use, PTSD, anxiety, and depression (Burnam et al., 1988; Kessler et al., 1995; Kilpatrick et al., 1985; Kilpatrick et al., 1998; Walsh et al., 2014). In addition, it may result in genital injuries, sexual health problems, and unintended pregnancies (McFarlane et al., 2005).

Although stereotypical ideas around sexual assault often involve images of deadly weapons or physical force being used by perpetrators, in reality many assaults are perpetrated using coercion or incapacitation of victims. Indeed, many victims of sexual assault do not bear any physical injuries – no black eyes or bruises – which may confound both formal (e.g. the police) and informal (e.g. friends or family) support providers when victims disclose their assault.

Fear of disbelief is often cited in victimisation surveys as a primary reason why victims do not report their victimisation to authorities. Likewise, sexual assaults perpetrated by strangers and/or that do include the use of a weapon are far more likely to be reported to authorities than 'typical' sexual assaults committed by known offenders or without the use of a weapon, because they are widely seen as somehow more 'legitimate' (Fisher et al., 2003). Victims also cite fear regarding how the perpetrator might react as a reason for not reporting (Wolitzky-Taylor et al., 2011). Such fears might be exacerbated when the victim knows, and has a prior or current relationship with, the perpetrator.

Activity 9.1: What is sexual consent?

Think about the legal definition of consent, as you understand it. For example, the UK Sexual Offences Act 2003 defines it as: 'a person consents if he agrees by choice and has the freedom and capacity to make that choice'.

- Within this definition, do you think there are circumstances where one, both or all of the individuals involved in the sexual activity cannot give consent?
- How might the definition of consent create self-doubt among sexual assault survivors regarding their culpability or role in their own victimisation? What therapeutic interventions do you think might help survivors to move past self-doubt or blame?

Support and therapy for adult sexual assault

A large body of research indicates that the majority of victims of sexual assault *do* tell someone, most often friends and/or family members. Fewer victims disclose to more formal support providers such as healthcare professionals, rape crisis centre staff, or the police. Although victims of sexual assault might need myriad resources or services to heal after their victimisation, a critical and acute need is for the disclosure recipient to listen and believe them. The sexual assault disclosure process is an important experience for victims and the response(s) that victims receive from those to whom they disclose can impact both their well-being and their future service acquisition. According to Starzynski and colleagues (2005), 'negative social reactions to initial disclosures may discourage subsequent disclosures and further traumatize the survivor' (p. 418).

As previously mentioned, a variety of psychotherapies have been developed for addressing trauma, including rape and sexual assault. A systematic review of studies comparing the effectiveness of TF-CBT, EMDR, stress management (SM), and other therapies (supportive therapy, non-directive counselling, psychodynamic therapy, and hypnotherapy) found that TF-CBT, EMDR, and SM were effective in the treatment of PTSD, while other non-trauma-focused psychological treatments did not reduce PTSD symptoms as significantly (Bisson & Andrew, 2007). Meta-analytic research which has compared Cognitive Processing Therapy (CPT), Prolonged Exposure (PE), Stress Inoculation Therapy (SIT), Supportive Psychotherapy (SP), and EMDR against no treatment in randomised controlled trials has provided tentative evidence that cognitive and behavioural interventions – specifically CPT, PE, SIT, and EMDR – are associated with decreased symptoms of PTSD, depression and anxiety in rape and sexual assault survivors (Regehr et al., 2013).

Trauma-focused psychotherapies, such as TF-CBT and EMDR, address trauma by reprocessing and reassessment of traumatic memories and thoughts or beliefs about the traumatic experience (Beck, 1995; Burns, 1980; Schiraldi, 2009). Traumatic memories often contain misinterpretations and inaccurate conclusions which were formed under great duress while strong emotions and arousal interfered with memory processing (Shapiro, 2001). Thought restructuring occurs in therapy by exposing unproductive ideas that maintain emotional distress and replacing these thoughts and beliefs with less distressing beliefs.

For example, one common dysfunctional cognitive process linked to trauma is abusive labelling (Burns, 1980; Schiraldi, 2009): a rape survivor may use a label or name to describe themselves, rather than seeing themselves as a complex person, for example, 'because of the rape, I am damaged goods'. In CBT, this type of thought would be examined, questioned, and replaced with a different, more adaptive thought, such as: 'I was raped; I am more than my wound'. The focus of this type of therapeutic strategy is to enable a rape survivor to develop the skills needed to identify troubling cognitive distortions, challenge the logic of such thoughts, and replace them with thoughts that are more accurate and less distressing (see Chapter 14 for more on CBT approaches).

Reporting sexual assault and abuse

Sexual assault is among the most under-reported of all 'person' crimes. The Crime Survey for England and Wales (CSEW) estimates that only around 15% of those who experience sexual violence choose to report it to the police (Ministry of Justice, 2013). Comparatively, in the United States, National Crime Victimization Survey data from 2011–2014 suggests that less than 35% of sexual assaults are reported to police annually (Bureau of Justice Statistics, 2016). Victims cite a range of reasons for not reporting sexual assault to the police, but the majority of such reasons are aligned with feelings of fear, shame, embarrassment, and anxiety that they will not be believed or taken seriously.

In the majority of cases of alleged sexual assault – cases that involve known victims and offenders – whether or not sexual contact occurred is not questioned. Instead, the central uncertainty concerns 'consent credibility' or whether the victim did or did not consent to the sexual contact. Because sexual assaults rarely take place in the presence of witnesses, such cases are considered 'he said, she said cases' (or he said/he said, or other relevant combinations of pronouns). This means cases where the only evidence that a sexual assault has occurred is the victim's claim that they were assaulted. As such, when victims of sexual assault attempt to report their assault to the police, they are often asked to recount their victimisation in great detail, multiple times, to multiple people, leading to feelings of revictimisation and distress at reliving the trauma. Police officers may also retraumatise the victim by asking questions that insinuate that they may share some of the blame for the assault or actively enticed the offender (e.g. by wearing revealing clothing or by consuming alcohol).

Research has indicated that when a trained advocate accompanies a victim to report their assault to the police, they have a more positive experience than when they report without an advocate (Campbell, 2006). Given that sexual assault robs victims of control over their own bodies, it is vital that they retain a sense of control in the reporting process. Victim advocates can help pace the experience by requesting breaks during the interview, redirect insensitive questions, and remind the victim of their rights, including stopping the interview at any time. Additionally, advocates can help victims navigate the complex criminal justice system and lend support during the lengthy process of a criminal prosecution.

Comparatively, while CSA can be reported directly to the police, allegations or suspicions of CSA are often first reported to a child welfare agency. CSA is most likely to be reported by a concerned adult (e.g. a family member, physician, teacher) rather than the child victim, and like cases of adult sexual assault, CSA is vastly under-reported. For example, based on retrospective studies of adults, it is estimated that only one in 20 cases of CSA comes to the attention of authorities (Kellogg, 2005). According to Kenny and Abreau (2015), mental health professionals are in a unique position to detect CSA among children with whom they have professional contact and to direct such children and their families to services, as well as to serve adults who were abused as children and find themselves ready to disclose and seek support. The forensic and therapeutic issues around remembering abuse and assault are covered in detail in Chapter 17.

Responses to perpetrators of sexual assault and abuse

Of course it is vital to consider the treatment of perpetrators as well as victims or survivors in this area if we are to prevent further sexual abuse and assault. Two promising practices for sex offender treatment include Cognitive Behavioural Therapy (CBT) and Multi-Systemic Therapy (MST). CBT focuses on dysfunctional thoughts and beliefs and their impact on behaviours and actions (Development Services Group, Inc., 2010). Comparatively, MST is family and community centric and focuses on interrupting the cycle of sexual abuse by working with the offender and their family to develop a safety plan and educating the individual and the family regarding risk factors associated with recidivism (Fanniff & Becker, 2006; Henggeler & Sheidow, 2012).

Research on the effectiveness of treatment for sexual offences – including CSA – is positive, but equivocal. For example, Hanson et al.'s (2002) meta-analysis, including a variety of sex offender treatment programmes and more than 9,000 sexual offenders, demonstrated an overall sexual re-offence rate of 12.3% among treatment participants in contrast to 16.8% among control group participants. A more recent analysis indicated an overall decline in recidivism of 10% among participants in sex offender treatment (Kim, Benekos & Merlo, 2016). Comparatively, an analysis of California's Sex Offender Treatment and Evaluation Project, a cognitive behavioural treatment and relapse prevention programme, demonstrated no significant impact of the programme on individuals who had committed sexual offences against children (Marques et al., 2005).

Intimate Partner Violence (IPV) researchers and treatment providers assert that there is a definitive need for individualised and targeted treatment protocols based on offender motivation for IPV (i.e. aggression or control and dominance) (Kelly & Johnson, 2008). Similarly, those who research and treat sex offenders argue for tailoring based on sex offender motivation, aggression, control and dominance, or sexual deviance (Reid et al., 2014; Wilcox, Garrett & Harkins, 2014). The inadequacy and low effectiveness of sex offender treatment may reflect a mismatch of treatment with offender need, and indicate the importance of individualised treatment strategies. We will consider this more now with the following activity.

Activity 9.2: Different perpetrator motivations

Exploring a perpetrator's motivations for committing crime is helpful in identifying individual treatment needs. Examine the quotes from anonymised perpetrators below. Using these statements, identify the underlying motivation for each perpetrator (aggression, control and dominance, or sexual deviance), and consider whether or not the same treatment would or would not work for all of them.

* Bob 'did not want to give children "that kind of love" but sexual impulses were too overwhelming' (Reid et al., 2014, p. 209).
* Steve was 'prowling near bars and nightclubs and would sometimes follow a victim for several days to learn her route ... he wanted to humiliate women because of the humiliation he felt from women who rejected him because of his unattractive appearance' (Reid et al., 2014, p. 210).

- Jim would 'watch porn for stimulation and to maintain sexual fantasies ... he then would hunt for someone to fulfil his fantasy scenarios' (Reid et al., 2014, p. 210).
- Sam stated 'he was angry and frustrated because of problems with his wife ... was looking for a victim the same age as his spouse ... feels that all women are whores' (Reid et al., 2014, p. 210).

Self-care for professionals doing rape work

Individuals who work with survivors of sexual victimisation often report experiencing 'vicarious trauma' (Martin, 2005). This may elicit negative emotions such as anger, fear, and loss of trust in others and impact upon their personal relationships. In addition, practitioners often experience professional burnout and can lose their energy for this kind of work.

Therefore, self-care is vital for individuals who work in the area of sexual offending. According to Wasco, Campbell and Clark (2002), 'self-care refers to proactive strategies, or routines, that professionals use to offset the negative aspects of working with trauma victims' (p. 734). Self-care coping strategies might tap into an individual's cognitive, physical, spiritual/philosophical, social, and/or physical resources. For example, practitioners might benefit from short-term methods such as meditation or deep breathing as well as long-term strategies like exercise, journalling, or expression via art or other forms of creativity. Many practitioners benefit from debriefing with a trusted support provider after particularly difficult interactions. Self-care also includes setting boundaries between home and work life and balancing the time and attention spent on one's work responsibilities versus personal life and enjoyable activities.

For practitioners with personal histories of sexual trauma, self-care is paramount. As a 'wounded healer', a practitioner has the unique ability to 'use the knowledge acquired through [their] own suffering in the service of clients' recovery' (Zerubavel & Wright, 2012, p. 489). The value of survivor-practitioners can be particularly salient when advocating for or treating survivors of sexual trauma, which has the potential to be uniquely stigmatising. However, helping others overcome tragedies similar to one's own can result in retraumatisation, relapse and impaired practice (Zerubavel & Wright, 2012). To prevent professional impairment, it is vital to cope with any cognitive and emotional reactions to triggers that may occur during the therapeutic process. For survivor-practitioners, it is critical to seek ongoing supervision, training, and a workplace where personal self-exploration and growth are encouraged, struggles are accepted and understood, and the myths of practitioner perfection and invincibility are debunked (Zerubavel & Wright, 2012).

In addition to personal strategies, self-care might include organisational activities such as guidelines regarding the number of survivors practitioners interact with each day, or the size of their overall caseload. Organisations might also encourage practitioners to set realistic expectations about their work with survivors and maintain limits regarding their workload and professional goals. Opportunities for ongoing training and professional development are also important to minimise burnout.

Conclusion

CSA and adult sexual assault are significant, global problems. While stereotypical images of 'legitimate' sexual violence often include strangers, weapons and force, in reality perpetrators of such abuse are often individuals with whom the victim has a prior acquaintance, and assaults rarely involve weapons or result in overt signs of violence. These differences between conventional notions of sexual violence and the overwhelming majority of experienced assaults – as well as the limited definitions and interpretations of consent – result in many survivors experiencing self-blame, doubt, and shame regarding their experiences. Such emotions may prevent them from reporting their experiences or seeking services for trauma. Additionally, the prevalence of polyvictimisation and additional life difficulties among survivors of sexual assault and abuse may further limit their access to formal and informal support providers.

When survivors seek support, counselling professionals have the unique opportunity to listen and believe their story. Research studies indicate that empirically-supported treatment modalities such as TF-CBT and EMDR are effective at resolving trauma-related symptoms suffered by those who have experienced sexual victimisation during childhood, adolescence, or adulthood. More research is needed to identify effective treatment for those who perpetrate sexual offences. Attending to self-care and ensuring organisational support are vitally important for those who provide care to sexual trauma survivors.

Suggestions for further reading

Friedman, J., & Valenti, J. (2008). *Yes means yes: visions of female sexual power and a world without rape*. Berkeley, CA: Seal Press.
A great book addressing cultural rape myths and the importance of enthusiastic consent.

Katz, J., & Moore, J. (2013). Bystander education training for campus sexual assault prevention: an initial meta-analysis. *Violence and Victims*, *28*, 1054–1067.
A useful paper to think more about the kind of training that might help to prevent sexual assault.

Richards, T. N., & Marcum, C. D. (Eds.) (2014). *Sexual victimization: then and now*. London: Sage.
This edited collection, by one of the authors, gives a lot more detail about sexual victimisation in all its forms.

10

SEX AND SEXUALITY IN THE THERAPY ROOM

AMANDA O'DONOVAN

Image 10 OK corner. With permission, Catriona Havard

Introduction

Sex and sexuality are central aspects of identity and experience for many people: ways in which they express their desires and key aspects of themselves, and seek pleasure, status, power and/or acceptance (de Botton, 2012). However, discussions around sex and sexuality are often neglected or marginalised in training and in the therapy room. Just as therapists need to be able to communicate about these issues with clients, investigative interviewers and forensic practitioners also need to be able to talk with offenders, suspects, victims and witnesses about sex and sexuality, particularly in the cases of sexual abuse and assault that we covered in the previous chapter. In this chapter we mainly focus on therapy and counselling contexts, but throughout you might like to reflect on how similar issues and suggestions are also relevant in criminal justice contexts.

This chapter explores what is difficult and challenging about talking about sex and sexuality and how and why these conversations can feel different from other aspects of therapeutic work. We then overview ethical concerns around sex and sexuality in the therapy room. These range from interpersonal challenges where feelings of attraction and arousal can affect professional practice, through to boundary transgressions such as sexual relationships with clients. In the second half of this chapter we overview working with sexual difficulties, and across sexual and gender diversity. Problems with sex may present as the primary focus of therapy or may co-occur with other health, psychological or forensic concerns. Past experiences of sexual violence or abuse, pain or difficulty during sex, concerns about sexuality and intimate relationships are not uncommon in people attending counselling. We also explore ideas around 'normal' sexual functioning and reflect on attitudes and expectations that may affect therapeutic work with sex and sexuality.

Factors that affect and shape consent are a continued theme, as in the previous chapter. It is helpful to think about how consent is negotiated around the therapeutic contract and process, and how skills and confidence in talking about sex can facilitate sexual consent. We also explore social understandings of sex and gender as these narratives powerfully shape the range of behaviours and identities we 'consent' to embody and enact.

Talking about sex and sexuality in therapy

Talking about sex and sexuality can be challenging for clients and counsellors alike. Despite the fact that sex is overtly visible and present in many aspects of daily life, therapists often feel that sexual matters are difficult to raise with clients (Verhoeven et al., 2003) or lie beyond the scope of their practice (Binik & Meana, 2009). Similarly, clients who are able to discuss many intimate aspects of their lives may struggle to name sexual difficulties or talk about sexuality (Quilliam, 2012). Understanding the many feelings that may be present in the therapy room may help these conversations feel less daunting.

Culture strongly shapes how we express sexuality and sex. Conversations about sex carry many layers of stigma and can be steeped in narratives of shame and secrecy that have historically dominated this landscape. There is something different, and difficult, about talking about sex – whether with friends, partners, health professionals, or clients with whom we are working.

Pause for reflection: Talking about sex

When was the last time you talked about your own sexual experiences? If you have ever discussed sex with a health professional, what was your experience like? If you have ever talked about sex with someone else, what was successful and why?

In the therapy room both therapists and clients may hold assumptions about who is best placed to raise sex as a topic for discussion. Clients may be anxious, embarrassed, ashamed or lack confidence in being able to talk about sexual matters or have concerns about being judged, dismissed or silenced even if they have discussed other intimate, difficult or distressing topics within therapy (Hook & Andrews, 2005; Verhoeven, 2003). They may be reluctant to initiate such a conversation due to innate power imbalances in the therapeutic relationship (see Chapter 1), and a sense that if sex were relevant then the therapist would ask about it (Quillian, 2012).

A number of different factors affect therapists' and other professionals' willingness to discuss sexual matters with clients. These include lack of appropriate skills or knowledge, time constraints, and concern about what language and terms to use. Emotional and psychological concerns that inhibit conversations include lack of confidence, anxiety and embarrassment about discussing sex, fear of offending or embarrassing the client, and concerns about being seen to be inappropriate or 'off-topic' (Lindau, et al., 2007; Stevenson, 2010). By avoiding asking about sex or sexuality the practitioner may inadvertently collude with a client's feelings of fear or shame.

Cultural factors such as gender, age, religion, and sexuality can facilitate or silence talking about sex in therapy, and various facets of identity are more or less visible and acknowledged or erased in clinical interactions (Butler, 2011). Understandably, therapists may experience an increased awareness of their own physicality/sexuality as well as those of their clients when talking about issues that are sexual or erotic, something we will come to shortly.

Talking about sex and sexuality can assist with assessment and understanding of a client's concerns. Sexual concerns can present as part of physical health diagnoses, mental health difficulties, relationship problems, or as a result of previous experience of assault or trauma (Petrak, 2002; Tarnowski, 2007; Wilmoth, 2007). In openly addressing issues around sex and sexuality, the counsellor models that sex is an acceptable issue to bring to therapy. As Quilliam (2012) notes, even if a client has a sexual issue but is not yet ready to talk about it, asking about sex and sexuality openly and confidently in the session creates a safe space for clients to bring these issues to therapy when they are ready.

Talking about sex in the therapy setting is also important as it provides a safe opportunity for clients to practice communication about their sexuality and sexual needs. Sexual assertion involves knowing your sexual preferences and kinks, likes and dislikes, and understanding your right to say no to sexual activity at any time, at any moment, for any reason (East & Adams, 2002). Communication around sex is central to issues of consent. It is not enough to assume a partner is willing to participate in sexual behaviour, and silence does not constitute agreement (Barker & Hancock, 2017).

How to talk about sex

Stevenson (2010) outlines useful guidelines for talking about sex in the therapeutic setting. These involve normalising discussion of sex, being transparent, and 'locating' your questions so clients understand the context for asking about these issues (e.g. 'Often when people are depressed it can affect how interested in sex they feel. Have you noticed that happening for you?'). Being alert to invitations and openings for conversations can also be helpful (e.g. 'You say things are very distant in your relationship, in what ways do you mean?').

Conversations about sex can be supported by therapist curiosity, reflectivity, and open-mindedness. Where possible therapists should avoid using language that may shut down conversations. This includes making assumptions about the following:

- Gender normativity – that they are cisgender – remaining in the sex they were assigned at birth (whereas trans people are not)
- Heteronormative – that they are heterosexual (whereas lesbian, gay and bisexual people are not)
- Monogamy – that relationships involve only one partner (whereas non-monogamous people's often involve more than one)
- The sexual imperative – that they experience sexual attraction (whereas asexual people do not).

Therapists may address clients' concerns by openly discussing what may be different or difficult about talking about sex and checking in with clients about how the conversation is going (Quilliam, 2012). As in all areas of therapeutic work, difficult or complex topics are more easily addressed within a good therapeutic relationship. Therapists need to consider the timing of conversations and establish close rapport before exploring areas where there may be particular anxieties or vulnerability.

Sexual feelings in the therapy room

Practitioners experience a wide range of feelings towards their clients. Sexual attraction towards a client does occur in therapy settings and can be part of a normal process in the therapeutic relationship. The challenge for therapists is to be mindful of sexual feelings such as attraction or fantasy and manage them appropriately (Fisher, 2004; Pope & Tabachnick, 1986). Sexual thoughts or feelings that occur in the therapy room commonly evoke shame, anxiety or embarrassment in the therapist (Rodgers, 2011). Unfortunately, ways of reflecting on these feelings and approaches to managing them are usually silenced or insufficiently considered in training. This can further exacerbate anxieties and reinforce the practitioner's concerns that such feelings are unprofessional, abnormal or unethical (Pope & Tabachnick, 1986).

There is a widely recognised need for more attention to these topics in education and training (Garret, 1998; Rodgers, 2011) as well as ongoing access to relevant literature, training and supervision. For therapists, recognising transference and countertransference (erotic and otherwise) is an important skill. Transference is when clients 'transfer' feelings from other relationships and experiences in their lives onto the therapist. This can facilitate powerful feelings towards the therapist, such as positivity, gratitude, dependence or resentment. Countertransference relates to the same process in the therapist's feelings towards the client. Such feelings and interactions can mimic or reflect the thoughts and sensations commonly encountered in the romantic or erotic domain. Cultivating an awareness of the often-fleeting but powerful array of feelings, thoughts and impulses that arise in the therapy room is essential. However, as Pope and Tabachnick (1986) observe, therapists often find it easier to discuss and reflect on their clients' difficult feelings than their own.

Sexual misconduct

'I will abstain from every voluntary act of mischief and corruption and further from the seduction of females or males' – Hippocrates, fourth century BCE

Despite prohibitions against sexual relationships dating back to the Hippocratic oath, sexual relationships between clinicians and patients were not explicitly proscribed until the late twentieth century due to changing societal attitudes and an awareness of the damaging effects of such relationships (Welfel, 2015). Garret (1998) found that 4% of clinical psychologists reported engaging in sexual contact with their clients and 23% had worked with clients who had been sexually involved with previous therapists.

Professional guidelines clearly prohibit sexual relationships with clients and state that a client who has been sexually assaulted by a therapist should report this to the relevant accrediting body as professional misconduct. Practitioners also have a duty to report colleagues who they know to engage in such behaviour (British Psychological Society (BPS), 2008; British Association for Counselling and Psychotherapy (BACP), 2016a; Health and Care Professions Council (HCPC), 2012; UK Council for Psychotherapy (UKCP), 2009).

Professional bodies also advise care and caution about entering into personal or business relationships with clients after therapy has ended. Power imbalances and/or psychological dependence will more than likely continue and engaging in other kinds of relationships (e.g. employment, social or sexual) with former clients is deemed inappropriate. Therapists need to consider the conflicts of interests that can arise from such dual relationships. Imbalances of trust or power also render sexual relationships inappropriate with individuals to whom practitioners owe a continuing duty of care, such as students, trainees or junior staff members (BACP, 2016a; BPS, 2008).

Sexual misconduct and the law

As you saw in the last chapter, sexual activity without consent is sexual assault and consent is only obtained if a person 'agree(s) by choice and has the freedom and capacity to make that choice' (Sexual Offences Act 2003).

In specific statutes relating to mental disorders, it is an offence to engage in sexual activity 'when that person, because of, or for a reason related to, a mental disorder is unable to refuse' (section 31). If a client wishes to pursue legal action for damages related to sexual misconduct, a case can be brought to the civil court.

Section 14 also addresses sexual offences with young persons that are considered abuses of positions of trust. Roles that are covered under this section include teachers, counsellors and social workers, and supervisors in forensic settings. Due to the inherent power imbalances in such relationships and duty of care, it is an offence for an adult in a position of trust to behave in sexual ways with a young person who is under 18 years of age (Sexual Offences Act 2003).

Risk factors for sexual misconduct and abuse

In audits of serious misconduct reports made to the BACP, the majority of complaints were from female clients who alleged sexual misconduct by their male therapist (Khele, Symons & Wheeler, 2008; Symons et al., 2011). Similarly, in a study of therapists in the US, Pope (2001) found that more male (7%) than female (2%) therapists self-reported engaging in sexual relationships with their clients.

Counsellors have an ethical, professional and legal duty to establish and maintain appropriate therapeutic boundaries. The literature notes that sexual misconduct often follows a 'slippery slope' pattern of other lesser boundary breaches and violations (Simon, 1999). Pope and Vasquez (2010) reported that the single biggest predictor of client sexual exploitation is therapist history of previous boundary violations. Boundary violations often begin seemingly innocently as boundary blurring which is perceived by the therapist as being beneficial for the client, such as longer sessions, flexibility in session arrangements, doing favours, etc. (Corey, Corey & Callanan, 2007). Gutheil and Brodsky (2011) note that departure from usual practice should be a trigger for reflection. There is a clear imperative for practitioners to guard against progressive boundary violations that themselves may be detrimental to client care, and that may also lead to more damaging behaviours, such as sexual misconduct (Gabbard, 1996; Gartrell et al., 2006).

A number of individual therapist factors have also been reported to increase the risk of boundary transgressions. These include a high level of stress, personal issues, problematic drug or alcohol abuse, and professional isolation (Gutheil & Brodsky, 2011). Regular consultation with peers, engagement with research evidence, personal therapy, and ongoing professional development and training are useful in mitigating against these and preventing burnout and poor practice (Lamb, Catanzaro &

Moorman, 2003; Martin et al., 2011). There is also consistent agreement among professional bodies that supervision is essential in assisting therapists to monitor and maintain appropriate boundaries (BPS, 2008; BACP, 2016a; UKCP, 2009). In a study of therapists who engaged in sexual misconduct, Gabbard (1996) observed that, paradoxically, the thoughts, feelings and behaviours that therapists were most likely to withhold or keep secret from a supervisor were the issues that most need to be bought to supervision.

Psychological effects of sexual misconduct

Sexual contact with therapists is damaging for clients and can have wide-ranging negative consequences (Pope & Vetter, 1991). The effects on clients are worse if the sexual contact occurs while the client is in therapy. They include depression, increased suicidality, experiences of isolation, emptiness, anger, abandonment, interpersonal difficulties in trust, and issues around sexuality and relationships (Pope & Vasquez, 2010). In addition, Welfel (2015) reflects that professional misconduct has negative legal and professional implications for the therapist and their ability to provide care, as well as calling into disrepute the therapeutic profession as a whole. Such cases, and the media coverage they attract, may prevent vulnerable individuals from attending counselling and exacerbate existing concerns about trust, power and safety.

Case example: Steve

A therapist, Steve, was working with Joanna, a young woman who had been referred for low mood, alcohol use and impulsive behaviour. Steve saw Joanna for several sessions, many of which ran over time. He was aware of his feelings of attraction for her. He gave her some money for taxis when she was concerned about getting home after their session. Steve felt flattered by Joanna's comments about how helpful their sessions were. They began to end their sessions with close hugs and soon embarked on a sexual relationship.

Activity 10.1: Better practice for Steve

Think about the following questions in relation to Steve, remembering the ideas you've just read about.

- How might Steve have identified that boundary violations were occurring over time?
- How could he have responded to this awareness?
- What could he have done differently?
- How could supervision have been helpful in this case?

Working with sexual problems

When we consider working therapeutically with sexual difficulties, we are confronted with the dilemma of what is 'good', 'healthy' or 'normal' sex. The behaviours and sensations we experience as being sexual and erotic are culturally determined and therefore part of an ever changing discourse – or set of understandings – in our wider culture (Butler & Byrne, 2010). Just as we have a biological need to eat, our culture defines what we eat and do not eat and with who, how, where and when; sexual activities are similarly driven by biology and shaped by cultural norms that change over time, such as the 'normalising' of sex before marriage or same-sex attraction. As sex is linked to reproduction, identity and freedom, it is essentially political and cannot be understood without reflection upon existing power structures (Foucault, 1976).

For millennia, sex and sexuality have been regulated and dictated by religious institutions. In Western society, these narratives eventually shifted from religious discourses to moral ones and sexual acts that were historically seen as sinful were repositioned as immoral. This is evidenced in the many shame-based narratives that still exist around sexuality (e.g. 'slut shaming' and the victim blaming that we touched on in the previous chapter). Early scientific work on sexuality reflected these ideas about sexual behaviours being undesirable, deviant or dangerous. Researchers focused on categorising sexual 'types' and there was little recognition that the act of 'discovering' and labelling illnesses was in fact a powerful force in constructing ideas about normality (Weeks, 2016).

In modern society, medical and psychiatric diagnoses and legal statutes continue to regulate and enforce ideas about what should be viewed as 'normal' sex (Barker, 2011). It was only as recently as 1991 that rape within a marriage was recognised as a criminal offence in the UK and male rape did not enter the legal statutes until 1994. Homosexuality was illegal in the UK until 1967 and was classified as a mental disorder by the World Health Organisation (WHO) until as recently as the early 1990s (Weeks, 2016). These legal and medical narratives impinge on individual expression, stigma and shame, and contribute significantly to the mental health burden felt by individuals.

Further discussion around sexual behaviours that have been marginalised, stigmatised and criminalised can be found in Chapter 11 which explores paraphilias and Chapter 12 which looks at understandings of transactional sex and sex work.

Activity 10.2: Constructing 'normal' sex

Reflecting on how narratives are constructed can help us to become aware of the assumptions we make around sex and sexuality. Think of some specific examples of how:

- The media socially constructs certain understandings of 'normal' and 'abnormal' sex.
- Schools socially construct sex.
- Religions socially construct sex.

Which of these institutions or experiences have influenced your ideas about sex, and how have your ideas, and societal assumptions, about sex and sexuality changed over your lifespan?

Sexual problems and their management

Many clients attend counselling exactly because they are concerned that they are not 'normal'. However, the variety in sexual desire, behaviours and expression is infinite. There is no 'normal' in human sexuality or sexual behaviour. Normative expectations of how sex should be performed can problematise sexuality and cause clients distress and concern (Greggoire, 1999; Moynihan, 2003).

The Diagnostic and Statistical Manual of Mental Disorders (DSM-V) (American Psychiatric Association, 2013) lists a range of sexual problems that can attract a formal diagnosis. Sexual dysfunctions listed include delayed ejaculation, erectile disorder, female orgasmic disorder, female sexual interest/arousal disorder, genito-pelvic pain/penetration disorder, male hypoactive sexual desire disorder, and premature ejaculation. These disorders are characterised by difficulties in a person's ability to respond sexually or to experience sexual pleasure (American Psychiatric Association (APA), 2013).

A formal diagnosis can facilitate care and access to services. However, it also impacts upon how people see themselves and how they are seen by others, and can have a stigmatising effect (Moynihan, 2003; Sungur & Gündüz, 2014; WHO, 2016). It is important to remember that the presence of a 'sexual dysfunction' like these may not always be problematic for the individual. For example, a person whose sexual pleasure doesn't rely on any form of penetration will not be troubled even if they have 'penetration disorder'. In determining whether a sexual problem warrants therapeutic intervention, counsellors need to be guided by whether the client and any partner/s they have are happy with the sex that they are – or are not – having.

As sexual difficulties are embodied and manifest themselves physically, it is also important to ensure that any physiological factors which may be contributing to, or causing, sexual problems are not overlooked. Sexual problems may be a consequence of an underlying illness, such as an infection, urogenital tract condition, or cancer (Juraskova et al., 2003; Lindau et al., 2007). For instance, female sexual pain can be due to undiagnosed vulval skin conditions, such as dermatitis or skin sensitivity, or thrush, and respond to topical treatment or lifestyle management (Welsh et al., 2002). Male erectile difficulties can be an early warning sign of diabetes or cardiovascular disease (Gandaglia et al., 2014; Malavige & Levy, 2009).

Sexual problems can also be a product of mental health difficulties such as depression or anxiety, or a medication side effect (Malavige & Levy, 2009). Sexual difficulties can occur in the context of previous experiences of abuse or may come embedded in attachment issues, trust or intimacy concerns, power imbalances, or abusive dynamics such as partner violence and sexual assault (Petrak, 2002; Read et al., 2006; Shepherd, Heke & O'Donovan, 2009). A careful assessment of these broader contexts is vital to formulation and therapeutic work.

Relationship factors can be important contributing factors even if they are not directly responsible for the development of sexual problems (Betchen, 2009; Meana, 2009). Where the client is in an established relationship, it is good practice to include their partner(s) in the therapeutic work, although relationship therapy may not always be possible (e.g. if the client hasn't disclosed they are attending therapy to a partner, or if a partner is unable to attend for practical reasons). Individual therapy may also be more appropriate if the focus of the work is on issues such as post-traumatic stress, trauma, previous sexual abuse, grief, depression, etc. (Petrak, 2002; Rellini & Meston, 2011).

Factors that impact negatively upon sexual arousal include: distraction, intrusive memories or flashbacks, anxiety, fatigue, pain or discomfort, self-consciousness, quality of sexual stimulation and lack of trust (Basson, 2002). People may report feeling unaroused even when their bodies show objective signs of physiological arousal (Chivers et al., 2010).

Judgemental thoughts of inadequacy, embarrassment, guilt and anxiety can draw attention away from the present moment and interfere with interoceptive – or body–mind awareness (Basson et al., 2005). Therapy for sexual problems includes skill building, exploring sexual identity, sexual communication, and developing awareness of physical and sensual sensations (Goldmeier & Mears, 2010; Silverstein et al., 2011). Symptoms and their meaning for clients should be explored to develop a shared understanding of the client's experience (Basson et al., 2005; Kashak & Teifer, 2002).

Many components of therapy for sexual problems can be integrated into counselling across a variety of therapeutic models (see Information box 10.1).

Information box 10.1: Components of therapy for sexual difficulties

- Psycho-education around the problem, including triggers and maintaining factors – biological, social, psychological, relational, societal
- Critical discussion of myths around 'normal' sex while respecting and validating the client's concerns and reasons for seeking therapy
- Discussion of models of arousal and desire
- Exploring thoughts and feelings around sex and related physical symptoms
- Sensate focus exercises to build intimacy, communication and turn-taking in touch
- Lifestyle and stress management
- Kegel exercises for pelvic floor muscles
- Relaxation skills training
- Graded desensitisation for pain or anxiety around sex.

Pause for reflection: Sexual myths

Listed below are some commonly held sexual myths. Think about which you are familiar with, where you hear them, and why they might be related to sexual problems, shame and/or non-consensual sex.

- Sex always means penetration
- Partner(s) should instinctively know what you like and enjoy
- Men should always initiate sex
- Sex should always end in (male) orgasm
- Sex should only occur within marriage or a committed relationship.

Working therapeutically with gender and sexual diversity

Recent decades have seen enormous shifts in understandings of sex and gender. Cultural narratives have significantly changed in recognition of how sexuality and gender are culturally shaped, named and owned (Richardson, 2015). As discussed in Chapter 6, gender encompasses multiple identities and experiences between and beyond the male/female binary, and sexuality between and beyond the gay/straight binary as 'identities which once seemed fixed and determined are increasingly seen as fluid; relational; people are bundles of possibilities' (Weeks, 2016, p. 37).

Gender and sexuality diverse (GSD) individuals attend counselling or forensic services for the usual problems that may bring any individual to these settings. Practitioners need to reflect on how their own attitudes, assumptions, knowledge and experience of diverse sexuality and gender may be relevant to work with these clients. Being aware of the wide-ranging and destructive effects of stigma and marginalisation is also central to ethical and affirmative working. This includes concerns with bullying and physical safety, psychological well-being, access to appropriate and respectful health services, and the upholding of basic human rights (APA, 2012, 2015; BPS, 2012). In the UK, it is a legal requirement under the Equalities Act to provide inclusive services within health and social care (Department of Health, 2006).

It is important to consider the intersections between sexuality and gender and aspects such as race, class, religion, age and geography (Butler & das Nair, 2012). The intersection of being GSD across these diverse cultural factors can create multiple experiences of stigma, repression or exclusion, for example a failure to recognise the sexuality of older or disabled people, or an assumption that men or women of certain racial groups are hypersexual. Therapists and practitioners need to be sensitive to these intersections to ensure the best possible and affirmative care for their clients.

People who are GSD may also seek help in understanding their identities and the social, familial or relational issues that these may impact (APA, 2009). It is important to note that it is unethical for therapists to offer 'conversion' therapies (UKCP, 2011, 2015). Such therapies are informed by inaccurate and unhelpful beliefs about 'abnormal sexuality' and are not only ineffective but are damaging to clients and perpetuate stigma (see Chapter 11 for further discussion).

Best practice also involves developing an awareness of any language used that may inadvertently be heterosexist or prejudiced. Therapists must pay attention to words or phrases that assume clients are heterosexual, monogamous or cisgender, such as asking female clients about pregnancy, using the term 'husband' to refer to partners of unknown gender, or asking intrusive questions about a trans person's body (Ansara & Hegarty, 2011). Therapists should use language that respects gender and sexual diversity in order to build therapeutic engagement and allow for open communication and person-centred care. Appropriate and respectful communication for working with GSD people includes enquiring about and using preferred pronouns and titles to develop a shared understanding and language with clients (APA, 2015; Department of Health, 2008; Long, 1996). Terminology that is gender neutral and avoids specific anatomical references should be used (Department of Health, 2007; Government Equalities Office, 2010).

GSD people are inevitably subject to many levels of stigma in a heteronormative culture which has binary gender role norms. It is important to recognise, understand and acknowledge the pervasive effects of shame and stigmatisation, minority stress and microaggressions that are commonly experienced by GSD individuals (Bersani, 1987). These multiple stressors increase risk of low mood, depression and suicidal thoughts (King et al., 2008) and should be attended to closely. Trans people are at greater risk of bullying and also interpersonal and sexual violence, from partners and strangers, as a result of transphobia or stigma and prejudice against trans people (Arcelus et al., 2016; Jauk, 2013; see Chapter 11 for more on this).

Conclusion

Therapeutic and forensic work related to sex and sexuality can be daunting in its complexity or unfamiliarity. Talking about sex and sexuality does feel different, but with appropriate support, space for reflection, practice and letting go of the need to 'get it right' it can become less challenging. Critical reflection can help practitioners to question normative assumptions and to understand their client's worlds.

Practitioners' attitudes, views and cultures will not always mirror those of their clients. However, practitioners should not allow their professional relationships with clients to be prejudiced by any personal views they may hold about sexuality, gender, age, disability, race, beliefs or culture (BACP, 2016a). Being able to reflect on, and articulate, sexual and gender values and norms help therapists and counsellors to become aware of assumptions they might make and prejudices they may inadvertently enact. Increased understanding of gender and sexual diversity can facilitate counselling and forensic work that is ethical, supportive and non-discriminatory. Good practice involves allowing space for the client to be expert and feeling able to ask for clarification/

explanation about concepts, terms or practices the practitioner is unfamiliar with (Stevenson, 2010), although it is unethical to expect clients to provide free education, and continued professional development in these areas is also vital.

Clinicians, counsellors and forensic staff need to be aware of their own beliefs and values around sex and sexuality as an essential part of developing reflective working practices. These areas are inherently complex due to the many social, political and relational contexts in which they are embedded and enacted. Awareness of our own cultures can help bring awareness to judging thoughts, unhelpful assumptions, and any difficult emotional responses that may arise. Practitioners can learn to sit with their own experiences and to cultivate a sense of gratitude at the trust shown, and intimacies shared, when working with sex and sexuality.

Suggestions for further reading

Butler, C., O'Donovan, A., & Shaw, E. (Eds.) (2010). *Sex, sexuality & therapeutic practice: a manual for trainers and clinicians*. London: Routledge. This is a useful text that examines issues of sexuality and diversity in a positive and affirming light and considers how these issues can be introduced into therapy and training in a wide variety of settings.

Richards, C., & Barker, M. (2013). *Sexuality and gender for mental health professionals: a practical guide*. London: Sage. An essential and accessible text that overviews normative and diverse sexualities, genders and relationships.

British Psychological Society (2012). *Guidelines and literature review for psychologists working therapeutically with sexual and gender minority clients*. Leicester: BPS. www.bps.org.uk/sites/default/files/images/rep_92.pdf This is a literature review and set of practice guidelines to support work with GSD clients and facilitate understanding of exclusion and stigmatisation.

11

'PARAPHILIAS'

JEMMA TOSH

Image 11   Man in handcuffs. With permission, Sarah Lamb

Introduction

This chapter outlines several psychiatric diagnoses relating to sex and sexuality, describing their history, their conflicting definitions, and criticisms of them. It encourages critical reflexivity around the context and ethics of categorising diverse sexualities as 'abnormal' or 'pathological'. Critical reflexivity means reflecting on our own understandings and their potential impact within our cultural context.

When there is an established way of talking about something, we can sometimes forget or be unaware of the many other ways that we could think about it. For example, it might sound strange to our ears that before we considered some forms of violence between strangers as a kind of mental health problem (e.g. 'sexual sadism'), it was a common view that such acts were committed by people who turned into beasts, such as werewolves or vampires (Gibson, 2012; Otten, 1986). This was within accepted explanations during the medieval period (fifth–fifteenth centuries) when people more often lived in small villages surrounded by woods (Walter, 2015). Sometimes these behaviours were explained as spiritual possession (e.g. by a demon or devil) that required a religious intervention such as an exorcism (Gibson, 2012; Otten, 1986). Many sexual activities that are not solely aimed at reproduction (e.g. sodomy and masturbation), were also positioned as sinful and to be feared (Bayer, 1981; Herek, 2010). Christian religious texts repeatedly emphasise(d) how sex for pleasure (rather than for having children) was an evil sin that should be avoided for fear of a wide range of consequences, which included criminal punishment for 'crimes against nature', such as execution (Robb, 2003).

Over time the influence of religious, spiritual and supernatural perspectives subsided in place of criminal explanations as the predominant, authoritative discourse. While religious and spiritual understandings continued to influence thought on what was 'appropriate' sexual behaviour, violent acts, or forms of sexuality that moved away from a strict reproductive focus (e.g. homosexuality), became largely labelled as criminal. Shortly thereafter, psychological and psychiatric viewpoints began to question whether these activities were the result of a criminal mind or if the individuals were in fact suffering from mental health problems and should not be deemed criminally responsible. Krafft-Ebing's highly influential book *Psychopathia Sexualis* (1892) examined this issue at length and defined many of the paraphilias that we are familiar with in psychological textbooks today.

Pause for reflection

Do you think that your culture still sees any forms of sexuality or sexual behaviour as criminal, or as pathological, today? If so, why do you think that is?

Many people were grateful for this change in focus, given that they had previously been thought of as 'monsters' and the psychological viewpoint seemed more sympathetic (Oosterhuis, 2000). Over time, however, we have seen how framing sexual difference and diversity as a 'mental health problem' can lead to stigma, shame and discrimination (Poole et al., 2012). Medicalising and pathologising behaviours and identities contributes to this context where diversity is viewed through the lens of 'abnormality', meaning that we look at people who are different from ourselves as something dangerous and to be feared. As you saw in Chapters 3 and 4, while people with a psychiatric diagnosis are at a far higher risk of being the victim of violence than a perpetrator (Mack, 2014; Maniglio, 2009; Weston-Parry, 2013), their psychiatric label can result in civil commitments, forced treatments and a loss of personal independence and bodily autonomy (Breggin, 1993; Pescoslido et al., 1999). How we choose to describe emotional distress and how we choose to respond to it can have serious consequences for a wide range of individuals and communities.

Stigma and prejudice were some of the reasons that another influential and controversial researcher, John Money (1986), introduced the word 'paraphilia'. He stated that this was an attempt to move away from judgemental terms, such as 'perversion' (previously used by individuals such as Krafft-Ebing and Freud). Unfortunately, 'paraphilia' had its problems too, as 'para' means 'abnormal' and 'philia' means 'love' (Moser, 2001). In other words, saying that someone has a paraphilia is defining their sexual activities as 'abnormal', and in doing so, replicates the problems of the previous terms.

Activity 11.1: Masturbation

During the nineteenth century it was a common view within sexology and psychiatry that masturbation was a perversion that could lead to madness. There was so much fear circulating at the time in relation to the terrible

(Continued)

(Continued)

consequences of 'self pleasure' that Hunt (1998) referred to it as the 'masturbation panic'. Over time, this 'panic' has subsided from academic spheres and masturbation is viewed as a 'normal' and even beneficial sexual activity. Moreover, masturbation was a key focus of feminist sexual liberation activities during the second wave of feminism (from the 1960s until the 1980s), with the publication of Dodson's (1974) celebrated work *Sex for One: The Joy of Selfloving*, and consciousness-raising groups that taught women how to masturbate.

Through this example we can see how strong views about sexual activities can change dramatically depending on the time period and context.

- Can you think of any current strong views regarding sexual activities or expressions that could change over time?
- What things do you think people will look back on in 100 years from now thinking that we were strange to have feared or condemned it?
- Thinking back to the previous chapters, what might such changes contribute to a culture where consent was the 'norm' and everyone's right to say 'yes' or 'no' to bodily contact was respected?

The topic of 'paraphilia' is marred with a lot of conflict. There continues to be debate regarding whether or not such activities should be seen as a crime or a mental health problem. Increasingly over time, there have also been those who argue that sexual difference or diversity are in fact neither. Rather than focus on the perceived 'abnormality' of the act, some have argued that what is more important is consent to that behaviour between individuals. They have also highlighted how criminalising or pathologising sexual diversity is generally unhelpful. Some have even stated that the concept of 'paraphilias' is so deeply flawed that it should be scrapped from the profession altogether (Moser, 2001). We will explore some of these debates in more detail in this chapter and look at examples of 'paraphilias' that have been the focus of controversy both inside and outside psychology.

Homosexuality

In Krafft-Ebing's landmark text, *Psychopathia Sexualis* (1892), he outlined many sexual activities and orientations as 'perversions'. Homosexuality[1] was included in this list, and he described the 'condition' as sexual activity and/or attraction between individuals of the same gender. It was also

---

[1]Or 'contrary sexual feeling' or 'sexual inversion'.

at this time that individual criminal behaviours (such as sodomy) became described and understood as internal and unchanging identities (i.e. the homosexual, Foucault, 1976). Subsequently, this changed the focus from temporary imprisonment for a 'bad decision', to medical treatment for a 'mental disorder'. Homosexuality was listed under the 'sexual deviations' section in the first and second editions of the Diagnostic and Statistical Manual of Mental Disorders (DSM) produced by the American Psychiatric Association (APA) in 1952 and 1968.

Not everyone shared this view. For example, Hirschfeld, Kinsey and Hooker were some of the people who studied homosexuality looking at the general population, instead of only studying those who were convicted or committed. Their results were starkly different. Kinsey, Pomeroy and Martin's (1948) survey that found 37% of the general population had engaged in sexual activity with someone of the same gender. Hooker (1957) compared homosexual and heterosexual individuals and found that the frequency of psychopathology was relatively similar. Hirschfeld (1914/2000) completed a comprehensive examination of homosexuality from biological and sociological perspectives that included a critique of various methods of classification, theories on causation, and treatment approaches. These researchers argued that homosexuality was not in itself pathological, and Hirschfeld and others actively campaigned to decriminalise homosexuality (Brennan & Hegarty, 2007).

At the same time, however, there were those who continued to view homosexuality purely as a 'disease' and worked towards finding a treatment. These treatments included giving men[2] electric shocks or drugs to induce nausea or vomiting when shown images of men (e.g. Freund, 1960; MacCulloch and Feldman, 1967). This was a behaviourist approach that aimed to create an association between homosexual arousal and pain, discomfort and displeasure. It was unsuccessful and widely criticised, both for its lack of ethics as well as its lack of success (Bancroft, 1974; Davison, 1976; Gittings, 2007). Other methods were used at this time, such as psychoanalytic therapies which were based on the belief that homosexuality was a stage of development before heterosexuality (Bayer, 1981). Based on this theory, some psychoanalysts tried to treat homosexual adults in the belief that they had developed the 'perversion' during their psychosexual development in childhood (e.g. Beiber et al., 1962).

This disagreement within the profession came to a head during the 1970s due to the accumulation of research that found treatment of same-sex attraction to be unsuccessful, increasing research

---

[2]As the majority of those seen were men, although they also treated individuals with other gender identities.

highlighting the relative 'normality' of same-sex relationships, as well as increasing pressure and protests both inside and outside the profession regarding gay rights. In 1973 the APA hosted a panel entitled 'Should homosexuality be in the APA nomenclature?' and a vote followed, which resulted in the removal of homosexuality as a mental health problem from future editions of the DSM (APA, 1973; Gittings, 2007).

This, unfortunately, is not the end of the story. There were similar diagnoses in the DSM some years after, such as 'ego-dystonic homosexuality', which described homosexual individuals who wanted to pursue heterosexuality (APA, 1980). This diagnosis was also widely criticised and removed from the nomenclature. Some therapists who try to change someone's sexual orientation still practise, mostly within religious contexts (i.e. reparative therapists), despite it being condemned by many professional organisations and, in some cases, illegal (e.g. Fang, 2015; Ferguson, 2015). Some of this criticism prompted the development of the gender and sexual diversity affirmative therapy approaches that you read about in Chapter 10.

Case example: John

While reparative therapies have been widely condemned and current guidelines frame such approaches as unethical (e.g. British Psychological Society, 2012; Keogh et al., 2015), the 'treatment' of 'feminine boys' continues. Moreover, a recent research survey found that 17% of UK therapists had tried to change a client's sexual orientation. In this study, 222 therapists reported trying to change a client's sexuality from homosexuality to heterosexuality from the 1960s onwards, including over 295 clients between 1994 and 2003 (Bartlett, Smith & King, 2009).

John was referred to a psychiatrist at the request of his parents. He was six years old and had been refusing to play with his brothers, choosing to spend his time socialising with three girls in his neighbourhood. He had come home on more than one occasion from the neighbour's house dressed in girls' clothing and had started asking his parents for toys that they considered to be inappropriate for boys (e.g. dolls). The parents were worried that their child would grow up to be sexually deviant. They had stated explicitly that they did not want their child to be gay or trans due to their religious beliefs. The psychiatrist informed the parents that there were no known successful therapies that change someone's sexual orientation, but that they could work together to encourage John to be more masculine.

Activity 11.2: Better practice with John

Think about the potential implications of parents and therapists encouraging a child to change in this way.

* If the child enjoys expressing femininity and shows no signs of emotional distress regarding his own behaviour, should a therapist intervene?
* Do you think this is an example of ethical practice? Why/why not?

Transvestism and autogynephilia

Some psychologists and psychiatrists have tried to 'treat' people for their gender expression when their appearance or behaviour has not matched the narrow definition of 'normality' that the profession has frequently promoted. Some of these diagnoses come under 'gender identity disorders', such as transsexualism or gender dysphoria, but others are listed as 'paraphilias'. The paraphilias include transvestism and an even more controversial term, 'autogynephilia'. Transvestism is a diagnosis that shows how those in psychology can confuse gender and sexuality. In Krafft-Ebing's (1892) attempt to describe homosexuality he included a phase where individuals presented or dressed as another gender. He also described a diagnosis of 'fetishism' which referred specifically to men who dressed in women's clothing. The terms used to describe 'cross-dressing' centred on these early diagnoses for many years, with the DSM including transvestism and fetishism in various guises since the first edition.

The diagnosis in the DSM-5 includes transvestism with autogynephilia. This latter term has amassed a large amount of criticism since Blanchard introduced it in the 1980s (e.g. Moser, 2009; Serano, 2010; Veale, Clarke & Lomax, 2011). He defined the diagnosis as when a man is sexually aroused at the thought of himself being a woman (Blanchard, 1989). This reaffirmed the already longstanding history of psychological approaches connecting cross-gender behaviour with 'perversion', which has a tendency to conflate sexual and gender identity. For those who do 'cross-dress' as a part of their sexual activity, there were criticisms and protests that such behaviour was not a mental health problem but a part of non-harmful, consensual sexual diversity. Similarly, criticisms were made from those who participated in 'cross-dressing' in a non-sexual way, as well as from trans communities, who argued that the diagnosis associated some gender expressions with sexuality and 'perversion', when their experience of their gender identity or expression was neither (Veale et al., 2011). Many pointed out the contradictions inherent in a diagnosis that pathologised male femininity but not female masculinity.

The difficulty in arguing for a non-pathologised recognition of those who 'cross-dress' either sexually or non-sexually is further complicated by psychological and media representations of the activity. Both mainstream mass media and some forensic psychology approaches have included a predominant focus on 'cross-dressing' as a frightening 'perversion' linked to serial killers. This has often been exaggerated further, to suggest or imply that trans people (who do not 'cross-dress' but are a different gender from that which was assigned at their birth) are violent predators. These narratives work to generate irrational fear, or transphobia. For example, the very successful *Silence of the Lambs* (Demme, 1991) film includes this trope of a man's desire to be female as evidence of his sociopathology, 'sickness' and inherent 'evil'. This trope is also reflected in a range of psychological texts, where 'cross-dressing' or transvestism is repeatedly associated with serial murder and violence in numerous case studies, despite acknowledging the rarity of this (e.g. Langevin, 2003; Lauerma, Voutilainen & Tuominen, 2010; Myers, 2004; Myers et al., 2008; Steiner, Sanders & Langevin, 1985; Zucker & Bradley, 1995).

The problem isn't in describing cases where individuals 'cross-dress' and murder, as they do exist. Rather, the problem is in making the association between two behaviours and assuming that they are in some way connected, or that one causes the other. In other words, there are many people who 'cross-dress' who do not commit violence (many, many more than those who do), and there are those who murder with no history of 'cross-dressing'. In fact, the majority of violence (including serial murder) is committed by men who do not 'cross-dress', do not have a psychiatric diagnosis, and are not trans (James & Smith, 2014; Kimmel & Mahler, 2003; Statistics Canada, 2015). Therefore, singling out 'cross-dressing' individuals as a particular group who kill is not only unethical, it is inaccurate. Nevertheless, psychology and psychiatry, and society more generally, continues to be fascinated by the 'cross-dressing' serial killer or the predatory transsexual lingering in public bathrooms (e.g. Jeffreys, 2014b). The fear is based on over a century of sensationalised media accounts and psychological research that created the concept of 'perversion' in the first place, and ignored the pleas and protests of the very communities and individuals it claimed to help.

The problem goes beyond just how we describe people or behaviours, and beyond an irrational interest. Those who do not conform to the norms of gender that psychology defines (trans people, non-binary individuals, etc.) experience stigma, shame, discrimination and violence.

It is increasingly well documented that these communities are under high threat of violence, such as assault, rape and murder (Stotzer, 2008; Turner, Whittle, & Combs, 2009; Wyss, 2004). Framing them as scary and threatening people just for being themselves makes it more difficult for them to access the support they need, to prevent violence, and to be believed if they have been hurt. We focus on the sensationalised fictional murderer, while turning a blind eye to the suffering of a real oppressed group (see Chapters 3 and 6 for more on the role of media representations and gender more broadly).

Sadism and masochism

Sadism was coined by Krafft-Ebing (1892) as a form of sexuality that combined violence with lust. While it was considered an unusual or 'abnormal' sexuality, there was much evidence in both his work, and that of others (e.g. Ellis, 1923; Freud, 1949), that masculine sexuality was viewed as 'normally' violent. Therefore, only those instances where the violence was perceived to be 'extreme' were framed as a mental health problem. This differentiation within psychology and psychiatry remains: artificially trying to separate what violence is 'normal' and what is not. For some, violence becomes 'abnormal' when it fails to serve a function or purpose, such as overpowering a victim (Freud, 1949). It becomes seen as a 'sickness' when it is considered to be unreasonable, impractical or for the purposes of pleasure. In other words, psychiatry positions violence as 'normal' if it is used to gain pleasure (such as to steal or force someone to do something you want) but abnormal if it is the violence itself which is deemed pleasurable (Tosh, 2015).

Sadism is a highly contested concept, particularly as the term was coined based on the work of Marquis de Sade. Sade (1791/2005) was known for his erotic fiction, such as *Justine*. Krafft-Ebing (1892) based the term on Sade's work, resulting in a complex relationship between psychiatry and erotica. 'Sadism' was taken up within psychiatry and psychology, as well as sexual subcultures, such as kink or BDSM (Bondage and Discipline, Dominance and Submission, and Sadomasochism) communities. However, the term is defined differently within these two very different areas. Within psychology it is considered to be a mental health problem with an emphasis on violence and non-consent. It is the kind of behaviour that tends to be the focus of popular crime shows, like *Criminal Minds* (Davis, 2005), and classic forensic texts based on convicted serial killers, like *Sexual Homicide* (Ressler, Burgess & Douglas, 1988). Both areas promote the idea of a dangerous psychopathic killer who tortures his victims, and thus is a 'sexual sadist'.

Activity 11.3: Psychiatric diagnoses and erotica

There are numerous examples of fiction and erotica influencing psychiatric thought, and of psychiatric diagnoses and theories inspiring erotica and pornography. Some examples are shown in Table 11.1.

Table 11.1   Psychiatric diagnoses and erotica

Erotica	Psychiatric diagnosis	Pornography
Justine (de Sade, 1791)	*Sadism* (Krafft-Ebing, 1892)	*120 Days of Sodom* (Pasolini, 1975); *The Story of O* (Jaeckin, 1975); *Fifty Shades of Grey* (Taylor-Johnson, 2015)
Venus in Furs (Sacher-Masoch, 1870)	*Masochism* (Krafft-Ebing, 1892)	*Belle de Jour* (Buñuel, 1967); *Venus in Furs* (Franco, 1969)
	Nymphomania (Bienville, 1771)	*Nymphomaniac: Vol. I* (Trier, 2013a); *Nymphomaniac: Vol. II* (Trier, 2013b)

- Do you think these diagnoses are likely to reflect accurate accounts of people's sexual behaviour, or their fantasies and sexual thoughts?
- Does listing something as 'perverse' and 'abnormal' make it more likely that people will stop the behaviour, or will it become more tempting?
- What do you think it says about psychiatry (and pornography) that this mutual influence exists?

The term 'sadism' is used within BDSM communities very differently, referring to a non-pathological sexual activity or interest, where consent is explicitly negotiated between partners. It includes a wide range of sexual activities (e.g. role play, bondage, biting, spanking, etc.) as well as many reasons why people find them enjoyable, such as physical pleasure, fun, personal growth, engaging with a community, confidence, and a freedom from everyday roles (Hébert & Weaver, 2015). That's not to say that non-consensual experiences don't happen; no community is immune to sexual abuse and assault (Barker, 2013a). Just as widespread domestic violence and rape occurs within heterosexual monogamous couples (Kelly, Lovett & Regan, 2005, see Chapter 6), we know that being in a kink relationship is not the reason for violence when it does occur. However, the situation is further complicated, particularly within legal contexts, where individuals can be deemed unable to consent to BDSM activities as they can be framed as 'assault'.

This was the outcome of the UK Spanner case (Regina vs. Brown, 1990) where 16 men were charged with either assault (the dominants/tops) or with aiding and abetting an assault (the submissives/bottoms). The law has not changed since then.

There has been a lot of debate and criticism about whether sadism is dangerous or 'normal' (Moser, 2011; Shindel & Moser, 2011). There are many problems with these kind of questions, mainly that they over-simplify complex aspects of people's lives and diverse communities. As the diagnosis can be used to commit someone under a range of laws[3] (such as the US Sexually Violent Predator Acts or the UK Mental Health Act), there can be very serious consequences depending on how we define sexual 'deviance' and if we consider it to be 'normal' or something to be feared.

Unfortunately, much of the work within psychiatry and psychology focuses on convicted serial killers. This is obviously more likely to find 'sadists' who aim to harm others. Psychologists working with consensual BDSM communities or clients come up with very different findings. Consequently, one of the most significant issues in these debates is the use of the same language (i.e. 'sexual sadism') to describe two very different things: (a) violent murderers and (b) consensual sexual diversity. Conflating these two diverse groups means that those who are in a BDSM relationship with a partner (or partners) can be labelled as 'mentally ill' or 'dangerous', and in some cases, committed or imprisoned under the assumption that everyone with this label is equally at risk of violence.

Conceptually, sexual sadism is rarely considered on its own. Krafft-Ebing (1892), Ellis (1923) and others (e.g. Freud, 1924/2001) often positioned it as opposite to another diagnosis: masochism. Krafft-Ebing coined both diagnoses, basing masochism on the works of Sacher-Masoch, another writer of erotic fiction. This diagnosis described those who experienced pleasure in receiving aggression (such as spanking, etc.), being humiliated, or creating an environment where they were (or were perceived to be) under the control of another person. Where sadism was thought to be related to 'norms' of masculinity due to its association with aggression, masochism was often aligned with femininity:

> What the woman secretly desires in intercourse is rape and violence, or in the mental sphere, humiliation. The process of childbirth gives her an unconscious masochistic satisfaction. ... Furthermore, as far as men indulge in masochistic fantasies or performances, these represent an expression of their desire to play the female role. (Horney, 1935/1973, p. 215)

---

[3]Obscenity laws can be enforced on representations of a wide range of sexual activities deemed 'abnormal' also.

The concept of masochism has also had much criticism and debate. Within the profession there is the same issue and disagreement regarding whether it is 'abnormal' or not, and masochism disorder remains in the current DSM-5 as a paraphilia (APA, 2013), alongside sexual sadism disorder. However, it has also come under scrutiny for attempts to create a personality disorder of the same name and idea, which would be predominantly applied to women (particularly those in abusive relationships) (Caplan & Gans, 1991; Ritchie, 1989).

The issues around gender relating to both of these concepts within psychiatry and psychology has led to much feminist input and discussion, mostly around how they are potentially harmful to women, such as labelling victims of domestic abuse as 'mentally ill' (Caplan, 2005; see Chapter 6). However, these disagreements and criticisms have also been an aspect of feminism itself, with different feminist communities also disagreeing over whether or not masochism and sadism are harmful, or even if they exist (Chancer, 2000). Some feminists argue that as sadism is aligned with masculinity and aggression, it is ultimately anti-feminist. Others state that the concepts were invented by psychiatrists to blame women for their victimisation and to justify the actions of violent men. However, this excluded the voices of BDSM feminists, who highlight how aggression and power relations can be subverted and deliberately performed within BDSM relationships and role plays. Again, we see the problems of discussing 'sexual sadism' or 'masochism' as if they mean only one thing, and the semantic arguments that result when a category like this is defined so broadly that it includes many kinds of people, and therefore many different variations of 'sadomasochism'.

Paraphilic coercive disorder

While some cases of sexual sadism refer to sexual violence, it wasn't until the 1980s that the American Psychiatric Association proposed a new diagnosis that specifically framed rape as a form of mental health problem. This new diagnosis, initially called 'paraphilic rapism' (Caplan, 1995; Thornton, 2010), was meant to refer to individuals who rape as their predominant means of sexual activity or fantasies, but never made it into the DSM. The profession struggled to differentiate between rapists as criminals and those who rape due to this particular diagnosis (Tosh, 2011a). One attempt made was to distinguish between these groups by the frequency of the behaviour. That is, those who raped less than three times were deemed to be 'normal' (or 'opportunistic') and those who raped more frequently than that were thought to represent a sub-group of men who had this disorder

(APA, 2010). This attempt to quantify sexual violence and pathology was highly contested and ultimately rejected.

What gets discussed less often, however, is the role of consent. While feminists and BDSM scholars and communities have considered the concept at length, often psychology and psychiatry assume a simple meaning to this complex concept. For example, the criteria for 'paraphilic coercive disorder' included sexual intercourse with 'non-consenting' people (APA, 2010), but never defined what was meant by 'non-consenting'. Within feminism there is much discussion around how women can freely consent within a patriarchal culture, or how coercion can take many forms beyond explicit violence (such as blackmail, emotional or financial abuse, threats of violence, and so on), and how many women engage in 'unwanted' sex for a wide range of reasons (Walker, 1997), including because they want to feel 'normal' (Tosh & Carson, 2016).

Pause for reflection

What reasons do you think that people have for having sex when they don't really want it? List as many as you can think of. You might reflect on whether these are related to power differences between people (e.g. if they are of different genders, cultural backgrounds or body-types), and the difficulties that poses for ensuring consensual sex.

The idea of diagnosing those who rape was met with a wealth of criticism and concern (Caplan, 1995; Frances, 2011a, 2011b; Tosh, 2011a; Zander, 2008), particularly in relation to how it could be misused within the legal system (a criticism voiced from forensic psychologists and psychiatrists) and used to justify or excuse the actions of a rapist (an argument from feminist academics and activists). There were even threats of legal action against the APA if it pursued the diagnosis for inclusion in the DSM (Caplan, 1995). The diagnosis was rejected by the APA in 1986, and did not make it into the DSM. It has been suggested several times since, most recently in 2010 (Tosh, 2011b). Each time criticisms and concerns drown out calls for inclusion, and the diagnosis goes back into the reject pile.

Nevertheless, the concept of a mental health problem based on repeatedly raping others remains a key area in forensic psychology and psychiatry (e.g. DeClue, 2006; Doren, 2002), despite the lack of consensus. For example, 'paraphilia not otherwise specified (NOS)' is often used to diagnose those who rape but do not fit under any other available diagnostic labels (like 'sexual sadism'). Paraphilia NOS is then used to commit individuals for their behaviours or fantasies (and in some cases, their role plays) under mental health legislation (Douard, 2007). This can also be used to enforce treatment, such as cognitive behavioural therapy, or the more controversial 'hormonal castration' (Money, 1986), where psychiatrists prescribe pharmaceuticals to reduce sex drive and induce impotence. These treatment methods are as contested and controversial as the diagnoses themselves.

Case example: Coercive sexual fantasies

Dave was increasingly worried about his sexual fantasies. He had been married to his wife for over a year and they had sex fairly regularly. Dave was happy with his relationship, but also fantasised while masturbating about raping her. Dave was scared to tell his wife, or anyone, about this desire. He sought the help of a psychiatrist, who diagnosed him as having 'paraphilia NOS' and prescribed him some anti-depressants. While his mood improved after this, the relationship with his wife deteriorated as Dave's sexual desire decreased and, on more than one occasion, he was unable to get an erection with her. Dave was concerned as he had not told his wife about the diagnosis, the treatments, or the side effects they could have. He became extremely distraught at the thought of hurting his wife and insisted that he did not find violence arousing. Dave's psychiatrist offered an alternative treatment of hormonal therapy, but Dave has started considering rape role play but is unsure if this would be a healthy choice for him.

- Do you think Dave's distress is because of a mental health problem or due to a fear of how others will react to his fantasy?
- Should we diagnose people based on their sexual fantasies?
- From this case study, is it possible to tell whether or not Dave is a rapist?

Conclusion

The paraphilias represent a contradictory concept where diagnoses reflect longstanding ideas that have changed very little since their initial definition, while simultaneously inspiring a wealth of debate, disagreement and protest over the years. They also show how diagnostic terms are often applied to broad and diverse groups of people, but are assumed to represent a universal and simple concept (see Chapter 4).

There are also problems with a profession that focuses its attention on certain kinds of sexual violence and positions the rest as 'normal'. As we saw in the previous chapter, those 'sadistic' serial killers that we hear about so often on television or within forensic psychology account for an extremely small number of violent incidents when compared to those committed by 'ordinary' (i.e. non-pathologised) people. So should psychology be more concerned with the 'normal' population? Similarly, why spend so much time analysing, convicting and treating those with 'unusual' sexual interests (according to psychiatrists) when we could be working towards the elimination of sexual violence, building a culture of sexual consent and celebrating sexual diversity?

Suggestions for further reading

Moser, C., and Kleinplatz, P. (2005). DSM-IV-TR and the paraphilias: an argument for removal. *Journal of Psychology and Human Sexuality, 17*(3/4), 91–109.
This paper provides a critical analysis of the concept of 'paraphilia'.

Oosterhuis, H. (2000). *Stepchildren of nature: Krafft-Ebing, psychiatry, and the making of sexual identity*. Chicago, IL: University of Chicago Press.
Robb, G. (2003). *Strangers: homosexual love in the nineteenth century*. London: Picador.
Two books describing the historical context and development of psychiatric diagnoses of sexuality.

Tosh, J. (2015). *Perverse psychology: the pathologization of sexual violence and transgenderism*. London: Routledge.
Zander, T. (2008). Commentary: inventing diagnosis for civil commitment of rapists. *Journal of American Psychiatry and Law, 36*, 459–469.
Two critical publications on the problems of psychiatry diagnosing sexual violence.

12

SEX WORK

ALLAN TYLER

Image 12   Twisted shadows. With permission, Kirsty Ann Harris

Introduction to sex work

For many people, the only knowledge they have about sex work comes from films (e.g. *Pretty Woman*, 1990), television (e.g. *The Secret Diary of a Call Girl*, Demange, et al., 2007) or news stories of murder investigations (e.g. BBC, 2006). Most people never study the topic of selling sex itself, so it is easy to understand how people rely on stereotypes and anecdotes of extreme cases – even in their professional roles (Hawthorne, 2011; see Chapter 3). This chapter addresses that gap between media representations and real sex work by presenting research on the experiences of sex workers, as well as discussing some of the legal and social structures around sex work which vary geographically. Sex work will be considered as a cluster of intersecting phenomena and practices rather than one unified behaviour.

This chapter looks critically at definitions of what sex work is, and how beliefs about people selling sex are informed or challenged. It will examine 'sex work' and 'prostitution' through legal and psychological perspectives as well as introducing some of the models that have been developed in psychology to understand sex work. It will go on to focus on concerns that people and organisations have about sexual exploitation before exploring this from the perspective of people who sell sex. Through the chapter you will have the opportunity to explore what 'sex' can mean in the context of sex work, how people have explained their decisions to sell sex, what kinds of sex work they will and will not do, and how these decisions can be affected by their environment and social contacts. Finally, you will consider examples of how forms of sex work have been utilised within therapeutic approaches.

It is crucial to keep in mind that legal and geographical variations create radically different contexts and priorities for the people who are engaged in, or are affected by, sex work. For example, in many countries it is illegal to sell sex. Alternatively, Sweden, Norway, Iceland and France have made it illegal to *pay* for sex. In most places in the United States, it is illegal to buy *or* sell sex (Weitzer, 2010a), while in New Zealand, selling sex was decriminalised in 2003.

New policies and legislation are being enacted nationally and locally, with no consensus about one best way to protect people from exploitation, or even what constitutes 'exploitation' when factors such as gender, race, age and nationality intersect with individual resources. This chapter uses a number of examples in the context of the current legal situation for people in Britain, acknowledging transnational movements and politics.

Turning to the issue of sexual consent, which was considered in the last three chapters, in the area of sex work tensions persist around understandings of choice, free-will and coercion. Some argue that sex workers freely consent in their work; others argue that they cannot possibly consent given the cultural and financial pressures they are under; some point out that *no* workers are free of such pressures and that this is in no way specific to sex work. The idea of *agency* indicates an ability to be self-directed and take action; however, all of our choices and behaviours take place within existing social *structures* such as those around class, gender and race (see Chapters 5–8). The tensions around structure and agency, and in ensuring consent within this, will be a theme that will be returned to throughout the chapter.

What is sex work?

Amnesty International (2016, p.15) defines sex work as 'situations where adults who are engaging in commercial sex have consented to do so'. Where consent is absent, such activities would be considered abuses of human rights and treated as criminal offences, 'including threat or use of force, deception, fraud, and abuse of power or involvement of a child' (Amnesty International, 2016, p. 15). This definition acknowledges the multiple ways in which criminal behaviour, including violence, can impact upon people who sell sex. However, from a counselling and forensic psychology perspective, it is also important to be mindful of the various ways that sex workers themselves are often considered to be criminals and/or mentally unwell, and are treated as such by health, legal, psychological and other social systems and professionals in ways that may perpetuate or compound distress through a circular relationship between societal norms and practices (Pilcher, 2016).

As we have seen, some people make assumptions that sex workers freely consent to what they do. Others assume that consenting to paid sex is itself a form – or consequence – of victimisation. It is important to remain mindful that the experiences of sex workers are as diverse and multifaceted as the experiences and beliefs of people who work with them.

Activity 12.1: Assumptions about sex workers

Think about the cultural assumptions that you are aware of around sex work.

* Make a list of common beliefs about people who sell sex.
* What information is used to support those beliefs?
* Which ones do you think could be generalised to all sex workers?
* Which ones do you think should be questioned? How might a psychologist go about challenging them?

The term 'sex work' is often used synonymously with prostitution, which means engaging in sex in exchange for payment or other benefits (Bernstein, 2007), although 'sex work' can also be used as an umbrella-term for a number of erotic labours, including lap dancing, stripping, telephone sex, escorting, compensated sex, domination/submission for pay (see Chapter 11), pornography, and sex tourism (Christina, 2004). This chapter's main focus is what is commonly referred to as prostitution, although many of these concepts and experiences overlap. It is also necessary to recognise that some people may be involved in more than one type of sex work at any given time, or at different points of involvement with the sex industry (Christina, 2004; Walby et al., 2012).

The language of 'sex work' and 'sex workers' is used to recognise the physical and emotional labour processes involved (Walby et al., 2012) and to escape from some of the negative connotations that may be associated with 'prostitution' (Walby et al., 2012). However, even this terminology is problematic. For a start, we can question what counts as 'sex' (Attwood, 2006; Plummer, 1995; see Chapter 10). While all 'sex work' may involve an erotic tone or sexualised atmosphere, it does not necessarily involve an explicitly sexual act. For example, an escort may be paid for time to share a romantic meal; a submissive may hire a dominating top for whipping and domination, but not genital sex. In the naming of 'sex' workers, there is a risk that a mythologised identity is created.

Information box 12.1: Shifting definitions of prostitution

'To be a prostitute is not and never has been a crime' (Brooks-Gordon, 2006, p. 29). Prior to the Sexual Offences Act 2003, prostitution was defined only within Clause 122 of the draft Criminal Code Bill. From the Sexual Offences Act 2003, the definition of prostitute became:

- A person who, on at least one occasion, and whether or not compelled to do so, offers or provides sexual services to another person in return for payment or promise of payment to (them) or a third person
- 'Payment' means any financial advantage including the discharge of an obligation to pay or the provision of goods or services (including sexual services) gratuitously or at a discount (Brooks-Gordon, 2006, p. 28).

> ## Pause for reflection
>
> Look at the definition in Information box 12.1 closely. According to British law any person who on one occasion offers sexual services to another person in return for free sexual services is a prostitute. By this logic, could two consenting adults who have reciprocally performed (or just agreed to) sexual acts for each other both be defined as 'prostitutes'? Think about what provision of goods and services are considered acceptable and unacceptable to provide in return for sex in wider culture.

One study of gay and bisexual men in Europe found that 5% of the men who responded had sold sex at least once in the past year (Weatherburn et al., 2013). Such data offers support for the reality that people who sell sex do not all identify with the description of 'sex worker' or see what they do as 'sex work' or 'prostitution'. Of men who had sold sex in the past 12 months, 52% had sold sex only once or twice. Fewer than 10% (of the original 5%) had sold sex more than 50 times in that 52-week period (0.5% of all respondents) (Weatherburn et al., 2013).

Sex work and exploitation

Between 2005 and 2010 the Police Service of Northern Ireland (PSNI) recorded a total of 18 offences, including 'exercising control over a prostitute, controlling prostitution for gain and paying for the sexual services of a child' (Hawthorne, 2011, p. 145) and seven offences of trafficking for exploitation. In interpreting these low numbers we could conclude that such crimes are difficult to detect because of various problems, including international jurisdiction and victim co-operation. To bring charges and obtain convictions against traffickers, the police need evidence and witnesses who are willing to testify in court. People may be afraid to make statements or testify for fear of being incriminated and, in some cases, deported. People who sell sex may be suspicious of agencies and professionals whose services have historically prosecuted sex workers or made support contingent on desistance (i.e. 'exiting' or 'rescue'). Those services may be regarded as unsafe or unhelpful to someone who does not wish to co-operate as a victim committed to proscriptive rehabilitation (Cornwall, 2014). Alternatively, people who have been coerced into sex work express fear of criminal retribution. Again, it is crucial to be open to hearing from sex workers themselves about their experiences and perspectives.

Psychology, sex work and the law

There are a number of cognitive, social, legal and embodied tensions for people who sell sex. While it is not illegal to 'be a prostitute', there are 35 possible offences related to selling sex. Two new measures that were introduced in the Anti-Social Behaviour, Crime and Policing Act 2014 were flagged as potential ways government might exercise jurisdictional regulation of the activities of sex workers: the Injunction to Prevent Nuisance and Annoyance (IPNA) and the Criminal Behaviour Order (CBO) (Lynch, 2014). The laws concerning sex work – and indeed many forms of sexual expression – are often unworkable, unenforceable, ineffective, ignored, contradictory and discriminatory (see Chapter 11).

Further legislation controls against managing, controlling and recruiting other sex workers. For example, conviction for keeping a brothel carries up to seven years in prison (Sanders, 2005), although charges of pimping brought against several massage parlours were thrown out unless a complaint was actually made against them (Sanders, 2005). The law and its practice are at odds with one another when local councils routinely inspect and license massage parlours where sex work takes place (Weitzer, 2010a, 2010b) while projects to control 'kerb crawling' and 'nuisance' move (mostly) women into isolated locations.

Legal contexts are historically gendered. For example, there have been uneven changes and challenges to women's rights and uneven recognitions of sexualities other than heterosexuality. Some LGBT+ politics (including decriminalisation of male homosexuality, employment rights, partner-recognition, and perhaps even gender recognition) have changed far more dramatically than social attitudes towards sex work (Tyler, 2015; Weeks, 2007).

Models of sex work

Given the limited cultural understandings of sex work, and the tendency to regard sex workers as one unified group who are all vulnerable, helping professionals in this area are at risk of viewing the people they work with purely as a 'sex worker' or 'prostitute' rather than as a complex human being with multiple roles and identities. Such a deficit model (Matthews et al., 2014) may also align sex workers with (possibly assumed) identities of 'victim', 'addict', 'foreigner' and/or 'illegal'.

Practices of 'supporting sex workers', 'rescuing' and 'exiting' can reinforce hierarchies of those who *do the helping* and those who *need help*. These hierarchies are often aligned with socio-economic status, education, access to financial and social capital, nationality and (mental) health. When a well-intended professional has identified a rationale which fits their self-definition as helper, they can unintentionally reinforce systems of power and privilege (cf. Rubin, 1993; Weeks, 2007). Ironically, these often feel much like the same systems which a sex worker may have been seeking to fit into or escape. This is the reason that sex worker activist slogans include 'save us from saviours' and 'our bodies, our business'. They highlight the importance of listening to sex worker experiences rather than starting from a set of narrow assumptions.

Research with sex workers themselves have informed some psychological and sociological models of sex work. For example, beyond the distinction between locations (on the street, in saunas or bars, residences, brothels), Vanwesenbeeck (2013) categorises motives for 'entry' into sex work as:

> financial, sexual, recreational motives, and coercion (i.e. trafficking). All of these are bound to play a role for women as well as for men but, noting that the sex work business is firmly rooted in (unequal) gender relations in sex and finance, most likely are not equally strong. For both sexes, however, the number one motive for engaging in commercial or exchange sex is, without a doubt, earning money. (Vanwesenbeeck, 2013, p. 12)

This builds on the social-cognitive model developed by Smith et al. (2013). Their findings indicate that there are reciprocal influences of behaviour, environment and cognition in motivations for engaging in sex work. In contrast to deficit models, Smith et al. explore expressions of self-efficacy related to specific behaviours in sex work, and the development of 'positive outcome expectations' with some experiences. However, self-efficacy can be limited when sex workers express 'moral conflict' and a lack of (physical) attraction to their clients. Cognitively, sex work was rationalised, however, 'because their values and self-perceptions were consistent with an opportunity to earn what appeared to them as a significant amount of money' (Smith et al., 2013, p. 9). Again, it is always worth comparing sex work with other forms of work where there are frequently conflicts between what we would ideally do and the challenges or mundanity that our job requires in order for us to be paid.

Narratives of people who have sold sex reveal that involvement in multiple aspects of sex work may happen for a number of reasons, including necessity, proximity, aptitude or opportunity (Christina, 2004). While these drivers are often written about singularly, or in opposition to one another, together they form an important framework to consider the interconnectedness of multiple drivers within any one person's reasons for selling sex.

Sex work or sexual exploitation? Definitions, practices and concerns with 'consent'

As we have seen, consent is core to distinguishing sex work from sexual exploitation, sexual violence, gender-based violence, human trafficking, and/or modern slavery (Amnesty International, 2016). Activists, clinicians and policy-makers disagree on definitions of consent (Scoular, 2010). Some consider paying for sex to be exploitative and violent by its very nature (Coy, Wakeling & Garner, 2011; Jeffreys, 1997), others would only regard it as exploitative if there was clear coercion. Under international law there is no clear definition of sexual consent. Amnesty International uses the term to mean 'the voluntary and ongoing agreement to engage in a particular sexual activity' (Amnesty International, 2016, p. 15).

Like any other person, a sex worker can change or remove their consent at any point. How this has been respected or ignored in psychology and law is critical to understanding the nexus of sex, work and crime. As in any other situation, 'where consent is not voluntary and ongoing, including when a person's changed or rescinded consent is not respected, this constitutes rape and is a human rights abuse and must be treated as a criminal offence' (Amnesty International, 2016, p. 15).

As you saw in Chapters 9 and 10, the Sexual Offences Act 2003 defines consent as being present if a person 'agrees by choice and has the freedom and capacity to make that choice'. This includes two key points: first, whether a person has capacity at the time to decide whether or not they should take part in the sexual activity (e.g. in terms of age and understanding); and second, whether they are in a position to have made their decision freely, without being constrained in any way.

However, the circular logic in this argument is apparent when considering the intractable interrelationship between structure and agency. While agency is often read as a straightforward synonym for 'choice' or 'the ability to choose', our abilities to choose are confined to the (perceived) options available. The argument of capacity to consent is additionally complicated when a person has become reliant on using drugs and alcohol, for example. By reframing these debates with reference to the limited options of real, lived experiences, theoretical discussions and interpretations of 'freedom', 'choice', 'agency' and consent become more fuzzy and more complex to define (CPS, n.d.). Consider these points when reading the following case example.

Case example: Marcos

Marcos has been working as an escort for four years in London. He identifies as gay and all his clients are men. He is 24 years old, but like many people who use online profiles, he advertises himself as younger. He has set an age limit on the clients he will see because men older than their mid-50s often seem to be seeking affection and not just sex. Marcos says he advertises as 'versatile' (giving or receiving anal penetration) because he does not want the pressure of having to maintain an erection if he is seeing several clients in one day. Marcos prefers the boundaries of his interactions with clients compared to a financially dependent long-term relationship with one man.

Marcos is from Brazil but also has an Italian passport. When he first arrived in the UK five years ago, he stayed with a friend who did escorting. With limited English and only a tourist visa, he struggled to find work. After working in retail, Marcos now works as a full-time escort. He has ads in several different magazines, and profiles on multiple websites and apps, but is unaware of how much he spends on advertising. He wants to save enough money to buy a house, after which he plans to stop escorting and go into another field of work, although he is unclear as to what that might be. He is quite specific that he does not want to work in an office, he would like to travel once or twice a month with time allowed for tourism, and any job he takes will have to be well paid. Despite his plans, Marcos spends all of his earnings on luxury car payments, insurance, rent, cosmetic surgeries and holidays. Marcos does not know what his total outgoing costs are, and he has debt and no savings, so is not successfully achieving his financial goal.

- Reflect on how Marcos's story compares to other accounts of other sex workers, and young people who have travelled that you're aware of.
- Ask yourself about the issues that could cause problems for Marcos now or in the future and the opportunities and resources that might be advantageous for him.

There is considerable debate about how people selling sex might be exercising agency or re-enacting sexual victimisation. In part this is because female street sex workers frequently report a level of historical sexual abuse, including child sexual abuse, which is much higher than that reported by people who sell sex in other contexts (Vanwesenbeeck, 2001, 2013). There are fewer studies of the life histories of other kinds of female sex workers, or of male sex workers, although associations have been made between child sexual abuse and male street sex workers who inject drugs (Vanwesenbeeck, 2013).

Experiences of sex workers

As we have seen, it is important to emphasise that 'sex work' is not a single, homogenous behaviour. In psychology and other social sciences, attempts have been made (and continue to be suggested) to construct models which categorise 'typologies' of sex workers (Allen, 1980; Caukins & Coombs, 1976) as if people's backgrounds and actions made them sub-types of an evolving species. These seem helpful as categories for predicting behaviours, risks, resiliences and needs, but they can be limiting and can even be harmful in how they (unintentionally) *objectify* people even further.

Others have identified a continuum of sex work practices (Altman, 1999), for example from people giving 'hand jobs' to men outdoors to those who provide specialised fetish services in custom-fitted accommodation (Christina, 2004). Because people who sell sex have multiple identities, multiple contexts, multiple behaviours and multiple motivations, more of a 'quantum, diffraction model' is preferable, where a person may occupy multiple, interrelated points.

Scarcity and utilising embodiment

For professionals working with people who sell sex, understanding the variety of contexts and experiences is crucial to understanding their significance to the individual. Many people are familiar with moral and legal prohibitions and some of the increased risks of exploitation associated with people whose decisions are made in a context of scarcity: poverty, conflict, lack of security or displacement (Amnesty International, 2016; Mullainathan & Shafir, 2013). Well-intended professionals and organisations with mandates and obligations to help people in distress need also to be mindful of the importance of individual agency and a person's own sense of self-efficacy.

Consider that in many contexts, a form of 'exchange' is not uncommon to how ordinary sexual encounters occur. This is often only made explicit in very low-income communities and/or where wealth distribution is recognisably uneven (Vanwesenbeeck, 2013, p. 13). For people with limited economic and social power, the body remains an available form of capital. Receiving money for sex is used to access material goods, social status and, in some cases, sexual experience (Vanwesenbeeck, 2013, p. 14). Pressures to be economically productive can lead to unwanted sex and coercion in contexts of gender inequality and poverty or other systems of scarcity (Vanwesenbeeck, 2013, p. 14).

Locations of contact

The places where sex work is done and where negotiations are made is another key component to evaluating risk and possible distress. Geography and environmental contexts can serve as indicators of co-occurring risks to a person who is doing sex work (as well as signalling a sense of agency or resilience). At the same time, it is important to understand how law enforcement in public/social spaces can impact the safety and risk-taking behaviours of people selling sex.

Generally, 'indoor' sex work is regarded as safer by sex workers and organisations who support sex workers (Sanders, 2005). Safety is related to the availability of immediate support for the sex worker. The absence or reduction of stigma experienced as threats, abuse and public 'outing' allows them to focus on earning money rather than self-protection. They have a greater sense of safety and express less distress about their working conditions.

Laws intended to protect people from slavery, trafficking and exploitation often have the consequence of criminalising people who work co-operatively. For example, some people do sex work in pairs or small groups. This can be safer than working alone in cases where clients/buyers might be under the influence of alcohol and/or drugs and become aggressive or violent. However, two sex workers working together is legally considered a 'brothel' in England and Wales (Hawthorne, 2011). People who do jobs which provide support to sex workers (e.g. receptionists, 'maids' and drivers) may face charges of brothel-keeping or 'pimping' and face maximum sentences of up to 14 years (Hawthorne, 2011).

Thus laws – often created with the aim of 'protecting' people from exploitation – can force sex workers to work alone and in secret. If they want or need to earn money without doing sex work themselves, they cannot use the networks they may have built, nor can they define themselves or their experience to employers in less stigmatised industries. Consider how a sex worker might talk about their experience and skills on a CV if they were applying for a job outside the sex industry.

Activity 12.2: Sex work and safety

To think a bit more about sex work and safety, consider the following questions:

- What actions can sex workers take to make it safer to make money?
- What are the risks or benefits of prohibiting buying or selling sex?

(Continued)

(Continued)

- What are the risks or benefits of two women working together? Or a man and a woman, or two men?
- What can psychology professionals learn about places where people do sex work that could be helpful to make sex workers feel safer?

Therapeutic approaches of sex work and body work

Up to this point we have considered sex work and psychology primarily through the lens of psychology as a tool for researching or working with sex workers. Now we will explore some of the ways that sex work overlaps with counselling and therapeutic work.

Sex work can be advertised in a variety of places, including websites, social networking 'apps' or more targeted sites like Gaydar or Grindr (Tyler, 2015). Sexual services may be referenced explicitly, or advertisements may take a more therapeutic tone. In some cases, the advertiser may use 'massage' as a way to manage the stigma of 'sex work' for the sex worker and/or their clients. Advertising other types of 'body work' (Twigg et al., 2011; Wolkowitz, 2011) might function to promote their brand discretely, to promote discretion as part of their brand, or to reinforce their own discretion in what consent is given and to whom (Tyler, 2014, 2015). However, what is on offer may be genuinely positioned as therapeutic.

Advertisements for 'sensual massage', 'tantric' or 'prostate' massages can signify that a form of sexualised touching is offered. However, it is important to clarify what is being negotiated and agreed. Masseurs who offer a more 'bounded' service (e.g. no mutual touching) may only be using sexualised imagery to expand their reach and/or to compete with sex workers who offer massage as a service. Nonetheless, the therapeutic effects of non-sexual touch are recognised as beneficial. Interpersonal touch may be interpreted as a source of existential security that is physically rather than symbolically signified (Koole, Sin & Schneider, 2014). Touch signifies security and care in infancy, thus touch retains a soothing and comforting effect through adulthood, in part from the physiological release of endorphins and hormones (Koole et al., 2014).

Some sex workers promote services which are specifically for people struggling with a range of issues, including social anxiety, moderate body image concerns, sexual problems or limited mobility (Owens, 2015). For example, male sex workers sometimes recall male clients who have sought out their first sexual experience with another man away from the disapproval of their family and community, whether as a one-time experience or another step towards acknowledging a closeted identity.

Sexual surrogates work alongside sex therapist practitioners to help somebody experiencing sexual problems, although there is still a lack of peer-reviewed research supporting its efficacy as a treatment. Legal and ethical considerations for using touch and sexual surrogacy as part of therapeutic interventions are other obstacles to its integration (Rosenbaum, Aloni & Heruti, 2013). Research using body therapy to aid recovery from sexual abuse may be useful to explore contexts and boundaries related to sex and therapy (Price, 2006, 2007).

Pause of reflection

What types of job or career involve touching other people? Why is touch used in these jobs? Who does the touching? Where do they touch? What makes touching sexual or not sexual? How does this impact on which professions we place in the 'therapeutic' or 'sex worker' categories? Might there be overlap between these categories?

Conclusion

Throughout this chapter, the diversity of experiences and contexts of sex work have been discussed. With regards the implications of this for counselling and forensic psychology, the criminalisation of people who sell sex produces barriers to the safety of individuals, as well as to ever entering other forms of employment, family networks and housing. Criminalisation of people who provide services to sex workers (e.g. rented accommodation, drivers, reception) can disrupt the ability of self-managed sex workers to work safely with the resources that protect them from potential dangers. This can make such relationships open to the possibility of exploitation, as with any relationship where the person is vulnerable. Such possibilities can be difficult to predict and/or assess without a detailed account of context.

The diversity of experiences and contexts of sex work also have implications in relation to mental health. In any interaction between a psychology professional and a sex worker, the following should be assessed: (1) What are the priorities of the person who is attending the service? Of the service itself? Of the psychology professional? (2) What change – if any – is desirable to the person selling sex? To the service?

(3) What change is possible for them in their context? (4) How might this impact their priorities (in the short term, medium term and longer term)? (5) What emotions, beliefs, thoughts, behaviours, reactions have they had, do they have, could they have?

Narrative approaches can be a useful way to help professionals in this area (Payne, 2006). Narrative, whether used for research analysis, interviewing or therapy (see Chapter 15), provides tools, structures and important spaces for professionals to learn about the characters, motivations, actions and significant events for people who have experienced sex work. Identifying the strengths and resilience, as well as the risks and scarcities, and experiences help to address feelings about self-efficacy and the power dynamics in supporting relationships. A narrative framework can explore an individual's unfolding story of the following actions that frame how sex work is experienced: how they address scarcity and what resources they have, including social networks; how they feel about sex, their body and their own sexual identity; and how their actions fit or disrupt possible plans for the future.

This chapter has introduced ways to think about, and understand, sex work that challenge commonly held assumptions. By thinking critically about how and why certain experiences are emphasised while others are ignored, psychologists and other professionals can develop ways of approaching this area with insight into how to assess the context and significance for every individual.

Suggestions for further reading

Laing, M., Pilcher, K., & Smith, N. (Eds.) (2015). *Queer sex work*. London: Routledge.
This edited volume explores diverse experiences and understandings of selling sex. Writers from various backgrounds discuss perspectives which are often ignored in many depictions of heterosexual, able-bodied, Anglo-American people, sex and work.

Weitzer, R. (Ed.) (2010a). *Sex for Sale: prostitution, pornography, and the sex industry*. Abingdon: Routledge.
This collection of chapters offers a useful overview of contemporary empirical social science research on sex work. It addresses different types of sex work and is edited to introduce readers to a number of perspectives.

PART IV

TREATMENT

13

ATTACHMENT-BASED APPROACHES

MARY HALEY

Image 13   Owls' eye. With permission, Nuria Outeiral

Introduction

Attachment theory, developed by Bowlby (1982), focuses on the quality of early relationships. How our physical and emotional needs were met in infancy and childhood can have a profound effect on how we develop as adults and on the quality of our emotional lives (Holmes, 2001). Early infant relationships with primary caregivers that are not sufficiently secure or sensitive to a child's physical and emotional needs have a dramatic impact on later development, relationships and interactions within the wider world. The kinds of 'real' attachment relationships we experience(d), whether secure, insecure or a mix of both, form part of an internalised 'unconscious'/out of awareness representation of what we think relationships are like (Bowlby, 1988).

Bowlby was a psychoanalyst and psychiatrist and the theory he developed has its origins in psychodynamic psychotherapy, which is a descendant of Freud's psychoanalytic theory (1963). Holmes (2001) and Finlay (2016) highlight the important theoretical contributions made by those working within a broadly relational psychoanalytic approach to our understanding of psychological distress. From this perspective, early relationship experiences with our primary caregivers form our patterns of relating which, seemingly long forgotten, can be re-experienced as if they were happening in the here and now. The psychoanalytically informed attachment approach aims to understand how our past relationships with primary caregivers affect our current behaviour and emotions (Bowlby, 1988). Survival in infancy requires adaptation to the environment and those within it and sometimes when our basic emotional and psychological needs are not met, we repress our 'true' needs and desires leading to 'unconscious' internal conflict. The need to conceal those parts of ourselves that are shamed and fearful, although unconscious, can provoke familiar feelings of anxiety and psychological distress which appear when we are under stress (Bateman, Brown & Pedder, 1991; Gomez, 1997). Consequently, unconscious defence mechanisms develop to help us manage this psychological distress. These include denial, repression (where the person has lost conscious memory of difficult experiences) and rationalisation (difficult feelings are explained and justified in a rational or logical manner to make them tolerable).

For the adult attachment-based practitioner, the focus of attention is on identifying and working with these defences and early infant relationships with attachment figures – particularly where they were unable to meet the child's psychological needs and offer a secure 'emotional' base (Holmes, 2001). This work encompassing adult relationships both in the past and present, importantly recognising that ways of being in adulthood are not fixed. As Howe (2011) points out, 'Changes, of course, can and do occur from secure to insecure, and insecure to secure' (p. 224).

In this chapter we will first provide an overview of attachment theory and its development. Following this, we will consider the role of the counsellor and psychotherapist in offering a different relational experience – an experience within which the therapeutic alliance offers a secure base from which to experience empathic attunement, holding, containment, mirroring and exploration of the client's past relationship experiences. The chapter concludes with a discussion of the relevance of attachment-oriented thinking in working therapeutically in forensic settings.

The development of attachment theory

Early studies

Attachment theory suggests that to survive, an infant looks to its main caregiver(s) for protection from potential/perceived threats. Once the threat has passed, a child will return to exploring its world. Thus the parent/caregiver is used as a 'secure base' from which to explore and interact with the external environment and, by doing so, develop a better understanding of it, and the child's own place within it. The quality of parent/caregiver responsivity to the child plays a major part in developing the child's views of the world. Bowlby (1982) called these representational understandings 'Internal Working Models' (IWMs). Taking two extremes as examples: if a caregiver's regular response was sensitive and appropriate to the child's needs, the child would internalise the world as a sensitive and supportive environment; if the response was neglectful or hostile, the child's model of the world would require caution.

Individual differences in attachment were a main focus of Mary Ainsworth's work (1973). She noticed that attachment behaviours were not uniform. Rather, as parents differ in their parenting skills and approaches, so infants develop different styles of attaching to their primary carers in order to elicit the best care possible. She recognised that attachment behaviours started in early infancy and that pre-verbal actions, such as smiling, crying, reaching out for the caregiver, are vital attachment cues and mechanisms and form the basis of the attachment bond. To explore this further Ainsworth developed the 'Strange Situation Test' (SST) (Ainsworth et al., 1978), in which observations were made of children, aged between 12 and 20 months, in a room with their mothers and some toys. Once settled they were joined by a

Table 13.1 Attachment styles in the Strange Situation Test*

Strange Situation Test: Mary Ainsworth

SST security class	At play	Towards stranger	On separation	On reunion
B: Secure	Plays freely; explores room and toys; looks back at mother; shows toys to her	Curious; uses mother as safe base; checks with mother if engaging in play with stranger	Follows mother to door, calls or cries; may be slightly comforted by stranger	Cries; reaches up clings; stops crying soon; re-engages in play
A: Anxious/ Insecure: Avoidant	Physically distant from mothers; seems confident but explores less; does not approach mother	Initially wary but may engage in play; may move subtly closer to mother	Watches mother go but does not follow or protest; does not cry but play is inhibited and there are physical signs of stress	Watches mother return; does not approach or protest; seems occupied with play
C: Anxious / Insecure: Ambivalent	Stays close to mother; may not play; checks back frequently	Wary; anxiety clearly raised; stays close to mother	Follows mother; cries; distressed; not comforted by stranger	Approaches with angry or distressed cries; clings; not soothed or re-engaged in play
D: Disorganised/ Disorientated (classified by Mary Main)	May seem distracted or stare into space; may have obsessive quality to play; may appear more stressed in PRESENCE of parent rather than absence	May superficially respond to stranger's entry as one of the categories above, or seem more relaxed and engaged with stranger than parent	May appear to relax a little in mother's absence, or may superficially react as one of the above categories	Attachment-seeking behaviour collapses, e.g. may freeze or start to follow then turn back; may rock or display bizarre behaviours; may approach backwards or veer aside or avert gaze

*With permission, Linda Cundy (2016)

pleasant stranger, followed by the mother leaving the room and returning later. This was repeated, with the child left either alone or with the
stranger until the mother returned. The test was designed to show how
much attachment versus exploratory behaviour the child would exhibit
under stressful conditions, i.e. either in the presence or not of the main
caregiver.

Based on her observations, Ainsworth classified responses into three
main attachment styles: Secure, Insecure-Ambivalent and Insecure-
Avoidant. Later a fourth style called 'Disorganised/Disorientated' was
added, which was found in the children who were thought to be most
'at risk' of neglect or abuse (Main & Soloman, 1986, 1990). These children showed no coherent behaviours indicating any particular
attachment style.

Table 13.1 provides a summary of these four attachment styles and
the related behaviours observed in the SST. Each security class identifies different responses from the child in terms of their level of anxiety
regarding the presence or absence of their caregiver and their responses
to the stranger, in particular whether or not the infant engages with the
caregiver and in what way.

Pause for reflection

Think for a moment about a fictional character (e.g. a soap opera, film or
book character) where you have some idea of their upbringing and the kind
of primary care relationship. From the information you have of this character
consider what their primary care relationship might have been like. What
factors do you think may impact on those individuals in terms of developing
an attachment style?

Self-development

The child's early relationship experiences and internal working model,
which is formed and mediated through the caregiver's sensitivity and
responses to a child's emotional needs, play an important role for the
shaping of the self (Wallin, 2015). Stern (1985) describes this responsivity as 'attunement', whereby a caregiver doesn't just soothe a distressed
infant crying loudly with soft words, but first 'mirrors' the child's
mood (e.g. by saying, 'Oh Dear!' or 'Poor love!' in a slightly raised
voice, echoing in a reduced way, the child's distress), before using
calmer words. The 'mirroring' of the distress helps the child to feel
recognised and understood, learning that they are not alone, either

actually or figuratively, and therefore feel safe enough to move from distress to calm. You will hear later in the chapter how therapists aim to mirror this attunement in the therapeutic relationship.

Importantly, attunement helps a child to recognise, over time, that emotions are not exact representations of the external world. This is essential to healthy development as it prevents the continuation of a mental state which Fonagy (2004) calls 'Psychic Equivalence', where an infant or toddler will view whatever is happening in their minds as wholly equivalent to external circumstances. Our ability to manage, or choose, our reactions to events is disabled if we cannot distinguish between the two and become overwhelmed by adverse experiences rather than developing resilience.

This self-development aspect of attachment theory emerged with the development of the Adult Attachment Interview (Main, Hesse & Goldwyn, 2008). Main's (1993) important contribution was in demonstrating how individual descriptions of their childhood histories is a key indicator of an adult's attachment style. Securely attached adults were able to reflect on their thoughts and feelings about events experienced as children, without re-experiencing old feelings. This level of reflection was not so available to those with insecure attachment styles who found themselves still immersed in their old emotions when talking about their childhood experiences.

Adult attachment

The Adult Attachment Interview (AAI) (Hesse, 2008) is a semi-structured interview tool used in counselling. The AAI asks about childhood relationships and experiences with parents and other caregivers, identifying adults' attachment styles – not so much from the *content* of their answers, but from the manner in which they are answered. The quality of their narrative is assessed in terms of whether it is lacking in detail or provides too much information, and whether it flows logically or moves between subjects randomly. The different narrative styles identified in the AAI can be related back to the main attachment styles that were conceptualised based on SST observations. Table 13.2 sets out these correspondences between the SST attachment styles and AAI classifications and provides an overview of different adults' attachments styles and how we might observe these in ourselves and others when considering qualities as parents and adult relationships.

When thinking about adult attachment styles it is important to remember that no one is totally fixed in any one of these 'boxes' and that most people have elements of different attachment styles. It is also vital to understand that there is no judgement of 'right' or 'wrong' in

Table 13.2 Adult Attachment Interview and attachment styles*

Adult Attachment Interview: Mary Main

SST classification	AAI classification	Narrative style	Qualities as parents	Adult relationships
B: Secure	Autonomous Secure	Balanced, realistic, detailed, coherent, does not idealise parents or minimise their shortcomings	Can tolerate conflict, allow child to express positive & negative emotions. Responds reliably to child's need for love, security, yet encourages autonomy	Co-operative, can be intimate and also separate. Conflict can be allowed and managed. Asks for support and is secure base for partner
A: Anxious/ Insecure Avoidant	Dismissing of relationships/ detached	Idealises childhood; contradictory, few details; denies need; anger; separation anxiety. Generalised, intellectualised, vague and brief	Aloof, unresponsive. Denies anxiety about child. Cannot allow child's negative feelings or needs for comfort. Encourages precocious independence	Distant. Avoids intimacy or conflict. Denies own needs. May resent partner's need – or encourage it. Anger may be out of context.
C: Anxious/ Insecure Ambivalent	Pre-occupied/ Entangled	Few happy memories. Unable to see parents objectively. Obsessive, long-winded	Unreliable, intrusive, angry. Child's autonomy arouses own separation anxiety so encourages dependence	Fear of abandonment; so clings. Angry, blaming, jealous. Craves intimacy and evidence of love
D: Disorganised/ Disorientated	Unresolved/ Disorganised	Incoherent, disjointed sentences, incomplete. Confused, confusing	Distracted, dissociated, disturbing, frightened, overwhelmed. May not notice baby's distress or may feel persecuted by the baby	Unpredictable, often chaotic. Easily overwhelmed or narcissistically wounded. Emotional, then numb/ dissociated. May be violent or withdrawn. (attacks on self)

* With permission, Linda Cundy (2016)

any of these styles. Infants act instinctively in ways most likely to provide the best possible care from the caregivers – given their limitations (parents of course went through similar developments when infants), and most, as adults and parents, do the best they can in the prevailing circumstances, in almost any situation.

A secure attachment style can either be developed as a child or 'earned' at a later stage in life. The latter occurs when we develop an insecure style of attaching as children, but have better relational experiences with, say, a partner, teacher, friend or counsellor, which had helped us reflect on our childhood experiences and make some sense of it. This notion of a later acquired secure style holds most relevance for counselling as it suggests that later therapeutic interventions can be remedial (Howe, 2011). In the following section we will explore how attachment theory can be applied to therapeutic practice, where the counsellor aims to provide a position of a 'secure base' – a caregiver sensitive to the emotional needs of the client – when working with the client.

Attachment-based counselling and psychotherapy

The task in attachment-based counselling is to support clients in recounting their childhood experiences so as to help them recognise (rather than be immersed in) their emotional needs and understand how current emotions are often a repetition of unmet childhood emotional needs and experiences (Bowlby, 1988: Renn, 2004). The aim is to assist clients in reflecting on their emotions and differentiating between external circumstances (i.e. current irritations, dilemmas or threats) and what are really 'left over' unhelpful habits and compulsions from childhood (i.e. 'Repetition Compulsion', Freud, 1920). This is primarily achieved through empathic attunement, much like a caregiver would give to their infant, and by listening to, acknowledging and taking in the client's feelings and feeding them back to the client in a moderated form.

For example, a person with emotionally distant caregivers may find themselves both wanting a loving relationship, but unable to allow themselves to commit to it fully as they are (unconsciously) fearful of being dismissed or rejected. As this dilemma and the related threat has its origins in pre-verbal life (Wallin, 2015), part of the person's infant experience is beyond their conscious memory and often just 'a feeling'. It is the role of the counsellor to help the client to get in touch with those feelings – i.e. to 'step back', recognise them and then explore them in ways that help the client to come to an understanding of their origins. The counsellor needs to be consistent and reliable (building security), responsive, attuned, mirroring the client's emotional states in order to help them recognise these themselves. Together, they work through perceived 'threats', helping the client distinguish between the past (when they may have had little control over events and responses) and the present, where they can now choose how to respond. The strategy of first providing safety and then helping to explore fears is needed both in the overall course of the therapy and in individual sessions (Wallin, 2015).

Information box 13.1 provides a list of typical elements in an attachment-based counselling process in the first and subsequent sessions.

Information box 13.1: Therapeutic elements in an attachment-based counselling process

- The counsellor listens carefully to the ways in which the client tells their story. The primary aim is to build the relationship and provide a secure base through empathic attunement, mirroring, acknowledgement and containment of any emotions that might occur.
- Observation of the client's demeanour: are they friendly, dismissive, making little eye contact, clingy, anxious? What is their narrative style (see Table 13.2)? Do they have a good level of self-care? These are clues to attachment style(s).
- Identification of the presenting problem, including 'unsaid' content (e.g. problems with a teenage child might be linked to their own teenage years).
- Help for the client to reflect on their emotions and when they experienced these, and when the past is impacting on current situations.
- The counsellor notes any countertransference feelings (see section below): How are they reacting to this client emotionally, physically? Who do they think they are for this client, what parts of them are brought into their relationship with this client?

The use of transference and countertransference in attachment-based counselling

In attachment-based counselling, client defences are identified and worked through using the concepts of transference and countertransference. As introduced in Chapter 10, transference simply means transferring one's feelings about an earlier person or situation onto a current one (Grant & Crawley, 2003). This is unconscious; for example, someone may dislike a neighbour but not know why. Later they come to recognise – through counselling – that something about the neighbour, or the situation, brings up familiar, uncomfortable feelings from their past – nothing specific, just a vague awareness of discomfort. These feelings re-occur when they are with the current neighbour. Recognising this 'baggage' from the past helps the client to distinguish between the past and the present and recognise the current circumstances.

Countertransference is the same mechanism, but it occurs in the counsellor when they notice feelings alien to themselves when they are with a client (Rowan & Jacobs, 2002). If recognised, this phenomenon can be very instructive in discovering what ails the client, as a counsellor who is aware can then 'name' these feelings for the client, allowing them to bring into consciousness what was formally 'hidden' (Rowan & Jacobs, 2002). An example of this was when a colleague of mine worked with a husband and wife who were seeking IVF treatment. They both appeared very practical and business-like, but my colleague felt an overwhelming sense of sadness. She decided to tell the couple what she was experiencing and the wife started to cry. When she was calmer, she said that she had no idea she had been supressing such sadness, but that 'naming' it has made it conscious. Counsellors can use their own countertransference feelings and emotional responses to the client and see if they are mismatched to the situation. If they are, they can decide whether to 'name' them now or not. The case example below illustrates how countertransference feelings can be employed in an attachment-based therapy process.

Case example: Victoria

Victoria is a 44-year-old woman, divorced, with an 18-year-old son. She has a good job with an airline company and her son does well at school. Her ex-husband has recently had a child with his new partner and appears to be spending less time with their son. She lives near her mother, but sees her very little as she has her own, busy, social life.

Victoria was an only child. Her mother was often sickly and her father, an airline pilot, was often away. She did well at school, but was thought of as aloof by her peers and so spent a lot of time alone. At home Victoria preferred studying to playing with friends. She dreamt of going to the places her father flew to and studied languages to help her in a future career. After reading Languages at university, she graduated and worked for the airline company, for whom she still works, in their Paris office. Here she met her husband, a pilot for the airline who, like her, lived in Paris. The marriage went well in the beginning, but on their return to England, when she was pregnant, their lives diverged, and the bond lessened until they were living parallel lives. When her husband left her for another woman eight years ago, she said it was something of a relief. While she was angry that he could just leave her alone with their son, she was a little sad that she didn't feel more, which made her feel short-changed by her own emotions.

Victoria comes to therapy saying 'I feel confused as to why I feel so low'. She reports that she often feels emotionally numb and that a friend had suggested she should try counselling as it 'gives you space to look at things'.

Throughout the course of therapy the therapist listens carefully to Victoria's story, responding empathically to her descriptions and expressions of feeling. The therapist notes her own unfamiliar feelings of distance and lack of emotional arousal (countertransference) and shares this with Victoria ('at times you seem distant and disengaged from me'). Victoria tells her about her early experience of attachment and loss, one minute someone is there for her and then they are gone. Mother was sickly and frequently unavailable; father, whom she probably idealised, was also frequently absent. As therapy progresses Victoria often misses sessions and appears distracted and impatient for them to end. The therapist begins to feel discounted, dismissed and irritable and wonders if this is how Victoria feels and whether her approach to therapy is a re-enactment of her early attachment difficulties.

Commentary

In listening to Victoria it becomes clear that she is used to caring for herself and is cautious about trusting the counsellor. It is important that she feels heard and tests counselling by missing sessions or being disengaged. Countertransference feelings of wanting the session to end and being preoccupied with one's own thoughts may be clues to Victoria's emotions. Victoria's 'relief' at her husband leaving is likely to be a misplaced feeling of safety; her father was absent physically and her mother emotionally ('This is familiar; I know I can survive it.'). Therapy should try to help her recognise her repressed need for connection and love and confront the sadness at not having these needs met as a child. She is likely to avoid looking at these issues and therapy will probably be long – if she doesn't give it up.

Activity 13.1

Having read the case example above, think about the possible attachment styles Victoria might have developed.

- What might be important aspects of her childhood to explore in therapy?
- What level of detail do you think she may give in her therapy sessions (try to relate this to attachment styles)?
- How would you work with missed sessions? (How may these link to her childhood?)

Attachment and the criminal justice system

Studies such as Frodi et al. (2001) and Fonagy (2004) suggest that poor early attachments appear to have an overwhelming impact on how we develop views of the world as hostile or friendly. These studies show that around 90% of psychiatric patients and prisoners who have committed severe violence have had strongly abusive childhood experiences. De Zulueta (2001) outlines how the lack of good caregivers in early childhood can produce physical changes in the brain which may leave a person more vulnerable to acting violently. The author also suggests that when good emotional care is lacking, we are more likely to fail to develop empathy sufficiently. Consequently, poor attachment histories can be seen not only to lead to a child growing up feeling insecure, but also to developing defence mechanisms to protect against feelings of anxiety and alienation.

An ambitious retrospective study on adverse childhood experiences involving 17,000 participants in the US (Adverse Childhood Experience Survey; see also Chapter 9) has shown how violent and/or abusive experiences in childhood (such as physical or emotional abuse, sexual abuse, family alcohol or drug use, violence, family depression or physical or emotional neglect) are related to difficulties in coping with problems in adult life (Felitti et al., 1998). The more adverse the childhood experiences, the higher the rate of problems in adulthood, including alcoholism, depression, illicit drug use, higher risk of intimate partner violence and suicide attempts. These findings suggest that the adult life 'choices' made after someone has experienced severe adverse experiences in childhood are more likely to be poor, and that the individual may suffer the consequences of these, thus unconsciously prolonging their own suffering.

The case example below illustrates some of the possible consequences of early repressed unconscious emotions as a result of relationship disruption, emotional neglect and physical abuse in childhood.

Case example: Mickey G

Mickey is a 39-year-old man serving a life sentence for the murder of a man whose house he was burgling. Mickey thought he was in the house alone but the victim was actually in bed and woke after hearing a noise. He caught Mickey going through the drawers. Mickey tried to run, but the householder stopped him by the door and a fight began. Mickey always carried a flick-knife which he pulled on the victim. He says he can't remember a lot but just knows he felt overwhelmed by anger and kept stabbing the victim, even after he had fallen to the floor and stopped moving. He then kicked the body and took some cigarettes which were on a table. He took nothing else. He said he walked away and at home he started to smoke a cigarette he had stolen but said it 'Didn't feel right' and so threw it away and rolled one of his own. The next day he went to a police station but turned away at the last minute. He was arrested two weeks later for the murder. He pleaded guilty to manslaughter, but denied murder.

Mickey was one of five children – three boys and two girls. He is the second child and his elder brother is his full sibling. Next are two half-sisters his mother had with another man. She left him as he was, like Mickey's father, a heavy drinker and would beat her and the boys regularly. Mickey said his only respite was the times his stepfather was in prison. The youngest boy was the son of his mother and her third partner – a man who did not drink and was not violent. This boy was spared the regular spectacle of violence to which Mickey and his other siblings were accustomed. Mickey's older brother is also in prison, but his sisters and younger brother have not been involved with the criminal justice system.

After the younger girl was born, Mickey's mother took herself and the children to a refuge, but she returned to her partner when he asked her to come back. After several years of more problems and unpredictability, his mother left her partner again and this time did not return to him. At this point his mother started drinking heavily too and Mickey and his elder brother would steal to get food for themselves and their sisters as their mother was unable to care for them. A few years later she met her current partner, a man some years older than her and finally had a settled life.

Mickey was pleased for his mother, but also felt a sense of loss as he and his brother had, until then, been her main support. He felt envy and humiliated when she told him he was no longer needed to protect her, and worse when she would tell him he was like his father and brought her only misery. Mickey left home at age 16, unable to face the fact that his mother had just had the son with her third partner. Since then he had drifted in and out of crime and began to misuse substances to 'escape' his feelings. His use of violence started at this time as he sought to ensure he didn't look weak or a victim to others.

Mickey was surprised at the level of violence he committed when stabbing the man. While he feels remorse and shame for his actions, part of him blames the victim for disturbing him and 'trying to be a hero'. Mickey often can't understand his feelings.

Commentary

Mickey's offences indicate an inability to reflect on his feelings and a tendency to fly into actions – often confused and impulsive actions. Safety in his therapy will be vital and he will need frequent reassurance of this in the

(Continued)

(Continued)

face of his likelihood to test it vigorously. It is likely to be very frightening as it will mean confronting feelings of vulnerability he has long repressed. It will probably be a long therapy process and his counsellor will need to be empathically attuned through being emotionally available and to show much patience and strength to bear his unbearable feelings and withstand the likely abuse he will throw out. Reliability, consistency and firm but fair boundaries will be a major part of helping him work through the chaotic defences he has established against the pain of his childhood.

Activity 13.2

Having read the case example above, think about the possible attachment styles Mickey might have developed.

- What are his survival strategies? Why might he have started to take substances (there could be more than one reason)?
- What views of himself and of other people might Mickey G have developed?
- How strong would trust, fear, connection or alienation be in his mind?

Both case examples in this section illustrate some of the issues therapists needs to take into account in forming and maintaining a therapeutic relationship, and how an understanding of the client's attachment history and style can inform therapeutic work. For example, clients with an avoidant attachment style are likely to be wary and need to be given time to gradually build the relationship, whereas ambivalent clients may be overly adapted, agreeable and eager to be in therapy, and lacking in awareness of their own needs.

Conclusion

This chapter has demonstrated how attachment theory and related concepts are relevant for therapeutic work, and for therapy in forensic settings more specifically. More and more professionals within the criminal justice system are recognising the importance of attachment histories to violent crime, and the role of counselling and psychotherapy in helping offenders to understand their emotions and so to manage them better is growing.

Attachment theory and practice doesn't start with symptoms and pathology and work backwards towards possible causes. Instead, from its inception it looked at normative development and attachment and tried to understand why this could go wrong. It is therefore not only of use in therapeutic work, but in understanding development in the broadest sense and contributing to our knowledge of who we are.

Suggestions for further reading

Cassidy, J., & Shaver, P. R. (Eds.) (2016). *Handbook of attachment: theory, research and clinical applications* (3rd ed.). New York: Guilford Press.
This is an essential book for anybody with a serious interest in attachment theory. It is a comprehensive guide to the history of attachment and the latest research.

Holmes, J. (2001). *The search for the secure base: attachment theory and psychotherapy*. Hove: Routledge.
This is an excellent summary of attachment theory and how it can be used to inform a clinical approach based on attachment ideas.

14

COGNITIVE BEHAVIOURAL THERAPY

MATT BRUCE

Image 14 Overthinking. With permission, Sarah Shipley

Introduction

While for centuries people have expressed their internal experiences by how they think, feel and behave, it was not until the twentieth century that pioneers in the field of psychology began to systematically study how these processes shape perceptions of oneself, others and the world. Cognitive behavioural therapy (CBT), born from the stormy marriage between cognitive and behavioural traditions, represents a broad approach to the conceptualisation and treatment of mental health problems. Its ever-increasing forms, foci and flexibility have made it a very popular psychotherapy. This chapter will chart the evolution of CBT, its core assumptions and principles, and its use in forensic settings. A generic individual CBT protocol will be outlined and illustrated with a case example, followed by considerations and challenges that counsellors and forensic psychologists face when implementing CBT in prison settings.

Evolution of cognitive behavioural therapy

A popular approach to charting the evolution of CBT has been to conceptualise three distinct 'waves', each arguably reflecting the socio-political shifts of Western society. The first wave was behaviourism, popularised by seminal works of behaviourists such as Watson and Rayner (1920), Pavlov (1941) and Skinner (1965), who focused their efforts on explaining how behaviours were learnt and shaped by measurable environmental factors. The 'mind as machine' metaphor – governed by a finite set of physical laws and observable mechanisms – was very popular at that time. The second wave, dubbed the 'cognitive revolution', proposed a radical new idea – it was not *what* happened, but instead *how* it was processed (or interpreted) that was key (Beck, 1963, 1969; Ellis, 1958). Arguably, the advent of the computer in the mid-twentieth century served as an ideal metaphor and catalyst for this cognitive evolution – examining human information processing and developing 'programming rules' for desired behaviour. The third wave, coined the 'third generation', emerged (or mutated) from traditional CBT (Hayes, 2004) and questioned narrow Western concepts of permanence, control and action. Heavily influenced by the metaphor of globalisation and Eastern philosophies, rather than challenge *what* or *how* we think (conceptualised as part of the problem), third-wave therapists sought to *accept* it. Examples of these include Acceptance and Commitment Therapy (ACT) (Hayes et al., 2006), Mindfulness for Stress Reduction (Kabat-Zinn et al., 1992), Mindfulness Based Cognitive Therapy (MBCT)

(Segal et al., 2002) and Dialectical Behaviour Therapy (DBT) (Linehan, 1993). Mindfulness and DBT will be explored further in Chapter 16.

Core assumptions of CBT

As discussed above, the second wave represents traditional CBT, founded on the ideas espoused by pioneers such as Beck and Ellis, and later augmented into a wider collection of common principles (see Information box 14.1) referred to collectively as cognitive behavioural therapies (Tafrate & Mitchell, 2014).

Information box 14.1: Common CBT principles

- A focus primarily on the present rather than the past
- Problems conceptualised as cognitions and behaviours
- Specific, clearly defined goals
- Collaborative and emphasises clients' expertise
- Cognitively and developmentally appropriate
- Tailored to meet individual needs of client
- Active and motivational stance on behalf of the therapist
- Requires implementation and practice in the real world
- Empirically grounded and supported
- Problem-focused and solution-oriented
- Time-limited and psycho-educational

Beck (1963, 1969) argued that depressed people develop negative schemata (or blueprints) – often as a result of traumatic early childhood experiences – that shape (and distort) how depressed people subsequently experience the world. Beck proposed that three primary mechanisms were responsible for reinforcing and maintaining depression: (1) the cognitive triad – three key forms of negative thinking about the self, the future and the world; (2) the negative self-schema – a set of beliefs and expectations about oneself that disrupts and distorts normal information processing; and (3) cognitive distortions – the consequent impairments in perception, memory and learning. Beck conceptualised ten fundamental errors or 'cognitive distortions' in information processing which are summarised in Table 14.1. Beck's cognitive model can also be understood topographically with three distinct levels of thought: (1) *core beliefs*, which are considered fundamental and unconditional truisms, usually outside an individual's consciousness and rarely verbalised (e.g. 'I am worthless'); (2) *underlying assumptions*, which refer to conditional beliefs or 'if–then' propositions that may or may not be outside the individual's awareness (e.g. 'If I'm not perfect, I'll be rejected'); and (3) *automatic thoughts*, which sit near the surface of awareness and spontaneously flow through the individual's mind in the moment (e.g. 'I'm totally useless, they think I'm stupid').

Table 14.1 Cognitive distortions (adapted from Burns, 1999)

Cognitive distortion	Description	Example
All-or-nothing thinking	Looking at things in black and white, absolute terms	'If it's not perfect, it must be total crap'
Over-generalisation	One negative event is applied across all situations	'Shit like this always happens to me!'
Mental filter	Scan for negatives and disregard positives	'But he said my pitch was a little off'
Disqualifying the positive	Discounting accomplishments and positives	'Anyone can change a car tyre'
Jumping to conclusions	Mind reading or fortune telling	'She's going to think I'm so boring'
Magnification or minimisation	Catastrophise errors or diminish success	'This isn't working, it's a complete disaster'
Emotional reasoning	Deducing pseudo facts from emotional sates	'I'm hurt, he's clearly trying to attack me'
'Should statements'	Criticising self and others on basis of 'oughts', 'musts', 'shoulds'	'She shouldn't go out with her friends without me'
Labelling	The use of pejorative global descriptors	'I'm an idiot'; 'He is a waster'
Personalisation or blame	Attribute too much responsibility on self or others for outcomes	'We didn't win because I'm a terrible player'

Ellis (1958, 1962) developed rational emotive behavioural therapy (REBT) that used the A-B-C model to conceptualise the relationship between *Antecedents (or activating events)* that are objective and measurable phenomena that trigger irrational *Beliefs (or interpretations)* that subsequently led to a succession of negative, self-defeating and self-reinforcing *Consequences*. Ellis argued that a belief was irrational if it distorts reality, is illogical, prevents achievement of goals, leads to unhealthy emotions and self-defeating behaviours. In contrast, Beck used therapist and client collaborative investigation, looking for evidence to support or reject negative thoughts, which can help and discredit negative self-schema and distorted cognitions. Ellis employed a more directive and emotive approach by actively *Disputing* the clients beliefs and prescribing an *Effective* thought. Accordingly, Ellis's approach became known as the A-B-C-D-E model.

Pause for reflection

Take five minutes to reflect on whether you hold any cognitive distortions or irrational beliefs (referring back to those listed in Table 14.1, if needed). Think about whether they might be connected to any negative early childhood experiences.

CBT in forensic settings

Historically delivered exclusively face-to-face in the therapists office, CBT can now be accessed via telemental health (e.g. telephone, video conferencing, Skype) services (Hilty et al., 2013); computerised cognitive behavioural therapy (CCBT) (NICE, 2006); self-help books (Mayo-Wilson & Montgomery, 2013); and group formats (Thimm & Antonsen, 2014). This ever-expanding portfolio of CBT permutations and delivery methods has unsurprisingly given rise to an equally growing number of therapeutic protocols. Within the criminal justice system, group programmes grounded in CBT principles have proved enormously popular and effective in reducing recidivism by improving social skills, problem solving, critical thinking, moral reasoning, cognitive style, self-control, behavioural inhibition and self-esteem (Landenberger & Lipsey, 2005). A key departure from traditional CBT is the additional focus of community responsibility in forensic settings – living in harmony with the community and contributing to positive societal outcomes (Milkman & Wanberg, 2007). The therapist must be cognisant of his or her need to sensitively balance sociocentric (public safety) and egocentric (client-focused) outcomes. Among the growing body of CBT group programmes are: Aggression Replacement Training, Reasoning and Rehabilitation, Enhanced Thinking Skills, and Relapse Prevention Therapy (see Milkman & Wanberg, 2007, for a detailed review). Broadly speaking, these programmes aim to address various characteristics associated with distorted thinking, such as an inability to consider the effects of one's behaviour, developmentally arrested thoughts, egocentric viewpoints, inability to accept blame, difficulty managing anger, use of force or violence to achieve goals (Clarke, 2010). While the use of large-scale manualised group programmes in forensic settings continues to flourish, their ability to offer tailored and client-centred CBT interventions remains poor. Figure 14.1 represents a generic CBT delivery protocol that can be used as a helpful foundation for approaching face-to-face therapy in both traditional and forensic settings.

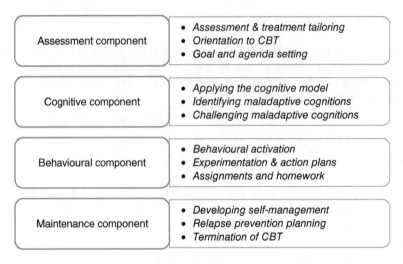

Figure 14.1   Generic CBT delivery protocol

In the next part of this section, a case illustration of Omar will be used to demonstrate how this protocol may be applied in clinical practice.

Case example: Omar

Omar is a 22-year-old man, recently involved in the criminal justice system, who has been referred to you for CBT assessment because he is struggling with low mood, feelings of hopelessness and helplessness, irritability, nightmares, flashbacks, self-harm, and difficulties maintaining intimate relationships.

As a child, Omar was subjected to regular beatings from his mother, who would repeatedly tell him he 'was a mistake', had 'ruined her life' and 'was useless'. He never met his biological father, whom his mother refused to talk about. From an early age he was also subjected to repeated sexual abuse from three of his mother's male acquaintances who often volunteered to 'look after him' when she was out of town. Omar became very withdrawn, isolated and found it difficult to make friends and trust adults. He did very poorly at school and is insecure about his reading and writing abilities which he attempts to hide for fear of being ridiculed and rejected. He recalled thinking that 'people would laugh at me and think I was stupid'.

While Omar was able to secure a number of temporary retail jobs, he would often quit or get fired following verbal altercations. He also reported a string of short-term relationships with men and women that ended due to his 'excessive dependency'. Omar reported feeling worthless, stating that 'everyone abandons me, I'm a freak'. His self-injurious behaviours and flashbacks have increased over recent months following a difficult relationship breakup with a man he had been seeing for eight months. He stated that recently he only feels safe in his room, and tries to avoid leaving, reporting 'I will only get into trouble, I can't do anything right'.

Assessment component

Assessment involves obtaining a detailed description of the presenting problem (e.g. the onset, duration, frequency and severity of Omar's low mood, nightmares, relationship difficulties, etc.), background history (e.g. his developmental milestones, key relationships, sexual abuse, psychiatric, medical, forensic and substance use history, unhelpful and helpful coping strategies), as well as his strengths and goals. Orientation is a further important initial step in order to educate Omar about the model of CBT, develop an initial conceptualisation and instil hope. Omar should understand the basic theory and principles that underlie CBT. For example, we might explain to Omar that events do not directly give rise to feelings, but instead indirectly via thoughts, e.g. not being able to read a job application (event) makes him think he is useless and stupid (thought) which consequently leaves him angry (feeling). Discussing the research evidence of CBT effectiveness, clarifying length and duration of sessions, structure of therapy and role of homework are important topics to cover to ensure that Omar's expectations are sufficiently managed. Goal and agenda setting constitutes a very good way of motivating ambivalent clients (Cox & Klinger, 2011; Miller & Rollnick, 2013), structuring the sessions, managing expectations and establishing markers of therapeutic success. Ideally, goals should be SMART (i.e. specific, measurable, attainable, realistic and time-bound) (Doran, 1981), relate to cognitive behavioural changes and linked to the presenting problems. Information box 14.2 illustrates an example of a session agenda plan adapted from Beck (1995).

> # Information box 14.2: CBT session agenda plan
>
> ## Start of session
>
> - Mood check
> - Review previous session
> - Review homework
> - Set the agenda
>
> ## Middle of session
>
> - Apply and reinforce cognitive model
> - Help challenge maladaptive cognitions
> - Demonstrate empathy and understanding
>
> ## End of session
>
> - Provide session summary
> - Set homework assignment(s)
> - Feedback and questions

Cognitive components

Applying the cognitive model requires us to examine Omar's three layers of cognition: his automatic thoughts, intermediate beliefs and core beliefs. Maladaptive automatic thoughts or 'hot thoughts' (Padesky & Greenberger, 1995) should be identified as they arise during the session and recorded. As 'hot thoughts' are those closely linked to negative emotions, it is important to identify and reflect non-verbal changes in Omar's tone of voice, physiological state and in session behaviours to assist him in gaining more awareness and mastery with respect to linking thoughts, feelings and behaviours. Rating the emotional intensity and/or believability (e.g. 0–100) of different hot thoughts will also help Omar to prioritise which to focus on during the session. Maladaptive cognitions can be challenged using a multitude of CBT strategies. As an exhaustive list of these strategies is beyond the scope of this chapter, we shall focus here on using a thought record (Greenberger & Padesky, 1995) with Omar. As can be seen in Table 14.2, Omar can use this record within and between sessions to practise identification and recording of problematic situations (column 1), automatic thoughts and degree of believability (column 2), feelings and their intensity (column 3). Omar is then required to select one hot thought from column 2 to

Table 14.2 Typical Thought Records used in CBT

Thought Record

1. Situation	2. Identify automatic thoughts	3. Identify & rate feelings	4. Facts supporting hot thought	5. Facts opposing hot thought	6. Balanced thought	7. Rate feeling now
(What were you doing? where? With who? When?)	(What thoughts or images went through your mind? what does this mean about you? Others? The world? For each, rate believability: 0–100)	(Identify and rate the intensity of each feeling: 0–100)	(Circle the hot thought in the second column related to the most intense feeling. Write supporting facts for this thought)	(Write facts that do not support this thought. What things have happened that make it untrue?)	(What could be the most balanced way to see the situation? What is the believability of this balanced thought? Rate: 0–100)	(Copy emotions from the third column. Re-rate (0–100) and add any new emotions)
Argument with Tom, at work, Tuesday morning	I'm a total waste of space (90) He's going to fire me (80) Images of begging in the street (70) I'd like to punch him in the face (60)	Fear (80) Anger (65) Sadness (60) Shame (75)	Mum calls me useless I can't read that well I've no qualifications I forgot to tell Tom about the order	I got a pay rise I pay bills on time I've got certificates Tom often asks me for advice	I can make mistakes but that doesn't mean I'm a total waste of space (80)	Fear (40) Anger (25) Sadness (40) Shame (35) Relief (80) Pride (30)

examine 'scientifically'. The therapist and Omar share the task of generating facts to support (coloumn 4) and refute (column 5) the hot thought. The following task is to generate a balanced thought (column 6) that is not polarised and instead a synthesis of columns 4 and 5 – a healthy, adaptive, rational thought – rating its believability (0–100). The final task (column 7) is for the client to re-rate the feeling(s) recorded in column 3 and introduce any new emotions. If the intensity ratings show little change, further examination of columns 4 and 5 may be required to increase believability scores.

Behavioural components

Behavioural activation can help improve mood in a number of ways, such as reducing avoidance, providing physical exercise, increasing activities, improving self-confidence, mastery, enjoyment and purpose. For example, the therapist might explain to Omar that avoiding his feared situation (e.g. leaving his room) prevents him from disconfirming the belief that he 'will only get into trouble' and denies him the opportunity for exercise, positive interactions and participation in enjoyable activities. Accordingly, the therapist and Omar will schedule activities to engage in between sessions that can be recorded on an activity chart for review. Experiments and action plans help gather information to examine the validity of client's automatic thoughts and beliefs as well as test new balanced thoughts or beliefs. Behavioural experiments are considered by some to constitute the most powerful method of bringing about change (Bennett-Levy, 2004). Conceived and conducted within or between sessions, Omar may be encouraged to engage in tasks which are predicted to end negatively (e.g. Omar disclosing to Tom, his co-worker, that he cannot read) and record the process and outcome. Similar to the dysfunctional thought record, a chart can be created for Omar with six columns which might look as follows when completed: (1) Prediction and likelihood (e.g. 'Tom will laugh at me and call me an idiot – 90%'); (2) Experiment (e.g. 'I will tell him that I cannot read well and ask him to read the instructions to me'); (3) Possible problems (e.g. 'I avoid him or start stuttering'); (4) Strategies to overcome problems (e.g. 'I coach myself just before, take deep breathes, think of something I'm good at'); (5) Outcome of experiment (e.g. 'I didn't stutter, he did not laugh and said he had educational difficulties too'); (6) How much does the outcome disconfirm the automatic thought tested (e.g. '80%'); and (7) Learning (e.g. 'not everyone will laugh at me, others have difficulties too'). Experiments may need to be broken down into smaller steps, repeated multiple times, and active problem solving is required when they do not turn out as hoped. The latter can be achieved with an action plan that should include a SMART goal, possible obstacles, coping responses, and a record of progress and learning (Greenberger & Padesky, 1995). Finally, homework provides Omar the opportunity to practise techniques outside therapy, facilitate skill acquisition, increase treatment adherence, mastery, autonomy and competence (Tee & Kazantzis, 2011). It is important to tailor assignments and homework to Omar's cognitive abilities, physical capabilities, motivation and access to resources.

Maintenance component

Self-management via self-directed learning, completion of thought records, experiments, action plans and CBT workbooks outside sessions are very important for increasing the client's self-efficacy, competence and sustaining treatment gains. An ever-expanding pool of CBT workbooks, self-help interventions (Gellatly et al., 2007) and smartphone apps (Bakker et al., 2016) are available to augment and transfer responsibility from the therapist's consultation room to the client's personal toolkit. Relapse prevention planning refers specifically to reducing the risks of setbacks or relapses and is often used for individuals living with addiction. While various relapse prevention methods exist, Butler and Butler (2005) outlined three principal aims of relapse prevention plans: (1) to develop an individual relapse picture that helps to identify 'at risk' mental states/situations (e.g. for Omar these might be strong feelings of threat, paranoia, restlessness, isolation, not sleeping); (2) to develop a relapse plan or 'relapse drill' (e.g. Omar may plan to monitor severity of symptoms, complete thought records, call a friend, contact a health-care professional, present to crisis service); and (3) to promote the client's understanding and self-control over re-occurring problems/symptoms (e.g. the plan itself may give Omar more confidence, awareness and reassurance). When approaching the end of CBT treatment, the therapist encourages the client to review learning and troubleshoot any concerns about ending sessions (Beck, 1995). Tapering of sessions (e.g. reducing the frequency of Omar's appointments) is a commonly used technique in CBT to decrease dependency on the therapist and increase self-management.

Specific challenges and issues in working therapeutically with forensic clients

Many individuals involved in the criminal justice system demonstrate elevated rates of physical health problems, mental illness, personality disorder, substance abuse, intellectual disability and suicide (Fazel et al., 2016). As these adversities are also strongly correlated with socio-economic disadvantage (Fergusson, Swain-Campbell & Horwood, 2004; see also Chapter 8), many criminologists argue that criminal behaviour is symptomatic of a larger complex social problem, with prisons representing ineffective solutions. The high level of psychiatric morbidity found in prisons is further exacerbated by a shortage of inpatient beds and failure to divert appropriately from court to hospital (Fazel & Baillargeon, 2011). Accordingly, the need for effective mental health provision by competent counsellors and counselling and forensic psychologists is enormous. Developing a good understanding of the complexities and challenges faced by this clinical population, particularly in relation to CBT delivery, is imperative and will be the focus of the remainder of this chapter.

Pause for reflection

Think for a minute about the paragraph above. What might be some of the internal (psychological) and external (environmental) factors that could complicate and challenge the process of delivering brief CBT to individuals in prison?

There are a number of internal and external factors that counsellors and forensic psychologists should pay special attention to when working with forensic clients (some of which are discussed in Chapter 1 and 19). As an exhaustive list is beyond the scope of this chapter, the following internal factors will be considered here: (1) motivational issues; (2) cognitive abilities; (3) cognitive styles; (4) social/moral development; and (5) emotional functioning; as well as external factors: (1) physical environment; (2) accessibility factors; and (3) therapist challenges.

Motivational issues

Individuals often come to the attention of forensic services via court orders, supervision directives or licence conditions. Typically, these pathways reflect a damaged relationship to 'help' and justice-involved individuals may perceive the world as a fearful, abusive and harmful place. Rather than treatment seeking, many are considered treatment-rejecting (Tyrer et al., 2003) or perhaps, more accurately, treatment-fearing. For many, crime has served as a self-preservative function and provided them with a sense of worth, self-esteem and peer acceptance. Accordingly, their goals are often unlikely to align with those who recommended or mandated the referral, which may focus on public safety outcomes rather than symptom relief. Justice-involved individuals are often resistant to admitting the extent of their offending, appreciating the impact on the victim, taking responsibility and committing themselves to change (Polaschek & Reynolds, 2004). Accordingly, it is important to be very clear about the purpose of the meeting, what will be covered and how CBT can be helpful.

Cognitive abilities

As reviewed above, individuals in the criminal justice system are at increased risk of individual, familial and social adversities than their non-justice-involved counterparts. Therefore it is not surprising that incarcerated offenders in the UK have a reading age at, or below, that expected of an 11 year old (Morrisroe, 2014). Cognitive behavioural therapy requires the use of logical analysis, rational disputation and abstract thinking (Ronen & Rosenbaum, 1998). For example, development of causal reasoning evolves from concrete and external relationships towards abstract and internal hypothetical relationships (an important part of being able to identify, link and challenge thoughts, feelings and behaviours). Cognitive behavioural therapy also requires metacognition (thinking about one's thoughts) and self-reflection (awareness of one's thoughts, feelings and behaviours). Delays or difficulties in these areas must be assessed and carefully considered when working with forensic clients. Handouts and assignments may require visual translation, the use of simple language and careful explanation.

Cognitive styles

Initial steps in CBT involve increasing awareness and identification of problematic thinking patterns that lead to negative or unhelpful emotional and behavioural outcomes. However, research suggests that individuals who commit offences may actually not engage in 'awfulising' or 'personalising'. Instead they may show a lack of concern and a tendency to underestimate danger and engage in overly optimistic predictions of likely behavioural outcomes (Mitchell, Simourd & Tafrate, 2014). Unlike depressive and anxious individuals, whose cognitive distortions cause them distress and suffering, for some individuals, these thinking patterns may serve a very useful, protective and egosyntonic (harmonious to self) function. Furthermore, the tendency for perpetrators to view themselves as victims (both before and after their offences) may reflect a wish to avoid punishment and maximise sympathy (Baumeister, 2001) or a genuine perception of events. The latter is consistent with Beck's notion of impaired or maladaptive core beliefs, dysfunctional attitudes and automatic thoughts, which leads to faulty information processing. Although rarely discussed in mainstream psychotherapy literature, individuals who have committed offences might have a tendency to engage in a number of cognitive distortions in order to minimise guilt, accountability and disapproval from others – known as neutralization theory (Sykes & Matza, 1957). It is important to be mindful of these and approach them sensitively and cautiously. Mitchell et al. (2014) review these and additional distortions or thinking styles which are illustrated in Information box 14.3.

Information box 14.3: Criminogenic cognitive styles with examples

- Denial of responsibility: 'I had no choice, they made me do it.'
- Denial of victim: 'They were asking for it.'
- Denial of injury: 'It didn't hurt him, it toughened him up.'
- Condemnation of condemner: 'They don't know shit.'
- Appeal to higher loyalties: 'I had family to take care of.'
- Excuses: 'It was a complete accident.'
- Justifications: 'That's the way the world works.'

Social/moral development

Offending behaviour can be conceptualised as violations of society's moral rules, laws and order. CBT pursues the acquisition and implementation of socially accepted and responsible responses to problems – a focus particularly prioritised in forensic settings. Many justice-involved individuals are considered to operate within the preconventional stage of moral development (Kohlberg, 1984), whereby they struggle to consider (or choose to ignore) others' perspectives and make decisions based on their own self-interest (Corriea, 2009). This may be a reflection of abusive and/or neglectful childhood environments in which looking out for oneself served a necessary self-preservative function. Accordingly, the CBT counsellor may have an additional task to assist the client to move from simplistic, egocentric-based moral reasoning towards more conventional society-oriented considerations (Kegan, 1982).

Emotional functioning

The ability to identify, label and regulate emotional experiences is an essential goal of CBT. Saarni (1999) described eight stages or skills of emotional competence associated with cognitive and social development (i.e. awareness of one's emotional state, discerning others' emotions, using an emotional vocabulary, capacity for empathy and sympathy, discriminating inner versus external emotional expressions, emotional regulation, emotional reciprocity and symmetry within relationships, and emotional self-efficacy). Many individuals involved in the criminal justice system exhibit higher rates of emotionally unstable personality disorder compared to the general population (Singleton, Meltzer & Gatward, 1998) and are at increased likelihood of developing trauma and hopelessness (Peters & Wexler, 2005). Accordingly, the degree of emotional competence should be assessed at the beginning of CBT, as it is likely to be related to the presenting problem, risk of recidivism, as well as treatment prognosis. Working with individuals involved in the criminal justice system may require a deeper focus on developing emotional competence in order to ensure emotion regulation strategies can be effectively acquired and applied.

Physical environment

The importance of creating a safe space to optimise therapeutic engagement and outcomes has been well established (Rogers, 1957). However, as described in Chapters 1 and 19, forensic settings are often associated with punishment, rejection and physical deprivation (Carr et al., 2006). Prisons can be violent, harsh and depriving environments that can be depersonalising and dehumanising (Peters & Wexler, 2005), placing incarcerated offenders at increased risk of developing 'prisonization' (Clemmer, 1940) – the process of assimilation by new inmates that encourages social disconnection, suspicion of others, opposition to prison personnel and the use of aggression and hostility to others. This process is likely to both reinforce and exacerbate existing cognitive distortions. Furthermore, forensic settings are often mandatory environments stripped of furnishings and artefacts due to safety and penal factors. The therapist is also likely to be restricted by prison processes, regimes and emergency operations (e.g. lock downs). They must carry keys, chaperone the client and unlock/lock doors, all of which emphasises a power imbalance, increases the likelihood of negative transference (Harvey & Smedley, 2010) and interferes with the development of a genuine collaborative therapeutic relationship characteristic of CBT.

Accessibility factors

Despite the high rates of mental illness and aspirations for equality of access to psychiatric care for incarcerated individuals, a third of prisons in England and Wales do not provide CBT (group or individual) (Cornford, Sibbald & Baer., 2007), fewer still provide this on an individual basis (Peters & Wexler, 2005). There are a number of factors that may prevent access to CBT in prisons, including budgetary constraints, space limitations, available healthcare professionals, frequent movement of prisoners and legislative barriers. Furthermore, restrictions on interpersonal encounters, pleasurable activities, work opportunities and liberty may limit the degree and range of behaviour activation or experimentation that is so critical for effective CBT (Niveau, 2007).

Therapist challenges

Within forensic settings the client, nature of their crime(s) and the surroundings are likely to constitute significant challenges for the therapist in remaining objective and unbiased. The client may engender fear, betrayal, disgust, anger, pity, arousal, attraction, which the therapist must carefully navigate. Indeed, counsellors and forensic psychologists working with clients should be cognizant of the dangers of their own automatic thoughts and cognitive distortions when working with clients. They should avoid labelling individuals as 'victims' and 'perpetrators', 'mad' or 'bad' – such distinctions are rarely helpful or accurate.

Having outlined a number of considerations that counsellors and forensic psychologists should be cognizant of when using CBT in criminal justice settings, take a few minutes to read the case example below.

Case example: Mr Bradford

Mr Bradford is a tall black British man serving a five-year prison sentence for grievous bodily harm (GBH), section 20 (the defendant caused serious bodily harm but did not intend to). Mr Bradford had head-butted the victim, causing a broken nose and fractured cheekbone. The victim's 10-year-old nephew witnessed the incident and subsequently reports nightmares and somatic complaints.

You have been asked to meet Mr Bradford in one of the prison interview rooms. Officers on his wing warn you that his behaviour has become increasingly challenging and they struggle to manage his outbursts and 'controlling and manipulative behaviour'. They also inform you that he has had repeated verbal and physical altercations with other inmates. As a result, he has spent an increasing amount of time in a segregation cell.

When you meet Mr Bradford he appears dishevelled, underweight and dressed in regular prison attire with a prominent scorpion neck tattoo. He appears irritable, hostile and defensive. You introduce yourself and ask him to read and sign a consent form for assessment. He refuses, rips up the form and tells you to go to hell.

- What were the 'automatic thoughts' that you might experience in this situation with Mr Bradford?
- What do you consider might be the key challenges in working with Mr Bradford? Do you notice any differences compared to the case example of Omar?

Activity 14. 1

Reflect once again on the two examples you have worked with in this chapter. Both actually referred to the case of Mr Omar Bradford, a 22-year-old black British man who was serving a five-year prison sentence for GBH, section 20, who attacked his boyfriend Dennis after discovering that he had been unfaithful. Take a few minutes to review the automatic thoughts, challenges and differences you noted when reading the case examples.

- Was your thinking influenced by our cultural tendency to view people as 'good' or 'bad', 'victim' or 'perpetrator'?
- Thinking back on what you have read in Chapter 5 about stereotyping, reflect on any biases or stereotypes that may have impeded your judgement.
- Is Mr Bradford's presentation more understandable in light of his background? How might it be possible to prevent, or mitigate, these reactions in the future?

Conclusions

Cognitive behavioural therapy reflects a large and diverse collection of interventions that can be applied to the full range of human experience from severe psychopathology to tertiary community prevention initiatives (Herbert & Forman, 2011), across multiple settings and delivered via numerous modalities. The 'third generation' CBT interventions, with their emphasis on holistic, contextual, mindful, and compassionate approaches, represent exciting new frontiers and are discussed in detail in Chapter 16. It is hoped that this chapter provides a sampling of the various principles, models, and techniques that fall under the rubric of CBT when applied to forensic settings. This chapter further aimed to orientate the reader to the various complexities and challenges faced by counsellor and forensic psychologists when working in forensic settings and the need to tailor CBT interventions accordingly.

Suggestion for further reading

Beck, J. S. (1995). *Cognitive therapy: basics and beyond*. New York and London: Guilford Press.
This arguably represents the 'gold standard' text for counsellors and psychologists wishing to deliver classic CBT.

Tafrate, R. C., & Mitchell, D. (2014). *Forensic CBT: a handbook for clinical practice*. Chichester: John Wiley & Sons.
This book addresses more advanced issues regarding the delivery of CBT interventions within forensic settings.

15

SYSTEMIC APPROACHES

ANDREAS VOSSLER, BRIGITTE SQUIRE AND CLARE BINGHAM

Image 15   Into the wood. With permission, Catriona Havard

Introduction

Systemic approaches to counselling and psychotherapy share the view that individual distress and mental health problems are not developed within individuals but in the relationships, interactions and language that emerge between individuals in social systems. Early systemic theories were interested in explaining individual and family behaviour and experiences in terms of the structure and organisation of systems (hence 'systemic' therapy), especially family and sub-systems, like parents or siblings (Shelton, 2010). A 'system' was defined as a unified whole which consists of interrelated parts (Nichols & Everett, 1986), with the whole system being different from the sums of its parts and changes in one part affecting the rest of the system (Vossler, 2010b). Later, the systemic focus was extended to include aspects of the wider client context (e.g. neighbourhood/community, cultural and religious context) and societal norms and understandings as conveyed through language.

With this understanding of problems as inter- rather than intrapersonal, systemic approaches have widened the traditional therapeutic setting and preoccupation with individual functioning and pathology. You will hear in this chapter that systemic therapists focus on the different social contexts individuals are embedded in – which includes not only the present family but also the family of origin, workplace and wider society (Vetere & Dallos, 2003). In working systemically with a client system, they aim to explore the relational dynamics, interaction pattern and belief systems that may be related to the problems and draw attention to the strengths and solutions in the stories their clients bring to therapy.

Pause for reflection: Implicit rules in social systems

What were the taken-for-granted rules in your family around the expression of anger and frustration (e.g. how to communicate with someone if you are angry with them)? What would happen if you wouldn't follow these rules or meet the expectations? How does this compare to the implicit rules in your peer group or your first place of work?

Systemic approaches are now firmly established in many areas of mental health provision in the UK, especially in working with children and young people (e.g. in Children and Adolescent Mental Health Services,

CAMHS) and in therapeutic work with couples and families. As we will show in this chapter, relationship and family-focused thinking is also very relevant when working therapeutically with clients in a forensic setting. While there haven't been many publications in this area, 'systemic work in these settings has been occurring in the UK for the past three decades' (Davies & Doran, 2012, p. 1).

In the following, we will first provide you with a brief overview of the development of systemic thinking and concepts in the last six decades. We will then explore how systemic ideas are applied in two forensic-mental-health practice settings – the work with young offenders and their families in community settings and systemic therapy with clients in a forensic mental-health inpatient context.

Key ideas in systemic counselling and therapy

While systemic therapy has never been a singular coherent therapy school, the different models and approaches developed under the 'systemic umbrella' are based on shared theoretical assumptions and working principles that we will introduce in this section. The term 'systemic therapy 'is used to describe both the general way of thinking systemically when working with clients as well as a set of systemically informed skills and techniques for therapeutic work (Dallos & Draper, 2015), some of which we will present below.

Information box 15.1 provides a brief overview of the development of systemic therapy, with the key systemic ideas emerging in each development stage (based on the more detailed accounts in Dallos & Draper, 2015; Parks, 2015; Shelton, 2010).

Information box 15.1: A short story of systemic ideas

The early pioneers of systemic therapy in the 1950s, like Gregory Bateson (Bateson et al., 1956), applied ideas and concepts derived from cybernetics and engineering to families. Similar to other biological or mechanical systems (like, for example, central heating systems), family functioning was seen as organised by a set of rules with feedback mechanisms employed to adapt and self-regulate the family system. Individual problems displayed by a family member were understood as serving a function in maintaining family balance and stability.

(Continued)

(Continued)

In the 1960s and 1970s, Strategic Family Therapy (Haley, 1963) and Structural Family Therapy (Minuchin, 1974) were developed based on the system analogy. These systemic schools drew attention to the organisational family structure (e.g. boundaries, hierarchies, coalitions) and the way family members interact with each other around problematic behaviours (interaction pattern). With directive and strategic interventions (including homework assignments), therapists aimed to move the family system from a dysfunctional state (e.g. weak hierarchies, inappropriate alliances, restrictive rules, children in overly powerful positions) to more functional structures and interaction dynamics.

In the late 1970s and 1980s the Milan and post-Milan schools became influential for the systemic therapy movement. The Milan team (Selvini-Palazzoli et al., 1978) shifted the therapeutic focus to the different ways family members see family life and the patterns of communications and underlying beliefs guiding families' actions. To stimulate change, therapists offered diverse hypotheses about the family dynamics based on their subjective observations in the therapy sessions. In embracing constructivism (philosophical perspective highlighting the uniqueness of individual perceptions and reality constructions), it was acknowledged in that period that it is not possible for therapists to take a non-involved expert position as they inevitably become part of the therapeutic system co-creating what they are observing (often described as shift from the 'first order' to 'second order' position).

Since the 1990s systemic thinking and practice has moved towards emerging social constructionist theories (beliefs and experiences are created or 'constructed' through social interaction; e.g. McNamee & Gergen, 1992) stressing the importance of the wider social and cultural context for family life and dynamics. From this perspective, individual perceptions and beliefs are not just shaped by the family context, but socially constructed through cultural discourses (e.g. the language used to describe 'mad/bad' behaviour) and shared societal norms and understandings. Seeing therapy as a collaborative process, systemic therapists became interested in helping clients/families to change the 'stories' they tell about themselves and their problems (Narrative Therapy; White & Epston, 1990) and focus on resources and solutions rather than problems and 'problem-saturated talk' (Solution-Focused Therapy; de Shazer, 2005). However, alongside these postmodern approaches there has been a resurge of modernist ideas in systemic practice more recently (Dallos & Draper, 2015), as illustrated by the introduction of attachment-based family therapy (Diamond, Diamond & Levy, 2014) and multi-systemic and functional therapies (e.g. Henggeler et al., 2009).

With the growing acceptance of systemic approaches in the twenty-first century the field seems to have 'moved away from several schools of thought to a unified practice' (Dallos & Draper, 2015, p. 169).

Contemporary systemic therapists often draw on concepts from different development stages of systemic approaches in a pragmatic and eclectic manner (Pinquart, Oslejsek & Teubert, 2016). While most of the early systemic therapists were predominantly seeing clients in the classical family setting (hence the often used term 'systemic family therapy'), contemporary systemic practice has become more flexible and includes work with individual clients (Athanasiades, 2008; Hedges, 2005), couples, part families and multi-family group therapy (Asen, 2002).

When working with their clients today, systemic practitioners share a set of guiding tenets and principles. Reflecting constructivist thinking and the idea of different or 'multiple' perceptions and realties in families, the therapeutic stance of neutrality and curiosity was first introduced by the Milan systemic school (see Information box 15.1). Systemic therapists aim to show equal and non-judgemental interest in the different and often contradicting views and beliefs expressed in the therapy room. Taking a neutral and curious stance can help to balance dominant and unhelpful narratives and pathological labelling of behaviour (e.g. as 'pathologic' or 'deviant'; Shelton, 2010) and facilitate the introduction of alternative descriptions and perspectives. However, we will see later in this chapter that it can be challenging for systemic therapists to take a 'neutral' stance when working in a forensic setting.

Table 15.1 provides an overview of three further key systemic principles that can be considered as relevant for therapeutic work in a forensic setting, together with one systemic technique epitomising each concept.

Table 15.1 Systemic principles and techniques

Systemic principle	Systemic technique
1. Focus on strengths and resources Each family/client system is considered as a system that owns a wealth of strengths and solutions in the face of difficult situations. Systemic therapists show appreciation of solution attempts and search for a constructive contribution even in destructive behaviour.	**1. Miracle question** De Shazer's (2005) miracle question invites the client to envision and describe in detail how the future will be different when the problem is no longer present, thus shifting the focus from problems to resources and possible solutions: *'Suppose that one night, while you are asleep, there is a miracle and the problem that brought you here is solved. However, because you are asleep you don't know that the miracle has already happened. When you wake up in the morning, what will be different that will tell you that the miracle has taken place? What else?'*

(Continued)

Table 15.1   (Continued)

Systemic principle	Systemic technique
2. Circularity	**2. Circular questioning**
Patterns of behaviour develop within systems, which are repetitive and circular in nature and also constantly evolving. Behaviour and beliefs that are perceived as difficulties will also therefore develop in a circular fashion, being affected by and affecting all members of the system. The behaviour of one person can be understood at the same time as the cause and effect of the behaviour of another person (A: 'I withdraw when you start nagging'– B: 'I start nagging when you withdraw'), which is distinct from linear or causal description ('A is cause of B').	Circular questioning (CQ) is aimed at looking at difference and is therefore a way of introducing new information into the system. CQ is effective in illuminating the interconnectedness of system members and invites people to consider relational aspects of the topic being investigated. There are different kinds of circular questions. An example of CQ is a question where a third person is asked about his/her perception of the meaning of the behaviours or feelings of one person for another person ('triadic question'): 'Emily, how do you think your Mum feels when your Dad starts crying?'
3. Meaning making and changing	**3. Reflecting teams discussions**
Reflecting constructionist ideas (each person has a unique and personal view of the world), systemic counselling and psychotherapy can be seen as a collaborative exploration of the different meanings and beliefs held by system members. In exploring meanings it is vital to understand the different contexts the client is living in as these contexts influence a person's identity and behaviour. This can help to challenge the dominant 'mad/bad' views and balance them with more constructive and positive views/ meanings (Shelton, 2010).	A 'reflecting team' (RT) (Andersen, 1987) consists of two or more observing therapists who are invited at some point during a session (or at the end of a session) to discuss their perceptions and ideas in front of the clients. RTs are employed to provide the clients with multiple perspectives and ideas about their situation. RT comments can be used to express reflections that are difficult to communicate within the client system, and the sharing of ideas can help to reveal new meanings and possibilities for the clients.

The following section will introduce a systemic intervention programme for the therapeutic work with young offenders and their families in a community setting.

Systemic practice in community work with young offenders and their families

In Chapter 7 we provided you with an overview of age-related vulnerabilities to developing mental health problems. In addition, cross-sectional and longitudinal studies (e.g. Elliott, Huizinga & Ageton, 1985; Liberman, 2008; Swenson et al., 2009) have identified key causes and correlates of anti-social behaviour in adolescents across multiple contexts, including family (e.g. high conflict/parenting problems), peer system (e.g. association with negative peers), school (e.g. low school attendance) and community (e.g. increased availability of weapons and drugs). Hence, the body of research evidence indicates that to address the risk factors for offending and anti-social behaviour in adolescents, multi-factorial interventions are needed to target problems in the multiple systems in which the adolescents are embedded.

Multi-Systemic Therapy: Intervening in systems to make individual behavioural change

In the last decades, some systemic intervention programmes have been developed and researched for their effectiveness with this aim in mind, such as Multi-Systemic Therapy (MST) and Functional Family Therapy. MST has a more extended socio-ecological approach, which is explained below.

MST (Henggeler et al., 2009) was developed in the 1970s by Scott Henggeler and colleagues at the Medical University of South Carolina and intensively researched in randomised controlled trials (RCTs) before it was disseminated to other areas in the USA and later to Europe and other countries. It is a treatment model for young people aged 11 to 17 with very serious behavioural problems and their families, based on Bronfenbrenner's (1979) theory of social ecology. Young people are seen to be embedded in multiple systems and behaviour is a function of individuals' interactions within and between these systems and these influences are bi-directional. So, the behaviour of a child will influence how the parents react to them and vice versa. One of the main assumptions of MST is that the caregiver is the primary catalyst for change and therefore the interventions will focus on empowering the caregivers to effectively manage their children's behaviour. As the parents' effectiveness increases, so will their impact on the peer, school and community systems, which will reduce the anti-social behaviour in the young person. Often the young person is so involved in anti-social activities, which can be reinforcing, that they are not engaging in any form of individual treatment. By working with the parents, change can still be achieved and can sometimes increase the young person's engagement with the treatment (Tighe et al., 2012).

MST is an intensive home and community-based treatment administered by a team of a half-time MST supervisor and three to four therapists working with four to six families. Therapists visit the family three or more times a week and treatment requires daily effort from the family members to reach the collaborative goals. The family has access to a 24-hour on-call system to assist and support them while addressing the problems. Considerable attention is devoted to the role of extra familial systems (e.g. peers, school, neighbourhood, family network) in trying to reduce identified problems, and social support systems will be utilised to generate pro-social contexts and sustain treatment gains. MST interventions are drawn from existing evidence-based techniques, such as behaviour management techniques, cognitive behavioural therapies and pragmatic family therapy approaches.

Systemic concepts and techniques used in MST to facilitate change

In the engagement and alignment process, reframing and positive connotations are powerful systemic techniques to reduce blaming and polarisation of positions as they can be used to 'describe problematic emotions or behaviours in a fundamentally different (mostly positive) frame' (Vossler, 2010b, p. 202). By the time a family is referred to MST, the caregivers have often given up hope of any possible change and often blame the young person's behaviour for the persistence of problems. The young people might attribute the lack of parental warmth, harsh punishment and family dynamics to their behaviour. By offering reframes and positive connotations, the family members are respectfully invited to see things differently and to expand each person's definition of the presenting problem. They are intended to propose new and often unexpected meanings for individual behaviours, the nature of a particular relationship and the collective interaction of a whole family system (Watzlawick, Weakland & Fisch, 1974). Reframing, for example, verbal aggression from the young person as a way to get closer to the parents or as anxiety about feeling rejected or as a desperate attempt to seek help, not only for them but for the whole family, can make the parent feel less angry and behave differently. Nagging can be reframed as behaviour showing that the other is important, that one cares and wants to be close to the other.

In the process of understanding the interactional dynamics that causes conflict and aggression the MST worker will do an in-depth sequence analysis by going in detail over the sequence of events leading to conflict from different family member's perspectives and may use the technique of circular questioning (see Table 15.1 above). Such an analysis of a conflictual incident between the adolescent and the parents gives a good insight in the interactional circularity of mutual influences. It can guide the MST therapist to advise all family members to change some steps in the sequence by thinking and behaving differently and thereby influence the impact and behaviour of the other.

Lack of parental monitoring and effective parenting disciplines are often strongly related to behavioural problems and an improvement in parental monitoring and management skills is related to better outcomes (Robinson et al., 2015). Techniques from Structural Family Therapy (Minuchin, 1974; see Information box 15.1 above) can be useful, such as appropriate boundary setting to help to restore the hierarchy in the home by promoting the parents to take joint authority and control in a warm but authoritative way and not allowing fear to shape the way they react to the adolescent. Setting up behaviour rules for certain desired behaviours, with appropriate rewards and consequences, is a tool that allows the parents to make clear expectations and gives the young person a choice on how to make decisions as they know exactly what will happen and how the parents will react. This reduces conflict and excessive punishments that are often used as a threat in an emotional encounter. Relational changes can motivate young people to comply and develop positive behaviours without needing the use of power and consequences.

The following case example illustrates some of the systemic techniques used in MST work and how they can facilitate change in a family system.

Case example: Tina and her family

Tina is 13 years old and was referred to MST because of significant verbal and physical aggression at home, ongoing non-attendance at school and many school exclusions due to aggressive behaviour towards staff. She was mixing with older anti-social peers and would come home late, intoxicated. Mum was battling with depression, having survived a domestic violence situation, but was refusing to take medication. She was instead using cannabis to relax and calm down. Mum struggled to regulate her

(Continued)

(Continued)

emotions and would shout a lot to try to have some influence on Tina. She was also worried about the impact Tina's disrespectful behaviour would have on the younger children.

The MST worker tried to empower mum's position in the family structure, encouraging her to set boundaries and monitor Tina's whereabouts by setting clear expectations and making rules with consequences as to her whereabouts and going to school. Many reframes were used to help mum to see Tina as a child wanting closeness and warmth, as mum had distanced and detached herself because she was feeling unable to cope and was using cannabis to chill out. By doing detailed sequence analyses of the ongoing conflicts and arguments, the MST worker helped the family to understand the reasons and triggers of the escalation and each perspective and motivation. This brought a better understanding of each position and increased the desire to spend some quality time with each other. As mum felt more in control, she was able to have direct conversations with the school to increase the monitoring of attendance and deal with the problems that Tina was facing there. She was placed in a special unit within school where she could get more individual assistance to catch up with her missed education. Her increased attendance made her less involved with the anti-social peers and she took up some after-school sport activities.

Systemic practice in a forensic-mental-health secure setting

There has been substantial development of the use of systemic approaches in secure services over the last 15 years. Although there is a history of systemic psychotherapy being offered to families in forensic services over the last 30 years (Davies & Doran, 2012), this was initially limited to a few discrete services and not provided routinely. In 2014, Davies et al. (2014) replicated a survey of medium secure units (MSUs) originally conducted by Geelan and Nickford in 1999. The 2014 study reported that 19 of the 49 MSUs which responded were offering family therapy and in 16 of these units, systemic psychotherapy was the main approach – in contrast to only nine out of 33 secure services offering family therapy in 1999 (with the main theoretical approach being cited as 'psycho-educational' rather than systemic) (Geelan & Nickford, 1999).

It is estimated that 72% of forensic 'service users' (a term often used as an alternative to 'clients' or 'patients') have regular contact with their relatives, and in 56% of cases families are involved in the service user's discharge planning (Absalom et al., 2010). In most cases, a forensic inpatient admission will only be warranted where there has been a conviction for a violent offence or where there is an ongoing risk of violence to others. Sometimes family members have been the victims of violence and the provision of systemic family therapy aims to alleviate some of the distress associated with past violent incidents (Robinson et al., 1991) and to reduce the risk of violence in future, as well as to improve family functioning and communication overall, in line with the families' own generated goals for therapy.

Systemic therapists use their skills in a variety of ways in secure forensic inpatient settings. They provide consultation to teams, to help them to think about their interactions with each other and with service users. They can think about wider organisational practices from a systemic perspective and provide supervision to other clinicians who are engaged with families or careers. In the main, though, systemic therapists work clinically with service users and their partners or families, providing systemic family therapy in a clinic setting. In the following we will introduce you to some key features of this type of work.

Working with the 'mad or bad' discourses of the forensic setting

The delivery of family therapy in secure forensic settings necessitates an awareness and understanding of the possible impact of the forensic inpatient context. Forensic contexts are complex institutions where multiple discourses overlap and impact on the service user (see Chapter 1). Service users and their families become a focus for powerful cultural discourses from both the criminal justice and psychiatric systems. The language of these systems sometimes contributes to the development of a rigid and problem-saturated identity for service users, which can limit opportunities for change. Terms relating to a person's mental health section, criminal conviction and mental health diagnosis (such as 'restriction order', 'schizophrenia', 'grievous bodily harm', etc.) are embedded in the communication about, with and between service users in forensic settings.

Social constructionist and narrative ideas (White & Epston, 1990; see Information box 15.1) can be especially helpful in deconstructing these dominant discourses and in thickening alternative descriptions coming from the family, which may generate more positive ideas about recovery and opportunities for change. Using these approaches, it is possible to invite a family to think outside 'mad or bad' terminologies and to bring their own ideas about the service user, which may be less problem-saturated. For example, a family might talk about the service user having been an extremely sensitive child or highly protective of someone in the family, which brings new insights and can help to provide a different and useful focus for therapeutic work. They may highlight an important relationship or skill which could be helpful in motivating and engaging the service user in working towards change.

Pause for reflection: Labels

Consider some of the labels which have been used to describe you. For example, labels may refer to your gender, your ethnicity, sexuality or marital status. What assumptions have been made about you because of those labels? In which ways have they been helpful or unhelpful?

Circularity and multiple positions

Often when families first come to therapy they struggle with the idea that the sessions are for thinking about the whole family system (as well as the wider context) and not just the family member who is in hospital. Some of the constructivist ideas from Milan and post-Milan schools of systemic therapy (see Information box 15.1) help to shift the focus away from the service user and enable more thinking about the family system and social and cultural factors which may have played a part in developing or maintaining some of the difficulties that are currently located in the service user.

An exploration of family scripts and beliefs can help to generate ideas about similarities and differences within a family, where these might have come from and how they might contribute to patterns of communicating and behaviour. The use of circular questioning (see Table 15.1) can assist the family in developing an understanding of difficulties which is more systemic, and acknowledges the impact of each part of the system on all other parts. From here, the hope is that families will be able to change unhelpful patterns of communicating and behaving and develop positive patterns which support the service user in making desired changes themselves. For example, a mother may have a belief that looking clean and tidy is very important. She may insist on doing laundry for her son, who is then interpreted as being excessively dependent on her and lacking skills in self-care. Exploring this mother's belief about being clean and tidy can help to understand where this might have come from and consider the impact on the wider system of her continuing to do the laundry. Circular questioning can also help to bring into therapy beliefs and perspectives of family members who may not be physically present in therapy.

In doing this work, it is also important for therapists to reflect on the 'second-order' position from the Milan and post-Milan schools (see Information box 15.1) and to consider the ways they may be impacting on the system in therapy. Therapists may find themselves occupying multiple positions in relation to the service user and their family. Clinicians are inevitably involved in the ongoing task of risk assessment, which is central to the function of the forensic service. As such, they may be involved in making decisions about when someone is ready to be discharged from hospital, or whether they can have more leave into the community or visit the family at home. This can sit uncomfortably with the task of building a trusting therapeutic alliance with families, who may find it difficult to open up knowing that this is the case. Therapy may be offered at the request of the family but often service users report that they feel they have to engage in order to be discharged. Even identifying goals for therapy with a family can involve untangling the priorities of the family and the organisation, for which risk is usually the 'highest context marker' (see Chapter 1).

Challenges of systemic work in a forensic-mental-health secure setting

Moving away from a focus on risk to engage families in new ways can leave clinicians feeling exposed and unsafe (Vivian-Byrne, 2001) and this is a challenge for systemic psychotherapy in secure forensic services. Some ideas which are central to systemic practice are difficult to apply in this context. For example, it is not ethical for therapists to attempt to maintain a stance of neutrality in relation to violence and the potential for future violence towards others. In forensic settings, taking a curious approach often feels more helpful and ethical than taking a position of neutrality when discussing issues relating to offending and violence (Goldner, 1998). A curious stance enables exploration of the psychological, relational, social and cultural factors which may have contributed to violent behaviour, while taking a position that the violence itself is unacceptable.

Taking a helpful position as a therapist is one of the biggest challenges to any therapy in a forensic setting. The aim is to form a trusting therapeutic relationship in which potential for change and recovery is recognised but without colluding with ideas and behaviour which may be risky and unhelpful. In systemic psychotherapy, it can be a challenge not to align oneself with a family member whom we may identify with or who may have been the victim of an offence. We may prioritise ideas about a service user needing to take responsibility for past violence to an extent that other opportunities for change are not explored. Sometimes, as described above, aspects of the forensic setting can seem counter-therapeutic and this may be frustrating as a therapist. However, it is important to guard against the potential for unhelpful polarisation within the professional system working with the service user and regular supervision can provide a helpful space for reflection on the positions we may be taking.

Conclusions

Systemic thinking and techniques have proven useful for many and varied clinical situations, and are 'increasingly used in various settings and with a variety of problems where the work does not simply or predominantly involve meeting with family members' (Dallos & Draper, 2015, p. 169). While it is acknowledged in the field that more research is needed (Pinquart et al., 2016), there is a growing body of evidence pointing to the efficacy of systemic approaches with different client groups (especially clients with eating disorders, mood disorders and schizophrenia). It is therefore no surprise that systemic ideas have also been employed in therapeutic work in different forensic settings, as illustrated above.

Systemic practice has traditionally been more common in community outpatient settings than in secure settings, which may reflect the specific challenges of practising healthcare in a custodial environment. However, systemic work now also seems to be well established in secure forensic settings, like medium-secure units (Bingham & Smith, 2012) and prisons (Shelton, 2010). We hope this chapter has shown that there is a clear rationale for systemic thinking and practice, with a focus on context and multiple perspectives, in all these forensic settings as systemic approaches can be used to work with clients on issues that can be applied to life and (family) relationships in and beyond forensic contexts (Shelton, 2010).

Suggestions for further reading

Dallos, R., & Draper, R. (2015). *An introduction to family therapy: systemic theory and practice* (4th ed.). Buckingham: Open University Press.
A great introduction to systemic family therapy, providing a comprehensive overview of the development of systemic approaches and their core concepts and techniques.

Shelton, D. (2010). Systemic psychotherapy in prison. In J. Harvey & K. Smedley (Eds.), *Psychological therapy in prisons and other secure settings* (pp. 130–149). Abingdon: Willan.
This book chapter illustrates how systemic concepts can be used in therapeutic work with young offenders in prison settings.

16

MINDFULNESS

MEG-JOHN BARKER AND TROY COOPER

Image 16   Seeing the light. With permission, Sue Cheval

Introduction

One of the biggest influences on counselling and psychology in recent years has been the huge therapeutic interest in adapting Buddhist mindfulness as a way of addressing mental health difficulties and improving well-being. Mindfulness is increasingly advocated by professional bodies and political parties as an approved way of tackling mental health problems (e.g. Mindfulness All-Party Parliamentary Group (MAPPG), 2015; National Institute for Health and Care Excellence (NICE), 2000). It is also increasingly being adopted in other areas, such as education, the workplace and – importantly for our purposes – the criminal justice system. Psychological research on this topic has also increased exponentially over the last decade and there is now a significant body of research evidence supporting the effectiveness of mindfulness in tackling both common mental health problems (e.g. Shonin, Van Gordon & Griffiths, 2015) and difficult offender behaviours (Shonin et al., 2013).

In this chapter we introduce you to mindfulness, if you're not already familiar with the subject, and overview the ways in which it is now being applied in both counselling and forensic psychology. In particular we focus in on the mindfulness-based approach of Dialectical Behaviour Therapy (Swales & Heard, 2009) and how that is being used in a forensic context (Berzins & Trestman, 2004).

What is mindfulness?

You will almost certainly be familiar with the term 'mindfulness' already, given there has been a huge amount of popular interest in the topic in recent years, with popular self-help books being published on the topic, not to mention newspaper reports, television documentaries, and the like.

> **Pause for reflection: Definitions**
>
> Think about the times that you have come across the word 'mindfulness'. What words and phrases do you associate with this concept? How would you define it if somebody asked you what it meant?

Mindfulness is a concept that comes from traditional Buddhist philosophy and has recently been embraced by many Western authors, therapists and psychologists. We might define mindfulness as something like 'giving open, curious attention to the way that things are, rather than attempting to avoid or grasp hold of any aspect of experience'. To help you to understand what that means better, try Activity 16.1.

Activity 16.1: Being mindful

The basis of most mindfulness approaches is this breathing practice. Have a go and then reflect on what the experience is like for you.

- Sit comfortably and quietly on a chair, shut your eyes and relax any tension in your body.
- Breathe in and out three times.
- Now just focus on your natural breathing for five minutes, not trying to control it in any way, but just noticing how it feels coming in and out of your body.
- You will probably get distracted many, many times, by thoughts, feelings, sounds or sensations. There is nothing wrong with this, it is part of the experience. Each time it happens, just notice you've been distracted and bring your attention gently back to your breath.

The idea of practices like this is not to get rid of distractions or to achieve any kind of blank mind. Rather, it is to become more aware of how people tend to become carried away by the stories they tell about their lives (such as going over the past or planning for the future), and to cultivate the ability to come back to the present moment. The idea with this is that the more people do practices like these the more able they will be to do the same thing when more difficult states, like anxiety or depression, arise.

People often confuse mindfulness with meditation because one way mindfulness is practised is through meditations like this one, or ones where you scan your bodily sensations or listen to the sounds around you. However, the point of meditation is really just to develop your capacity to be mindful. The idea is to try to apply this way of being to all of your everyday life. Indeed, many teachers suggest deliberately doing everyday tasks like eating, brushing your teeth or washing the dishes mindfully (Nhat Hanh, 1975/1991). A mindfulness practitioner might meditate formally for half an hour every day, but they would also try to pause regularly during their day to bring themselves back to the present moment (Williams, 2016), and they might also take a break for mindfulness any time things became particularly difficult (Chödrön, 1994).

Mindfulness, mental health and counselling

In the world of counselling and psychology, the word 'mindfulness' has taken on a somewhat broader meaning to encompass a number of new forms of counselling which draw upon Buddhist ideas, often weaving them together with modern Western psychotherapy. While one main focus is on cultivating the mindful capacity to attend to experience as it is in the present moment, such approaches also often draw in other aspects of Buddhist philosophy, particularly the importance of developing compassion and kindness – for yourself and for others (e.g. Gilbert, 2010; Salzberg, 2011).

While all the main counselling and psychotherapy approaches have engaged with Buddhism to some extent (Barker, 2013b), when people refer to 'the mindfulness movement' they are often talking about the 'third wave' of cognitive behavioural therapy (CBT) approaches (see Chapter 14) which have drawn upon mindfulness and other aspects of Buddhist theory and practice. Mindfulness Stress Reduction Therapy, Mindfulness-Based Cognitive Therapy, Acceptance and Commitment Therapy, Compassion-Focused Therapy (which also draws on attachment theory, see Chapter 13), and Dialectical Behaviour Therapy are just some of the mindfulness-based forms of CBT which have emerged in recent years (Germer, Siegel & Fulton, 2005).

As well as being something that can be used in one-to-one therapy with clients, mindfulness CBT is often taught to people in group training formats, such as eight-week courses, where a trainer takes a group through the materials and they also practise alone between sessions (Crane, 2009). There are many self-help manuals, videos and audio materials to help people to develop their own mindfulness practices (e.g. Heaversage & Halliwell, 2012; Williams & Penman, 2011) as well as computer programs and apps (Glück & Maercker, 2011).

Mindfulness understandings of mental health problems

Reviews or the research and meta-analyses (which amalgamate the data across research studies) so far find evidence that mindfulness-based interventions are effective across a number of different common mental and physical health conditions, notably preventing relapse from depression and easing chronic pain conditions (MAPPG, 2015; Shonin et al., 2015).

So what is the theory behind these practices being so helpful? Why do we try to cultivate that open, curious attention to the way things are? Going back to the original Buddhist understanding of distress, the idea there is that suffering is rooted in craving: the approach where we try to get everything we want and to avoid everything we don't want. Martine Batchelor explains it well with this metaphor:

> Let's imagine that I am holding an object made of gold. It is so precious and it is mine – I feel I must hold onto it. I grasp it, curling my fingers so as not to drop it, so that nobody can take it away from me. What happens after a while? Not only do my hand and arm get cramp but I cannot use my hand for anything else. When you grip something, you create tension and limit yourself.
>
> Dropping the golden object is not the solution. Non-attachment means learning to relax to uncurl the fingers and gently open the hand. When my hand is wide open and there is no tension, the precious object can rest lightly on my palm. I can still value the object and take care of it; I can put it down and pick it up; I can use my hand for doing something else. (Batchelor, 2001, p. 96)

Applying this metaphor to our everyday lives, we could say that suffering happens whenever we fall into that habit of grasping things and/or hurling them away, whether that is our own thoughts or emotions, aspects of our identity, relationships with others, material things, or anything really.

For example, you might notice this happening with feelings. Something happens which gives you a little anxious feeling: just a twinge. That feeling is unpleasant so – maybe without even noticing – you try to deny it is happening and just get on with things. However, the anxiety seems to get larger in the background so soon it's really quite frightening. You worry about the fear which you now can't avoid: 'what's wrong with me that I'm suddenly so scared?' You try to think the feeling away, telling yourself it's irrational, but it doesn't work and now you're panicked about why you're making such a huge deal out of something so minor. Maybe it's a terrible sign that you have to do something major to address it. The idea of that is so scary that you end up in even more of a panic.

Buddhists call this the 'second arrow': the idea that it's often not the initial feeling, thought, experience, or whatever that is the problem (the first arrow), but rather it is all of the feelings, thoughts and behaviours that we engage in after that (the second arrows). For example, imagine you were in a meeting and said something you thought was a bit foolish. The first arrow would be that brief flush of embarrassment. The second arrows would be telling yourself you were stupid, worrying what everybody thought of you, feeling angry with yourself, tensing your body, etc. 'Staying with' the first arrow means allowing yourself to feel the embarrassment without hitting yourself with all those additional thoughts and feelings about it.

Second arrows don't just happen with 'negative' experiences like fear, we're just as bad with 'positive' experiences, like finding something that makes us feel good, and then trying to get that experience more and more, and protecting it because we're so scared of not having it again (a common pattern in addictions and compulsions).

Pause for reflection: Second arrows

Can you remember a recent time when you experienced something like the spiral of thoughts and/or feelings described here?

The alternative, as we saw in Batchelor's metaphor, is turning towards the initial experience and trying to be with it as it is, instead of layering all those other things on top of it. That's why, during meditation, we try to notice each thought, feeling or sensation as it bubbles up, and let them go: not itching a scratch, following a fantasy, or trying to block off a negative thought.

So mindful therapies for anxiety tend to advocate 'approaching' rather than 'avoiding' frightening experiences, and learning to 'stay with' the experience, noticing with curiosity how it unfolds over time (Orsillo & Roemer, 2011). Mindful therapies for addiction encourage 'urge surfing': slowing down and noticing the urges when they come, rather than either trying to avoid them or giving into them (Bowen, Chawla & Marlatt, 2010). Mindful therapies for pain note how we tend to clench up around physical pain and focus on eliminating it, in a similar way to the way we relate to emotional pain. Again, trying to be with the sensation openly and spaciously, so we're aware of our whole experience and how it shifts over time, seems to be helpful (Kabat-Zinn, 1996).

It is important to remember that with all mental and physical health issues it is generally a lot more difficult to be mindful when things are hard than it is at other times. For this reason many approaches advocate training in mindfulness when things aren't so tough (e.g. before a relapse, when you're not feeling anxious), and then slowly applying it to the difficult situation. Many approaches also emphasise strongly the need to cultivate self-compassion and kindness so that mindfulness doesn't just become another stick to beat yourself with when you – inevitably – find it difficult (e.g. Chödrön, 2001; Magid, 2008).

Mindfulness approaches in counselling

You should have got the sense, from the section above, that Buddhist approaches don't draw much distinction between everyday experiences and mental health problems, or between different kinds of distress (depression, anxiety, addiction, psychosis, etc.). The 'mindless' craving way of being is seen as something that we all do in various ways, and which results in both the everyday and extreme forms of suffering that we experience. And the way of addressing this – through mindfulness, meditation, compassion, etc. – is the same regardless.

Buddhist approaches also challenge distinctions between therapist (well) and client (sick). Because we all engage in the same patterns, mindfulness would be just as important for the practitioner as for the person they're working with. It can be a great way of cultivating the focused attention, self-awareness, empathy for others, and ability to 'stay with' difficult material which is required in therapy (Barker, 2013b). A mindful therapist can model these abilities for their client and offer a mindful relationship in the therapy room which is beneficial in itself (Nanda, 2005).

Of course, mindfulness ideas and practices can also be offered to clients as something to try for themselves, either in addition to regular therapy, or as the whole focus of therapy sessions: practising both with support within sessions and as 'homework'.

Case example: Mindful therapy

Paul is a man in his late 50s who comes for counselling. He says he's suffered from periods of depression every few years for most of his adult life and he'd really appreciate some help with it. A lot of the time he's fine – getting on with his work, his hobbies, and the home he's made with his husband Michael. But when depression hits he becomes withdrawn and anti-social and finds himself questioning everything he does, becoming irritable with Michael and despondent about the future.

Before reading on, you might like to reflect from what you've read already how mindful approaches might understand Paul's difficulties, and how a mindful therapist might work with him. The evidence so far suggests that mindfulness is particularly effective at preventing relapse from depression in people who've experienced it before (Shonin et al., 2015) so it could be particularly beneficial for Paul to work with a counsellor one-to-one or in a group to learn mindful techniques before depression hits again (Segal, Williams & Teasdale, 2002).

If Paul is currently experiencing depression, a therapist might encourage him to try 'staying with' his irritable or despondent feelings rather than trying to grasp them or hurling them away. With awareness he might notice the barrage of 'second arrows' which tend to come in whenever he starts to feel low. He might cultivate the capacity to come back to his whole experience

(Continued)

(Continued)

in the present moment instead of ruminating over the past and worrying about the future (Williams, Teasdale, Segal & Kabat-Zinn, 2007). A therapist might also like to draw in more compassion-based practices, such as meditations designed to get Paul feeling more kind, and less critical, towards himself and the rest of the world (e.g. Gilbert, 2010).

Mindfulness in the criminal justice system

As we have seen, mindfulness has become important in therapy, but it is also now broadly influential in public policy proposals for increasing the well-being of society. In 2008, the UK's Government Office for Science published a report entitled *Mental capital and wellbeing: making the most of ourselves in the 21st century* as an overview of how to increase 'mental capital'. Central to the project was the idea of mindfulness techniques at all stages of life to promote personal well-being and better mental health and functioning, from childhood school and adolescent learning and leisure settings, to older adults in work, in education or training, and after work in older age.

This focus was further developed in the Mindfulness All-Party Parliamentary Group (MAPPG) report *Mindful nation UK* (MAPPG, 2015). The report was produced by a group of members of parliament who had been offered mindfulness sessions by The Mindfulness Initiative: a group of teachers, economists, theorists and others influenced by mindfulness, who try to raise awareness of the uses of mindfulness practices throughout society.

Considering the cost to the state and research evidence, the report identified four areas in which mindfulness could be a key resource. One was the criminal justice system, particularly in relation to the rehabilitation of offenders and the prevention of recidivism (reoffending by prisoners once they are released). The report noted the evidence that prison populations have higher levels of depression and anxiety and a higher suicide rate than the rest of society; higher levels of negative feelings, anger and inability to self-regulate; higher incidence of childhood histories of emotional, sexual or physical abuse (see Chapter 13); and higher levels of substance abuse.

These factors are all linked to offending, and are therefore understood as *criminogenic* and should be addressed in a 'what works' approach to rehabilitation and prevention of recidivism (Howells, Day & Thomas-Peter, 2007). Howells et al.'s report also noted that there was now significant research to support mindfulness-based training and practice in prison being effective in ameliorating the occurrence and effects of these factors. Mindfulness-Based Cognitive Therapy was therefore recommended as standard therapy in the UK criminal custodial system, and the report called for further investigation of the effectiveness of mindfulness-based interventions with offenders.

Meditation and mindfulness in prison systems

Grounded in Hindu philosophy, Transcendental Meditation was one of the earliest meditation programmes to achieve huge popularity across Western society after the Second World War. Introduced into US prison from the 1970s onwards, its practice involved repetition of a mantra once or twice for 15–20 minutes a day to produce a 'wakeful condition of alertness [and] a restful physiological condition' (Himelstein, 2011, p. 648). The focus of its introduction in prisons was reduction of levels of anger and aggressive behaviour, but there were a range of additional benefits, including reduced use of narcotic drugs and addiction behaviours, and recidivism.

Orme-Johnson (2011) notes a series of research studies in which follow-up of these, and Buddhist-based meditation, programmes found impressive effects on levels of aggression, well-being, self-esteem, negative thoughts, optimism, pro-social behaviour, and empathy with others. Offenders in these programmes were between 33% and 47% less likely to be convicted of a further crime following release from prison.

Prison environments are alien, alienating, noisy, cramped, regimented, and sometimes chaotic and threatening (Scott-Whitney, 2002). These are huge barriers to activities requiring stillness, silence and reflection. As a prisoner in US high security prisons over 20 years, Maull (2005) movingly details his journey to develop Buddhist meditation practice to survive this environment, to found a meditation self-help group for other prisoners, and his use of mindfulness in hospice care for prisoners with terminal illness. In 1987 he founded the Prison Dharma Network, which is now a global organisation working to promote support for Buddhist prison meditation groups and practices across the world.

Vipassana is the usual form of mindful and 'Buddhist informed' meditation used in prisons. It involves an initial ten-day training period of total silence and retreat with sitting meditational exercises – no mean feat in a prison environment – followed by regular group practice. Two documentaries have been made in the very different contexts of the US and India (Ariel & Menahami, 1997; Philips, Kukura & Stein, 2007) to show the actuality and practice of such groups and the issues and difficulties they encounter.

Lyons and Cantrell (2015) detail the continuing success of such volunteer-based programmes, but in particular how the mindfulness-informed therapeutic approaches mentioned earlier are now being combined with CBT techniques in a range of prison therapeutic regimes. For example, they describe the adaptation of Mindfulness-Based Stress Reduction into Mindfulness-Based Relapse Prevention, which develops the capability for acceptance and non-reactive observation of the desire to use drugs – 'urge surfing' (Bowen & Marlatt, 2009). This appears to be effective in lessening the severity of negative emotional states which cue drug use, and enabling tolerance of these. Substance misuse and addiction is a big problem in US prisons and intersects directly with the race issues covered in Chapter 5. In relation to gender (see Chapter 6), research suggests that for women prisoners in particular, mindfulness-based interventions are effective in addressing substance misuse and serious psychological trauma (Katz & Toner, 2013).

Research into the outcomes of mindfulness and meditation-based interventions was cited extensively in the MAPPG report, *Mindful Nation UK* (MAPPG, 2015). However, the difficulties of conducting research in prisons and custodial settings are considerable, from the practical to the methodological and ethical. This means that individual studies vary hugely in the conditions, quality, measured outcomes and controls that are applied (Howells et al., 2010; Shonin et al., 2013).

However, systematic reviews and meta-analyses of these studies show a qualified but consistently positive impact of interventions in relation to the following: alleviation of feelings of low self-worth and low self-efficacy; excessive self-focus and inability to relate closely with others; habitually high levels of negative thought, feeling and anger improving behaviour relating to poor self-management; lowering of impulsivity; and better emotional self-regulation (Auty, Cope & Liebling, 2015; Dafoe & Stermac, 2013). There is also reasonably consistent evidence that prisoners who have taken part in substantial and sustained programmes of this kind have significantly lower rates of recidivism.

Focus on Dialectical Behaviour Therapy (DBT)

Marsha Linehan (Linehan, 1993; Linehan et al., 1991) developed Dialectical Behaviour Therapy (DBT) to address the deeper individual developmental history and emotional issues of her clients. She had found that clients often felt misunderstood and invalidated in CBT (see Chapter 14), and withdrew from it or got angry with the continual emphasis on change. She proposed this is because CBT focuses on acquiring scripts and techniques to apparently change thought and behaviours, without acceptance or exploration of the individuality of a client's emotions or the history and experience of their particular lives.

DBT introduces the 'dialectic' of balancing *acceptance* of who an individual client is with the need or goal of *change* in particular ways. The key mindful therapeutic addition to CBT here is *radical acceptance*. This involves recognising that many of the significant judgements that we make about ourselves and others – particularly the negative judgements which often lead to self-destructive actions – are emotional and unreasonable. It is about accepting painful and unpleasant emotions, but not allowing them to build up through judgements about what they mean into suffering. In this way, it involves recognising and accepting the 'first arrow' feelings behind the 'second arrows'. The client can then choose to change or to accept particular areas of their life which cause pain, and to enable either choice using skills development.

In DBT there are four skill areas which practitioners and clients work on together to develop this dialectic for both change and acceptance of what is (McKay, Wood & Brantley, 2007). They are:

1. Distress tolerance to cope better with painful emotions and to build new resiliencies so that the events or circumstances that provoke pain do not also build up into suffering.
2. Mindfulness to experience the present moment more fully and focus less on painful or frightening events in the past or possibilities in the future. Part of this involves reviewing and overcoming habitual negative judgements made about the self or others.
3. Emotional regulation to recognise feelings clearly and be able to experience and modulate them without feeling overwhelmed, which often causes destructive behaviour.
4. Interpersonal effectiveness to express beliefs and needs, to set limits and to negotiate problems while protecting relationships and maintaining respect.

In a standard format, DBT involves group sessions for the first three months working on these skills in a structured form, with practice sessions, homework and record keeping. These are followed by individual sessions and (ideally) availability of the therapist to clients on the phone for coaching for several additional months up to a year. This has been modified and trialled within many contexts and with many mental health issues, but should always follow a particular format of treatment stages and a hierarchy of target behaviours so that therapy is safe, structured and progressive, and not just used as a reactive crisis management service (Pederson, 2015).

DBT has been used extensively with community clients diagnosed with borderline personality disorder (BPD), eating disorders, substance abuse, depressive disorders, and self-harm, with consistently positive results (Panos et al., 2014; see Chapter 18). It has been particularly impressive in its successful use with BPD, which within psychiatric services is often considered to be an untreatable condition.

Within the growing evaluation literature, it has been frequently noted that DBT is particularly successful with women clients, and it has been trialled with impressive results with long- and short-term women prisoners across custodial contexts and countries (Berzins & Trestman, 2004; Gee & Reed, 2013; Nee & Farman, 2007). It is now also being adapted and trialled, with some success, with male prisoners diagnosed with psychopathy and other issues (Galietta & Rosenfield, 2012). It is, however, an intensive and sustained form of therapy, and one whose literature is rich in the tensions and issues which arise from implementing therapeutic practices grounded in Buddhist spiritual philosophy into a secular, Western, materialist system of practice.

Critical perspectives

Throughout this chapter we have generally presented a pretty positive view of mindfulness-based interventions and their effectiveness at helping people in both counselling and forensic psychology contexts. However, it is important to inject a note of caution here. Mindfulness-based therapies are a very new thing (even if they are based on an ancient approach), and this means that they still haven't been researched as thoroughly as other therapies or over such a long period of time. There are also some serious criticisms coming to light of the limitations of the mindfulness movement in its current form.

In relation to the research, studies in this area suffer from many of the problems of research on therapy more broadly, including the fact that they tend to be conducted by people who are invested in their approach to mindfulness, who will therefore tend to find more positive results; that significant results tend to be published while non-significant ones do not; and that it is very hard to create comparison groups who go through everything else that the mindfulness group goes through, except the mindfulness itself, and with the same practitioner (Cooper, 2008). Shonin, Van Gordon and Griffiths (2010) suggest that some of the effectiveness of mindfulness may well be because it is currently so fashionable. They also point out that 'mindfulness' is being used to refer to many different therapies and techniques, and that it is also very difficult to determine whether clients are actually engaging in the practices they've been taught.

A spate of critical articles and programmes have also pointed out some serious issues with the ways in which the current mindfulness movement operates (e.g. Beyond Belief, 2014; Foster, 2016; Purser & Loy, 2013). There isn't space to go into all these in detail here, but Information box 16.1 provides a brief list of some of the concerns.

Pause for reflection

Before reading the list in Information box 16.1, take a moment to think about any criticisms you have thought of while engaging with this chapter.

Information box 16.1: Problems with the mindfulness movement

* Mindfulness and/or meditation may increase rather than decreasing distress for some people, particularly if done as a one-size-fits-all approach without support or a thorough understanding (Farias & Wikholm, 2015).
* There's no accreditation to ensure that mindfulness trainers are well trained and ethical (Foster, 2016).
* There are ethical issues with people repackaging, trademarking and selling ancient ideas and practices which were originally given away for free to whoever wanted to engage with them (Barker, 2013b).
* Difficulty meditating or being mindful can become another reason for people who are struggling to be self-critical (a major element of mental health problems) if not combined with compassion (Chödrön, 2001; Magid, 2008).
* By locating problems internally, rather than externally, mindfulness can potentially encourage people to accept toxic circumstances – such as relationships, workplaces or criminal justice systems – instead of addressing them (see Chapter 15; Stanley, 2012).
* 'McMindfulness' often presents a quick-fix solution to reduce costs (e.g. MAPPG, 2015), which denies the social and material causes of much of mental ill-health and criminal behaviour (e.g. structural inequalities, austerity measures, discrimination) (Purser & Loy, 2013).
* The current social, political and economic systems of consumer capitalism and neoliberalism actively encourage people to police themselves as individuals and to try to get everything they want and avoid things they don't want in order to be 'successful' and 'happy'. We can question the capacity of individuals to shift these patterns if there is no wider change in the society and institutions around them (Barker, 2015).

Conclusion

In this chapter you have learned about the roots of mindfulness in the Buddhist approach, which locates suffering in our human tendency to try to get all the things that bring us pleasure and to avoid or eradicate all the things that bring us pain. The radical approach of mindfulness involves accepting our thoughts, feelings and emotions as they are instead of trying to cling on to them or hurl them away. Therapies which draw this approach together with Western therapy – often in the form of CBT – have been found to be effective with depression, anxiety and addiction, as well as in reducing difficult offender behaviour and addressing recidivism.

However, like everything, from the Buddhist perspective, the current wave of mindfulness therapies needs to be held lightly, rather than grasped hold of as a panacea, or hurled away as dangerous and damaging (Batchelor, 2001). If we do this, we can engage with such therapies creatively and critically, as well as reflecting cautiously about how and where we apply them.

Suggestions for further reading

Barker, M-J. (2013b). *Mindful counselling & psychotherapy: practising mindfully across approaches and issues.* London: Sage.
Provides you with a good overview of mindfulness, how it has been used in therapy and how it can work with common mental health problems.

Mindfulness All-Party Parliamentary Group (MAPPG) (2015). *Mindful nation UK: report by the Mindfulness All-Party Parliamentary Group (MAPPG).* London: The Mindfulness Initiative. Accessed 19 November 2015 from www.themindfulnessinitiative.org.uk/images/reports/Mindfulness-APPG-Report_Mindful-Nation-UK_Oct2015.pdf
This is a thorough review of the research evidence for the use of mindfulness in mental health, criminal justice and other settings.

Prison Mindfulness Institute: www.prisonmindfulness.org
Inside Out: insight-out.org
These websites are useful in exploring current developments in use of mindfulness in prisons.

Pederson, L. D. (2015). *Dialectical behavior therapy: a contemporary guide for practitioners.* Chichester: John Wiley & Sons.
This book is an accessible introduction to DBT particularly.

PART V

DICHOTOMIES IN FORENSIC AND THERAPEUTIC PRACTICE

17

MEMORY

NADIA WAGER

Image 17   Pause for thought. With permission, Sue Cheval

Introduction

This chapter discusses a highly controversial topic, that of reports of recovered memories of childhood sexual abuse. The chapter will begin with a real-life case study, before exploring the debate around this phenomenon.

> ### Case example: Reported recovered memory
>
> Ellie claimed that at the age of 27 she spontaneously recovered memories of being repeatedly sexually abused between the approximate ages of two months and 14 years, by her grandfather, who had died when she was 20. She reported that one evening, after having had friends to dinner (no alcohol had been consumed as she was still breastfeeding her youngest child), as she undressed for bed, she had a series of flashbacks relating to a number of different instances during her childhood when her grandfather was abusing her. She claimed the memories were highly vivid, yet fragmented, but that for some of them she could discern roughly when and where the abuse happened. The experience of these flashbacks was extremely traumatic – it left her questioning her relationships with all family members and with a shattered sense of self. During the flashbacks she recalled remembering the abuse on two previous occasions: when her grandfather was in a coma in an intensive care unit and she was saying goodbye to him before the life-support machine was switched off; and when she was giving birth to her first child. She said that although these previous recollections were both associated with her becoming hysterical, both were immediately forgotten again. On discussing this with her ex-husband, he said that she had also told him that she had been abused when they were arguing one night about her fears of becoming pregnant for the second time. However, she had remained amnesic (i.e. had no conscious memory) with regards to memories for these events. For two years after this incident Ellie claims that she was frequently and unexpectedly troubled with additional memories – each new memory that surfaced was associated with extreme distress and for these two or more years she could hardly function in her role as wife and mother. She and her husband divorced. In an attempt to seek an understanding of the remembered events Ellie turned to popular psychology literature written for survivors of child sexual abuse (CSA), and found it gave her the strength to continue living and to strive to ensure that her own children had happy and safe lives. After two years she finally discussed these memories with her mother. Her mother confirmed that the family had known about the abuse. Indeed, it was her mother who told her that the abuse had begun when she was only a very young baby.

Activity 17.1: Impressions of the case example

Thinking about Ellie's case, how does her remembering, forgetting and remembering again fit with your own understanding of memory for events?

The case example was based on an interview with someone who reported experiencing abuse for which she had no enduring memory until she reached the age of 27 years. I have referred to her inability to remember as amnesia, but strictly speaking this should be referred to as either psychogenic amnesia (because there was no physical cause, such as brain damage) or dissociative amnesia (which suggests that dissociation, or rather the inability to integrate thoughts, memory and sense of identity, is causally related to the amnesia).

Ellie's experience will be discussed throughout this chapter in an endeavour to explore the issue of recovered memories of CSA, particularly in relation to the debate around whether such memories should be considered 'recovered memories' or 'false memories', which has become known as the 'memory wars'.

The emergence of the 'memory wars'

According to Gold, Hughes and Swingle (1999) prior to 1992 clinically experienced psychiatrists and clinical psychologists widely accepted that a significant proportion of adult survivors of CSA would present as having experienced a period of amnesia for memories of their abuse; and the literature at the time was largely related to the healing needs of survivors. Subsequently, Loftus (1993) and other cognitive psychologists began to argue that such recovered memories were in fact likely to be 'false memories'. False memories were seen to arise due to either the actions of overzealous therapists implanting fictitious memories in the minds of their clients (referred to as an iatrogenic illness) or suggestible individuals (those who are readily and often unconsciously influenced by the assertions made by others) being persuaded by the self-help literature that their problems in living stemmed from being sexually abused as a child (Belli & Loftus, 1994).

So what happened in 1992 to cause this shift? It appears that the pivotal moment was in 1990 when Professor Jennifer Freyd (a cognitive psychologist) accused her father of sexually abusing her as a child, after recovering memories of the alleged abuse as an adult. Within almost two years of the accusation her mother and father, Pamela and

Peter Freyd, established the False Memory Syndrome Foundation (FMSF) in the US, which advocated for people accused of sexual offending. They invited some of the most eminent cognitive psychologists (including Elizabeth Loftus) to become members of the scientific advisory board for the Foundation. In the UK, the British False Memory Society was founded in 1994 (it is interesting to note that the UK organisation did not use the term 'syndrome' in its title). Both organisations have over the years gathered collections of case studies of either highly improbable accounts of recovered memories or instances where individuals have been wrongly convicted on the grounds of evidence given by complainants.

The impact of the establishment and political activity of the FMSF challenged the recovered memory concept and this had a number of repercussions, one of which being the change in focus of the academic literature. Beckett (1996) reported that prior to 1991 the vast majority (80%) of the literature on child sexual abuse pertained to the victims and their needs, whereas just three years later the predominant focus of the literature (80%) was on the problem of false memories of CSA and the potential for the wrongful conviction of innocent people erroneously accused of CSA.

While these issues are clearly pertinent and deserving of recognition, many of these publications could be perceived as fairly damning and dismissive of genuine victims of CSA. Thus, the 'memory wars' were born, as there was little consideration given to the possibility that both perspectives might be valid and of exploring ways of ensuring justice for both the accused and the complainants.

The arguments proposed by the FMSF

Dallam (2001) outlined six key assumptions proposed by the memory foundation and presented counter-evidence in relation to each one. The assumptions and counter-arguments included:

- *A recovered memory is likely to be a false memory.* However, amnesia for abuse-related memories is evident in a proportion of legally documented cases (e.g. Duggal & Stroufe, 1998; Williams, 1994, 1995). Corroborating evidence is available for a significant proportion of the abuse allegations that relate to recovered memories (e.g. Andrews et al., 1999). Misremembering (that is, remembering details of events incorrectly) is more likely to be characterised as forgetting than 'remembering' events that did not occur (Brewin, Andrews & Gotlib, 1995). Recovered memories have been found to be as accurate as continuous memories (Duggal & Stroufe, 1998; Smith et al., 2003).

- *False memories result as a consequence of therapists engaging in inappropriate memory work.* From the cases presented by the FMSF it is clear that there are a number of cases where this has happened. However, it has been argued that memory recovery techniques are not common among mainstream clinicians (Andrews et al., 1999). A significant proportion of people who report recovered memories have never participated in therapy (Albach, Moormann & Bermond, 1996; Chu et al., 1999). When memories do arise in the context of participating in therapy it often happens outside the therapy and without the use of memory recovery techniques (Andrews et al., 2000; Elliot, 1997). A significant proportion of people enter therapy as a consequence of recovering memories (Andrews et al., 1999).
- *It is easy to implant false memories of traumatic events.* Due to ethical considerations, no study has attempted to implant traumatic experiences. What studies such as Loftus's 'Lost in the Shopping Mall' experiments demonstrate is that it is possible to implant false autobiographical memories (Loftus & Pickrell, 1995). However, the ability to do so is largely dependent on the strength of the suggestive influences (authority figures or people who report having been present at the time) and the perceived plausibility of the event (Lindsay, 1998; Pezdek, Finger & Hodge, 1997; Porter, Yuille & Lehman, 1999).
- *People who recover memories are highly suggestible.* Studies which have compared patients with recovered memories and those without history of CSA in terms of their suggestibility scores have not consistently supported this assumption (Leavitt, 1997). Even a two-year, longitudinal comparison of high and low suggestible patients in therapy, which investigated the potential differences in propensity for recovering memories, found no support for this assumption (Leavitt, 1999).
- *False memory syndrome is common among psychotherapy patients who claim to recover memories of CSA.* So far there has been no epidemiological study which has explored the prevalence rates of false memories, and thus the proportion of recovered memories which are in fact false memories has not been established (Dallam, 2001; Pope, 1996).
- *Alleged perpetrators are immune from developing false memories, except in cases where they have 'falsely' confessed.* It appears that the key 'diagnostic criteria' for the so-called false memory syndrome is the denial of the allegations of those accused. Their denials are never seen as untrue and they are taken at face value, even though there is a substantial body of literature on the rates of denial and minimisation within the convicted sex offender population (e.g. Gibbons, de Volder & Casey, 2003; Ware, Marshall & Marshall, 2015).

Additional points of contention between the recovered and the false memory proponents include issues around the nature of memory and whether there is a separate memory system for traumatic memories. Those on the side of the false memory argument argue that the normal processes of forgetting and remembering apply to memories for traumatic events, whereas those situated on the recovered memory side suggest that there are different processes for traumatic memories.

Activity 17.2: Reflections on the case study

Returning to Ellie's case, if I now tell you that 11 years prior to recovering her memories of abuse Ellie had undergone six sessions of hypnotherapy to help her overcome debilitating agoraphobia (an inability to leave the house), would you want to change your opinions on her case? Think, first, in terms of being a therapist and then in terms of being an investigating officer.

Luckily in Ellie's case there were corroborating accounts of the abuse from others who witnessed it. Without this it is possible that both therapists and investigating officers might have been more sceptical of the account since hypnotherapy is the type of therapy most likely to be associated with the creation of false memories.

Researching recovered and false memories

The different research methods employed by the opposing sides of this debate are partly responsible for the ongoing divide in opinions. Uba (2002) highlighted that researching trauma ethically means that we have been unable to conduct rigorously controlled, experimental studies on traumatic memories. Instead, we have had to compromise and rely on phenomenological studies exploring individuals' own experiences, correlational studies or experimental investigation of ordinary information processing that is then generalised to explain the trauma processes. Each of these methods has its own limitations. Phenomenological studies (e.g. interview studies that explore people's own accounts of their experiences) are often seen as subjective and thus lacking 'scientific objectivity'. Correlational studies (where we find that differences in one variable are related to differences in another variable) are unable to establish causal relations between the variables being investigated. Finally, the laboratory studies tend to lack ecological validity, since they are unable to experimentally manipulate conditions that emulate the trauma of protracted CSA and the duration between the incident and the recall of memories.

Information box 17.1: The 'Lost in the Shopping Mall' study (Loftus & Pickrell, 1995)

This study involved making contact with a close family relative (e.g. parent) of each of 24 participants (18–53 years). The relatives were asked whether the associated participant had ever been lost in a shopping mall as a child for more than just a few minutes. For all those who responded negatively to this question, they were then asked to describe three other events that they believed would be memorable for the participant.

The researchers then asked the participants if they could recall four events – three were events described by their respective relatives and the fourth was being lost in the shopping mall. Participants completed booklets which entailed reading what their relatives had said about each event and writing what they themselves remembered. The participants were asked to indicate if they did not remember the event. The participants were then interviewed on two follow-up sessions 1–2 weeks later and then 2–4 weeks later.

The results showed that 68% of the 'true events' were recalled at each of the three recall phases. Additionally, 29% of the false events were recalled in the booklet phase and 25% of the false events were recalled at the follow-up interviews.

While the Loftus and Pickrell (1995) study has far greater real-world applicability than many laboratory studies that examine the phenomenon of false memories (particularly the fact that it does show that a whole new memory can be implanted), I still believe there are a few problems with applying it to CSA. These are related to a number of significant differences between the study and abuse-related contexts. First, the study involved a one-off incident, whereas abuse (especially that associated with psychogenic amnesia) tends to be repeated multiple times. Second, the participants were aware that the stories of the events had been provided by a family member – someone who was there at the time of the alleged event and who had no reason to be telling an untruth. As such, the participant might defer to their relative and be persuaded that the story must be true and thus incorporate this into their own memories. Furthermore, and unlike CSA, being lost in a mall is not traumatic and there were no serious consequences to falsely remembering such an event.

Pezdek and Lam (2007) conducted a systematic review of 198 false memory research studies (published between 1994 and 2004) that employed an experimental paradigm and identified five main experimental techniques. The most used technique (41.4% of the articles) was the Deese, Roediger and McDermott (DRM) paradigm (Roediger & McDermott, 1995), which involves presenting participants with a list of semantically related words (e.g. tired, pillow, yawn). When asked to recall or to recognise words from such lists, many people remember a strongly related word (e.g. sleep) even though it was not present in the original list.

Furthermore, Pezdek and Lam (2007) concluded that among cognitive psychologists there was no longer a universally accepted definition of 'false memory'. Prior to 1992 the term 'false memory' was used exclusively for implanting a new memory of a fictitious event. However, post-1992 it appears that the term has been used in relation to both the implanting of a completely new memory and the ability to change an existing memory in some way. They contend that the latter might be more appropriately referred to as a flawed memory rather than a false memory and that a clearer distinction between the two would be beneficial as it would foster smoother communication between clinical and cognitive psychologists and help multidisciplinary researchers/practitioners who might erroneously assume the generalisability of research on flawed memory to memories of CSA.

In 1997, Pezdek, Finger and Hodge replicated Loftus's shopping mall study, with a couple of changes. They reduced the number of true events to be recalled to two and randomly allocated the research participants to one of two false event conditions: being lost in the shopping mall or receiving a rectal enema. Of the participants in the 'lost in the mall' condition, 15% falsely recalled this event. While less than the proportion found by Loftus, this was still consistent with the earlier finding. However, none of the participants in the rectal enema condition falsely recalled the event. Pezdek et al. (1997) concluded that these findings suggest that it may be possible for family members (e.g. people who were also present during the alleged event) to implant pseudo-memories of common, and thus plausible, events but not more unusual events.

With regards to researching recovered memories or amnesia for memories of CSA there are three principal methods that have been utilised: retrospective self-report surveys and prospective studies of officially recognised cases of CSA (be they hospital admissions or alleged victims in prosecutions) have both been used to estimate prevalence rates, and qualitative phenomenological studies, including case studies, have been used to explore the experience and contexts of recovering memories.

Information box 17.2: Linda Williams' prospective study of amnesia for memories of documented CSA

The seminal work by Linda Williams (1994, 1995) is one example of a prospective study. She created a sample using hospital records of children who had attended an accident and emergency department for the collection of forensic evidence following reports of CSA between 1973 and 1975. At the time of the hospital attendance the children were aged between ten months and 12 years. The hospital records contained the details of the forensic examinations and interviews with the child and/or the caregiver. Follow-up interviews were conducted in 1991 when the now-grown children were 18 to 31 years. Interviews were conducted with 129 women on the pretext that the study was exploring the lives and experiences of people who had received medical treatment from the city hospital in childhood. No reference to child abuse was given when introducing the study to the participants. When asked a series of 14 questions to explore whether they recalled ever having experienced CSA, 38% did not report the offence and thus were considered to be amnesic for the memories of the abuse. Furthermore, 10% of the total sample reported the experience of recovering memories at some time prior to the interview. Williams anticipated possible criticisms of her study and thus conducted additional analyses to test the alternative explanations for the failure to report the abuse to the researcher. She tested the following reasons for the failure to report the index abuse:

*   *Embarrassment* – but those who did not recall the abuse were no less likely to discuss other confidential or embarrassing information about their sexual history.
*   *Infantile amnesia* – although age was related to amnesia, amnesia rates were still high for the group who had been aged 11 to 12 years at the time of hospitalisation.
*   *The abuse never actually happened* – of 23 cases that met the highest standards of forensic validity, 52% were associated with failure to report.

One of the strengths of Williams (1994, 1995) research is that it used documented cases of CSA and then followed up the people in adulthood, rather than relying on uncorroborated accounts of events from many years previously. However, its weaknesses include that we cannot be certain that abuse actually occurred. Equally, the interviewees being able to discuss other intimate issues but failing to mention the abuse-related incident may not always be indicative of amnesia. Rather, the stigma associated with being a victim of CSA might have made some of the interviewees reluctant to report this even when able to discuss other embarrassing, but not stigmatising, issues.

Amnesia and recovered memories

Wolf and Nochajski (2013) noted that the fourth edition of the Diagnostic and Statistical Manual of Mental Disorders (American Psychiatric Association, 2000) included reference to dissociative amnesia which was characterised by the temporary full or partial loss of memories for traumatic events. The manual described how the amnesia might be reversible, with delayed memories for the trauma being consciously recalled at a later date and that these delayed recollections may be full or partial, conscious or unconscious (e.g. appear when dreaming) and verbal or non-verbal (e.g. bodily sensations or visual images.). In Scheflin and Brown's (1996) review of 25 studies of memory for CSA, almost 50% of the studies reported cases of partial amnesia where the individuals remembered that they had been abused but were unable to recall specific incidents or details of this abuse. A review of 30 studies (Brown, Scheflin & Hammond, 1998) indicated that the mean prevalence rate for amnesia was 29.6% of CSA survivors.

When recovered memories are discussed in the literature, the authors are generally referring to two different types of recovery process. The first type are memories that spontaneously become accessible to an individual, often following exposure to a trauma-specific reminder (Herman & Harvey, 1997). These memories often surface as fragmented images or sensations, which occur over a protracted period of time rather than as a single event (Crowley, 2008). Additionally, some survivors report experiencing momentary periods of being able to recall their memories, which are then immediately forgotten again. Thus, some individuals report amnesia for prior episodes of remembering (Milchman, 2008). This process has been referred to as a lack of meta-awareness, which is a difficulty recognising how much one remembers or has forgotten (Schooler, 2001). However, Ellie was very clear that her previous episodes of remembering were just fleeting recollections in response to highly emotive situations, which were then immediately out of conscious awareness again. The second type are memories of abuse that first begin to emerge during the course of therapy. Such memories might arise as a direct consequence of active memory work (e.g. hypnosis, directed imagination, thought association or dream analysis), or in response to finding a safe context in which the memories are free to surface.

Assessing the authenticity of 'recovered' memories of abuse

Currently, there is no reliable way of distinguishing between true recovered memories and false memories of CSA. However, a number of methods have been tried and tested by psychotherapists, cognitive scientists and forensic psychologists. Two such strategies will be examined here: the Rorschach projective imagery test, which is employed by psychoanalytic therapists; and Statement Validity Analysis, which is a tool used in forensic contexts in a number of countries (though not in England and Wales) to assess the credibility of children who are alleged victims of CSA.

The Rorschach projective imagery test allows for the projective assessment of personality and mental distress and consists of ten stimulus cards, each depicting an artistically enhanced inkblot. When presented, the participant is asked to report what they see. The theoretical basis for the test is that the descriptions arise out of the integration of memory traces from previous experiences and the nature of the stimulus image. The method used for interpreting and scoring the test results was amended (Meyer et al., 2011) to enhance the test's applicability in different cultural contexts and age groups (Giromini et al., 2015) and to improve the consistency of scores given by different people (Viglione et al., 2012). While the test is rarely used in forensic contexts (Raynor & McIvor, 2008), it appears to be more readily employed by clinical psychologists (Weiner & Greene, 2008). Rorschach-based expert testimony is deemed admissible in American courts (Gurley et al., 2014), despite the debate as to whether it meets the threshold of scientific acceptance for admissibility (Erard, Meyer & Viglione, 2014; Gurley et al., 2014). However, it appears that it is used less in England and Wales than it is in the US, though this may change as a result of the production of normative data based on an English sample (British Rorschach Society).

Studies have found that the imagery visualised by abused and non-abused samples is consistently different (Kamphuis, Kugeares & Finn, 2000; Kikuchi et al., 2010; Leavitt & Labortt, 1996). Identified differences have included issues related to oppression, dominant colours, blood, sexual anxiety, damaged bodies, fearfulness, victimisation, texture and dissociation (where an object is difficult to see as it is veiled, in the far distance or its form is seen as shifting).

Leavitt and Labortt (1996) examined Rorschach imagery in female psychiatric inpatients who claimed to have recovered memories of CSA to determine whether their imagery patterns were distinguishable from those reported by patients with continuous memories of CSA, and those who claimed not to have been abused. The recovered memory group was subdivided on the basis of whether they experienced dissociative symptoms, the rationale being that recovered memories combined with dissociative symptoms were more likely to be true memories of abuse. The responses were scored on the basis of 13 signs of CSA found in previous studies. Only 16% of the non-abused group gave any response associated with CSA, compared with 97% of the patients with continuous memories of abuse, 100% of the dissociative patients and 50% of the non-dissociative patients. This suggested that it would be unlikely that a non-dissociative recovered memory patient would be categorised as a genuine case of CSA. However, an alternative explanation is that the non-dissociative recovered memory group experienced a period of amnesia for reasons other than dissociation. Since 56% of the non-dissociators said their abuse-related memories were for events occurring before the age of three years, the validity of these memories is questionable as we tend not to have memories before this age.

Statement validity analysis (SVA) is another method that has been used to distinguish between true and false allegations of CSA. It is a 'verbal veracity assessment tool' which originated in Sweden in 1963 and was refined by Köhnken and Steller in 1988. The theoretical rationale of SVA is based on the Undeutsch hypothesis, which contends that statements that are the product of lived experience will have additional characteristics to statements based on products of the imagination. SVA became a standardised procedure that is considered admissible as valid evidence in criminal courts in a number of countries (Amado, Arce & Farina, 2015) and in family courts in England and Wales. While it was developed as a method to determine the credibility of child witnesses in CSA cases, its use has been extended to adult complainants of sexual abuse (Amado, Arce, Farina & Vilarino, 2016).

Steller and Boychuck (1992) outlined five stages to conducting the analysis. In the initial stages, there is a review of the relevant case information, a preserved semi-structured interview with the complainant, an analysis of the transcribed interview using criterion-based content analysis (CBCA), validity checks on any additional case information and the production of a systematic summary of the content analysis and associated validity checks.

CBCA entails analysing the content of the interview on the basis of 19 characteristics, such as whether there is a logical structure, the quantity of detail provided and the presence of unusual details. From Vrij's (2005) review of 37 studies of the CBCA component of the tool, it appears the correct classification rates for truth tellers and liars is between 65% and 90%. Vrij (2005) concluded that while the tool may not be accurate enough to be admitted as expert scientific evidence in criminal courts, it might be useful in police investigations. However, more recent meta-analyses have found that the CBCA component is accurate in distinguishing between memories of fabricated and ficti- tious events in both children and young people under the age of 18 years (Amado et al., 2015), and adults (Amado et al., 2016).

CBCA has been evaluated using experimental studies. For example, Blandon-Gitlin et al. (2009) used the Loftus 'lost in the shopping mall' research paradigm to implant a false memory for putting the toy 'Slime' into a primary school teacher's desk. The accounts from participants who falsely recalled the incident were compared with accounts pro- duced by people who had really experienced a particular incident and those who intentionally fabricated an account. The findings indicated that the CBCA scores were significantly higher for true events compared to fabricated events, but there was no significant difference between the accounts for the implanted event and either the true or the fabricated accounts. Volbert and Steller (2014) suggested the reason for this finding is that people with false memories are not engaged in effortful deception, rather they are just mistaken. Consequently, the way in which they con- struct their statements is likely to be similar to those giving true statements. Volbert and Steller therefore expressed reservation about using CBCA in cases of suspected false memories.

Conclusion

While some academics have argued that there is an increasing middle ground of consensus between the proponents of the two sides of the memory wars (e.g. Milchman, 2012a, 2012b, 2012c), others whose interest is more practical rather than theoretical prefer to err on the side of caution by positioning themselves on the false memory side. For example, Ring's (2012) exploration of legal precedent and evidentiary standards in US criminal prosecutions in cases of recovered memories of CSA resulted in her concluding that, in the interests of due process, no case of recovered memory (irrespective of the manner in which the memory arose) should be proceeded within criminal courts. The debate clearly has significant implications for both complainants' and defend- ants' ability to gain justice and thus warrants continued academic interest. The past denigrations by cognitive psychologists of observa- tions and case studies drawn from clinical work and the equal distrust of laboratory-based findings by clinicians have been unhelpful in moving towards a resolution to the debate, suggesting that one way forward might be to have multidisciplinary research teams employing a range of methods.

Suggestions for further readings

Bernstein, D. M., & Loftus, E. F. (2009). How to tell if a particular memory is true or false. *Perspectives on Psychological Science*, 4(4), 370–374.
This paper provides a brief overview of the different broad approaches to distinguishing between true and false memories, including the relatively new methods being trialled by cognitive neuroscientists.

Geraerts, E., Raymaekers, L., & Merckelbach, H. (2008). Recovered memories of childhood sexual abuse: current findings and their legal implications. *Legal and Criminological Psychology*, 13(2), 165–176.
A review of the differences between spontaneously recovered memories and those recovered in therapy, which discusses the legal implications of the findings.

Madill, A., & Holch, P. (2004). A range of memory possibilities: the challenge of the false memory debate for clinicians and researchers. *Clinical Psychology and Psychotherapy*, 11, 299–310.
This is a brief review of the key issues that are disagreed upon by the opponents on the two sides of the memory debate. The issues and the possible solutions are discussed from the position of clinical psychologists and therapists.

18

SELF-HARM AND SUICIDE

ANDREW REEVES AND PAUL TAYLOR

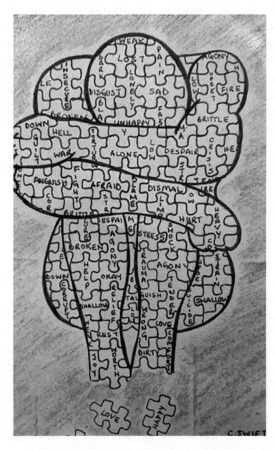

Image 18   Broken. With permission, Cat Swift

Introduction

Understanding reasons for, and offering interventions to prevent, self-harm and/or suicide are a routine concern for those working in therapeutic fields. Acts of self-harm have historically often been hidden from public view and the tragedy of a self-inflicted death is publically understood as a rarity. As time has progressed, though, public awareness of these self-injurious behaviours has expanded, not least through campaigning for awareness, media insights and explanations, and the growth of clinical and therapeutic expertise in the management of such behaviours.

Wilfully causing damage to one's own body, fatally or not, arouses both public sympathy and suspicion in equal measure. Often such behaviours are culturally earmarked as deviant; that is, they are seen as conflicting with social norms, values and/or belief structures. Indeed, suicide (self-murder) had been a punishable crime in England from the mid-thirteenth century until 1961. Attempts to interpret *why* an individual would consider committing such violent action against themselves has become an expanded area of medical and therapeutic specialism through the late twentieth and twenty-first centuries. This chapter will explore psychological interventions in the context of the risk of suicide and self-harm/injury, looking at practice implications of working with such risk, while additionally contextualising such behaviours within the medicalisation of human experience.

Definitions

Suicide

The World Health Organisation (WHO, 2016) defines suicide as, 'the act of deliberately killing oneself', while De Leo et al. (2006, p. 12) offer a definition as 'an act with fatal outcome, which the deceased, knowing or expecting a potentially fatal outcome, has initiated and carried out with a purpose of bringing about wanted changes'. In many ways, the act of suicide is relatively simple to define, but determining whether someone has died through suicide is altogether more difficult. Many factors can contribute to someone's death and differentiating a factor that, beyond doubt, demonstrates that the individual intended to bring about their own death is challenging. For therapists, however, the most difficult presentation in practice is determining the likelihood that a client will act on suicidal thoughts: in other words, their 'degree of suicidality'.

Self-harm and self-injury

Defining self-harm/injury is a relatively complex matter given the range of behaviours that may be self-harming or injurious. Indeed, a differentiation between self-harm, and self-injury is a critical consideration. Broadly, the National Institute for Health and Care Excellence (NICE) (2011, p. 3) define self-injury as:

> ...any act of self-poisoning or self-injury carried out by an individual irrespective of motivation. This commonly involves self-poisoning with medication or self-injury by cutting. There are several important exclusions that this term is not intended to cover. These include harm to the self arising from excessive consumption of alcohol or recreational drugs, or from starvation arising from anorexia nervosa, or accidental harm to oneself.

Other definitions have taken issue with this, as it is relatively narrow and explicitly excludes behaviours such as disordered eating, which do involve elements of self-harm. Reeves (2013) offers a summary of the key aspects of self-harm/injury that capture a broader array of behaviours. Self-harm/injury can:

- be directed against the body (e.g. cutting, burning), which might be termed as self-injury
- include behaviours without immediate impact, such as eating disorders, risky sexual behaviour
- be planned and form part of a habitual pattern, or may be unplanned and spontaneous
- be about coping, living, surviving and self-worth
- have a relationship with suicide potential, particularly in the context of other risk factors.

Here we can see an important difference emerging between self-harm and self-injury (even though the literature often uses these terms interchangeably):

- *Self-harm*: to include behaviours with indirect or deferred consequence, such as over-exercise, eating disorders, smoking, alcohol and drug use, sexual risk-taking, for example.
- *Self-injury*: to include behaviours with direct and immediate consequence, such as cutting, burning, banging, ingesting dangerous substances (including of medication), for example.

The differentiation between self-harm and self-injury is not simply a matter of definitions, but also has considerable therapeutic significance in that it can both shape and inform the nature of intervention offered to clients. If one of the tasks that therapy seeks to accomplish is to help clients understand their harming behaviour and to explore the meanings and communications behind it, then thinking about harm and injury in the context of the definitions offered here is very important. For example, a client self-injuring will generally be quite aware that they injure, even if they may be unclear as to *why* they injure, while a client who is self-harming may not be consciously aware of their actions as harmful until a therapist brings that to their attention. You can well imagine that working with a client who has been cutting themselves (self-injury) could be quite different from one who has been either working or exercising to an excessive degree (self-harm).

A final but fundamentally important aspect of differentiating between injury and harm is that it enables us all to reflect on our own self-harming actions. It might not be that we all self-injure, but most of us may self-harm at some point in our lives. That is, it is likely that most of us will be able to identify a time when we simply could not find a way of expressing powerful and overwhelming feelings, causing us to 'do them' instead, often to the detriment of our physical and emotional well-being. This might include drinking to excess following a traumatic end to a relationship, or working excessively as a way of coping with bereavement. The more we can challenge the 'them and us' of self-harm/injury – and understand it as an 'us' – the more we can empathically engage with it in others.

The medicalisation of suicide and self-harm

Medicalising self-harm, attempted suicide and suicidal ideation means trying to understand such behaviours through frameworks of medical language and discourse (see Zola, 2011, for an overview of the processes of medicalisation), and this has been one of the defining features of the medical and therapeutic field's evolution. Interpreting aspects of everyday life that conflict with societal norms through a medical lens is well established and the medicalisation of behaviours, feelings and experiences is widely considered as a beneficial methodology that will alleviate suffering and secure the health and well-being of a population.

Preventing self-harm and/or suicide is a key constituent of modern psychiatric and therapeutic work. But the idea that medical specialists are legitimate and justified in their pursuit to understand, explain and manage self-injurious behaviours through medical terminology is not universal. Indeed, some, such as Cohen (1985), have argued that medical interventions can lead to the very real risk of unintended consequences occurring, such as increased stigmatisation and unnecessary compulsion/treatment under mental health legislation. Specifically, in the area of suicide, medicalisation means that the 'rationality' of those with suicidal ideas comes under scrutiny. This can lead to disagreement over whether suicidal intent is a manifestation of a mental health problem or whether such action is the product of *free will*, in other words, a rational choice made in the face of an intolerable world (Lieberman, 2003). Suicide as a subject has, for centuries, challenged philosophical debates over *free will* and the extent to which *we* are actually *free* at all. Although taking one's life may well be considered to reflect a point of utter despair and crisis, authors such as Lorentzon (2005) point out that conversely the act of suicide can also be conceived as an act of taking control amid a life that is experienced as out of control.

The debate about the role of free will in suicide is important to therapy, as although therapeutic intervention might seem a logical step for someone considering suicide as a result of a mental health problem, it is less clear if it is a result of a rational decision. As a result, the idea that those who 'choose' to take their own life or injure themselves are in some way 'irrational' or are in need of medical/therapeutic expertise has long been a matter of critical debate. For some, such suicidal thoughts or behaviours fall into matters of civil or human rights. What is meant by this is that any 'interference' by agencies of the state (e.g. medical experts, social care professions) is uncalled for, and breaches that individual's freedom. Such a point of view is often seen as unpalatable on the basis of popular questions such as 'why wouldn't we try to prevent somebody harming themselves?'. It might be tempting to expect those in favour of intervention by medical and other agencies to be predominantly part of such organisations, and those who question such intervention to be from outside those organisations, but this is not the case.

Indeed, scholars such as Thomas Szasz (see, for example, Szasz, 1997) have opened rich debates on the territorial parameters of psychiatric and medical power, while at the same time actively working as a psychiatrist. So instead of all practitioners being of a like mind, a spectrum of standpoints exist within the profession as to the extent to which medical professionals should be responsible for, and have a right to exercise, control over their 'patients' (for example, through diagnosis, therapy and legal coercion). If relevant ethical guidelines mean that members of the medical field are required to 'do no harm', then it follows that as practitioners they must respect the rights of others. However, if a society adopts an ethical approach that does require practitioners to respect the rights of others, then it cannot also maintain a moral right to interfere, as doing so would violate the human rights of the person.

Decisions regarding intervening or preventing self-injurious behaviour while also respecting the rights of an individual are a complex matter both intellectually and in practice. On the one hand, *not* intervening when opportunities arise to do so may be seen as neglectful, while, on the other hand, intervention can risk not respecting the rights of the individual. The matter is made even more complex when you take into account the different reasons why an individual might consider suicide. In cases where a mental health problem (with a biological cause) exists, it is relatively easy to justify intervention. But what about if the root cause is non-biological and what if the individual is able to clearly attribute their suicidal ideas or behaviour to rational choice, or to ideology or martyrdom? In these cases, if we truly respect the rights of the individual, then it is difficult to also justify medical or therapeutic intervention.

Understanding and working with suicide risk

Prevalence

The UK statistics on suicide, like those internationally, do not necessarily provide a true or complete record of the number of deaths resulting from suicide.

Pause for reflection

From what you have read so far about suicide, what problems do you think occur in trying to use official statistics to establish the true prevalence of suicide?

As outlined above, determining beyond doubt that death occurred as a direct intention of the individual is a difficult process and, as such, unless the 'beyond doubt' benchmark can be met, a recorded verdict of death through suicide is not possible. Additionally, the cultural and societal tolerance to suicide will shape and influence how information is interpreted; the less 'tolerant' a culture is to suicide the less likely a verdict of suicide will be reached, and vice versa.

However, the UK statistics do provide some extremely valuable information in that they show males to be the highest risk group for completed suicide across the lifespan, with a ratio of deaths through suicide of males to females as high as about 3:1, particularly around the 35–49 age group. They also show risk to be significant across the lifespan for both males and females, with numbers peaking around the 30–55 age group. Finally, despite UK policy recently becoming more focused on suicide prevention, we see an increase in the number of completed suicides over the last decade.

Legal considerations

The law as it relates to suicide varies significantly internationally. In the UK, suicide was decriminalised in the 1961 Suicide Act and while there is not a general duty to report concerns of potential suicide, many practitioners would do so either through their employment contractual expectations (and the policies and procedures that determine the nature of practice in different contexts), or through choice. The latter point, action through choice, is likely to be informed by many factors, including the individual practitioner's own perspectives on suicide (a moral position); the subsequent contracts they make with clients at the outset of therapy (a practice position); and the guidance offered by professional organisations in protecting the well-being of clients (an ethical position).

While mental health legislation is important in determining the nature and form of interventions with potentially suicidal clients who additionally demonstrate some evidence of underlying mental health problems, it is legislation (such as the 2005 Mental Capacity Act in England and Wales and the 2000 Adults with Incapacity Act in Scotland) concerning *capacity* that informs practitioner decisions concerning risk. These Acts are based on the principle that adults have the right to self-determination, including the right to die through suicide, if they have the capacity to do so. However, practitioners can act to protect the well-being of the client if a contract with a client is established at the outset of therapy, which limits confidentiality with regards to the risk of suicide. Information provided to the client by the organisation or individual responsible for delivering the therapy can act in a similar way to such a contract. While mental capacity legislation applies to adults over 18 years of age, 16–18 year olds are additionally assumed to have capacity, although the High Court or Court in Session can over-rule that in certain situations. When thinking about client consent and capacity, in general terms (and in addition to the issues discussed in Chapters 9 and 10), Bond and Mitchels (2014) offer some helpful guidance (see Information box 18.1).

Information box 18.1: Determining consent and capacity

Bond and Mitchels (2014) offer the following guidance on determining consent and capacity:

* For what action is consent being sought?
* Have all the potential benefits, risks and consequences of taking or not taking that action been fully explained and understood?
* Has the person retained the information long enough to properly evaluate it when making the decision?
* Can the person clearly communicate their decision (with help as appropriate) once it has been made?
* Is the consent sought for the individual concerned, or is it for the treatment of another person?
* If consent is sought for another person, is that person an adult or a child?
* If consent is sought for a child, does the person giving consent have parental responsibility for the child?

Working with suicide risk in therapy

The predominant research in working with the potential for suicide focuses on the identification of risk factors (factors that make suicide more likely), with some attention (albeit less so) on protective factors (factors that make suicide less likely). Practitioners are often required to use risk assessment tools to determine the presence of risk and protective factors, and decide on a course of action accordingly (see Chapter 1). However, it must be noted that NICE state the following regarding the scales involved in such risk assessment: 'The sensitivity and specificity of these scales are, at best, modest' (NICE, 2011, p. 29).

While the use of such tools can contribute to some understanding of client potential, they do not provide the answers practitioners (and organisations) typically look for in any certain way. It is important to recognise that fear of getting it wrong – of completed suicide – is a significant fear for many practitioners (Reeves, 2010), making approaches that seem to offer the certain prediction of suicide risk based on the actions of the client very attractive. In reality, of course, the only certain thing that can be said of human behaviour is just how unpredictable it is.

Activity 18.1

Jason is a 53-year-old financial consultant who was made unemployed one year ago. His relationship has ended and he lost his home. He has limited social support and has been drinking alcohol heavily to cope with feelings. He attends counselling and has found early sessions helpful. During one session he says he sometimes feels quite overwhelmed and wants to 'go' to get out of the way. He has one good friend, with whom he maintains contact, and desperately wishes for things to be different.

In applying a 'risk factor approach' to understanding Jason's risk, the first step would be to determine what risk factors might apply. As well as factors that may place Jason at risk, there are also factors that could act to protect him. Read the description above again and see what risk and protective factors you can identify.

Below are some of the factors we identified:

- Gender: male
- Age: 53 and so in the age group where suicide is most prevalent
- Loss of employment
- Loss of relationship
- Loss of home
- Limited social support
- Increasing use of alcohol to cope
- Expressed suicidal thoughts.

There are also some protective factors too:

- Attendance in counselling
- Finding some early counselling sessions helpful
- Willingness to disclose suicidal thoughts
- Supportive friend
- Hopeful feelings for the future.

While this information is undoubtedly helpful, we can immediately see that it, in itself, does not provide us with an insight into Jason's thoughts and feelings, nor the likelihood of him acting on his thoughts. Working with suicide risk, therefore, should always be about suicide *exploration*, rather than simply suicide *assessment*. The capacity of the therapist to be prepared to ask Jason about his suicidal feelings will be critical in informing both the therapist and

Jason of the likelihood of suicide and, perhaps most importantly, how Jason might begin to support himself.

The nature of harm to self

Prevalence

Working out the prevalence of self-harm/injury is very difficult indeed. For one thing, there are several methodological problems:

- The terms self-harm and self-injury are used to describe similar, but also sometimes different things; it can be difficult to measure *how* statistics are collected and about *what* type of behaviour
- Self-harm/injury statistics are often collected from regional research centres and, as such, offer a national perspective based on extrapolated, rather than actual, data
- Statistics that are collected are usually obtained from Accident and Emergency (A&E) or primary care settings; a great many people who self-injure do not attend such units for treatment and, as such, what we see is a tip of the iceberg.

In summary, we know from those statistics that self-harming/injury is: a wide-ranging phenomenon; is seen in both males and females; is culturally defined and informed; is not a 'young person' issue but is rather seen right across the lifespan; is not an 'attention-seeking' process; and can mean different things for different people at different times.

Legal considerations

The legal parameters informing actions around self-harm/injury are less clear, although they are not too dissimilar to the legal context of suicide. That is, people have the right under law to inflict injuries on themselves (as opposed to on others), but therapists might consider intervention should the level of injury or harm jeopardise life. Given that self-harm/injury is typically conceptualised as an action intended for self-support (through relief, purging, expression, focusing of pain, etc.), where the level of harm or injury has reached a sufficient level of risk, some intervention might be required to safeguard the client's well-being. However, it is not uncommon for clients not to realise the extent to which their behaviour is self-harming until a therapist is able to have this discussion.

The fact that a behaviour is more about self-harm, rather than self-injury, does not make it any less of a risk for a client (severe eating disorders can be life-threatening, for example). As such, the therapist will need to pay attention to parameters that inform their working role, such as policies and procedures around risk that constitute part of their employment relationship with an agency. Likewise, therapists who are members of professional organisations whose work is informed by ethical principles need to ensure they work within them, whether employed, voluntary or self-employed.

Working with self-harm/injury in therapy

While the perception is often that clients attend therapy wanting specific help in reducing or stopping self-harming or injurious behaviour, that is generally not the case. While some clients will want particular advice and support around self-harm/injury, many instead wish to use therapeutic input to address the underlying issues causing their distress, and thus impacting the self-harm. The therapeutic 'task', therefore, is no different from a more general therapeutic task of attending to emotional turmoil and mental health distress. Therapists can be drawn into seeing the extent of self-harm/injury as some 'barometer' of the efficacy of intervention: a reduction in self-harm = effective therapy; an increase in self-harm = ineffective therapy. This over-simplified way of viewing both therapy and self-harm is mostly incorrect, and misses a more meaningful opportunity to explore the client's experience of therapy and whether their goals are being attended to.

Case example: Jasmine

Jasmine is a 24-year-old female client from Singapore. Her relationship ended abruptly recently and she has found the transition from living in Singapore to the UK difficult. She has some social contacts but feels a pressure on her to look as if everything is going well. As such, Jasmine has developed an effective mechanism of protecting her own vulnerability and defending against any perception of her not coping. She explains in therapy that, as a teenager, she used to cut herself on her arms and while this stopped a few years ago, she has now started to do it again, particularly when she feels distressed, angry or isolated.

It is clear from Jasmine's story that there are a number of factors for her to attend to:

* Relationship breakdown
* Transition and cultural change

(Continued)

(Continued)

- Social expectations
- Personal expectations, including internalised messages of 'coping'
- Presenting a 'managed' public self vs. a personal struggle
- Re-emergence of her previous self-injury.

From the information given, we can identify at least six clear areas of potential focus, with a possibility of there being more, when Jasmine feels sufficiently comfortable to talk about them. Focusing on self-injury might be of help to Jasmine but, in all likelihood, it would not be her immediate priority to address. Clearly, the therapist would need to ascertain from Jasmine her desired focus for therapy, but should not assume that self-injury will be the priority, even though it might be the therapist's as a consequence of their own anxiety regarding the client. Should Jasmine wish to specifically focus on her self-injury, the therapist might use a number of interventions, including those from cognitive behavioural therapy (CBT) (see Chapter 14) and narrative work (see Chapter 15).

Clinical implications

We have talked here of the uncertainties that underpin working with risk in relation to suicide and self-harm/injury, particularly in the context of relevant policy seeming to expect risk to be established with certainty. These uncertainties can place therapists in a difficult therapeutic conundrum. However, in addition to following ethical guidance of respective professional associations, practitioners can also work to a number of principles to help ensure they remain in therapeutic connection with their clients (Reeves, 2015):

- Therapists must be qualified (or in advanced training) and drawing on a core theoretical model (or an integration of models) to support their practice.
- Regular supervision must be in place, meeting at least the minimal requirements of supervision set by their professional body.
- Therapists must work within the context of a clear ethical framework.
- Therapy must be carefully contracted, including clearly setting the boundaries around time, availability between sessions and the limits of confidentiality, in this context, as defined by risk.
- Therapists must be reflective practitioners in relation to risk, with a willingness to identify personal and professional areas for development and to seek resources to support that development, as appropriate.

- Therapists must be able to engage with a dialogue around risk and be aware of any existing policies or procedures (where they exist), and work accordingly.
- Therapists need to be aware of issues that relate to suicide and self-harm/injury, including definitions, aetiology and key research findings informing practice.
- Therapists must be willing to communicate clearly with clients about suicidal ideation and self-harm/injury.
- While therapists need to be carefully attentive to risk, they need to ensure they do not become risk-driven, missing important therapeutic possibilities or losing therapeutic contact with clients.
- Therapists must not judge, but instead be empathic, compassionate and understanding, and willing to be congruent in line with the teaching of their core theoretical model(s).
- Therapists must be willing to name risk as it presents, and to work proactively and collaboratively with clients to engage with the risk in a way that is respectful of the client's well-being and autonomy, where possible.

Other factors, too, will inform the nature of the therapeutic relationship when a client presents at risk, but these provide a helpful basis from which therapy may be conducted.

Suicide as an act of terrorism

A challenge to common understandings and professional expertise of suicide is the case of the suicide-terrorist (see Weatherston & Moran, 2003). There is a long history of explaining criminal conduct generally through medical frameworks and, as a result, legal systems have evolved to take account of medical expertise in investigative, judicial and punishment contexts. Causal relationships between the presence of mental health problems and criminality are difficult to demonstrate and cultural narratives that depict individuals with mental health problems as violent and high risk are hugely damaging, especially when those with mental health problems are more likely to be victims of crime rather than perpetrators (Peay, 2011).

The example of the suicide-terrorist illustrates the advancement of medical opinion in a relatively new territory. Schouten (2010) poses an important question which highlights some complexities of the area when asking whether cases should be categorised as 'terrorist acts' or 'acts of violence related to mental health problems/mental illness?'. Topics such as the question of whether ideology does in fact interact with suicidal ideation (that is already held by the individual), resulting in an act of murder-suicide, has been well developed by Lankford (2011, 2012). 'Psychiatrising' terrorism is not an easy task but studies have been conducted with pre-emptively arrested suicide-terrorists and organisers (see Merari et al., 2009). Findings have shown that the social circumstances in which some suicide-terrorists live are important and that some have shown clinical features of depression (more than half of the sample of the martyrdom bombing group), and some demonstrate comorbidity with post-traumatic stress disorder (20%). While this study does locate differing background factors and motivations of suicide, it also shows that in some cases suicidality may be a contributing factor in a minority of terrorist martyrs.

Lankford (2011) draws attention to issues of intent, questioning whether a suicide-terrorist is actually suicidal, or is instead motivated by martyrdom, and highlighting how difficult it is to reach a conclusion either way. Indeed, cultural narratives and popular representations may lead to a common view of suicide-terrorism as an act underpinned by politically, culturally or religiously motivated goals. To identify all murder-suicide actors in this way, as Lankford (2011) suggests, would be misleading, and in fact it may well be plausible to suggest individual motivations (which may be suicidal) can be overlooked.

Our intellectual understandings of suicide-terrorism as a psychiatric/ psychological issue remain in a developmental phase and the practical usefulness of understanding these acts through a medical lens is in the balance. However, amid a political and social context of increased concerns of terrorism, extremism and radicalisation, the relevance of this area in the practice of clinical or therapeutic work is becoming ever more important. A very real practical responsibility has been placed on service practitioners (across the delivery of psychological therapies, including health, social care, education and in the third sector) in mitigating against the risk of terrorism. Section 26 of the Counter-Terrorism and Security Act 2015 places a duty on certain bodies, in the exercise of their functions, to have 'due regard to the need to prevent people from being drawn into terrorism'. This places a duty on bodies outlined in Schedule 6 of the Act to adhere to the PREVENT strategy (published by the UK government in 2011). Schools, further and higher education, policing, prisons and probation, and the health sector are all required to implement this duty, which consists of preventing the risk of people being drawn into terrorism (implementing the UK government's anti-radicalisation plan).

Many critical voices have emerged in opposition to this duty (see Davies, 2016), not least concerns over how identification of, and tolerance of thresholds in, indications of extremism and radicalisation. For some, the duty placed on these sectors, including health providers, requires an adoption of techniques of surveillance and monitoring (imbued with racial prejudice) in the therapeutic domain.

Conclusion

Risk dominates contemporary practice in the therapeutic field. In a society increasingly concerned with addressing matters of potential insecurity, risk has firmly set itself in the lexicon of modernity. The practical challenges that this brings can be substantial. The boundaries of clinical expertise are constantly being redefined and, as critical commentaries have compellingly argued, medical dominion can, and does, bring with it unintended consequences if critical reflection is not applied at every stage. The practitioner's ability to negotiate the dilemmas of their own moral position, duties placed on them by their employer, and legal duties placed on them by governments raise important considerations, not least against a backcloth of disciplinary advancement and social insecurity.

Working with suicide potential and self-harm/injury brings focus to these challenges in a very real-world way. The uncertainty of risk, set against the dominance of the risk assessment and mitigation discourse, places practitioners in a difficult position between a policy imperative of a search for certainty set against the unpredictability of human behaviour. However, a relational connection between client and therapist, with a willingness on the therapist's part to talk about risk and its meaning, can help create a good enough context for work with risk to be undertaken.

Suggestion for further reading

Mitchels, B., & Bond, T. (2010). *Essential law for counsellors and psychotherapists.* London: Sage.
This text provides a comprehensive overview of key legislation for counsellors and psychotherapists.

Reeves, A. (2015). *Working with risk in counselling and psychotherapy.* London: Sage.
This text offers a full consideration of working with risk in a therapeutic setting, including that of suicide and self-injury.

Szasz, T. S. (1997). *The manufacture of madness: a comparative study of the inquisition and the mental health movement.* Syracuse, NY: Syracuse University Press.
A seminal text critiquing the philosophical underpinning of mental health: diagnoses, systems and the medicalisation of human experience.

19

CONTEXTS

HENRY STRICK VAN LINSCHOTEN

Image 19 Dead slow (abandoned psychiatric hospital). With permission, Sarah Lamb

Introduction

As stated in Chapter 1, the context of a prison, young offender institution or high-security hospital is very different from the contexts in which most psychotherapy is conducted, whether in private accommodation or in an agency. Although psychotherapy in prison is the responsibility of the NHS, the overall context and framework is still quite different from that in other NHS environments.

In this chapter I will cover the impact on therapy of this context, especially the centrality of considering the offence committed, and of adapting therapy to the specific characteristics and needs of the offender. I will set out the institutional context in England and Wales, with Scotland as a contrasting example, and discuss the relationship between psychotherapy and the probation system. I will also introduce the main therapeutic alternatives to prison in the UK, such as democratic therapeutic communities and high-security psychiatric hospitals.

Punishment (retribution, revenge, retaliation) and rehabilitation are often seen as the most important goals for imprisonment, with (temporary) incapacitation also being important. Deterrence is often mentioned, but there is little evidence as to the effectiveness of prison as a deterrent. In some cultures, notably in the USA, rehabilitation is seen as less important than the primary punitive purpose. As psychotherapy can hardly be enlisted as a form of punishment, it fits best into the goal of rehabilitation, and so will only be welcome in a prison environment in which rehabilitation is seen as a major priority – which is rarely the case.

Pause for reflection

Spend some time thinking for yourself about the goals of or justifications for imprisonment – depriving a person of their liberty and a substantial part of their rights. How would you feel about working in a prison? If you feel prisons should be about rehabilitation, would you be happy working in a system that places the emphasis on punishment? The more your views about the reasons for imprisonment differ from the goals of the institution, the likelier it is that sooner or later you will find yourself in internal or actual conflict with prison authorities.

A major purpose of rehabilitation is often regarded as the reduction or minimisation of reoffending (see Chapter 1). Reoffending is a major problem. In the UK, for instance, almost half of released prisoners will reoffend within 12 months – the shorter the sentence, the more chance there is of reoffending. Sex offenders and committers of fraud are categories of offenders who are low on reoffending (Ministry of Justice, 2016). Traditionally, rehabilitation is seen as a major role for the probation service, although the 'probation' terminology is not always used, for instance not in Scotland.

A country's criminal justice system (CJS) provides an environment with a strong structure, and with heavy institutional features. The CJS substantially affects the context for psychotherapy, and systems differ widely from country to country. This chapter will focus mainly on the CJS in England and Wales, with some descriptions of the CJS in Scotland, and only occasional references to other countries.

Challenges of therapeutic work in a forensic context

It is well known that the therapeutic relationship is probably the most important factor for the effectiveness of psychotherapy (Norcross, 2011; Wampold & Imel, 2015). In a forensic context, the therapeutic relationship for the psychotherapist and for the client will be affected, often heavily, by the institutional environment. This can be an issue if the institution is mostly focused on punishment and security, with only a secondary eye towards rehabilitation, and little interest in psychotherapy as such (as outlined in Chapter 1 and in the chapters in Part IV on treatment).

A psychotherapist who is introduced to working with clients in prison is always told that they can never ignore two issues: security, and the offence committed by the prisoner. These two factors directly and significantly impact the therapeutic relationship. Security, its impact on confidentiality in the therapy room, and its relationship with anxiety levels in the therapist, have already been covered in Chapter 1, so we will continue with reviewing how the emphasis on the offence affects the therapeutic work and relationship.

Most people will understand and agree that the therapist needs to know what offence their client has committed. This implies a previous flow of information to the psychotherapist, and a reliance on other inputs than what they are told by the client – which in itself, in many schools of psychotherapy, is already seen as somewhat problematic. What varies further is how the information is treated, with different therapeutic approaches and different supervisors having different ideas as to the best treatment of this information.

The once popular idea that there might be an advantage in 'making' the client feel guilty about their 'crime' has been mostly abandoned.

Similarly, therapy is not seen as a vehicle for eliciting more information about the crime, though, as mentioned in Chapter 1, if new information is revealed in therapy, and the therapist believes this affects current security issues, they must inform the prison authorities. If the information is historical and does not affect current security, different psychotherapy supervisors will have different views about the proper course of action for the psychotherapist, even as to whether they have any freedom as to how to deal with such information. The more freedom allowed, the more the therapist is forced to deal with dilemmas that their standard training, and non-forensic practice, have not really prepared them for (see Chapter 1, where some of these dilemmas have been discussed).

Pause for reflection

How do you believe you would act as a psychotherapist in a high-security facility in the following situations?

- You are working with a sexual offender, and having spent many long sessions in which you believe your client has shared very openly what has happened, you come to the conclusion that they are innocent of the (very serious) offence for which your client has been convicted.
- You work with a violent offender, who is convicted of a crime during which others were present. You come to the conclusion that a certain named other person, who has been cleared of involvement, should also have been prosecuted and convicted.

If for either of these instances you would consider contacting prison or other law enforcement personnel, think about how that might affect your relationship with the client and the therapeutic process.

As a general 'rule of thumb', most supervisors would consider it important in working with a client that the offence comes up and gets a significant amount of attention in therapy – it is felt that if you don't, this needs to be carefully considered, and would usually mean that something is not going 'right' in the therapy. How this could be addressed will significantly depend on the therapeutic approach being used.

The reason to bring the offence into therapy is the (sometimes unspoken) idea that psychotherapy should be part of rehabilitation, and that the main goal for rehabilitation should be the reduction of reoffending. This line of thinking has led to a substantial volume of research in a number of countries. In the 1960s, in the UK especially, there was a wave of enthusiasm for the deemed success of rehabilitation in reducing reoffending. Then Lipton, Martinson and Wilks's (1975) survey was published in the USA, and had a major world-wide impact, including in the UK. It was an early form of meta-analysis that analysed a large number of research studies and concluded that the effectiveness of rehabilitation in reducing reoffending had been exaggerated and heavily overestimated. Under the slogan of 'Nothing works', this played a big role in reducing the trust in, and budgets for, probation and rehabilitation, and shifted penal systems in many countries towards a more punitive position. Although there had been early voices saying that the conclusions of this research were overstated, it took probably until McGuire (1995) – 20 years later and in the UK, not the USA – before the idea of the ineffectiveness of probation and rehabilitation was overturned. Some even argue that political as well as popular support for rehabilitation has never fully recovered (see Robinson & Crow, 2009).

In parallel with the above, since the early 1990s in Canada several researchers have organised a systematic long-term effort to collect and analyse new research into the effectiveness of methods for reducing reoffending (Andrews & Bonta, 2010). Andrews and Bonta set out their conclusions about what the research evidence shows in the form of the Risk-Need-Responsivity (RNR) model. According to this model, the intensity of treatment should match the *Risk* of the offender and meet their *Needs* (often related to the reason the crime was committed), which should be targeted and turned into strengths. In addition, rehabilitation programmes should be *Responsive* to the service setting and to relevant individual characteristics of the offender. The model retains considerable influence (see, for example, a recent evaluation in Polaschek (2012)), but in England and Wales it has substantially lost support since about 2010. In the recent update of a government policy paper (Ministry of Justice, 2015a) the RNR model gets no mention, and some of the main actions proposed are listed as (quotations from Ministry of Justice, 2015a):

- payment by results to private providers of probation and rehabilitation services ('incentivise innovation, paying providers by results for delivering reductions in reoffending')
- a diverse range of rehabilitation providers from the private, voluntary and social sectors (including potential mutuals) through 21 Community Rehabilitation Companies (CRCs)
- extension of probationary supervision ('statutory rehabilitation') to 45,000 short-sentenced offenders, most of whom will be low-to medium-risk.

In Canada and Scotland, the very substantial evidence-base for the RNR model sustained its support by professionals and the relevant authorities.

The next most popular rehabilitation model with a reasonable evidence base is the Good Lives model, associated with Tony Ward and Shadd Maruna. This is described in Ward and Maruna (2007), and is compared with the RNR model by the main proponents of RNR in Andrews, Bonta and Wormith (2011). The Good Lives model supplements RNR by focusing on the strengths of the offenders, and uses part of the interaction with prisoners to put together a life plan for living outside prison which is both attractive for the offender and incompatible with further offending.

In more detail, once a decision has been made to support the availability of psychotherapy for prisoners, it is usually felt that a choice has to be made between the (many) different psychotherapy approaches. The continued claims by the followers of many approaches or groups of psychotherapy schools that their school is more effective than the others, is continued, and perhaps intensified, within the prison context. All the main categories of CBT, humanistic therapies, integrative approaches, psychoanalytic and psychodynamic ways of working, group therapy, and systemic therapy, have their proponents for forensic purposes, and a number of them are described in Chapters 13–16. The strong research evidence for the overall equivalence of different psychotherapy approaches (Lambert, 2013; Wampold & Imel, 2015) is rarely accepted, and even less so in a forensic context.

One major difference between schools of psychotherapy is the distinction between insight-oriented and behavioural approaches. Psychoanalytic and psychodynamic psychotherapy are the original insight-oriented methods, but gestalt therapy and most other humanistic therapies are also mostly insight-oriented. In contrast, cognitive behavioural therapy (CBT) is, as the name suggests, substantially focused on behaviour as an outcome. If one accepts that the main goal of forensic psychotherapy is the reduction of reoffending, this would suggest a behavioural focus, which sits less well with the insight-oriented approaches to psychotherapy. Nevertheless, it must be noted that in England and Wales psychoanalytic and psychodynamic approaches are widely used in prisons. This is also a result of the influence of the International Association of Forensic Psychotherapy (IAFP) in the UK, which is mainly psychoanalytically oriented. The contrast between insight-oriented and more behaviourally focused approaches is not an argument to use CBT or its variants only. It is possible, and in my view necessary, even when mainly using an insight-oriented model, to adapt and expand it to include a clear emphasis on the offence committed, and to keep in mind the desirability of reducing the risk of reoffending.

Other factors that influence psychotherapy in a forensic context include an emphasis on diagnostic categories and the influence of the Mental Health Act 1983 and the Mental Capacity Act 2005, due to (mental) healthcare in prison being managed by the NHS, and the major decisions about treatment often being sanctioned by a (forensic) psychiatrist. In addition, psychotherapy in prison has to take into account that many inmates are dealing with various disorders, of which alcohol and substance use, personality disorders, PTSD and dissociation are the most common.

Apart from a large proportion of offenders being in prison for drug-related offences, alcohol and drugs often play a role in the committed offence. Working with offenders who in parallel with the psychotherapy are also part of a drug treatment programme is common, and produces extra challenges to the psychotherapist, who may not be accustomed to these factors and so-called 'dual diagnoses'. 'Dual diagnosis' (or, less frequently, 'comorbidity') is the term used for people with two separate mental health diagnoses. As there is a frequent co-occurrence of addictive disorders (alcohol and substance abuse) with other mental health problems, dual diagnosis is sometimes used as short-hand for this combination specifically (although its main official meaning continues to be the co-occurrence of any two disorders). There is a separate research literature about the effectiveness of treatment and therapeutic protocols for helping people with these dual diagnoses, as there may be interactions between the diagnoses, and lack of progress with one may make it harder or impossible to work with the other (Atkins, 2014; Gournay, 2016; Phillips, McKeown & Sandford, 2010).

Case examples: Forensic and voluntary settings

Forensic setting

John Smith is 25 years old and has a history of petty offending, but he is in prison at present following convictions for actual bodily harm and drug-related offences. He was unemployed and was a regular user of cannabis and alcohol, which he shared with friends in their houses in his neighbourhood. Some of his offending involved him in violent affrays while under the influence. He has now been offered psychotherapy to help with the challenges of his offending, which he accepted. He is cooperating with therapy but at times becomes aggressive and menacing with his female therapist,

(Continued)

(Continued)

when and if she puts challenging notions back to him about his life. He then apologises and asks for further help. The therapist will be asked to give her opinion during case reviews and eventually when John is being considered for parole. The therapist is currently concerned because John has begun to talk about his access to Class A drugs within prison and of increasingly aggressive interactions with fellow inmates.

Voluntary setting

Jack Smith is 25 years old and is seeing a student counsellor at his university. He has sought out counselling as he is worried that he may be abusing cannabis and alcohol. About 18 months ago he began to share cannabis with a group of friends in his neighbourhood. Subsequently, he started selling illegal substances on a number of occasions and also became involved in a number of violent confrontations with other drug users and sellers. He is worried that his substance use and lifestyle is interfering with his studies to the point where he may fail his end-of-year exams. Although he is very cooperative with the therapeutic process, he can sometimes become aggressive with his female therapist if she challenges certain notions about his life. However, he is always apologetic following such outbursts and is quick to ask for more help. The therapist is currently concerned because Jack has begun to talk about selling Class A drugs within the university, and of increasingly aggressive interactions with some of his fellow students.

In many ways these two clients have similar issues, but think about how the role of the therapist is different because of the different contexts they are working in. In thinking about the impact that context can have, consider:

- How might the matter of voluntarism be played out in both cases?
- How is confidentiality affected by the two settings?
- What are the different implications for the duty of care of the professionals in the two settings?
- Can the worker in the forensic setting devote herself unconditionally to the needs of the prisoner?
- How optimistic are you about progress in each case?

After drug and alcohol issues, the most frequent and ubiquitous mental health problems relevant for forensic psychotherapy are personality disorders, post-traumatic stress disorder (PTSD) and dissociation, either as a symptom or in the form of dissociative disorders. They are much more frequent for offenders than for people not in contact with the CJS. Ideally, these diagnoses would be systematically taken into account in the psychotherapy of offenders, and influence the way of working, as well as the training and experience level expected from the psychotherapist. In practice, however, this is rarely the case. Statistics suggest that well over 50% of offenders in prison may be diagnosable with personality disorders, especially borderline personality disorder and anti-social personality disorder. Similarly, PTSD and dissociation are heavily over-represented in forensic settings. Many (though not all) schools of psychotherapy would agree that their way of working needs to be adapted to be effective with personality disorders, and with PTSD, dissociation and other forms of trauma.

Psychotherapy for offenders with personality disorder has a number of implications. It needs to be accepted that treatment will take a considerable time – mostly it is thought that one has to think about a period of uninterrupted treatment of one or two years, sometimes even more. The way of working needs to be adapted – special models, such as Dialectical Behaviour Therapy (see Chapter 16) and Mentalization-Based Treatment, have been developed (NICE Guidelines for Personality Disorder; NICE, 2009). These special models often recommend more than once weekly treatment and/or a combination of individual psychotherapy with group therapy and psycho-education sessions. Teamwork among the therapy providers and between-session availability of carers are further components of most complete treatment models. All this 'special treatment' is usually difficult or impossible to make available in a standard prison environment. Despite that, there is good evidence (Dowsett & Craissati, 2008; McMurran & Howard, 2009; Willmot & Gordon, 2011) that such specialised models are necessary to make an impact on borderline personality disorder, and that untreated, personality disorder may make reoffending more likely.

Psychotherapy in prisons

The organisational context of psychotherapy in prisons is different for the countries of the UK, and is regularly changed. In England, the prison service and probation service have been combined (in 2008) in one overall organisation, the National Offender Management Service (NOMS), an executive agency of the Ministry of Justice. As part of NOMS, a new National Probation Service maintains a separate profile for high-risk offenders. Prison healthcare, of which psychotherapy, psychiatry and psychology form a part, has been provided by the NHS (National Health Service) since 2002. A National Partnership Agreement between NOMS, NHS England and Public Health England (NOMS, 2015) gives useful details of the country-wide organisation, responsibilities and history of the way in which prison healthcare is organised.

You can take away from this formal organisational description that in England and Wales the prison service and the probation service (most directly associated with the goal of rehabilitation) have been merged into one organisation, whereas healthcare, including psychotherapeutic provision, formerly managed by the prison service, is now under the responsibility of the NHS. In contrast, prisons in Scotland are run by the Scottish Prison Service and probation services are now carried out by 'criminal justice social workers', especially in the community.

The major contacts for an imprisoned offender in the context of an English prison are the prison officers, and, when allocated, a probation officer. This means that any contact between psychotherapist and client has been preceded by setting up appointments via the prison officers, and that every single psychotherapy appointment will be known and visible to the prison officers – and in fact often be visible to other offenders on the same 'wing', too. This is a far cry from the privacy that is usually associated with non-forensic psychotherapy. Further, while prisoners are rarely directly compelled to attend psychotherapy, they can be and regularly are pressured into psychotherapy, or at a minimum will feel under pressure to attend, as it may 'look good' on their record. There is also the overall association between psychotherapists in prison and the other prison staff: for example, the psychotherapist in a high-security environment must be able to move around, which means that they wear a belt with a bunch of keys – a very visible sign of their involvement with the prison regime, and the difference in power between the psychotherapist who is free to lock and unlock doors and move around, as opposed to the prisoner, who is confined. All these factors together amount to a much heightened and more visible power differential between the offender-client and the psychotherapist (see also Chapter 1). This will need to be taken into account in the psychotherapy process, according to the modality of the psychotherapist.

The competing agendas for the prison system and the psychotherapist have been described in this book in Chapter 1, and referred to repeatedly in other chapters. Other imposed adaptations of the normal psychotherapeutic framework are imposed by the prison environment and by security considerations. Prison officers are always entitled to take a look in to see if there might be 'problems', and occasionally do, depending on their assessment of a prisoner and their state of mind. If there is an alarm, or a need for a 'lock-down', therapy might be interrupted or need to be abruptly ended. Sometimes other inmates 'by mistake' open the door and wander in – for obvious reasons, the door needs to be kept unlocked. Finally, in many prisons space is at such a premium that there are no dedicated therapy rooms, so a waiting room, conference room, or canteen space is used instead. At first, the contrast between this and the 'normal' carefully managed and stabilised therapy environment is striking. However, in practice, most therapists get accustomed to it reasonably quickly, and find that therapy is still possible. After all, these factors, and especially the lack of personal freedom, are representative of the daily life of the prisoner anyway – so their reproduction in the therapy situation is not surprising, and may also 'integrate' therapy better with their life.

The quality of the therapeutic relationship is crucial for therapeutic effectiveness, a factor that can be affected by the insecure attachment style of many offenders, with a high proportion falling into the disorganised attachment category (see Chapter 13). Currently in England and Wales, little attention is paid to this when decisions are made to transfer prisoners to other locations, or when they leave prison. Attachment security issues are powerfully raised when treatment is ended. Potentially, if notice is given, and there is time to complete a period of psychotherapy, the impact on the attachment system and on separation anxiety can be processed in therapy with positive effect. However, this is often not the case, and decisions are frequently made by the prison authorities for independent reasons of offender management which ignore the requirements of psychotherapeutic effectiveness.

In addition, therapy and reoffending rates would be improved if there could be continuity of psychotherapeutic treatment between locations and 'through the gates'. The latter means that at the time of release of prisoners, during the all-important transition period between prison and return to the community, psychotherapy should be continued and sustained by the same psychotherapist. In reality this is only rarely the case and it only needs brief thinking about the high rate of reoffending after release from prison, before a year is over, to realise that this is a major unutilised opportunity. It is, therefore, a positive move that looking at the 'through the gates' option has been announced as a policy target in England and Wales (Ministry of Justice, 2015a).

This chapter has paid little attention to socio-cultural factors, other than the reference in the RNR model to the importance of individual responsivity. In fact, as you saw in Chapters 5 and 6 (on race and gender), these factors are extremely important. The special considerations influencing work with women prisoners are at least well known and discussed (e.g. in Blanchette & Brown, 2006; Motz, 2001; Sheehan, McIvor & Trotter, 2007). Black people are heavily over-represented in prison (see Chapter 5), which is a noticeable part of the prison experience, for psychotherapists too. There is a much lower uptake of psychotherapy by black people in prison (personal experience). The reasons for this may be similar to those in British society in general (Keating & Robertson, 2004).

Directly therapeutic environments

'Therapeutic community' (TC), sometimes 'democratic therapeutic community', is the term used to describe a model where a medium-security prison (or certain wings only) is turned into a community, still subject to security and separated from the free world, but run according to somewhat democratic principles, and with a substantial provision of psychotherapy, particularly group therapy. This is seen as being especially effective for rehabilitation and the reduction or prevention of reoffending. It has been developed and used mostly in the UK, having started shortly after the Second World War. In the USA, the same term of therapeutic community is used for a completely different model, as it pertains to hierarchically run institutions developed to work with drug and alcohol use problems.

The most well-known of these facilities in the UK, and the longest surviving one, is HMP Grendon. Despite their promise, and the long period over which therapeutic communities have successfully run, they have been criticised for not resulting in a significant reduction in reoffending and at the same time costing more than standard prisons and for compromising security (there have been a few highly-publicised escapes over the years). Shuker (2010) and Rutter and Tyrer (2003) illustrate the discussions about research evidence for the effectiveness of the Grendon TC model, where a lack of unequivocal evidence for a reduction in reoffending continues to be problematic. It is unfortunate, in terms of diversity of models, that the pressure on HMP Grendon keeps mounting and shows how important objective evaluation is when implementing a non-standard model.

England has three high-security psychiatric hospitals: Broadmoor, Ashworth and Rampton. Scotland has one, the State Hospital at Carstairs, South Lanarkshire. They are clearly different from prisons, as the inmates have been placed there because their actions are considered to have been caused by their mental health problem. As a result, the role of psychotherapy in treating a disorder, and the role of the disorder as the reason for the person being locked up, are more aligned than in prisons. Nevertheless, inmates of high-security psychiatric hospitals have usually committed very serious crimes, and the high-security regime under which they are held is there to prevent escape, and to reduce their freedom to repeat their actions. The high-security environment itself means that there are many similarities with the constraints and adaptations that are necessary for psychotherapy in prisons.

The best-known and highest-profile high-security psychiatric hospital in England is Broadmoor Hospital in Berkshire, England, managed by the West London Mental Health Trust, and currently undergoing a major redevelopment. It houses over 200 people – all male, since the female wing was closed in 2007. Most patients stay there for well under five years. Therapies provided are mainly forms of group therapy or group activity, and arts therapy. In the late twentieth century, patients also received individual psychotherapy, but this has been largely discontinued.

Conclusion

This chapter has covered different contextual factors of psychotherapy in prison, and the adaptations required of therapists and their methods for effective working. The offence is usually central in therapy, as well as the goal of reducing reoffending. Prison can be an inhospitable environment for psychotherapy. Despite the excellent evidence-base brought together in the RNR model of Andrews and Bonta (2010), in England and Wales this has been substantially defocused as an approach to including psychotherapy in rehabilitation. Models that have been used in the UK's Therapeutic Communities and high-security psychiatric hospitals have not been based on strong research evidence, nor has there been a systematic policy of publishing research about the work that is being done. I want to leave you with the conclusion that there are real missed opportunities in the failures to link what is done to reduce reoffending by British prisoners more closely to research findings and review.

Working as a psychotherapist in a prison or high-security environment is not easy and requires special training, supervision, adaptability, and a strong determination to fully tailor one's way of working to the unique institutional context, and the unique requirements and needs of individual prisoners.

Suggestions for further reading

Andrews, D. A., & Bonta, J. (2010). *The psychology of criminal conduct* (5th ed.). New Providence, NJ: LexisNexis.
A fundamental book by the two Canadian researchers originating the RNR model. It is based on strong research evidence, and has a wealth of information about offenders and their relationship with crime.

Bell, E. (2013). Punishment as politics: the penal system in England and Wales. In V. Ruggiero & M. Ryan (Eds.), *Punishment in Europe: a critical anatomy of penal systems* (pp. 58–85). London: Palgrave Macmillan.

(Continued)

(Continued)

An excellent summary of the English and Welsh penal system from a number of broader perspectives.

Maruna, S. (2001). *Making good: how ex-convicts reform and rebuild their lives*. Washington, DC: American Psychological Association.
A good combination with Andrews and Bonta (2010). It sets out the Good Lives model in a readable fashion and explains a lot about the rehabilitation of offenders.

20

PREVENTION

NADIA WAGER AND GRAHAM PIKE

Image 20   On patrol. With permission, Sarah Lamb

Introduction

In previous chapters we have looked at many different examples of 'mad' or 'bad', exploring how people who are experiencing mental health problems or who commit criminal offences are classified and treated by formal medical and criminal justice systems. The focus of these chapters has tended to be on the treatment of people after a diagnoses or verdict, but here we turn our attention to how mental health and offending behaviour might be prevented, and to discern the synergies and contrasts between the different approaches and the aspirations of prevention. In addition, we will concentrate on childhood and adolescence, in part because it is simply not possible to deal with every aspect of prevention in a single chapter, but also because it is often most effective to conduct interventions at this stage of life. However, this focus is not meant to suggest that approaches to prevention in adulthood are not worth conducting, as they have certainly proved to be effective.

Levels of prevention

It is proposed that there are essentially three levels of prevention: primary, secondary and tertiary (Leavell & Clark, 1965). Primary prevention has been likened to a public health strategy where the intervention is universally applied to the whole population with a view to preventing a few from becoming perpetrators of crime or having to deal with mental health problems. Strategies employed by those seeking primary prevention could include protective policies that tackle structural causal factors such as marginalisation from employment or discrimination, or that encourage individuals to change their behaviour through media campaigns. In secondary prevention, the intervention efforts target either indicated or selected groups of individuals. Indicated individuals are those who are showing early signs of mental health problems, but the signs have not met the criteria for a particular diagnosable disorder, or those who have engaged in anti-social or delinquent behaviour (which is often seen as a precursor to offending behaviour). Selected groups are those who, by dint of characteristics that broadly match risk factors for offending behaviour or developing mental health issues in the future, are deemed to be the populations of interest. Thus, delivery of the intervention is targeted to subsections of the population, particularly those who are deemed to be the most likely to benefit. Finally, tertiary prevention targets those who have already offended or who have already manifested mental health issues. The aims of the interventions here are to reduce the likelihood of reoffending or to restore mental health/reduce symptoms to facilitate adaptive functioning.

Case example: Peter Woolf

Peter's description of his early childhood, given in his autobiography – *The Damage Done*, paints a brutal picture of his family and neighbourhood environments. Peter was born in 1957 in a socio-economically deprived area of London. The people he had grown up believing were his mother and father were in fact his grandparents and his 'sisters' were actually his mother and aunt. His mother-figure is described as possibly alcoholic. Peter reported that both parental figures routinely engaged in corporal punishment and would regularly attempt to sedate Peter the toddler by adding alcohol to his bottle. He describes one particularly memorable incident in which his 'mother' savagely beat him with a fire poker after he unwittingly swore at her when he was aged almost five years. During his early years he witnessed frequent domestic violence between his 'parents', a suicide attempt by his 'mother' and was bullied and humiliated by his 'sisters'. His 'father' encouraged him to use violence as a means of resolving conflict and theft for securing his material desires. With regards to the wider social environment, his parents' friends were notorious armed criminals. Peter claimed that by the age of five years he had developed an imaginary friend as a way to ward off the self-imposed loneliness that has remained with him for most of his life. He portrayed his family life as loveless and characterised by their failure to display affection, which he asserted left him feeling excluded from others. He was also forbidden to show emotions, particularly those that indicated distress, fear or upset, as these were seen as signs of weakness. Additionally, he learnt that violence and the fear that it evoked in others could be used as a means of establishing and maintaining power over others. At the age of seven his 'parents' demanded that he leave home to live with his 'sister' (his birth mother). Here he was not only left unattended, but he also became the minder for a neighbour's child, who was still in nappies, while the two mothers went out socialising.

Peter claimed that by the age of six he had started stealing and by the age of ten he had started taking drugs, which ultimately lead to him becoming an intravenous drug user and hardened criminal. By the age of 44 Peter had spent 18 years in prison, was living rough, committing more and more crime in order to support his drug addiction and regularly thinking of committing suicide. Following a conviction for burglary, he asked to take part in the Rehabilitation for Addicted Prisoners Trust (RAPt) programme at Norwich prison, which helped him both stop taking drugs and committing crimes.

Pause for reflection

Consider the case of Peter Woolf in terms of the three levels of prevention. At which points in his life could interventions have been made, and how might these have affected his later life?

It can be tempting to see the earliest intervention as likely to be the most effective, but do you think there might be any disadvantages associated with primary and secondary levels of prevention, or are they always preferable to tertiary levels of prevention?

Conceptualising mental health

Mental health is typically conceptualised as the absence of negative mental health problems (e.g. depression, anxiety, psychosis, etc.). However, the World Health Organisation argues that psychological well-being is more than just a lack of *negative* mental health, but should also include provision for *positive* mental health (WHO, 2004). For instance, the WHO (2001, p. 1) define mental health as 'a state of well-being in which the individual realises his or her own abilities, can cope with the normal stresses and is able to make a contribution to his or her community'. Within psychology, the positive psychological approach, which focuses on what makes people flourish and be happy, argues that rather than being placed on the same continuum, positive and negative mental health are two distinct, yet related qualities each with their own continuum (Joseph, 2015).

Consequently, from this perspective, focusing on preventing negative mental health issues only would be insufficient to promote mental health (Keyes, 2007). However, there is some evidence to suggest that initiatives that promote positive mental health can also lead to a reduction in negative mental health issues, but that initiatives which target negative mental health are less likely to also have an impact on positive mental health (Jane-Llopis et al., 2005).

The difference between positive and negative mental health is therefore an important one and to concentrate solely on the prevention of negative health outcomes is to ignore a considerable part of the picture. Nonetheless, although there is an ever-growing focus upon mental well-being in many societies, as we will see, the primary focus of prevention programmes tends to be on the avoidance of negative health outcomes.

Preventing mental health issues

Proponents of preventative psychiatry contend that since many treatments have limited efficacy in terms of ameliorating the symptoms and enhancing functioning for a proportion of patients who experience mental health problems, it might be prudent to direct efforts towards the prevention of the emergence of these issues (Trivedi et al., 2014). If we consider that the onset of more than half of all diagnosable mental health problems commences in early adolescence, around the age of 14 (Kessler et al., 2007), it would seem wise to direct preventative interventions towards factors that impact on children and childhood circumstances. Indeed, a review of age of onset and timing of intervention for mental health problems concluded that there is emerging evidence that early intervention might be able to reduce the persistence and severity of initial mental health problems and to prevent the emergence of secondary problems (McGorry et al., 2011).

The development of preventative interventions is informed by the existing knowledge of risk factors that contribute to the mental health prognosis, and protective factors that are associated with resilience (see Chapter 7). Here, prognosis is conceptualised in terms of the severity of symptoms, the age of onset of symptoms, the duration of the episode(s) and the responsiveness to treatment, while resilience is deemed to be the ability to maintain mental health despite exposure to multiple risk factors for negative mental health. Importantly, protective factors that have been found to increase resilience are also associated with positive mental health (Davydov et al., 2010). Consequently, there are two broad approaches to preventing mental health problems, which are based on two different models of mental health: the disease and the building resilience models.

The disease-based model focuses on the reduction of risk for specific diseases which are deemed to have genetic or neurobiological origins. In contrast, the resilience-building model aims to build the individual's psychological resilience and social strength to enable the developing child to be better able to cope with potential adverse events that might occur later in life. The effectiveness of interventions which aim to enhance resilience in young people have been associated with fewer depressive symptoms for the treated samples. For example, Brunwasser, Gillham and Kim's (2009) meta-analysis of a group-based, cognitive-behavioural intervention, known as the Penn Resiliency Programme, was found to demonstrate positive effects in both targeted and universally applied programmes. Additionally, the benefit of the programme on depressive symptoms appeared to remain at one-year follow-up for both genders, and irrespective of baseline levels of symptoms and who provided the intervention. Consistent with the notion that preventative interventions are best delivered in childhood, the analysis also revealed that the benefits were less evident for older adolescents and adults.

There is evidence to suggest that the attachment behavioural system (see Chapter 13) mediates the individual differences found in the way individuals cope with life stressors and their capacity for maintaining resilience in the face of adversity (Mikulincer & Shaver, 2007). This is exemplified by the fact that insecurely attached children have been shown to experience difficulty in coping with the transition points in their education, for example starting nursery school or moving between schools (Coie, 1997).

The strategies used for building children's resilience have included training in interpersonal problem solving, building social competencies, raising self-esteem and enhancing the availability of social support (Bloom, 1997). Guralnick and Neville (1997) proposed that between the 1970s and 1990s the predominant focus of prevention work with children focused on developing social competence. Social competence is rooted in the ability to form secure emotional attachments to others (Egeland, 2009). In turn, secure attachments facilitate the ability to trust others, regulate one's own emotions and to develop the capacity to mentalise and empathise, and to be self-reflective (see Chapter 13). All of these attributes are seen as essential to permitting adaptive functioning when confronting the turmoil and uncertainty of adult life.

Insecure attachments, on the other hand, have been associated with a number of attributes which reduce the individual's ability to cope with stress and uncertainty. Two broad categories of attributes that render the individual more vulnerable are destructive self-representations and the poor capacity to regulate emotions. With regards to problematic self-representations, insecurely attached individuals have a propensity for being self-doubters, perfectionists, overly self-critical and depend on the approval of others, and for being troubled by sensations of hopelessness and helplessness (Wei, Heppner & Russell, 2006). The problems with emotional regulation manifest differently for anxious and avoidant insecure attachment styles. Individuals with avoidant attachment are more likely to suppress negative emotions and less likely to seek social support to deal with life stressors (Berant, Mukulincer & Shaver, 2008). Conversely, individuals who demonstrate anxious attachment experience exaggerated emotional responses to negative events which trigger their attachment hypersensitivity. This can result in excessive worrying, depression proneness, intrusion symptoms of post-traumatic stress disorder (e.g. flashbacks and nightmares), impulsivity and explosive outbursts of anger (Mikulincer & Shaver, 2007).

Indication of the protective quality of secure attachments comes from Turanovic and Pratt's (2015) analysis of the data from America's National Longitudinal Study of Adolescent Mental Health. The data consisted of an average of a seven-year follow-up of 13,555 young people from early adolescence until their early-to-mid-twenties. The findings revealed that positive attachment to both family and school mitigated the risk posed by violent victimisation in adolescence leading to adverse outcomes in early adulthood. The outcomes assessed in the study included negative mental health issues (e.g. depression, anxiety, suicidality, etc.) and substance misuse, as well as revictimisation and adult offending. Turanovic and Pratt speculate that the pro-social attachments formed can lead to a protective effect, and that this effect may be the result of the individual developing adaptive coping resources. The authors contend, therefore, that secure attachments bestow developmental advantages to young people which are not only enduring, but which may also accumulate over time. They refer to this notion as 'cumulative continuity'.

Conceptualising offending behaviour and offenders

While officially 'offending behaviour' is that which breaks a particular law of the country, it is also possible to include other behaviours which breach moral codes or social norms in the definition. For example, many young people are deemed to be 'at risk' for offending due to their anti-social or delinquent behaviour. Importantly, this broader definition can also mean that young people are at risk of being labelled as offenders for engaging in what are deemed age-inappropriate behaviours (under-age drinking, smoking and sex, truanting from school, running away from home/going missing). These are known as 'status-offences' and it is questionable as to whether they should be labelled as 'offences' due to the negative implications this can have for the young person who carries such a label.

Pause for reflection

Think about examples of anti-social, delinquent and offending behaviour. Where would you draw the lines between these categories? Would the type of preventative intervention that might be needed differ according to which category it fell in?

In 2009 the Prison Reform Trust declared that the UK incarcerated more children than anywhere else in the Western world. They claimed that the number of children incarcerated trebled between 1991 and 2006. However, a large proportion of these young people had not technically committed a criminal offence. Paylor (2011) suggests that many children are being incarcerated for the breach of Anti-Social Behaviour Orders (ASBO). She states that 42% of all ASBOs are breached and 55% of all breaches result in a custodial sentence. As you saw in Chapter 7, while adult men accounted for the majority of ASBOs, a disproportionately high number were applied to children aged 10–17 (Home Office and Ministry of Justice, 2014). Moreover, young people aged 15–17 years were one of the age groups most likely to breach their ASBO, meaning that the introduction and use of ASBOs was an important factor in the criminalisation of young people in mid-to-late adolescence.

In Chapter 7 you were introduced to Moffitt's (1993) approach to categorising offending behaviour across, and in relation to, the lifespan. Moffitt's developmental taxonomy of offenders would clearly separate out those who commit status offences from those who commit more serious types of crime. The taxonomy split the population into three groups based on their potential for criminality. These included abstainers, adolescent-limited offenders (which would include the status offenders) and the life-course persistent offenders.

In Moffitt's original conceptualisation of abstainers, this group were seen as somewhat abnormal and their abstinence from offending was seen as a consequence of their life circumstances that prevented their inclusion in peer groups (e.g. responsibilities as a carer, having a disability which precluded an age-appropriate level of independence, or having a characteristic that rendered them vulnerable to being rejected by peers). However, later research by Piquero, Brezina and Turner (2005) found that abstainers were in fact embedded into peer groups, but that these peer groups appeared to have a greater involvement in pro-social behaviour. Additionally, parental monitoring of the young person and the young person's attachment to their teachers were both factors associated with engagement with pro-social peer groups that are likely to have also acted to limit the potential for criminality.

For adolescent-limited offenders, offending is limited to this life stage. In other words, the onset of offending coincides with puberty and desistance coincides with the attainment of adult social roles. Offending in this group tends to be committed as a group and to be relatively minor. However, when violent offences do occur these are likely to be status-oriented (e.g. to be about 'saving face') rather than instrumental (e.g. to be a means of getting a desired object or behaviour from others). Importantly, Moffitt (1993) referred to a number of factors that could delay or prevent desistance for 'what would have been' adolescent limited-offenders. These 'snares' included gaining a criminal record, a truncated education, unwanted pregnancy, drug or alcohol dependency and incarceration.

Finally, life-course persistent offenders tend to begin offending at an earlier age, offend alone, have a higher frequency and variety of offending, be more likely to engage in violent crime and be less likely to desist in adulthood. As was described in Chapter 7, the interaction between the person (particularly through vulnerabilities to offending resulting from specific bio-psycho-social factors) and their environment shaped a personality structure that supported criminal behaviour (Moffitt, 1993). More recently, research has also pointed to the importance of genetic factors in explaining life-course-persistent offending (Barnes, 2012). Although the presence of neurobiological and genetic factors might appear to be problematic for the creation of effective prevention programmes, it is important to remember that environmental factors have been found to exert significant ameliorative or exacerbating effects on the long-term outcomes of such neurobiological challenges. One of the modifiable exacerbating factors is the quality of parenting, particularly attachment bonds to caregivers in early childhood. Importantly, if we are considering preventing serious offending, this is possibly the group who are most likely to be targeted for interventions.

Preventing offending

The Crime and Disorder Act 1998 established that the primary aim of the Youth Offending Service was to identify and manage or reduce the risk factors that were linked to offending. According to Paylor (2011), the rationale for this emphasis on what is known as the 'risk factor prevention paradigm' (Farrington, 2007) was a response to the perceived inefficiency and costliness of the existing youth justice system. The prevention paradigm became focused on risk assessment and the identification of variables that predict offending. In the UK this led to the introduction of two actuarial risk assessment tools, Asset and Onset, which are used to identify young people at risk of offending. Asset was introduced in 2000 and was used by all Youth Offending Teams on young people who had already come into the service due to their offending behaviour. The tool was used to ensure that the level of intervention received by the young person was proportionate to the risk that they posed and that the interventions selected targeted the risk factors that were present for each particular individual, thereby ensuring the most cost-effective use of resources. Onset, which is a little more controversial, was introduced in 2006. This is also an actuarial risk assessment tool, but on this occasion the tool is used on younger children who have not yet shown signs of offending.

Paylor (2011) was highly critical of the use of these tools and the implications they had for conceptualisations of youth offending. She contends that the Home Office erroneously interpreted factors that predict risk as being aetiological factors (i.e. causal factors). Paylor goes on to point out that despite many researchers concluding that it is virtually impossible to assess whether the relationship between a specific factor and the probability of reconviction is causal or not (e.g. Garside, 2009), the Home Office lists some of the risk factors included in Asset under the heading of 'What Causes Crime?' (Home Office, 2010b).

In addition, there is a concern that the inevitable over-emphasis of negative factors (since the tool takes little account of protective factors) could potentially encourage practitioners to adopt narrow and hopeless views of the young people with whom they work (Smith, 2007). An additional impact of this erroneous interpretation of the risk factors is that the focus on individualised factors meant that structural barriers to health, well-being and community participation (e.g. school exclusion, poverty, unemployment, etc.), drifted out of focus for policy-makers, despite these being the strongest predictors in adolescence. Instead, young people came to be viewed as possessing multiple needs rather than being subjected to them, their behaviour became problematised and exploration of the causes of their behaviour became obsolete (Barry, 2007).

We mentioned earlier in this chapter the distinction between status offences and criminal offences. This distinction, combined with Moffitt's taxonomy of offenders, has implications for intervening to prevent offending. Indeed, it is questionable as to whether or not we should consider intervening in offending that is limited to adolescence, particularly when this relates specifically to status offences. For example, Jennings, Gibson and Lanza-Kaduce's (2009) analysed the Klein and Maxson's (2010) data which examined the effectiveness of three different types of intervention for young people who had engaged in status offences in the US. The three approaches employed by the interventions were: deterrence, treatment and normalisation. They found that the treatment approach was associated with the poorest self-concept, whereas the normalisation model was associated with the best self-concept. A negative correlation was found between number of prior arrests and self-concept, which might lend some support for the notion of a stigmatising effect of involvement with the criminal justice system; a 'snare' according to Moffitt (1993) for would-have-been adolescent-limited offenders. Finally, positive associations were found between self-concept and time spent with family, support from extended family and level of engagement in homework. Overall, the findings suggested that agencies that adopted the normalisation approach, which viewed status offences as just part of normal adolescent behaviour, had a favourable impact on young people's self-concept that was twice that found to be associated with agencies that adopted deterrence-based interventions (e.g. those that deliver quick and severe penalties for transgressions).

Promoting positive mental health and preventing offending behaviour

While most parents automatically form secure attachments with their off-spring, there are others who are likely to experience difficulty in this endeavour. Factors that have been found to impact on the quality of the emotional bond between parents and their young children can be classified as being parent-related, child-related or contextual issues. Parent-related factors are those that are more highly associated with insecure attachments and include teenage parenthood, maternal depression, having a period of out-of-home care, unresolved trauma or loss, learning disability, chronic/enduring mental illness, substance misuse, dysfunctional attitudes towards the child and own lack of security. Child-related factors include premature birth, low birth-weight and difficult temperament. Social factors relate to the availability of role models and social support, poverty, poor education and lack of employment opportunities for the parents of the child.

Importantly, most risk factors do not manifest in isolation. Rather, one risk factor is likely to be associated with a host of other risk factors. For example, women who have experienced out-of-home care are more likely to have unresolved trauma, become teenage parents (which poses a greater risk of having a premature and hence low birth-weight baby), to have their own attachment insecurities, to live in poverty and to lack social support from the wider family. This means that there are some groups of individuals who are likely to be seen as 'risky' parents by dint of their own life circumstances. Although this is not to say that all people with these combinations of circumstances will be bad parents.

There are three levels of intervention that have been developed to assist such parents to create secure and protective environments for their children (Svanberg, 1998). These are educational, social and emotional support, and psychological treatments and therapy. More recently, Egeland (2009) proposed that there are just two broad types of intervention programmes that aim to enrich the quality of the relationship between infants and their primary caregivers:

- First, there are interventions which aim to assist caregivers to become appropriately responsive to the infant's needs and able to more accurately recognise their signalling cues. Such interventions are most likely to take the form of psycho-educational training, which can be applied to groups of parents, particularly those who are deemed at risk for experiencing difficulties with parenting.
- Second, there are the interventions which aim to encourage parents (particularly mothers) to reflect on and possibly alter their own perspectives of being the object of parenting. This type of intervention aims to assist parents to resolve their own experiences of insecure attachments. The rationale for this comes from evidence of the intergenerational transmission of attachment insecurity. For example, a child's attachment style at one year, as indicated by their reaction in the Strange Situation Test (SST, see Chapter 13), has been predicted pre-birth purely on the basis of the mother's description of her own childhood experiences and relationships with caregivers, with accuracies of 75% (Steele, Steele & Fonagy, 1996) and 81% (Beniot & Parker, 1994). This type of intervention is more likely to consist of individual counselling or psychotherapeutic sessions.

With regards to the effectiveness of the interventions, Egeland (2009) contends that the longer-term cost-benefits of attachment interventions remain largely speculative. That is, there is a paucity of research which prospectively assesses the impact of early interventions on later mental health or offending outcomes. Rather, most of the intervention evaluations have been based on fairly limited periods of follow-up and the outcomes assessed have typically been restricted to changes in parental sensitivity and infant attachment. One such comparative evaluation was conducted by Cicchetti and colleagues and the results were published in 2006 and 2013. The study examined the potential differential impact of two different interventions to a no-intervention control group for mothers of infants who had been abused. The two interventions were infant–parent psychotherapy (IPP) (Lieberman, Weston & Pawl, 1991) and the Nurse Family Partnership Programme (Olds et al., 1986), a psycho-educational training programme which focused on parenting skills, stress management and social support.

Information box 20.1: Infant–parent psychotherapy

Infant–parent psychotherapy (IPP) is based on the work of Fraiberg, Adleson and Shapiro (1975) and has proven to be effective in engendering secure attachment in high-risk families, particularly immigrant families with a low income (Lieberman, 1992). Rather than see problems as arising from a lack of parenting knowledge or skill alone, IPP focuses on the idea that maltreating parents may have difficulties relating to their infant because of internal, insecure models that arose due to their own experiences in childhood. Moreover, interactions with the infant can evoke memories and emotions from the parent's relationship with their own parents, which in turn can be projected onto the infant, leading to distorted perceptions and insensitive care. Rather than an individual (a parent or infant) being the patient, in IPP it is the relationship between the mother and the infant that is central. Sessions involve the mother and therapist jointly observing the infant and exploring the parent's understanding and misperceptions of the infant. The therapist attempts to allow any distorted emotions and perceptions of the infant that are displayed by the mother to become associated with emotions and perceptions from the mother's own childhood. The aim of this process, which is conducted through an unfailingly positive, supportive and non-directive approach (which also includes developmental guidance), is for the mother to learn to differentiate their current relationship with their infant from their own past relationships, and ultimately to form positive representations of their current relationship with their infant.

The study recruited 137 infants, who were approximately 12 months old, from maltreating families, and a non-maltreated comparison group of 52 infants. Both interventions were delivered for a 12-month period, during which time both interventions were equally associated with improvements in both parent sensitivity and an increase in attachment security in comparison to the no-intervention control group (Cicchetti, Rogosch & Toth, 2006). However, at the subsequent 12-month follow-up the psychotherapeutic intervention demonstrated a superior impact above that found for both the educational training programme and the no-intervention condition (Stronach et al., 2013).

However, these findings have not always been replicated. A number of meta-analyses have been conducted on the effectiveness of attachment interventions to enhance parental sensitivity and the infants' attachment security (e.g. Van Ijzendoorn et al., 1992). These have produced inconsistent findings regarding which type of intervention is preferable.

Conclusion

Throughout this chapter we have explored possible factors, and preventative interventions, that can help individuals avoid negative health outcomes and offending behaviour. It is worth remembering that all too often prevention programmes, particularly those provided through state agencies, focus on stopping negative outcomes rather than on fostering positive outcomes, and that although prevention is usually preferable to treatment, there are downsides to models that locate problems at an individual level and ignore structural problems such as poverty. Nor should the power of labelling be ignored, and it is critical that in designing and implementing prevention programmes, marginalised and at-risk individuals and families are not demonised further by being branded with yet another negative label.

In the end, though, it certainly seems likely that a far greater emphasis needs to be placed on prevention rather than treatment, in the case of both mental health and offending behaviour. We began the chapter by looking at the case of Peter Woolf, and it is worth reflecting just how different his life might have been if the intervention that eventually helped him had been introduced *before* the addiction and criminal offending that ruined the first part of his life.

Suggestions for further reading

Paylor, I. (2011). Youth justice in England and Wales: a risky business. *Journal of Offender Rehabilitation, 50,* 22–33.
This text provides a useful description and critique of risk factor-based research and prevention paradigms.

Stronach, E. P., Toth, S. L., Rogosch, F., & Cicchetti, D. (2013). Preventive interventions and sustained attachment security in maltreated children. *Development and Psychopathology, 25*(4pt1), 919–930.
This article provides more detail on the PPI and other intervention models, and describes a study exploring their effectiveness.

CONCLUSION

Over the course of this book you have been introduced to the fascinating themes and debates at the intersections of counselling and forensic psychology, and mental health and crime. You have considered who is seen as 'mad' or 'bad' by professionals, mainstream media and by society more widely, and what this means for how people are then treated. You have learned more about the ways in which criminal behaviour and mental health struggles are influenced by race, gender, age and class, and you have examined issues around sex and sexuality in both forensic and therapeutic settings. You have explored the tensions and challenges of working therapeutically in these settings and been introduced to four therapeutic approaches and how they are applied in a forensic context. Finally, you have examined some of the current debates in forensic and therapeutic practice, as well as the importance of prevention of mental health problems and offending behaviours. At the end of this book we very much hope that reading the twenty chapters has helped you to develop a much greater knowledge and understanding of the vital relationship between counselling and forensic psychology, and related fields of practice.

We now want to take a critical look back over some of the key themes and tensions running through the book before providing you with a table of helpful resources and services for coping with mental health difficulties and for victims and perpetrators of crime – which you will find at the end of this conclusion.

Throughout the preceding chapters, hopefully the similarities between mental health difficulties and criminal behaviour and activities have become apparent. Both kinds of problems tend to be categorised and treated as forms of deviance from established social norms and rules. Also, similar social forces impact on the perception of behaviour as criminal or mentally disturbed, for example stereotypes around race, gender, class and age. The media plays a central role in defining which kind of behaviour should be seen as 'normal' (meaning in line with social norms and expectations) or deviant (Chapter 3), as well as in reinforcing these kinds of stereotypes. Diagnoses used in the medical and criminal justice system have the power to cement the categorisation of a behaviour as either unlawful or mentally abnormal, or indeed as both (Chapter 4).

The view of mental health difficulties and offending as different types of social deviance implies that both kinds of problems are to a good deal socially constructed and affected (Gregoriou, 2012). We have seen that the way society looks at crime and mental health has changed over time (think, for example, of how the views about sexual activities have changed dramatically depending on time period and context – Chapter 11) and will continue to change in the future. Whether someone is classified as having mental health problems (and therefore in need of psychiatric or therapeutic treatment) or being criminal (and therefore in need of criminal justice intervention) depends on the prevailing social norms, rules and laws in a society. We have seen that this will also be impacted by the socially constructed view of a person's race, gender, age and class and the social labelling of actions and behaviours as problematic (Chapters 5–8). Finally, broader structural factors, such as poverty, social exclusion and deprivation, have been proven to play a crucial role in the onset and persistence of mental health problems and crime (Chapter 8).

However, in the wake of the medicalisation of crime and mental health problems in our Western societies (Chapter 18), a rather individualised view of people with mental health problems, as well as perpetrators and victims of crime, often prevails. This perspective largely ignores social influences and structural disparities, and instead locates the causes of mental health problems and offending, and the focus of treatment, within the psychology and minds of individuals (Harvey & Smedley, 2010). We explored examples of some of the effects of this approach throughout this book, including the victimisation of people who experience sexual or domestic violence, who are often blamed or regarded as personally culpable for the assault (Chapter 10), and also the development of concepts such as psychopathy and personality disorder that are used to explain anti-social and criminal behaviour through individual dysfunction (Chapters 2 and 4). Mills and Kendall (2010) argued that forensic services and the 'therapunitive' prison (combining punishment and therapy for inmates) 'also serves to individualise crime and to deflect attention away from structural issues, such as poverty, racism, sexism, violence and poor educational attainment, involved in both crime and punishment' (p. 42).

Counsellors and psychotherapists, whether working in forensic settings or other contexts, need to be aware of the risk that therapeutic work, with its focus on individual functioning and how people perceive the world, may unwillingly reinforce individualised views of crime and mental health problems. For example, David Smail (1998) argued that counselling and psychotherapy are in danger of taking the focus away from broader socio-political issues and the real-life problems people are experiencing. This highlights the need for professionals working in mental health and criminal justice services to pay attention to different levels of social context (from the individual to the broader society) 'rather than developing an individual pathological model of behaviour' (Harvey & Smedley, 2010, p. 15). As we have seen throughout the book, adopting a contextual and systemic approach (Chapter 15) can enable practitioners and service users to consider the social relatedness of mental health problems and criminal behaviour.

We hope this book has helped to deconstruct dominant ideas, like the individualised view of crime and mental health problems, in our society and that it will allow practitioners and service users alike to think outside and beyond 'mad or bad' terminologies and understandings.

The *Mad or Bad?* editor team

LISTS OF HELPFUL RESOURCES AND SERVICES

Please find below a table with helpful resources and services for coping with mental health difficulties and for victims and perpetrators of crime. More detail and services can be found at the 'Information & Support' section of the website of the mental health charity Mind (www.mind.org.uk/information-support/).

General mental health problems	*Samaritans* www.samaritans.org 24-hour freephone helpline: 116 123 jo@samaritans.org 24-hour emotional support for anyone struggling to cope
	Elefriends elefriends.org.uk Elefriends is a friendly, supportive online community for people experiencing a mental health problem.
	British Association for Counselling and Psychotherapy (BACP) Tel: 01455 88 33 00 itsgoodtotalk.org.uk BACP is the membership body for counsellors and therapists. They provide information on different types of therapy and you can search for a therapist by area.
	Mind Infoline Tel: 0300 123 3393 (Monday to Friday 9am to 6pm) info@mind.org.uk Details of local Minds, other local services, and Mind's Legal Advice Line.

(Continued)

(Continued)

	Rethink Mental Illness Tel: 0300 5000 927 rethink.org Information for carers including a carer's assessment pack, message board and sibling support network. *Carers Trust* carers.org matter.carers.org (online community for young carers aged 16-25) Information and support for carers, including an online chatroom.
Domestic violence	*Refuge* Helpline: 0808 2000 247 (Freephone 24-hour National Domestic Violence Helpline. Run in partnership between Women's Aid and Refuge) info@refuge.org.uk / refuge.org.uk *Women's Aid (England)* helpline@womensaid.org.uk *Welsh Women's Aid* Helpline: 0808 80 10 800 Email: via website: welshwomensaid.org.uk *Men's Advice Line* Helpline: 0808 801 0327 (Monday– Friday 10am–1pm and 2pm– 5pm) info@mensadviceline.org.uk / mensadviceline.org.uk Confidential helpline for all men (whether in heterosexual or same-sex relationships) experiencing domestic violence by a current or ex-partner. *National LGBT Domestic Abuse Hotline* Helpline: 0800 999 5428, Email: help@galop.org.uk www.galop.org.uk/domesticabuse/ Confidential helpline for LGBT people experiencing domestic abuse.
Sexual abuse	*CIS'ters (Childhood Incest Survivors)* PO Box 119, Eastleigh SO50 92F Tel: 023 8033 8080 admin@cisters.org.uk Help and support for adult women who suffered incest as a child. Workshops and conferences to raise awareness on the issues surrounding incest, particularly mental distress. *Rape Crisis (England and Wales)* National freephone helpline: 0808 802 9999 (12–12.30pm, 7–9.30pm every day of the year) Email: info@rapecrisis.org.uk rapecrisis.org.uk

	Lists local organisations throughout England and Wales with contact details, services offered and opening times. Services are available to women who have been sexually abused at any time in their lives. *Mankind* Tel: 01273 911 680 Email: admin@mankindcounselling.org.uk mankindcounselling.org.uk Provides one-to-one counselling, therapeutic groups and couple counselling to men (age 18+) who have experienced sexual abuse at any time in their lives. *Survivors UK* Text: 020 3322 1860, Email: help@survivorsuk.org www.survivorsuk.org Provides support for men who have been raped or sexually abused. Also provides face-to-face counselling and support groups in some areas. *Sexual Assault Casework & Support Service* Tel: 0207 704 2040, Email: referrals@galop.org.uk www.galop.org.uk/sexualviolence/ Confidential advice and support for LGBT people who have experienced sexual assault.
Victims of crime	*Victim support* www.victimsupport.org.uk Provides support for victims of all kinds of crime in moving forward. *UK Government Resources* www.gov.uk/get-support-as-a-victim-of-crime
Perpetrators	*Respect* Tel: 0845 122 8609, Email: info@respectphoneline.org.uk www.respectphoneline.org.uk Helpline offering information and advice to people who are abusive towards their partners and want help to stop.
	StopSO Tel: 07473 29983 www.stopso.org.uk/ Specialist treatment organisation for the Prevention of Sexual Offending, working with those at risk of sexual offending or reoffending to enable them to stop acting.

REFERENCES

8 ER 718, [1843] UKHL J16. (1843). United Kingdom House of Lords Decisions. Daniel McNaughtan's Case. May 26, June 19, 1843. British and Irish Legal Information Institute. Retrieved from www.bailii.org/uk/cases/UKHL/1843/J16.html.

Absalom, V., McGovern, J., Goodiung, P. A., & Tarrier, N. (2010). An assessment of patient need for family intervention in forensic services and staff skill in implementing family intervention. *The Journal of Forensic Psychiatry and Psychology, 21*, 350–365.

Ainsworth, M. D. S. (1973). The development of infant mother attachment. In B. Caldwell & H. Ricciuti (Eds.), *Review of child development research* (Vol. 3, pp. 1–94). Chicago, IL: University of Chicago Press.

Ainsworth, M. D. S., Blehar, M. C., Waters, E., & Wall, S. (1978). *Patterns of attachment: assessed in a strange situation and at home.* Hillsdale, NJ: Lawrence Erlbaum.

Albach, F., Moormann, P., & Bermond, B. (1996). Memory recovery of childhood sexual abuse. *Dissociation, 9*, 261–273.

Aleman, A., Kahn, R. S., & Selten, J. P. (2003). Sex differences in the risk of schizophrenia: evidence from meta-analysis. *Archives of General Psychiatry, 60*(6), 565–571.

Allen, D. M. (1980). Young male prostitutes: a psychosocial study. *Archives of Sexual Behavior, 9*(5), 399–426.

Allen-Collinson, J. (2009). A marked man: a case of female-perpetrated intimate partner abuse. *International Journal of Men's Health, 8*(1), 22–40.

Altemus, M., Sarvaiya, N., & Neill Epperson, C. (2014). Sex differences in anxiety and depression clinical perspectives. *Frontiers in Neuroendocrinology, 35*(3), 320–330.

Altman, D. (1999). Foreword. In P. Aggleton (Ed.), *Men who sell sex: international perspectives on male prostitution and HIV/AIDS* (pp. xiii–xix). London: UCL Press.

Amado, B. G., Arce, R., Farina, F., & Vilarino, M. (2016). Criteria-based content analysis (CBCA) reality criteria in adult: a meta-analytic review. *International Journal of Clinical and Health Psychology, 16*(2), 201–210.

Amado, B. G., Arce, R., & Farina, F. (2015). Undeutsch hypothesis and criteria-based content analysis: a meta-analytic review. *The European Journal of Psychology Applied to Legal Context, 7*, 3–12.

American Psychiatric Association (1952). *Diagnostic and statistical manual of mental disorders.* Washington, DC: APA.

American Psychiatric Association (1968). *Diagnostic and statistical manual of mental disorders* (2nd ed.). Washington, DC: APA.

American Psychiatric Association (1973). Homosexuality and sexual orientation disturbance: proposed change in DSM-II, 6th printing, page 44 Position Statement. Retrieved 8 March 2011 from www.psychiatryonline.com/.

American Psychiatric Association (1980). *Diagnostic and statistical manual of mental disorders* (3rd ed.). Washington, DC: APA.

American Psychiatric Association (2000). *Diagnostic and statistical manual of mental disorders* (4th ed.). Washington, DC: APA.

American Psychiatric Association (2009). *Report on gender identity and gender variance*. Washington, DC: APA.

American Psychiatric Association (2010). Paraphilic coercive disorder: proposed revision. Retrieved 6 November 2010 from www.dsm5.org.

American Psychiatric Association (2012). The guidelines for psychological practice with lesbian, gay and bisexual clients. *American Psychologist, 67*(1), 10–42. Retrieved 21 December 2016 from www.apa.org/pi/lgbt/resources/guidelines.aspx

American Psychiatric Association (2013). *Diagnostic and statistical manual of mental disorders* (5th ed.). Washington, DC: APA.

American Psychiatric Association (2015). Guidelines for psychological practice with transgender and gender nonconforming people American Psychological Association. *American Psychologist, 70*(9), 832–864.

Amnesty International (2016). Decision on state obligations to respect, protect, and fulfil the human rights of sex workers. The International Council Decision. Amnesty International. Retrieved 24 January 2017 from www.amnesty.org/en/policy-on-state-obligations-to-respect-protect-and-fulfil-the-human-rights-of-sex-workers/.

Andersen, T. (1987). The reflecting team: dialogue and meta-dialogue in clinical work. *Family Process, 26*, 415–428.

Anderson, I., & Doherty, K. (2007). *Accounting for rape: psychology, feminism and discourse analysis in the study of sexual violence*. London: Routledge.

Andrews, B., Brewin, C. R., Ochera, J., Morton, J., Bekerian, D. A., Davies, G. M., & Mollon, P. (1999). Characteristics, context and consequences of memory recovery among adults in therapy. *British Journal of Psychiatry, 75*, 141–146.

Andrews, B., Brewin, C. R., Ochera, J., Morton, J., Bekerian, D. A., Davies, G. M., & Mollon, P. (2000). The process of memory recovery among adults in therapy. *British Journal of Clinical Psychology, 39*, 11–26.

Andrews, D. A., & Bonta, J. (2010). *The psychology of criminal conduct* (5th ed.). New Providence, NJ: LexisNexis.

Andrews, D. A., Bonta, J., & Wormith, J. S. (2011). The risk-need-responsivity (RNR) model: does adding the Good Lives Model contribute to effective crime prevention? *Criminal Justice and Behavior, 38*, 735–755.

Angermeyer, M. C., & Matschinger, H. (2003). The stigma of mental illness: effects of labelling on public attitudes towards people with mental disorder. *Acta Psychiatrica Scandinavica, 108*(4), 304–309.

Annsseau, M., Fischler, B., Dierick, M., Albert, A., Leyman, S., & Mignon, A. (2008). Socio-economic correlates of generalised anxiety and manic depression in primary care. *Depression and Anxiety, 25*, 506–513.

Ansara, Y. G., & Hegarty, P. (2011). Cisgenderism in psychology: pathologizing and misgendering children from 1999 to 2008. *Psychology & Sexuality*, iFirst, 1–24. doi: 10.1080/19419899.2011.576696.

Appignanesi, L. (2008). *Mad, bad and sad: a history of women and the mind doctors from 1800 to the present day*. London: Virago.

Arcelus, J., Claes, L., Witcomb, G., Marshall, E., & Bouman, W. (2016). Risk factors for non-suicidal self-injury among trans youth. *Journal of Sexual Medicine, 13*, 402–412.

Archer, M. (2000) *Being human: the problem of agency*. Cambridge: Cambridge University Press.

Ariel, E. (director/producer), & Menahemi, A. (director) (1997). *Doing time, doing Vipassana* [Film]. India: Karuna Films.

Armstrong, E. A., Hamilton, L. T., Armstrong, E. M., & Seeley, J. L. (2014). Gender, social class, and slut discourse on campus. *Social Psychology Quarterly, 77*(2), 100–122.

Arnett, J. (2007). Emerging adulthood: what is it, and what is it good for? *Child Development Perspectives, 1*(2), 68–73.

Arseneault, L., Moffitt, T., Caspi, A., Taylor, P., & Silva, P. (2000). Mental disorders and violence in a total birth cohort: results from the Dunedin Study. *Archives of General Psychiatry, 57*(10), 979–986.

Asen, E. (2002). Multiple family therapy: an overview. *Journal of Family Therapy, 24*, 3–16.

Athanasiades, C. (2008). Systemic thinking and circular questioning in therapy with individuals. *Counselling Psychology Review, 23*, 5–13.

Atkins, C. (2014). *Co-occurring disorders: integrated assessment and treatment of substance use and mental disorders*. Eau Claire, WI: PESI Publishing.

Attwood, F. (2006). Sexed up: theorizing the sexualization of culture. *Sexualities, 9*(1), 77–94.

Auty, K. M., Cope, A., & Liebling, A. (2015). A systematic review of meta-analysis of yoga and mindfulness meditation in prison: effects on psychological well-being and behavioural functioning. *International Journal of Offender Therapy and Comparative Criminology, 60*(13), 1–22.

Babiak, P., & Hare, R. D. (2006). *Snakes in suits: when psychopaths go to work*. New York: Regan Books.

Bakker, D., Kazantzis, N., Rickwood, D., & Rickard, N. (2016). Mental health smartphone apps: review and evidence-based recommendations for future developments. *JMIR Mental Health, 3*, e7.

Bamshad, M., Wooding, S., Salisbury, B. A., & Stephens, J. C. (2004). Deconstructing the relationship between genetics and race. *Nature Reviews Genetics, 5*, 598–609.

Bancroft, J. (1974). *Deviant sexual behaviour: modification and assessment*. Oxford: Oxford University Press.

Bandura, A. (1977). Self-efficacy: toward a unifying theory of behavioural change. *Psychology Review, 84*, 191–215.

Barker, M-J., & Hancock, J. (2017). *Enjoy sex (how, when and if you want to): a practical and inclusive guide*. London: Icon.

Barker, M-J., & Richards, C. (2015). Further genders. In M-J. Barker & C. Richards (Eds.), *The Palgrave handbook of the psychology of sexuality and gender* (pp. 166–182). London: Palgrave Macmillan.

Barker, M-J. (2011). Existential sex therapy. *Sex & Relationship Therapy, 26,* 33–47.

Barker, M-J. (2013a). Consent is a grey area? A comparison of understandings of consent in *Fifty Shades of Grey* and on the BDSM blogosphere. *Sexualities, 18*(8), 896–914.

Barker, M-J. (2013b). *Mindful counselling & psychotherapy: practising mindfully across approaches and issues.* London: Sage.

Barker, M-J. (2015). Social mindfulness. Retrieved 30 January 2016 from http://rewritingtherules.files.wordpress.com/2015/07/socialmindfulnesszine.pdf.

Barker, M-J., Vossler, A., & Langdridge, D. (2010). Conclusions. In M-J. Barker, A. Vossler, & D. Langdridge (Eds.), *Understanding counselling and psychotherapy* (pp. 327–343). London: Sage.

Barnes, J. C. (2012). Analyzing the origins of life-course-persistent offending: a consideration of environmental and genetic influences. *Criminal Justice and Behavior, 40*(5), 519–540.

Barr, B., Kinderman, P., & Whitehead, M. (2015). Trends in mental health inequalities in England during a period of recession, austerity and welfare reform 2004 to 2013. *Social Science & Medicine, 147,* 324–331.

Barraclough, B. M., & Mitchell-Heggs, N. A. (1978). Use of neurosurgery for psychological disorder in the British Isles during 1974-6. *British Medical Journal, 2*(6152), 1591–1593.

Barry, M. (2007). Youth offending and youth transitions: the power of capital in influencing change. *Critical Criminology, 15,* 185–198.

Bartlett, A., Smith, G., & King, M. (2009). The response of mental health professionals to clients seeking help to change or redirect same-sex sexual orientation. *BMC Psychiatry, 9,* 11.

Basson, R. (2002). A model of women's sexual arousal. *Journal of Sex and Marital Therapy, 28,* 1–10.

Basson, R., Brotto, L., Laan, E., Redmond, G., & Utian, W. (2005). Assessment and management of women's sexual dysfunctions: problematic desire and arousal. *Journal of Sex and Marital Therapy, 2,* 291–300.

Batchelor, M. (2001). *Meditation for life.* London: Frances Lincoln.

Bateman, A., Brown, D., & Pedder, J. (1991). *Introduction to psychotherapy: an outline of psychodynamic principles and practice* (2nd ed.). London: Routledge.

Bateson, G., Jackson, D., Hayley, J., & Weakland, J. (1956). Towards a theory of schizophrenia. *Behavioural Science, 1,* 173–198.

Batrinos, M. L. (2012). Testosterone and aggressive behavior in man. *International Journal of Endocrinology and Metabolism, 10*(3), 563–568.

Baumeister, R. F. (2001). *Evil: inside human violence and cruelty.* New York: Henry Holt.

Bayer, R. (1981). *Homosexuality and American psychiatry: the politics of diagnosis.* Princeton, NJ: Princeton University Press.

BBC (2006). Man charged with Suffolk murders. *BBC News.* 21 December 2006. Retrieved 21 December 2016 from http://news.bbc.co.uk/1/hi/england/suffolk/6194351.stm

Beck, A. T. (1963). Thinking and depression. I. Idiosyncratic content and cognitive distortions. *Archive of General Psychiatry, 9,* 324–333.

Beck, A. T. (1969). *Depression: clinical, experimental, and theoretical aspects.* London: Staple Press.

Beck, J. S. (1995). *Cognitive therapy: basics and beyond.* New York and London: Guilford Press.

Beckett, K. (1996). Culture and the politics of signification: the case of child sexual abuse. *Social Problems, 43*(1), 57–75.

Beckley, A., Caspi, A., Harrington, H., Houts, R., Mcgee, T., Morgan, N., Schroeder, F., Ramrakha, S., Poulton, R., & Moffitt, T. (2016). Adult-onset offenders: is a tailored theory warranted? *Journal of Criminal Justice, 46,* 64–81.

Beiber, I., Dain, H., Dince, P., Drellich, M., Grand, H., Gundlach, R., ... & Bieber, T. (1962). *Homosexuality: a psychoanalytic study of male homosexuals.* New York: Basic Books.

Beitel, M., Ferrer, E., & Cecero, J. J. (2004). Psychological mindedness and cognitive style. *Journal of Clinical Psychology, 60*(6), 567–582.

Bell, E. (2013). Punishment as politics: the penal system in England and Wales. In V. Ruggiero & M. Ryan (Eds.), *Punishment in Europe: a critical anatomy of penal systems* (pp. 58–85). London: Palgrave Macmillan.

Belli, R. F., & Loftus, E. F. (1994). The pliability of autobiographical memory: misinformation and the false memory problem. In D. C. Rubin (Ed.), *Remembering our past: studies in autobiographical memory* (pp. 157–179). New York: Cambridge University Press.

Bennett-Levy, J. (2004). *Oxford guide to behavioural experiments in cognitive therapy.* Oxford: Oxford University Press.

Benoit, D., & Parker, K. C. H. (1994). Stability and transmission of attachment across three generations. *Child Development, 65,* 1444–1456.

Bensley, L. S., Eenwyk, J. V., & Simmons, K. W. (2000). Self-reported childhood sexual and physical abuse and adult HIV-risk behaviours and heavy drinking. *American Journal of Preventive Medicine, 18,* 151–158.

Bentall, R. P. (2004). *Madness explained: psychosis and human nature.* Hammondsworth: Penguin.

Berant, E., Mikulincer, M., & Shaver, P. R. (2008). Mothers' attachment style, their mental health, and their children's emotional vulnerabilities: a seven-year study of children with congenital heart disease. *Journal of Personality, 76,* 31–66.

Bernstein, E. (2007). Sex work for the middle classes. *Sexualities, 10*(4), 473–488.

Bersani, L. (1987). Is the rectum a grave? *AIDS: Cultural Analysis/Cultural Activism, 43,* 197–222.

Berzins, L. G., & Trestman, R. L. (2004). The development and implementation of dialectical behavior therapy in forensic settings. *International Journal of Forensic Mental Health, 3*(1), 93–103.

Betchen, S. (2009). Premature ejaculation: an integrative, intersystem approach for couples. In K. Hertlein, G. Weeks, & N. Gambescia (Eds.), *Systemic sex therapy* (pp. 131–152). New York: Routledge.

Beyond Belief (2014). Mindfulness. *Beyond Belief.* Radio 4, 26 May. Accessed 30 January 2016 from www.bbc.co.uk/programmes/b044gp6f.

Bhui, K. (Ed.) (2002). *Racism and mental health: prejudice and suffering.* London: Jessica Kingsley Publishers.

Bienville, M. (1771). *La nymphomanie ou traité de la fureur uterine.* Amsterdam: M. M. Rey.

Bingham, C., & Smith, R. (2012). Including families in therapy: challenges and opportunities. *Context, 124,* 25–28.

Binik, Y., & Meana, M. (2009). The future of sex therapy: specialization or marginalization? *Archives of Sexual Behaviour, 38,* 1016–1027.

Birch, M. (2012). *Mediating mental health: contexts, debates and analysis.* Farnham and Burlington: Ashgate.

Bisson, J., & Andrew, M. (2007). *Psychological treatment of post-traumatic stress disorder (PTSD)* (Review). New York: Wiley.

Black, M. C., Basile, K. C., Breiding, M. J., Smith, S. G., Walters, M. L., Merrick, M. T., & Stevens, M. R. (2011). *National intimate partner and sexual violence survey.* Atlanta, GA: Centers for Disease Control and Prevention.

Blackman, L., & Walkerdine, V. (2001). *Mass hysteria: critical psychology and media studies.* Basingstoke: Palgrave.

Blanchard, R. (1989). The concept of autogynephilia and the typology of male gender dysphoria. *Journal of Nervous and Mental Disease, 177,* 616–623.

Blanchette, K., & Brown, S. L. (2006). *The assessment and treatment of women offenders: an integrative perspective.* Chichester: John Wiley.

Blandon-Gitlin, I., Pezdek, K., Lindsay, D. S., & Hagen, L. (2009). Criteria-based content analysis of true and suggested accounts of events. *Applied Cognitive Psychology, 23*(7), 901–917.

Bloom, S. (1997). *Creating sanctuary: toward the evolution of sane societies.* London: Routledge.

Bohart, A. C., & Wade, A. G. (2013). The client in psychotherapy. In M. J. Lambert (Ed.), *Bergin and Garfield's handbook of psychotherapy and behavior change* (6th ed.) (pp. 219–257). Hoboken, NJ: Wiley & Sons.

Bond, T. (2010). *Standards and ethics for counselling in action* (3rd ed.). London: Sage.

Bond, T., & Mitchels, B. (2014). *Confidentiality and record keeping in counselling and psychotherapy.* London: Sage.

Borochowitz, D. Y. (2008). The taming of the shrew: batterers' constructions of their wives' narratives. *Violence Against Women, 14,* 1166–1180.

Bourdieu, P. (2002). The forms of capital. In N. W. Biggart (Ed.), *Readings in economic sociology* (pp. 280–291). Oxford: Blackwell.

Bowen, S., Chawla, N., & Marlatt, G. A. (2010). *Mindfulness-based relapse prevention: a clinician's guide.* New York: Guilford Press.

Bowen, S., & Marlatt, A. (2009). Surfing the urge: brief mindfulness-based intervention for college student smokers. *Psychology of Addictive Behaviors, 23,* 666–671.

Bowl, R. (2007a). The need for change in UK mental health services: South Asian service users' views. *Ethnicity and Health, 12*(1), 1–19.

Bowl, R. (2007b). Responding to ethnic diversity: black service users' views of mental health services in the UK. *Diversity in Health and Social Care, 4,* 201–210.

Bowlby, J. (1982). *Attachment and loss. Vol. 1: Attachment.* London: Hogarth Press and the Institute of Psycho-Analysis. (Original work published in 1969.)

Bowlby, J. (1988). *A secure base: clinical applications of attachment theory.* London: Routledge.

Bowling, B., & Phillips, C. (2007). Disproportionate and discriminatory: reviewing the evidence on police stop and search. *Modern Law Review, 70,* 936–961.

Bradley Report (2009). *Lord Bradley's review of people with mental health problems or learning disabilities in the criminal justice system.* London: Department of Health.

Braslow, J. T. (1999). History and evidence-based medicine: lessons from the history of somatic treatments from the 1900s to the 1950s. *Mental Health Services Research, 1*(4), 231–240.

Breggin, P. (1993). *Toxic psychiatry: drugs and electroconvulsive therapy, the truth and better alternatives.* London: Harper Collins.

Brennan, T., & Hegarty, P. (2007). Who was Magnus Hirschfeld and why do we need to know? *History and Philosophy of Psychology, 9*(1), 12–28.

Brewin, C., Andrews, B., & Gotlib, I. (1995). Psychopathology and early experience. *Psychological Bulletin, 113,* 82–98.

British Association for Counselling and Psychotherapy (2016a). *Ethical framework for the counselling professions.* Rugby: BACP.

British Association for Counselling and Psychotherapy (2016b). *Ethics and standards.* Rugby: BACP. Retrieved 31 July 2016 from www.bacp.co.uk/ethical_framework/ethics.php.

British Psychological Society (2008). *Professional practice guidelines: overview of general good clinical practice guidelines including confidentiality, note-keeping and supervision.* Leicester: BPS.

British Psychological Society (2012). *Guidelines and literature review for psychologists working therapeutically with sexual and gender minority clients.* Leicester: BPS. Retrieved 31 July 2016 from www.bps.org.uk/sites/default/files/images/rep_92.pdf.

Bronfenbrenner, U. (1979). *The ecology of human development: experiments by design and nature.* Cambridge, MA: Harvard University Press.

Brookman, F. (2005). *Understanding homicide.* London: Sage.

Brooks-Gordon,B. (2006). *The price of sex: prostitution, policy and society.* Cullompton: Willan.

Brown, D. P., Scheflin A. W., & Hammond, D. C. (1998). *Memory, trauma treatment and the law.* New York: W. W. Norton.

Brown, E., & Males, M. (2011). Does age or poverty level best predict criminal arrest and homicide rates? A preliminary investigation. *Justice Policy Journal, 8*(1), 1–30.

Brown, K. (2011). Beyond 'badges of honour': young people's perceptions of their anti-social behaviour orders. *People, Place & Policy Online, 5*(1), 12–24.

Brunwasser, S. M., Gilham, J. E., & Kim, E. S. (2009). A meta-analytic review of the Penn Resiliency Programme's effect on depressive symptoms. *Journal of Consulting and Clinical Psychology, 77,* 1042–1054.

Buckland, R. (2016). The decision by approved mental health professionals to use compulsory powers under the Mental Health Act 1983: a Foucauldian discourse analysis. *British Journal of Social Work, 46*(1), 46–62.

Buñuel, L. (1967). *Belle de Jour* [Film]. Paris: Paris Film Productions.

Bureau of Justice Statistics (2016). Percent of rape/sexual assaults by reporting to the police, 2011–2014. Generated using the NCVS victimisation analysis tool at www.bjs.gov. Retrieved 11 July 2016.

Burnam, M. A., Stein, J. A., Golding, J. M., Siegel, J. M., Sorenson, S. B., Forsythe, A. B., & Telles, C. A. (1988). Sexual assault and mental disorders in a community population. *Journal of Consulting and Clinical Psychology, 56*(6), 843–850.

Burns, D. D. (1980). *Feeling good: the new mood therapy.* New York: New American Library.

Burns, D. D. (1999). *Feeling good: the new mood therapy.* New York: Avon Books.

Busfield, J. (1994). The female malady? Men, women and madness in the nineteenth century. *Sociology, 28*(1), 259–277.

Busfield, J. (2011). *Mental illness.* Cambridge: Polity Press.

Butler, C. (2011). Breaking taboos: acknowledging therapist arousal and disgust. *Psychotherapy and Politics International, 9,* 61–66.

Butler, C., & Byrne, A. (2010). Culture, sex and sexuality. In C. Butler, A. O'Donovan, & E. Shaw (Eds.), *Sex, sexuality & therapeutic practice: a manual for trainers and clinicians* (pp. 160–180). London: Routledge.

Butler, C., & das Nair, R. (2012). *Intersectionality, sexuality and psychological therapies: working with lesbian, gay and bisexual diversity.* London: Wiley.

Butler, E., & Butler, J. (2005). The effect of structured relapse prevention planning on attitudes to recovery from depression: a review of the literature and programme planning. *Advancing Practice in Bedfordshire, 2,* 8–17.

Callaghan, J. E. M., & Clark, J. (2007). Feminist theory and conflict. In K. Ratele (Ed.), *Intergroup relations: a South African perspective* (pp. 87–110). Cape Town: Juta.

Campbell, R. (2006). Rape survivors' experiences with the legal and medical systems: do rape victim advocates make a difference? *Violence Against Women, 12,* 30–45.

Cantor-Graae, E., & Selton, J. (2005). Schizophrenia and migration: a meta-analysis and review. *American Journal of Psychiatry, 162,* 12–24.

Caplan, P. (1995). *They say you're crazy: how the world's most powerful psychiatrists decide who's normal.* Reading, MA: Addison-Wesley.

Caplan, P. (2005). *The myth of women's masochism.* Lincoln, NB: iUniverse.

Caplan, P., & Gans, M. (1991). Is there empirical justification for the category of 'self-defeating personality disorder'? *Feminism & Psychology, 1,* 263–278.

Care Quality Commission (2010). *Monitoring the use of the Mental Health Act 1983 in 2009/10.* London: CQC.

Care Quality Commission (2015). *Monitoring the use of the Mental Health Act 2014/15.* London: CQC.

Carr, W. A., Rotter, M., Steinbacher, M., Green, D., Dole, T., Garcia-Mansilla, A., Goldberg, S., & Rosenfeld, B. (2006). Structured Assessment of Correctional Adaptation (SACA): a measure of the impact of incarceration on the mentally ill in a therapeutic setting. *International Journal of Offender Therapy and Comparative Criminology, 50,* 570–581.

Caukins, S. E., & Coombs, N. R. (1976). The psychodynamics of male prostitution. *American Journal of Psychotherapy, 30*(3), 441–451.

Cemlyn, S., Greenfields, M., Burnett, S., Matthews, Z., & Whitwell, C. (2009). *Review of inequalities experienced by Gypsy and Traveller communities*. London: Equalities and Human Rights Commission (EHRC). Accessed 1 July 2016 from www.equalityhumanrights.com/en/publication-download/research-report-12-inequalities-experiences-gypsy-and-traveller-communities.

Centre Forum (2016). *Education in England: annual report 2016*. London: Centre Forum.

Chancer, L. (2000). From pornography to sadomasochism: reconciling feminist differences. *Annals of the American Academy of Political and Social Science, 571*(1), 77–88.

Cheshire, J. (2012). Lives on the line: mapping life expectancy along the London tube network. *Environment and Planning A, 44*(7). doi: 10.1068/a45341.

Chivers, M. L., Seto, M., Lalumiere, M. L., Laan, E., & Grimbos, T. (2010). Agreement of self-reported and genital measures of sexual arousal in men and women: a meta-analysis. *Archives of Sexual Behaviour, 39*, 5–56.

Chödrön, P. (1994). *The places that scare you: a guide to fearlessness*. London: HarperCollins.

Chödrön, P. (2001). *The wisdom of no escape: how to love yourself and your world*. London: HarperCollins.

Christakis, N., & Fowler, J. (2010). *Connected: the amazing power of social networks and how they shape our lives*. London: Harper Press.

Christina, G. (Ed.) (2004). *Paying for it: a guide by sex workers for their clients*. Oakland, CA: Greenery Press.

Chu, J., Frey, L., Ganzel, B., & Matthews, J. (1999). Memories of childhood abuse: dissociation, amnesia, and corroboration. *American Journal of Psychiatry, 156*, 749–755.

Cicchetti, D., Rogosch, F. A., Gunnar, M. R., & Toth, S. L. (2010). The differential impacts of early physical abuse and sexual abuse and internalizing problems on daytime cortisol rhythm in school-aged children. *Child Development, 81*, 252–269.

Cicchetti, D., Rogosch, F. A., & Toth, S. L. (2006). Fostering secure attachment in infants in maltreating families through preventive interventions. *Development and Psychopathology, 18*, 623–649.

Clark, C., Pike, C., McManus, S., Harris, J., Bebbington, P., Brugha, T., ... Stansfeld, S. (2012). The contribution of work and non-work stressors to common mental disorders in the 2007 Adult Psychiatric Morbidity Survey. *Psychological Medicine, 42*(4), 829–842.

Clarke, P. (2010). Preventing future crime with cognitive behavioural therapy. *National Institute of Justice, 265*, 22–25.

Classen, C. C., Palesh, O. G., & Aggarwal, R. (2005). Sexual revictimisation: a review of the empirical literature. *Trauma, Violence, & Abuse, 6*, 103–129.

Clemmer, D. (1940). *The prison community*. New York: Holt, Rinehart and Winston.

Cohen, J., Mannarino, D., & Deblinger, A. (2006). *Treating trauma and traumatic grief in children and adolescents*. New York: Guilford Press.

Cohen, S. (1985). *Visions of social control: crime, punishment and classification*. Cambridge: Polity Press.

Coie, J. D. (1997). Testing developmental theory of antisocial behaviour with outcomes from the Fast Track Prevention Project. Paper presented at the meeting of the American Psychological Association, Chicago, IL.

Colaizzi, J. (1989). *Homicidal insanity, 1800–1985*. Tuscaloosa, AL: University of Alabama Press.

Colman, R. A., & Widom, C. S. (2004). Childhood abuse and neglect and adult intimate relationships: a prospective study. *Child Abuse & Neglect, 28*(11), 1133–1151.

Cooper, C., Morgan, C., Byrne, M., Dazzan, P. et al. (2008). Perceptions of disadvantage, ethnicity and psychosis. *British Journal of Psychiatry, 192*, 185–190.

Cooper, C., & Roe, S. (2012). *An estimate of youth crime in England and Wales: police recorded crime by young people in 2009/10*. Research report 64. London: Home Office.

Cooper, M. (2008). *Essential research findings in counselling and psychotherapy: the facts are friendly*. London: Sage.

Corey, G., Corey, M., & Callanan, P. (2007). *Issues and ethics in the helping professions* (7th ed.). Belmont, CA: Thompson Brooks/Cole.

Cornford, C., Sibbald, B., & Baer, L. (2007). *A survey of the delivery of health care in prisons in relation to chronic diseases*. Manchester: Prison Health Research Network, Primary Care.

Cornwall, A. (2014). *Women's empowerment: what works and why?* (No. 2014/101). Helsinki: UNU-WIDER.

Corriea, K. M. (2009). *A handbook for correctional psychologists: guidance for the prison practitioner*. Charles C. Thomas.

Corrigan, P. (2004). How stigma interferes with mental health care. *American Psychologist, 59*, 614.

Cox, W. M., & Klinger, E. (2011). *Handbook of motivational counseling: goal-based approaches to assessment and intervention with addiction and other problems*. Chichester: Wiley-Blackwell.

Coy, M., Wakeling, J., & Garner, M. (2011). Selling sex sells: representations of prostitution and the sex industry in sexualised popular culture as symbolic violence. *Women's Studies International Forum, 34*(5), 441–448.

CPS (Crown Prosecution Service) (n.d.). *Rape and sexual offences*. Chapter 3: Consent. London: CPS. Retrieved 1 April 2016 from www.cps.gov.uk/legal/p_to_r/rape_and_sexual_offences/consent/.

Crane, R. (2009). *Mindfulness-based cognitive therapy*. London: Routledge.

Creeber, G. (2015). Killing us softly: investigating the aesthetics, philosophy and influence of Nordic Noir television. *Journal of Popular Television, 3*(1), 21–35.

Crenshaw, K. (1991). Mapping the margins: intersectionality, identity politics, and violence against women of color. *Stanford Law Review, 43*(6), 1241–1299.

Crenshaw, K. (1994). Mapping the margins: intersectionality, identity politics, and violence against women of color. In M. Fineman & R. Mykitiuk (Eds.), *The public nature of private violence* (pp. 93–118). New York: Routledge.

Crewe, B. (2009). *The prisoner society: power, adaptation and social life in an English prison*. Oxford: Oxford University Press.

Criminal Justice Act (1991). London: HMSO.

Crimmins, E. M., Hayward, M. D., & Seeman, T. E. (2004). Race/ethnicity, socioeconomic status, and health. In N. B. Anderson, R. A. Bulatao & B. Cohen (Eds.), *Critical perspectives on racial and ethnic differences in health in late life* (pp. 310–352). Washington, DC: National Academies Press (US).

Critcher, C. (2008). Moral panic analysis: past, present and future. *Sociology Compass, 2*(4), 1127–1144.

Cross, S. (2010). *Mediating madness: mental distress and cultural representation.* Basingstoke: Palgrave Macmillan.

Cross, S. (2014). Mad and bad media: populism and pathology in the British tabloids. *European Journal of Communication, 20*(4), 460–483.

Crowley, M. S. (2008). Three types of memory for childhood sexual abuse: relationships to characteristics of abuse and psychological symptoms. *Journal of Child Sexual Abuse, 17*, 71–88.

Cuddy, A., & Fiske, S. (2004). Doddering but dear: process, content and function in stereotyping of older persons. In T. D. Nelson (Ed.), *Ageism: stereotyping and prejudice against older persons.* Cambridge, MA: The MIT Press.

Cundy, L. (2016). Lecture notes (personal correspondence). Unpublished.

Dafoe, T., & Stermac, L. (2013). Mindfulness meditation as an adjunct approach to treatment within the correctional system. *Journal of Offender Rehabilitation, 52*(3), 198–216.

Daigneault, I., Hébert, M., & McDuff, P. (2009). Men's and women's childhood sexual abuse and victimisation in adult partner relationships: a study of risk factors. *Child Abuse & Neglect, 33*(9), 638–647.

Dallam, S. J. (2001). Crisis or creation? A systematic examination of 'false memory syndrome'. *Journal of Child Sexual Abuse, 9*(3/4), 9–36.

Dallos, R., & Draper, R. (2015). *An introduction to family therapy: systemic theory and practice* (4th ed.). Buckingham: Open University Press.

Davies, A., & Doran, J. (2012). Systemic practice in forensic settings. Editorial for special issue. *Context, 124*, 1–2.

Davies, A., Mallows, L., Easton, R., Morrey, A., & Wood, F (2014). A survey of the provision of family therapy in secure units in Wales and England. *Journal of Forensic Psychiatry and Psychology, 25*(5), 520–534.

Davies, L. (2016). Security, extremism and education: safeguarding or surveillance? *British Journal of Education Studies, 64*(1), 1–19.

Davis, A. (2012). Gathering momentum: working systemically in forensic settings. *Context, 124*, 2–4.

Davis, J. (2005). *Criminal minds* [Television series]. Burbank, CA: ABC Studios.

Davison, G. (1976). Homosexuality: the ethical challenge. *Journal of Consulting and Clinical Psychology, 44*, 157–162.

Davydov, D. M., Stewart, R., Ritchie, K., & Chaudieu, I. (2010). Resilience and mental health. *Clinical Psychology Review, 30*(5), 479–495.

de Botton, A. (2012). *How to think more about sex.* London: School of Life.

De Leo, D., Burgis, S., Bertolete, J. M., Kerkof, A. J., & Bille-Braha, U. (2006). Defintions of suicidal behaviour: lessons learnt from the WHO/EURO multicentre study. *Crisis, 27*, 4–15.

De Shazer, S. (2005). *More than miracles: the state of the art of solution-focused therapy.* Binghamton, NY: Haworth Press.

De Zulueta, F. (2001). *From pain to violence: the traumatic roots of destructiveness.* London: Whurr Publishers.

DeClue, G. (2006). Paraphilia NOS (nonconsenting) and antisocial personality disorder. *Journal of Psychiatry & Law, 34,* 495–514.

Demange, Y., Tully, S., Lydon, P., Macdonald, F., Harris, O., Moo-Young, C., ... Yip, W. (2007). *The secret diary of a call girl* [Television series]. London: Independent Television (ITV). Retrieved 30 December 2016 from www.imdb.com/title/tt1000734/.

Demme, J. (Director) (1991). *Silence of the lambs* [Film]. Los Angeles, CA: Orion Pictures.

Department of Health (2006). *Core training standards for sexual orientation: making national health services inclusive for LGB people.* London: DH.

Department of Health (2007). *Improving access to health and social care for lesbian, gay, bisexual and trans (LGBT) people.* London: DH.

Department of Health (2008). *Guidance for GPs, other clinicians and health professionals on the care of gender variant people.* Londo: DH.

Development Services Group, Inc. (2010). *Cognitive behavioural treatment.* Washington, DC: Office of Juvenile justice and Delinquency Prevention. Retrieved 30 December 2016 2016 from https://www.ojjdp.gov/mpg/litreviews/Cognitive_Behavioral_Treatment.pdf.

Diamond, G. S., Diamond, G. M., & Levy, S. A. (2014). *Attachment based family therapy for depressed adolescents.* Washington, DC: American Psychological Association.

Division of Clinical Psychology (2011). *Good practice guidelines on the use of psychological formulation.* Leicester: British Psychological Society.

Division of Clinical Psychology (2013). *Classification of behaviour and experience in relation to functional psychiatric diagnosis: time for a paradigm shift.* Leicester: British Psychological Society.

Dobash, R. E., & Dobash, R. P. (1992). *Women, violence and social change.* New York: Routledge.

Dodson, B. (1974). *Sex for one: the joy of selfloving.* New York: Crown.

Dong, M., Anda, R. F., Dube, S. R., Giles, W. H., & Felitti, V. J. (2003). The relationship of exposure to childhood sexual abuse to other forms of abuse, neglect, and household dysfunction during childhood. *Child Abuse and Neglect, 27,* 625–639.

Doran, G. T. (1981). There's a S.M.A.R.T. way to write management's goals and objectives. *Management Review, 70*(11), 35–36.

Doren, D. (2002). *Evaluating sex offenders: a manual for civil commitments and beyond.* Thousand Oaks, CA: Sage.

Douard, J. (2007). Loathing the sinner, medicalizing the sin: why sexually violent predator statutes are unjust. *International Journal of Law and Psychiatry, 30,* 36–48.

Dowler, K., Fleming, T., & Muzzato, S. L. (2006). Constructing crime: media, crime and popular culture. *Canadian Journal of Criminology and Criminal Justice, 48*(6), 875–850.

Dowsett, J., & Craissati, J. (2008). *Managing personality disordered offenders in the community.* Hove: Routledge.

Dube, R., Anda, R. F., Felitti, V. J., Chapman, D. P., Williamson, D. F., & Giles, W. H. (2001). Childhood abuse, household dysfunction, and the risk of attempted suicide throughout the life span. *Journal of the American Medical Association, 286*, 1–21.

Duggal, S., & Sroufe, L. A. (1998). Recovered memory of childhood sexual trauma: a documented case from a longitudinal study. *Journal of Traumatic Stress, 11*(2), 301–321.

Dunne, R. A., & McLoughlin, D. M. (2012). Systematic review and meta-analysis of bifrontal electroconvulsive therapy versus bilateral and unilateral electroconvulsive therapy in depression. *The World Journal of Biological Psychiatry, 13*, 248–258.

East, P., & Adams, J. (2002). Sexual assertiveness and adolescents' sexual rights. *Perspectives on Sexual and Reproductive Health, 34*, 212–213.

East, W. N., & de Bargue Hubert, W. H. (1939). *Report on the psychological treatment of crime*. London: HMSO.

Eaton, W. W. (1980). A formal theory of selection for schizophrenia. *American Journal of Sociology, 86*(1), 149–158.

Egeland, B. (2009). Attachment based intervention and prevention programmes for young children. *Encyclopaedia on early childhood development*. Retrieved 30 December 2016 from www.child-encyclopedia.com/attachment/according-experts/attachment-based-intervention-and-prevention-programs-young-children.

EHRC (2015). *Is Britain fairer?* Report. Rome: European Convention on Human Rights. Accessed 17 September 2016 from www.equalityhumanrights.com/en/britain-fairer/britain-fairer-report.

Eigen, J. P. (1995). *Witnessing insanity: madness and mad-doctors in the English court*. New Haven, CT: Yale University Press.

Eleftheriadou, Z. (2010). Cross-cultural counselling psychology. In R. Woolfe, S. Strawbridge, B. Douglas & W. Dryden (Eds.), *Handbook of counselling psychology* (pp. 195–212). London: Sage.

Elliott, D. L., Huizinga, D., & Ageton, S. S. (1985). *Explaining delinquency and drug use*. Beverly Hills, CA: Sage.

Elliott, D. M. (1997). Traumatic events: prevalence and delayed recall in the general population. *Journal of Consulting and Clinical Psychology, 65*, 811–820.

Ellis, A. (1958). Rational psychotherapy. *Journal of General Psychology, 59*, 35–49.

Ellis, A. (1962). *Reason and emotion in psychotherapy*. New York: Lyle Stuart.

Ellis, H. (1923). *Studies in the psychology of sex: erotic symbolism; the mechanism of detumescence; the psychic state in pregnancy*. Philadelphia, PA: F. A. Davis Company Publishers.

Equality Act (2010). (Specific Duties) Regulations 2011; SI 2011 No. 2260. London: HMSO.

Erard, R. E., Meyer, G. J., & Viglione, D. J. (2014). Setting the record straight: comment on Gurley, Piechowski, Sheehan and Gray (2014) on the admissibility of the Rorschach Performance Assessment System (R-PAS) in court. *Psychological Injury and Law, 7*(2), 165–177.

Eschold, S., Mallard, M., & Flynn, S. (2004). Images of prime time justice: a content analysis of 'NYPD Blue' and 'Law and Order'. *Journal of Criminal Justice and Popular Culture, 10*(3), 161–180.

Esnard, C., & Dumas, R. (2013). Perceptions of male victim blame in a child sexual abuse case: effects of gender, age, and need for closure. *Psychology, Crime & Law, 19*(9), 817–844.

Estroff, A., & Zimmer, C. (1994). Social networks, social support, and violence among persons with severe, persistent mental illness. In J. Monahan & H. E. Steadman (Eds.), *Violence and mental disorder: developments in risk assessment* (pp. 259–295). Chicago, IL: University of Chicago Press.

Evans, K. (2012). Media representations of male and female 'co-offending': how female offenders are portrayed in comparison to their male counterparts. *Internet Journal of Criminology, 6743*, 1–26.

Fang, M. (2015). The country's first openly bisexual governor bans gay conversion therapy in her state. *The Huffington Post*. Retrieved 31 July 2016 from www.huffingtonpost.com/2015/05/19/oregon-gay-conversion-therapy-ban_n_7337350.html.

Fanniff, A., & Becker, J. (2006). Developmental considerations in working with juvenile sexual offenders. In R. E. Longo & D. S. Prescott (Eds.), *Current perspectives: working with sexually aggressive youth and youth with sexual behaviour problems* (pp. 119–141). Holyoke, MA: NEARI Press.

Farber, B. A., Berano, K. C., & Capobianco, J. A. (2004). Clients' perceptions of the process and consequences of self-disclosure in psychotherapy. *Journal of Counseling Psychology, 51*(3), 340–346.

Farias, M., & Wikholm, C. (2015). Ommm… aargh. *New Scientist, 226*(3021), 28–29.

Faris, R. E. L., & Dunham, H. W. (1939). *Mental disorders in urban areas: an ecological study of schizophrenia and other psychoses*. Oxford: University of Chicago Press.

Farrington, D. P. (2007). Childhood risk factors and risk-focussed prevention. In M. Maguire, R. Morgan & R. Reiner (Eds.), *The Oxford handbook of criminology* (4th ed.) (pp. 602–640). Oxford: Oxford University Press

Fazel, S., & Baillargeon, J. (2011). The health of prisoners. *Lancet, 377*, 956–965.

Fazel, S., Hayes, A. J., Bartellas, K., Clerici, M., & Trestman, R. (2016). Mental health of prisoners: prevalence, adverse outcomes, and interventions. *Lancet Psychiatry, 3*(9), 871–881. doi: 10.1016/S2215-0366(16)30142-0. Epub 14 July 2016.

Fazel, S., & Seewald, K. (2012). Severe mental illness in 33,588 prisoners worldwide: systematic review and meta-regression analysis. *The British Journal of Psychiatry, 200*(5), 364–373.

Fazel, S., Sjöstedt, G., Längström, N., & Grann, M. (2006). Risk factors for criminal recidivism in older sexual offenders. *Sexual Abuse: A Journal of Research and Treatment, 18*(2), 159–167.

Felitti, V., Anda, R. E., Nordenberg, D., Williams, D. F., Spitz, A. M., Edwards, V., Koss, M. P., & Marks, J. S. (1998). The relationship of adult health status to childhood abuse and household dysfunction. *American Journal of Preventive Medicine, 14*, 245–258.

Ferguson, R. (2015). Ontario becomes first province to ban 'conversion therapy' for LGBTQ children. *The Star*. Retrieved 31 July 2016 from www.thestar.com/news/canada/2015/06/04/ontario-becomes-first-province-to-ban-conversion-therapy-for-lgbtq-children.html.

Fergusson, D., Swain-Campbell, N., & Horwood, J. (2004). How does childhood economic disadvantage lead to crime? *Journal of Child Psychology and Psychiatry*, *45*, 956–966.

Fernando, S. (2003). *Cultural diversity, mental health and psychiatry: the struggle against racism*. Hove: Routledge.

Fernando, S. (2010). *Mental health, race and culture* (3rd ed.). London: Palgrave Macmillan.

Fernando, S. (2014). *Mental health worldwide: culture, globalization and development*. Basingstoke: Palgrave Macmillan.

Ferrito, M., Vetere, A., Adshead, G., & Moore, E. (2012). Life after homicide: accounts of recovery and redemption of offender patients in a high secure hospital – a qualitative study. *Journal of Forensic Psychiatry and Psychology*, *23*(3), 327–344.

Fink, M., & Miller, Q. (2013). Trans media moments: Tumblr, 2011–2013. *Television & New Media*, *15*(7), 611–626.

Finkelhor, D., Hammer, H., & Sedlak, A. (2008). *Sexually assaulted children: national estimates and characteristics* (Publication No. NCJ 214383). Bulletin: National Incidence Studies of Missing, Abducted, Runaway, and Thrownaway Children Series. Retrieved 30 December 2016 from https://www.ncjrs.gov/pdffiles1/ojjdp/214383.pdf

Finkelhor, D., Shattuck, A., Turner, H. A., & Hamby, S. L. (2014). The lifetime prevalence of CSA and sexual assault assessed in late adolescence. *Journal of Adolescent Health*, *55*, 329–333.

Finkelhor, D., Turner, H., Shattuck, A., Hamby, S., & Kracke, K. (2015). *Children's exposure to violence, crime, and abuse: an update*. Juvenile Justice Bulletin: NCJ 248547. Washington, DC: US Government Printing Office.

Finlay, L. (2016). *Relational integrative psychotherapy: engaging process and theory in practice*. Chichester: Wiley Blackwell.

Fisher, B., Daigle, L., Cullen, F., & Turner, M. (2003). Reporting sexual victimisation to the police and others: results from a national-level study of college women. *Criminal Justice and Behaviour*, *30*, 6–38.

Fisher, C. (2004). Ethical issues in therapy: therapist self-disclosure of sexual feelings. *Ethics & Behavior*, *14*, 105–121.

Fitzpatrick, M. R., Janzen, J., Chamodraka, M., & Park, J. (2006). Client critical incidents in the process of early alliance developments: a positive emotion-exploration spiral. *Psychotherapy Research*, *16*, 486–498.

Fonagy, P. (2004). The developmental roots of violence in the failure of mentalization. In G. Adshead & F. Pfafflin (Eds.), *A matter of security* (pp. 13–56). London: Jessica Kingsley Publishers.

Forrest, G. G. (2010). *Self-disclosure in psychotherapy and recovery*. Plymouth, MA: Jason Aronson.

Forrester, A., Ozdural, S., Muthukumaraswamy, A., & Carroll, A. (2008). The evolution of mental disorder as a legal category in England and Wales. *Journal of Forensic Psychiatry and Psychology*, *19*, 543–560.

Foster, D. (2016). Is mindfulness making us ill? *The Guardian*, 23 January 2016. Accessed 30 January 2016 from www.theguardian.com/lifeandstyle/2016/jan/23/is-mindfulness-making-us-ill.

Foucault, M. (1976). *The history of sexuality. Vol. 1: An introduction.* (Robert Hurley, trans.). London: Allen Lane.

Foucault, M. (1977). *Discipline and punish: the birth of the prison.* New York: Random House.

Fountain, J., & Hicks, J. (2010). *Delivering race equality in mental health care: report on the findings and outcomes of the community engagement programme 2005–2008.* Harrington: ISCRI.

Fraiberg, S., Adelson, E., & Shapiro, V. (1975). Ghosts in the nursery: a psycho-analytic approach to impaired infant–mother relationships. *Journal of the American Academy of Child Psychiatry, 14,* 387–421.

Frances, A. (2011a). The rejection of paraphilic rape in DSM III: a first hand historical narrative. *Psychology Today.* Retrieved 10 April 2011 from www.psychologytoday.com/blog/dsm5-in-distress/201103/the-rejection-paraphilic-rape-in-dsm-iii-first-hand-historical-narrative.

Frances, A. (2011b). DSM-5 rejects coercive paraphilia: confirming yet again that rape is not a mental disorder. *Psychology Today.* Retrieved 1 June 2013 from www.psychologytoday.com/blog/dsm5-in-distress/201105/dsm-5-rejects-coercive-paraphilia.

Franco, J. (1969). *Venus in furs* [Film]. Paris: Cinematografica Associati (CIAS).

Frese, F. J. (2010). On the impact of being diagnosed with schizophrenia. *Journal of Mental Health, 19*(4), 376–378.

Freud, S. (1919). Advances in psycho-analytic therapy. In J. Strachey (Ed.), *The standard edition of the complete psychological works of Sigmund Freud* (pp. 157–168). London: Hogarth Press.

Freud, S. (1920/2001). *Beyond the pleasure principle.* In J. Stachey, A. Freud, A. Stachey & A. Tyson (Eds.), *The standard edition of the complete psychological works of Sigmund Freud (Vol. xviii (1920–1922)* (pp. 7–64). London: Vintage Books.

Freud, S. (1924/2001). The economic problem of masochism. In J. Stachey, A. Freud, A. Stachey & A. Tyson (Eds.), *The standard edition of the complete psychological works of Sigmund Freud (Vol. xix (1923–1924)* (pp. 159–172). London: Vintage Books.

Freud, S. (1949). *Three essays on the theory of sexuality.* London: Imago Publishing.

Freud, S. (1963). *An outline of psychoanalysis.* (J. Strachey, trans.). New York: W. W. Norton. (Original work published 1940.)

Freund, K. (1960). Some problems with the treatment of homosexuality. In H. J. Eysenck (Ed.), *Behaviour therapy and the neuroses* (pp. 312–314). New York: Pergamon Press.

Frodi, A., Dernevik, M., Sepa, A., Philipson, J., & Bragesto, M. (2001). Current attachment representations of incarcerated offenders varying in degree of psychopathy. *Attachment & Human Development, 3*(3), 269–283.

Fung, L., Bhugra, D., & Jones, P. (2009). Ethnicity and mental health: the example of schizophrenia and related psychoses in migrant populations in the Western world. *Psychiatry, 8,* 335–341.

Gabbard, G. (1996). Lessons to be learned from the study of sexual boundary violations. *American Journal of Psychotherapy, 50,* 311–322.

Gajwani, R., Parsons, H., Birchwood, M. J., & Singh, S. P. (2016). Ethnicity and detention: are black and minority ethnic (BME) groups disproportionately detained under the Mental Health Act 2007? *Social Psychiatry and Psychiatric Epidemiology, 51*, 703–711. Accessed 17 September 2016 at http://wrap.warwick.ac.uk/77457/1/WRAP_art%253A10.1007%252Fs 00127-016-1181-z.pdf.

Gale, F. (2007). Tackling the stigma of mental health in vulnerable children and young people. In P. Vostanis (Ed.), *Mental health interventions and services for vulnerable children and young people* (pp. 58–80). London: Jessica Kingsley Publishers.

Galietta, M., & Rosenfield, B. (2012). Adapting dialectical behaviour therapy (DBT) for the treatment of psychopathy. *International Journal of Forensic Mental Health, 11*(4), 325–335.

Gandaglia, G., Briganti, A., Jackson, G., Kloner, R., Montorsi, F., Montorsi, P., & Vlachopoulos, C. (2014). A systematic review of the association between erectile dysfunction and cardiovascular disease. *European Urology, 65*, 968–978.

Gans-Boriskin, R., & Wardle, C. (2005). Mad or bad? Negotiating the boundaries of mental illness on law & order. *Journal of Criminal Justice and Popular Culture, 12*(1), 26–46.

Garner, S. (2010). *Racisms: an introduction*. London: Sage.

Garret, T. (1998). Sexual contact between patients and psychologists. *The Psychologist, May*, 227–229.

Garside, R. (2009). *Risky people or risky societies? Rethinking interventions for young adults in transition*. Transition to Adulthood, No. 1. London: Centre for Crime and Justice Studies.

Gartrell, N., Heran, J., Olarte, S., Feldstein, M., & Localio, R. (2006). Psychiatrist–patient sexual contact: results of a national survey. I: Prevalence. *American Journal of Psychiatry, 143*, 1126–1131.

Gee, J., & Reed, S. (2013). The HoST programme: a pilot evaluation of modified dialectical behaviour therapy with female offenders diagnosed with borderline personality disorder. *European Journal Counselling and Psychotherapy, 15*(3), 233–253.

Geelan, S., & Nickford, C. (1999). A survey of the use of family therapy in medium secure units in England and Wales. *The Journal of Forensic Psychiatry, 10*, 317–324.

Gellatly, J., Bower, P., Hennessy, S., Richards, D., Gilbody, S., & Lovell, K. (2007). What makes self-help interventions effective in the management of depressive symptoms? Meta-analysis and meta-regression. *Psychological Medicine, 37*, 1217–1228.

Germer, C. K., Siegel, R. D., & Fulton, P. R. (Eds.) (2005). *Mindfulness and psychotherapy*. New York: Guilford Press.

Gibbons, P., de Volder, J., & Casey, P. (2003). Patterns of denial in sex offenders: a replication study. *Journal of the American Academy of Psychiatry and Law, 31*, 336–244.

Gibson, D. (2012). *Legends, monsters, or serial murderers? The real story behind an ancient crime*. Oxford: Praeger.

Gilbert, P. (2010). *Compassion focused therapy*. London: Routledge.

Giromini, L., Viglione, D. J., Brusadelli, E., Reese, J. B., & Zennaro, A. (2015). Cross-cultural validation of the Rorschach Developmental Index. *Journal of Personality Assessment, 97*(4), 348–353.

Gittings, B. (2007). Preface: Show-and-tell. In J. Drescher and J. Merlino (Eds.), *American psychiatry and homosexuality: an oral history* (pp. xv–xix). London: Harrington Park Press.

Glover, G., & Evison, F. (2009). *Use of new mental health services by ethnic minorities in England*. Durham: North East Public Heath Observatory.

Glover-Thomas, N. (2011). The age of risk: risk perception and determination following the Mental Health Act 2007, *Medical Law Review, 19*, 581–605.

Glück, T. M., & Maercker, A. (2011). A randomized controlled pilot study of a brief web-based mindfulness training. *BMC Psychiatry, 11*(1), 175.

Gold, S. N., Hughes, D. M., & Swingle, J. M. (1999). Degrees of memory of childhood sexual abuse among women survivors in therapy. *Journal of Family Violence, 14*(1), 35–46.

Goldmeier, D., & Mears, A. (2010). Meditation: a review of its use in western medicine and, in particular, its role in the management of sexual dysfunction. *Current Psychiatry Reviews, 6*, 11–14.

Goldner, V. (1998). The treatment of violence and victimization in intimate relationships. *Family Process, 37*(3), 263–286.

Gomez, L. (1997). *An introduction to object relations*. London: Free Association Books.

Gournay, K. (2016). Reflections on 20 years of dual diagnosis research. *Journal of Psychiatric and Mental Health Nursing, 23*, 243–244.

Government Equalities Office (2010). *Factsheet: lesbian, gay, bisexual and transgender equality*. London: Government Equalities Office.

Government Office for Science (2008). *Mental Capital and Wellbeing: Making the most of ourselves in the 21st century*. Final project report – executive summary. London: Government Office for Science.

Grant, J., & Crawley, J. (2003). *Transference and projection: mirrors to the self*. Maidenhead: Open University Press.

Green, M. J., & Benzeval, M. (2011). Ageing, social class and common mental disorders: longitudinal evidence from three cohorts in the west of Scotland. *Psychological Medicine, 41*(3), 565–574.

Greenberg, S. A., & Shuman, D. W. (1997). Irreconcilable conflict between therapeutic and forensic roles. *Professional Psychology: Research and Practice, 28*(1), 50.

Greenberger, D., & Padesky, C. A. (1995). *Mind over mood: change how you feel by changing the way you think*. New York and London: Guilford Press.

Greenwald, A. G., & Krieger, L. H. (2006). Implicit bias: scientific foundations. *California Law Review, 94*, 945–967.

Greggoire, A. (1999). ABC of sexual health: male sexual problems. *British Medical Journal, 318*, 245–247.

Gregoriou, C. (Ed.) (2012). *Constructing crime: discourse and cultural representations of crime and 'deviance'*. London: Palgrave Macmillan.

Grey, T., Sewell, H., Shapiro, G., & Ashraf, F. (2013). Mental health inequalities facing UK minority ethnic populations causal factors and solutions. *Journal of Psychological Issues in Organizational Culture, 3*, 146–157. Accessed 17 September 2016 at http://onlinelibrary.wiley.com/doi/10.1002/jpoc.21080/epdf.

Guralnick, M. J., & Neville, B. (1997). Designing early intervention programs to promote children's social competence. In M. J. Guralnick (Ed.), *The effectiveness of early intervention* (pp. 579–610). Baltimore, MD: Brookes.

Gurley, J. R., Sheehan, B. L., Piechowski, L. D., & Gray, J. (2014). The admissibility of the R-PAS in court. *Psychological Injury and Law, 7*(1), 9–17.

Gutheil, T. G., & Brodsky, A. (2011). *Preventing boundary violations in clinical practice*. New York and London: Guilford Press.

Guy, W. A. (1869). On insanity and crime; and on the plea of insanity in criminal cases. *Journal of the Statistical Society of London, 32,* 159–191.

Haddad, P. M., & Sharma, S. G. (2007). Adverse effects of atypical antipsychotics. *CNS Drugs, 21,* 911–936.

Haley, J. (1963). *Strategies of psychotherapy*. New York: Grune and Stratton.

Hall, S., Critcher, C., Jefferson, T., Clarke, J., & Roberts, B. (1978). *Policing the crisis: mugging, the state, and law and order*. London: Macmillan.

Hanson, K. (2002). Recidivism and age: follow-up data from 4673 sexual offenders. *Journal of Interpersonal Violence, 17*(10), 1046–1062.

Hanson, R. K., Gordon, A., Harris, A. J. R., Marques, J. K., Murphy, W., Quinsey, V. L., & Seto, M. C. (2002). First report of the collaborative outcome data project on the effectiveness of psychological treatment for sex offenders. *Sexual Abuse: A Journal of Research and Treatment, 14*(2), 169–194.

Hare, R. D., & Neumann, C. S. (2008). Psychopathy as a clinical and empirical construct. *Annual Review of Clinical Psychology, 4,* 217–246.

Harper, S. (2009). *Madness, power and the media: class, gender and race in media representations of mental distress*. Basingstoke: Palgrave Macmillan.

Harvey, J., & Endersby, L. (2015). Young people's self-disclosure in secure forensic settings. In A. Rogers, J. Harvey & H. Law (Eds.), *Young people in forensic mental health settings: psychological thinking and practice* (pp. 344–355). Basingstoke: Palgrave Macmillan.

Harvey, J., & Smedley, K. (Eds.) (2010). *Psychological therapy in prisons and other secure settings*. Abingdon: Willan.

Hawthorne, E. (2011). Women in Northern Ireland involved in prostitution. *Irish Probation Journal, 8,* 142–164.

Hayes S. C. (2004). Acceptance and commitment therapy and the new behavior therapies: mindfulness, acceptance and relationship. In S. C. Hayes, V. M. Follette & M. Lineman (Eds.), *Mindfulness and acceptance: expanding the cognitive behavioral tradition* (pp. 1–29). New York: Guilford Press.

Hayes, S. C., Luoma, J. B., Bond, F. W., Masuda, A., & Lillis, J. (2006). Acceptance and commitment therapy: model, processes and outcomes. *Behaviour Reserach and Therapy, 44,* 1–25.

Health and Care Professions Council (2012). *Standards of conduct, performance and ethics*. London: HCPC.

Heaversage, J., & Halliwell, E. (2012). *The mindful manifesto*. Carlsbad, CA: Hay House.

Hébert, A., & Weaver, A. (2015). Perks, problems, and the people who play: a qualitative exploration of dominant and submissive BDSM roles. *Canadian Journal of Human Sexuality, 24*(1), 49–62.

Hedges, F. (2005). *An introduction to systemic therapy with individuals: a social constructionist approach*. Basingstoke: Palgrave Macmillan.

Heimer, K., Lauritsen, J. L., & Lynch, J. P. (2009). The national crime victimization survey and the gender gap in offending: redux. *Criminology, 47*(2), 427–438.

Henggeler, S. W., Schoenwald, S. K., Borduin, C. M., Rowland, M. D., & Cunningham, P. B. (2009). *Mutisystemic therapy for antisocial behavior in children and adolescents.* New York and London: Guilford Press.

Henggeler, S. W., & Sheidow, A. J. (2012). Empirically supported family-based treatments for conduct disorder and delinquency in adolescents. *Journal of Marital and Family Therapy, 38*(1), 30–58.

Henriques, R. (2016) *An independent inquiry into allegations made against Lord Greville Janner.* London: Crown Prosecution Service. Available at www.cps. gov.uk/publications/reports/henriques_report_190116.pdf.

Herbert, J. D., & Forman, E. M. (2011). *Acceptance and mindfulness in cognitive behavior therapy: understanding and applying the new therapies.* Hoboken, NJ: John Wiley & Sons.

Herek, G. (2010). Sexual orientation differences as deficits: science and stigma in the history of American psychology. *Perspectives on Psychological Science, 5*(6), 693–699.

Herman, J. L., & Harvey, M. R. (1997). Adult memories of childhood trauma: a naturalistic clinical study. *Journal of Traumatic Stress, 10,* 557–571.

Herman, J. L., Perry, C. J., & Van der Kolk, B. A. (1989). Childhood trauma in borderline personality disorder. *American Journal of Psychiatry, 146*(4), 490–495.

Hesse, E. (2008). The adult attachment interview: protocol, method of analysis, and empirical studies. In J. Cassidy & P. R. Shaver (Eds.), *Handbook of attachment: theory, research, and clinical applications* (2nd ed.) (pp. 552–598). New York: Guilford Press.

Hiday, V. (1995). The social context of mental illness and violence. *Journal of Health and Social Behavior, 36,* 911–914.

Hilty, D. M., Ferrer, D. C., Parish, M. B., Johnston, B., Callahan, E. J., & Yellowlees, P. M. (2013). The effectiveness of telemental health: a 2013 review. *Telemedicine Journal and E-Health, 19,* 444–454.

Himelstein, S. (2011). Meditation research: the state of the art in correctional setting. *International Journal of Offender Therapy and Comparative Criminology, 55*(4), 646–661.

Hinshaw, S. (2006). *The mark of shame: stigma of mental illness and an agenda for change.* Oxford: Oxford University Press.

Hirschfeld, M. (1914/2000) *The homosexuality of men and women.* (M. Lombardi-Nash, English trans., 2000). Amherst, NY: Prometheus Books. (Original edition: *Die Homosexualität des Mannes und des Weibes.* Berlin: Louis Marcus.)

Hodgins, S., & Janson, C.-G. (2002). *Criminality and violence among the mentally disordered: the Stockholm Metropolitan Project.* Cambridge: Cambridge University Press.

Hollingshead, A. B., & Redlich, F. C. (1958). *Social class and mental illness: a community study.* Hoboken, NJ: John Wiley & Sons.

Hollway, W. (1984). Gender difference and the production fo subjectivity. In J. Henriques, W. Hollway, C. Venn & V. Walkerdine (Eds.), *Changing the subject.* London: Methuen.

Holman, D. (2014). 'What help can you get talking to somebody?' Explaining class differences in the use of talking treatments. *Sociology of Health & Illness, 36*(4), 531–548.

Holmes, J. (2001). *The search for the secure base: attachment theory and psychotherapy.* Hove: Routledge.

Holwerda, T. J., van Tilburg, T. G., Deeg, D. J. H., Schutter, N., Van, R., Dekker, J., Stek, M. L., Beekman, A. T. F., & Schoevers, R. A. (2016). Impact of loneliness and depression on mortality: results from the Longitudinal Ageing Study Amsterdam. *The British Journal of Psychiatry, 209*(2), 127–134.

Home Office (2010a). *Crime in England and Wales 2009/10: findings from the British Crime Survey.* London: Home Office.

Home Office (2010b). Youth crime website. Available at www.homeoffice.gov.uk/crime-victims/reducing-crime/youth-crime/.

Home Office and Ministry of Justice (2014). *Anti-social behaviour order statistics England and Wales 2013.* London: Home Office.

Honigmann, J. (2013). The Equality Act 2010: the letter and the spirit of the law. In H. Sewell (Ed.), *The Equality Act 2010 in mental health: a guide to implementation and issues for practice.* London: Jessica Kingsley Publishers.

Honor, G. (2010). CSA: consequences and implications. *Journal of Pediatric Health Care, 24*(6), 358–364.

Hook, A., & Andrews, B. (2005). The relationship of non-disclosure in therapy to shame and depression. *British Journal of Clinical Psychology, 44,* 425–438.

Hooker, E. (1957). The adjustment of the male overt homosexual. *Journal of Projective Techniques, 21*(1), 18–31.

Horney, K. (1935/1973). *Feminine psychology.* New York: W. W. Norton.

Horsley, M. (2014). White-collar crime. In R. Atkinson (Ed.), *Shades of deviance: a primer on crime, deviance and social harm.* London: Routledge.

Howard, A. (1996). *Challenges to counselling and psychotherapy.* London: Macmillan.

Howe, D. (2011). *Attachment across the lifecourse: a brief introduction.* Basingstoke: Palgrave Macmillan.

Howells, K., Day, A., & Thomas-Peter, B. (2004). Changing violent behaviour: forensic mental health and criminological models compared. *The Journal of Forensic Psychiatry and Psychology, 15*(3), 391–406.

Howells, K., Tennant, A., Day, A., & Elmer, R. (2010). Mindfulness in forensic mental health: does it have a role? *Mindfulness, 1,* 4–9.

Hudson, C. G. (2005). Socioeconomic status and mental illness: tests of the social causation and selection hypotheses. *The American Journal of Orthopsychiatry, 75*(1), 3–18.

Humphrey, J. A., & White, J. W. (2000). Women's vulnerability to sexual assault from adolescence to young adulthood. *Journal of Adolescent Health, 27,* 419–427.

Hunt, A. (1998). The great masturbation panic and the discourses of moral regulation in nineteenth and early twentieth century Britain. *Journal of the History of Sexuality, 8*(4), 575–615.

Hunter, J. A., Goodwin, D. W., & Wilson, R. J. (1992). Attributions of blame in CSA victims: an analysis of age and gender influences. *Journal of CSA, 1*(3), 75–89.

Hurvitz, N. (1973). Psychotherapy as a means of social control. *Journal of Consulting and Clinical Psychology, 40*(2), 232–239.

Jaeckin, J. (1975). *The story of O* [Film]. Paris: A. D. Creation.

James, A., & Smith, B. (2014). There will be blood: crime rates in shale-rich US counties. Oxford: Oxford Centre for the Analysis of Resource Rich Economies, University of Oxford. Retrieved 15 September 2015 from www.oxcarre.ox.ac.uk/files/OxCarreRP2014140.pdf.

Jane-Llopis, E., Barry, M., Hosman, C., & Patel, V. (2005). Mental health promotion works: a review. *Promotion and Education* (Supplement 2), 2–25, 61, 67.

Jauk, D. (2013). Gender violence revisited: lessons from violent victimization of transgender identified individuals. *Sexualities, 16*, 807–825.

Jay, A. (2014) *Independent inquiry into child sexual exploitation in Rotherham (1997–2013)*. The Jay Report. London: Home Office. Available at www.rotherham.gov.uk/downloads/file/1407/independent_inquiry_cse_in_rotherham.

Jeffreys, S. (1997). *The idea of prostitution*. Melbourne, Vic.: Spinifex.

Jeffreys, S. (2014a). *Gender hurts: a feminist analysis of the politics of transgenderism*. New York: Routledge.

Jeffreys, S. (2014b). The politics of the toilet: a feminist response to the campaign to 'degender' a women's space. *Women' Studies International Forum, 45*, 42–51.

Jennings, W. G., Gibson, C., & Lanza-Kaduce, L. (2009). Why not let the kids be kids? An exploratory relationship between alternative rationales for managing status offending and youths' self-concepts. *American Journal of Criminal Justice, 34*, 198–212.

Jennings, W. G., Richards, T. N., Tomisch, E., Gover, A. R., & Powers, R. (2013). A critical examination of the causal link between child abuse and adult dating violence perpetration and victimisation from a propensity-score matching approach. *Women and Criminal Justice, 23*(3), 167–184.

Jewkes, V. (2011a). Prisons. In M. Tonry (Ed.). *The Oxford handbook of crime and criminal justice*. Oxford: Oxford University Press.

Jewkes, Y. (2011b). *Media and crime* (2nd ed.). London: Sage.

Jewkes, Y. (2015). *Media and crime* (3rd ed.). London: Sage.

Johnson, M. P. (2005). Domestic violence: it's not about gender – or is it? *Journal of Marriage and Family, 67*, 1126–1130.

Johnson, M. P. (2006). Conflict and control: gender symmetry and asymmetry in domestic violence. *Violence against Women, 12*(11), 1003–1018.

Johnstone, L., & Dallos, R. (Eds.) (2013). *Formulation in psychology and psychotherapy: making sense of people's problems*. London: Routledge.

Johnstone, L., & Gregory, L. (2015). Youth violence risk assessment: a framework for practice. In A. Rogers, J. Harvey & H. Law (Eds.), *Young people in forensic mental health settings: psychological thinking and practice* (pp. 96–122). Basingstoke: Palgrave Macmillan.

Jones, B. (2013). Adult mental health disorders and their age at onset. *The British Journal of Psychiatry, 202*(s54), 5–10.

Jones, K. (1993). *Asylums and after: a revised history of the mental health services from the early eighteenth century to the 1990s*. London: Athlone Press.

Jones, O. (2012). *Chavs: the demonization of the working class*. London: Verso.

Joseph, S. (Ed.) (2015). *Positive psychology in practice: promoting human flourishing in work, health, education, and everyday life* (2nd ed.). Chichester: Wiley.

Junginger, J. (1995). Command hallucinations and the prediction of dangerousness. *Psychiatric Services, 46,* 911–914.

Juraskova, I., Butow, P., Robertson, R., Sharpe, L., McLeod, C., & Hacker, N. (2003). Post-treatment sexual adjustment following cervical and endometrial cancer: a qualitative insight. *Psychooncology, 12,* 267–279.

Kabat-Zinn, J. (1996). *Full catastrophe living: how to cope with stress, pain and illness using mindfulness meditation.* London: Piatkus.

Kabat-Zinn, J., Massion, A. O., Kristeller, J., Peterson, L. G., Fletcher, K. E., Pbert, L., Lenderking, W. R., & Santorelli, S. F. (1992). Effectiveness of a meditation-based stress reduction program in the treatment of anxiety disorders. *American Journal of Psychiatry, 149,* 936–943.

Kamphuis, J. H., Kugeares, S. L., & Finn, S. E. (2000). Rorschach correlates of sexual abuse: trauma content and aggression indexes. *Journal of Personality Assessment, 75,* 212–224.

Kashak, E., & Teifer, L. (2002). *New view of women's sexual problems.* New York: Routledge.

Katz, D., & Toner, B. (2013). A systematic review of gender differences in the effectiveness of mindfulness-based treatments for substance use disorders. *Mindfulness, 4,* 31–331.

Keating, F., & Robertson, D. (2004). Fear, black people and mental illness: a vicious circle? *Health and Social Care in the Community, 12,* 439–447.

Kegan, R. (1982). *The evolving self: problem and process in human development.* Cambridge, MA: Harvard University Press.

Kellogg, N. (2005). The evaluation of sexual abuse in children. *Pediatrics, 25,* 506–512.

Kelly, J. B., & Johnson, M. P. (2008). Differentiation among types of intimate partner violence: research update and implications for interventions. *Family Court Review, 46*(3), 476–499.

Kelly, L., Lovett, J., & Regan, L. (2005). *A gap or a chasm? Attrition in reported rape cases.* London: Home Office Research, Development and Statistics Directorate.

Kendall, F. (2012). *Understanding white privilege: creating pathways to authentic relationships across race.* Abingdon: Routledge.

Kendler, K. S., & Gardner, C. O. (2014). Sex differences in the pathways to major depression: a study of opposite-sex twin pairs. *American Journal of Psychiatry, 171,* 426–435.

Kenny, M. C., & Abreau, R. L. (2015). Training mental health professional in CSA: curricular guidelines. *Journal of CSA, 24*(5), 572–591.

Kent, D. (2003). *Snake pits, talking cures & magic bullets: a history of mental illness.* Minneapolis, MN: Twenty-First Century Books.

Keogh, B., Calderwood, C., Ruddle, A., Newell, R., Hawkins, A., Lousada, J. ... Weisz, J. (2015). Memorandum of understanding on conversion therapy in the UK. Retrieved 31 July 2016 from www.psychotherapy.org.uk/UKCP_Documents/policy/MoU-conversiontherapy.pdf.

Kessler, R. C., Sonnega, A., Bromet, E., Hughes, M., & Nelson, C. B. (1995). Posttraumatic stress disorder in the National Comorbidity Survey. *Archives of General Psychiatry, 52*(12), 1048–1060.

Kessler, R., Amminger, G., Aguilar-Gaxiola, S., Alonso, J., Lee, S., & Ustun, B. (2007). Age of onset of mental disorders: a review of recent literature. *Current Opinion in Psychiatry, 20*(4), 359–364.

Keyes, C. L. M. (2007). Promoting and protecting mental health as flourishing: a complementary strategy for improving national mental health. *American Psychologist, 62*(2), 95–108.

Khele, S., Symons, C., & Wheeler, S. (2008). An analysis of complaints to the British Association for Counselling and Psychotherapy, 1996–2006. *Counselling and Psychotherapy, 8*, 124–132.

Kikuchi, K., Kikuchi, Y., Horikawa, Y., & Horikawa, K. (2010). Verification of Rorschach indications of sexual abuse. *Yonago Acta Medica, 53*, 53–59.

Kilpatrick, D. G., Best, C. L., Veronen, L. J., Amick, A. E., Villeponteaux, L. A., & Ruff, G. A. (1985). Mental health correlates of criminal victimisation: a random community survey. *Journal of Consulting and Clinical Psychology, 53*(6), 866–873.

Kilpatrick, D. G., Resnick, H. S., Saunders, B. E., & Best, C. L. (1998). Rape, other violence against women, and posttraumatic stress disorder: critical issues in assessing the adversity-stress-psychopathology relationship. In B. P. Dohrenwend (Ed.), *Adversity, stress, & psychopathology* (pp. 161–176). New York: Oxford University Press.

Kim, B., Benekos, P. J., & Merlo, A. V. (2016). Sex offender recidivism revisited: review of recent meta-analyses on the effects of sex offender treatment. *Trauma Violence Abuse, 17*, 105–117.

Kimmel, M., & Mahler, M. (2003). Adolescent masculinity, homophobia, and violence: random school shootings, 1982–2001. *American Behavioral Scientist, 46*: 1439–1458.

King, M., Semlyen, J., See Tai, S., Killaspy, H., Osborn, D., Popelyuk, D., & Nazareth, I. (2008). A systematic review of mental disorder, suicide, and deliberate self-harm in lesbian, gay and bisexual people. *BMC Psychiatry, 8*, 70–87.

Kingham, M., & Gordon, H. (2004). Aspects of morbid jealousy. *Advances in Psychiatric Treatment, 10*(3), 207–215.

Kinsey, A., Pomeroy, W., & Martin, C. (1948). *Sexual behaviour in the human male.* Bloomington, IN: Indiana University Press.

Kirkbride, J. B., Barker, D., Cowden, F., Stamps, R., Yang, M., Jones P. B., & Coid, J. W. (2008). Psychosis, ethnicity and socio-economic status. *British Journal of Psychiatry, 193*, 18–24.

Klein, M. W., & Maxson, C. L. (2010). *Street gang patterns and policies.* Oxford: Oxford University Press.

Kohlberg, L. (1984). *The psychology of moral development: the nature and validity of moral stages.* Essays on moral development (Vol. 2). New York: Harper & Row.

Köhnken, G., & Steller, M. (1988). The evaluation of the credibility of child witness statements in the German procedural system. In G. Davis and

J. Drinkwater (Eds.), *The child witness: do the courts abuse children?* (pp. 37–45). Leicester: British Psychological Society.

Koole, S. L., Sin, M., & Schneider, I. K. (2014). Embodied terror management: interpersonal touch alleviates existential concerns among individuals with low self-esteem. *Psychological Science, 25*(1), 30–37.

Krafft-Ebing, R. (1892). *Psychopathic sexualis with especial reference to contrary sexual instinct: a medico-legal study*. Philadelphia, PA: F. A. Davis.

Kruttschnitt, C. (2013). Gender and crime. *Annual Review of Sociology, 39*, 291–308.

Lamb, D., Catanzaro, S., & Moorman, A. S. (2003). Psychologists reflect on their sexual relationships with clients, supervisees, and students: occurrence, impact, rationales, and collegial intervention. *Professional Psychology: Research and Practice, 34*, 102–107.

Lambert, M. J. (2013). Outcome in psychotherapy: the past and important advances. *Psychotherapy, 50*, 42–51.

Lambert, M. J., & Barley, D. E. (2001). Research summary on the therapeutic relationship and psychotherapy outcome. *Psychotherapy: Theory, Research, Practice, Training, 38*(4), 357.

Landenberger, N. A., & Lipsey, M. (2005). The positive effects of cognitive-behavioral programs for offenders: a meta-analysis of factors associated with effective treatment. *Journal of Experimental Psychology, 1*, 451–476.

Langevin, R. (2003). A study of the psychosexual characteristics of sex killers: can we identify them before it is too late? *International Journal of Offender Therapy and Comparative Criminology, 47*(4), 366–382.

Lankford, A. (2011). Could suicide terrorists actually be suicidal? *Studies in Conflict & Terrorism, 34*(4), 337–366.

Lankford, A. (2012). A psychological autopsy of 9/11 ringleader Mohamed Atta. *Journal of Police and Criminal Psychology, 27*(2), 150–159.

Lantz, C. (2011). *Psychology student employability guide*. The Higher Education Academy Psychology Network. Retrieved 8 August 2016 from www.heacademy. ac.uk/sites/default/files/employability_guide_0.pdf.

Lauerma, H., Voutilainen, J., & Tuominen, T. (2010). Matricide and two sexual femicides by a male strangler with a transgender sadomasochistic identity. *Journal of Forensic Sciences, 55*(2), 549–550.

Leavell, H. R., & Clark, E. G. (1965). *Preventative medicine for the doctor in his community: an epidemiologic approach* (3rd ed.). New York: McGraw-Hill.

Leavitt, F. (1997). False attribution of suggestibility to explain recovered memory of childhood sexual abuse following extended amnesia. *Child Abuse & Neglect, 21*, 265–272.

Leavitt, F. (1999). Suggestibility and treatment as key variables in the recovered memory debate. *American Journal of Forensic Psychology, 17*, 5–18.

Leavitt, F., & Labortt, S. M. (1996). Authenticity of recovered sexual abuse memories: a Rorschach study. *Journal of Traumatic Stress, 9*, 251–257.

Lees, P. (2016). Placing a transgender woman in a men's prison is a cruel punishment. *The Independent*, 10 March. Retrieved from www.independent. co.uk/voices/comment/paris-lee-placing-a-trans-woman-in-a-mens-prison-is-a-cruel-and-unusual-punishment-a6923831.html#commentsDiv.

Liberman, A. M. (Ed.) (2008). *The long view of crime: a synthesis of longitudinal research*. New York: Springer.

Lieberman, A. F. (1992). Infant–parent psychotherapy with toddlers. *Development and Psychopathology, 4*, 559–574.

Lieberman, A. F., Weston, D. R., & Pawl, J. H. (1991). Preventive intervention and outcome with anxiously attached dyads. *Child Development, 62*, 199–209.

Lieberman, L. (2003). *Leaving you: the cultural meaning of suicide*. Chicago, IL: Ivan R. Dee.

Liggan, D., & Kay, J. (2006). Race in the room: issues in the dynamic psychotherapy of African-Americans. In R. Moodley & S. Palmer (Eds.), *Race, culture and psychotherapy: critical perspectives in multicultural practice* (pp. 100–115). Hove: Routledge.

Lindau, S., Schumm, L., Laumann, E., Levinson, W., O'Muircheartaigh, C., & Waite, L. (2007). A study of sexuality and health among older adults in the United States. *New England Journal of Medicine, 357*, 762–774.

Lindsay, D. S. (1998). Depolarizing views on recovered memory experiences. In S. J. Lynn & K. M. McConkey (Eds.), *Truth in memory* (pp. 481–494). New York: Guilford Press.

Linehan, M. M. (1993). *Cognitive-behavioral treatment of borderline personality disorder*. New York: Guilford Press.

Linehan, M. M., Armstrong, H. E., Suarez, A., Allmin, D., & Heard, H. L. (1991). Cognitive-behavioral treatment of chronically parasuicidal borderline clients. *Archives of General Psychiatry, 48*, 1060–1064.

Lipton, D. S., Martinson, R. M., & Wilks, J. (1975). *The effectiveness of correctional treatment: a survey of treatment evaluation studies*. New York: Praeger.

Liu, S. (2015). Is the shape of the age-crime curve invariant by sex? Evidence from a national sample with flexible non-parametric modeling. *Journal of Quantitative Criminology, 31*(1), 93–123.

Liu, W. M. (2011). *Social class and classism in the helping professions: research, theory, and practice*. London: Sage.

Loftus, E. F. (1993). The reality of repressed memories. *American Psychologist, 48*, 518–537.

Loftus, E. F., & Pickrell, J. E. (1995). The formation of false memories. *Psychiatric Annals, 25*, 720–725.

Logan, C., & Johnstone, L. (2013). *Managing clinical risk: a guide to effective practice*. Abingdon: Routledge.

Long, J. K. (1996). Working with lesbians, gays and bisexuals: addressing heterosexism in supervision. *Family Process, 35*, 377–388.

Lorentzon, F. (2005). Free will, determinism and suicide. *Philosophical Communications, 36*. Retrieved 30 December 2016 from www.phil.gu.se/posters/iccp.pdf.

Loughnan, A., & Ward, T. (2014). Emergent authority and expert knowledge: psychiatry and criminal responsibility in the UK. *International Journal of Law and Psychiatry, 37*(1), 25–36.

Lynch, T. (2014). Regulating street sex workers: a reflection on the use and reform of anti-social behaviour measures. In M. Wasik & S. Santatzoglou (Eds.), *Who knows best? The management of change in criminal justice* (pp. 186–208). Basingstoke: Palgrave Macmillan.

Lyons, T., & Cantrell, W. D. (2015). Prison meditation movements and mass incarceration. *International Journal of Offender Therapy and Comparative Criminology, 60*, doi: 10.1177/0306624X15583807.

MacCulloch, M., & Feldman, M. (1967). Aversion therapy in the management of 43 homosexuals. *British Medical Journal, ii*, 594–597.

Mack, T. (2014). The mad and the bad: the lethal use of force against mad people by Toronto police. *Critical Disability Discourse, 6*, 7–52.

Maffi, M. (1995). *Gateway to the promised land: ethnic cultures on New York's Lower East Side.* New York: New York University Press.

Magid, B. (2008). *Ending the pursuit of happiness.* Boston, MA: Wisdom Publications.

Maguire, M., Morgan, R., & Reiner, R. (Eds.) (2012). *The Oxford handbook of criminology* (5th ed.). Oxford: Oxford University Press.

Main, M. (1993). Metacognitive knowledge, metacognitive monitoring and singular (coherent) vs. multiple (incoherent) model of attachment: findings and directions for future research. In C. Parkes, J. Stevenson-Hinde & P. Marris (Eds.), *Attachment across the life cycle* (pp. 127–159). London: Routledge.

Main, M., Hesse, E., & Goldwyn, R. (2008). Studying differences in language usage in recounting attachment history: an introduction to the AAI. In H. Steele & M. Steele (Eds.), *Clinical applications of the adult attachment interview* (pp. 31–68). New York: Guilford Press.

Main, M., & Solomon, J. (1986). Discovery of an insecure disorganized/disoriented attachment pattern: procedures, findings and implications for the classification of behavior. In T. Braxelton & M. Yogman (Eds.), *Affective development in infancy* (pp. 95–124). Norwood, NJ: Ablex.

Main, M., & Solomon, J. (1990). Procedures for identifying infants as disorganized/disoriented during the Ainsworth Strange Situation. In M. Greenberg, D. Cicchetti & E. Cummings (Eds.), *Attachment in the preschool years: theory, research and intervention* (pp. 121–160). Chicago, IL: University of Chicago Press.

Malavige, L., & Levy, J. (2009). Erectile dysfunction in diabetes mellitus. *Journal of Sexual Medicine, 6*, 1232–1247.

Mangalore, R., & Knapp, M. (2012). Income-related inequalities in common mental disorders among ethnic minorities in England. *Social Psychiatry and Psychiatric Epidemiology, 47*(3), 351–359.

Maniglio, R. (2009). Severe mental illness and criminal victimization: a systematic review. *Acta Psychiatrica Scandinavica, 119*(3), 180–191.

Mann, F., Fisher, H. L., Major, B. et al. (2014). Ethnic variations in compulsory detention and hospital admission for psychosis across four UK Early Intervention Services. *BMC Psychiatry.* Accessed 17 September 2016 at https://bmcpsychiatry.biomedcentral.com/articles/10.1186/s12888-014-0256-1.

Marmot, M. G., Allen, J., Goldblatt, P., Boyce, T., McNeish, D., Grady, M., & Geddes, I. (2010). *Fair society, healthy lives: strategic review of health inequalities in England post-2010.* London: The Marmot Review.

Marques, J. K., Wiederanders, M., Day, D. M., Nelson, C., & van Ommeren, A. (2005). Effects of a relapses prevention program on sexual recidivism: final results from California's sex offender treatment and evaluation project (SOTEP). *Sexual Abuse: A Journal of Research and Treatment, 17*(1), 79–107.

Martin, C., Godfrey, M., Meekums, B., & Madill, A. (2011). Managing bound-aries under pressure: a qualitative study of therapists' experiences of sexual attraction in therapy. *Counselling and Psychotherapy Research, 11*, 248–256.

Martin, G., Bergen, H. A., Richardson, A. S., Roeger, L., & Allison, S. (2004). Sexual abuse and suicidality: gender differences in a large community sam-ple of adolescents. *Child Abuse & Neglect, 28*(5), 491–503.

Martin, P. Y. (2005). *Rape work: victims, gender, and emotions in organization and community context*. New York: Routledge.

Maschi, T., Sullivan Dennis, K., Gibson, S., MacMillan, T., Sternberg, S., & Hom, M. (2011). Trauma and stress among older adults in the criminal jus-tice system: a review of the literature with implications for social work. *Journal of Gerontological Social Work, 54*, 390–424.

Matthews, R., Easton, H., Young, L., & Bindel, J. (2014). *Exiting prostitution: a study in female desistance*. Basingstoke: Palgrave Macmillan.

Mattheys, K., Bambra, C., Warren, J., Kasim, A., & Akhter, N. (2016). Inequalities in mental health and well-being in a time of austerity: baseline findings from the Stockton-on-Tees cohort study. *SSM – Population Health, 2*, 350–359.

Maull, F. (2005). *Dharma in hell: the prison writings of Fleet Maull*. Boulder, CO: Prison Dharma Network.

Mayo Clinic (2009). Popular television shows inaccurately portray violent crime, researchers find. *ScienceDaily*, 22 May. Available at www.science daily.com/releases/2009/05/090519134835.htm.

Mayo-Wilson, E., & Montgomery, P. (2013). Media-delivered cognitive behav-ioural therapy and behavioural therapy (self-help) for anxiety disorders in adults. *Cochrane Database System Review, 9*, CD005330.

McCarthy, D., & Rapley, M. (2001). Far from the madding crowd: psychiatric diagnosis as the management of moral accountability. In A. McHoul & M. Rapley (Eds.), *How to analyse talk in institutional settings: a casebook of methods* (pp. 159–167). London: Continuum.

McClennen, J. C. (2005). Domestic violence between same-gender partners: recent findings and future research. *Journal of Interpersonal Violence, 20*(2), 149–154.

Mcfarlane, H. (2013). Masculinity and criminology: the social construction of criminal man. *Howard Journal of Criminal Justice, 52*(3), 321–335.

McFarlane, J., Malecha, A., Watson, K., Gist, J., Batten, E., Hall, I., & Smith, S. (2005). Intimate partner sexual assault against women: frequency, health consequences, and treatment outcomes. *Obstetrics & Gynecology, 105*(1), 99–108.

McGorry, P. D., Purcell, R., Goldstone, S., & Amminger, G. P. (2011). Age of onset and timing of treatment for mental and substance use disorders: implications for preventative intervention strategies and models of care. *Current Opinion in Psychiatry, 24*, 301–306.

McGowen, R. (1995). The well-ordered prison: England, 1780–1865. In N. Morris & D. J. Rothman (Eds.), *The Oxford history of the prison* (pp. 79–109). Oxford: Oxford University Press.

McGuire, J. (Ed.) (1995). *What works: reducing offending*. Chichester: Wiley.

McIntyre, J. (1967). Public attitudes toward crime and law enforcement. *The Annals of the American Academic of Political and Social Sciences, 374*(November), 34–46.

McKay, M., Wood, J. C., & Brantley, J. (2007). *The Dialectical Behavior Therapy skills workbook: practical DBT exercises for learning mindfulness, interpersonal effectiveness, emotion regulation, and distress tolerance.* Oakland, CA: New Harbinger Publications.

McLeod, J. (2003). *Introduction to counselling.* Maidenhead: Open University Press.

McManus, S., Meltzer, H., Brugha, T., Bebbington, P., & Jenkins, R. (2009). *Adult psychiatric morbidity in England 2007: results of a household survey.* London: NHS Information Centre for Health and Social Care. [Online] Accessed 11 August 2016 at www.hscic.gov.uk/pubs/psychiatricmorbidity07.

McMurran, M., & Howard, R. C. (Eds.) (2009). *Personality, personality disorder and violence.* Chichester: Wiley-Blackwell.

McMurran, M., Khalifa, N., & Gibbon, S. (2009). *Forensic mental health.* London: Routledge.

McNamee, S., & Gergen, K. (1992). *Therapy as social construction.* London: Sage.

McRae, L. (2015). The Offender Personality Disorder Pathway: risking rehabilitation? *Medical Law Review, 23,* 321–347.

Meana, M. (2009). Painful intercourse: dyspareuenia and vaginismus. In K. Hertlein, G. Weeks & N. Gambescia (Eds.), *Systemic sex therapy* (pp. 237–263). New York: Routledge.

Melville, S. (2012). Reflections on conversations about risa, risc and risco. *Context, 124,* 23–24.

Mental Health Act Commission (2006). *Count me in: the National Mental Health and Ethnicity Census: 2005 service user survey.* London: MHAC.

Mental Health Foundation (2015). *Fundamental facts about mental health 2015.* Accessed 2 June 2016 at www.mentalhealth.org.uk/sites/default/files/fundamental-facts-15-exec-summ.pdf.

Merari, A., Diamant, I., Bibi, A., Broshi, Y., & Zakin, G. (2009). Personality characteristics of 'self martyrs'/'suicide bombers' and organizers of suicide attacks. *Terrorism and Political Violence, 22*(1), 87–101.

Merton, R. K. (1968). *Social theory and social structure.* London: Simon & Schuster.

Mevissen, L., Lievegoed, R., & de Jongh, A. (2011). EMDR treatment in people with mild ID and PTSD: four cases. *Psychiatric Quarterly, 82*(1), 43–57.

Meyer, G. J., Viglione, D. J., Mihura, J. L., Erard, R. E., & Erdberg, P. (2011). *Rorschach Performance Assessment System™: administration, coding, interpretation, and technical manual.* Toledo, OH: Rorschach Performance Assessment System, LLC.

Mikulincer, M., & Shaver, P. R. (2007). Boosting attachment security to promote mental health, prosocial values, and inter-group tolerance. *Psychological Inquiry, 18,* 139–156.

Milchman, M. S. (2008). Does psychotherapy recover or invent child sexual abuse memories? A case history. *Journal of Child Sexual Abuse, 17*(1), 20–37.

Milchman, M. S. (2012a). From traumatic memory to traumatized remembering: beyond the memory wars, part 1: agreement. *Psychological Injury and the Law, 5,* 37–50.

Milchman, M. S. (2012b). From traumatic memory to traumatized remembering: beyond the memory wars, part 2: disagreement. *Psychological Injury and the Law*, 5, 51–62.

Milchman, M. S. (2012c). From traumatic memory to traumatized remembering: beyond the memory wars, part 3: an integrative schema. *Psychological Injury and the Law*, 5, 63–70.

Milkman, H., & Wanberg, K. (2007). *Cognitive-behavioral treatment: a review and discussion for correction professionals.*Washington, DC: Department of Justice, National Institute of Corrections.

Miller, W. R., & Rollnick, S. (2013). *Motivational interviewing.* New York: Guilford Press.

Mills, A., & Kendall, K. (2010). Therapy and mental health in-reach teams. In J. Harvey & K. Smedley (Eds.), *Psychological therapy in prisons and other secure settings* (pp. 26–47). Abingdon: Willan.

Mind (2013). *We still need to talk: a report on access to talking therapies.* Accessed 2 June 2016 from www.mind.org.uk/media/494424/we-still-need-to-talk_report.pdf.

Mindfulness All-Party Parliamentary Group (MAPPG) (2015). *Mindful nation UK: report by the Mindfulness All-Party Parliamentary Group (MAPPG).* London: The Mindfulness Initiative. Accessed 19 November 2015 from www.themindfulnessinitiative.org.uk/publications/mindful-nation-uk-report.

Ministry of Justice (2013). *An overview of sexual offending in England and Wales.* Ministry of Justice, Home Office and Office for National Statistics Statistics Bulletin. London: Ministry of Justice.

Ministry of Justice (2014). Statistics on women and the criminal justice system. *National Statistics* (November), 1–85. http://doi.org/10.1177/0264550515570194b.

Ministry of Justice (2015a). 2010 to 2015 government policy: reoffending and rehabilitation. London: Ministry or Justice. Accessed 2 July 2016 from www.gov.uk/government/publications/2010-to-2015-government-policy-reoffending-and-rehabilitation/2010-to-2015-government-policy-reoffending-and-rehabilitation#appendix-4-transforming-rehabilitation.

Ministry of Justice (2015b). *Offender Management Statistics Bulletin, England and Wales.* Quarterly Bulletin, January to March 2015. London: Ministry of Justice.

Ministry of Justice (2015c). *Race and the criminal justice system 2014: a Ministry of Justice publication under Section 95 of the Criminal Justice Act 1991.* Accessed 17 September 2016 at www.gov.uk/government/uploads/system/uploads/attachment_data/file/480250/bulletin.pdf.

Ministry of Justice (2016). *Proven reoffending statistics.* Quarterly Bulletin, July 2013 to June 2014, England and Wales. Accessed 30 June 2016 at www.gov.uk/government/uploads/system/uploads/attachment_data/file/519643/proven-reoffending-2014Q2.pdf.

Minuchin, S. (1974). *Families and family therapy.* Cambridge, MA: Harvard University Press.

Miranda, J., Bernal, G., Lau, A., Khon, L., Hwang, W., & La Framboise, T. (2005). State of science on psychosocial interventions for ethnic minorities. *Annual Review of Clinical Psychology*, 1, 113–142.

Mitchell, D., Simourd, D. J., & Tafrate, R. C. (2014). Introduction: critical issues and challenges facing forensic CBT practioners. In R. C. Tafrate & D. Mitchell (Eds.), *Forensic CBT: a clinical handbook for clinical pratice* (pp. 1–11). Chichester: John Wiley & Sons.

Mitchels, B., & Bond, T. (2010). *Essential law for counsellors and psychotherapists.* London: Sage.

Moffitt, T. E. (1993). Adolescence-limited and life-course-persistent antisocial behavior: a developmental taxonomy. *Psychological Review, 100*(4), 674–701.

Mohan, R., McCrone, P., Szmukler, G., Micali, N., Afuwape, S., & Thornicroft, G. (2006). Ethnic differences in mental health service use among patients with psychotic disorders. *Social Psychiatry and Psychiatric Epidemiology, 41,* 771–776.

Moncrieff, J. (2003). *Is psychiatry for sale? An examination of the influence of the pharmaceutical industry on academic and practical psychiatry.* Maudsley Discussion Paper. London: Institute of Psychiatry. Accessed 19 August 2016 at www.critpsynet.freeuk.com/pharmaceuticalindustry.htm.

Money, J. (1986). *Lovemaps: clinical concepts of sexual/erotic health and pathology, paraphilia, and gender transposition in childhood, adolescence and maturity.* New York: Irvington Publishers.

Morgan, C., McKenzie, K., & Fearon, P. (Eds.) (2008). *Society and psychosis.* Cambridge: Cambridge University Press.

Morrisroe, J. (2014). *Literacy changes lives 2014: a new perspective on health, employment and crime.* London: National Literacy Trust.

Moser, C. (2001). Paraphilia: a critique of a confused concept. In P. Kleinplatz (Ed.), *New directions in sex therapy: innovations and alternatives* (pp. 91–108). New York: Brunner-Routledge.

Moser, C. (2009). When is an unusual sexual interest a mental disorder? *Archives of Sexual Behavior, 38,* 323–325.

Moser, C. (2011). Yet another paraphilia definition fails. *Archives of Sexual Behavior, 40*(3), 483–485.

Motz, A. (2001). *The psychology of female violence: crimes against the body.* Hove: Brunner-Routledge.

Moynihan, R. (2003). The making of a disease: female sexual dysfunction. *British Medical Journal, 326,* 45–47. www.bmj.com/cgi/content/full/326/7379/45.

Mullainathan, S., & Shafir, E. (2013). *Scarcity: why having too little means so much.* London: Allen Lane.

Mullen, P. E., Pathé, M., Purcell, R., & Stuart, G. W. (1999). Study of stalkers. *The American Journal of Psychiatry, 156*(8), 1244–1249.

Mullers, E. S., & Dowling, M. (2008). Mental health consequences of CSA. *British Journal of Nursing, 17*(22), 1428–1433.

Myers, W. (2004). Serial murder by children and adolescents. *Behaviorial Sciences and the Law, 22,* 357–374.

Myers, W., Bukhanovskiy, A., Justen, E., Morton, R., Tilley, J., Adams, K. … Hazelwood, R. (2008). The relationship between serial sexual murder and autoerotic asphyxiation. *Forensic Science International, 176*(2/3), 187–195.

Namaste, V. (2000). *Invisible lives: the erasure of transsexual and transgendered people.* Chicago, IL: University of Chicago Press.

Nanda, J. (2005). A phenomenological enquiry into the effect of meditation on therapeutic practice. *Existential Analysis, 16*(2), 322–335.

National Children's Advocacy Center (2015). *Position paper on the use of human figure drawings in forensic interviews*. Huntsville, AL: National Children's Advocacy Center. Retrieved 30 December 2016 from http://calio.org/resources/research-briefs-research-to-practice/ncac-position-papers.

National Institute for Health and Clinical Excellence (NICE) (2000). *Depression: the treatment and management of depression in adults*. NICE Clinical Guidelines 90. London: NICE. Accessed 21 January 2012 at www.nice.org.uk/nicemedia/live/12329/45888/45888.pdf.

National Institute for Health and Care Excellence (NICE) (2006). Depression and anxiety – computerised cognitive behavioural therapy (CCBT). Accessed 23 May 2016 from https://www.nice.org.uk/guidance/ta97.

National Institute for Health and Care Excellence (NICE) (2009). *Borderline personality disorder: recognition and management*. NICE Clinical Guidelines 78. London: NICE.

National Institute for Health and Care Excellence (NICE) (2011). *Self-harm in over 8s: long-term management*. London: NICE.

National Institute for Health and Care Excellence (NICE) (2013). *Antisocial behaviour and conduct disorders in children and young people: recognition and management*. Clinical Guidelines. London: NICE. Available at http://nice.org.uk/guidance/cg158.

Nazroo, J., & Williams, D. (2006). The social determination of ethnic/racial inequalities in health. In M. Marmot & R. Wilkinson (Eds.), *Social determinants of health* (pp. 238–266). Oxford: Oxford University Press.

Nee, C., & Farman S. (2007). Dialectical behaviour therapy as a treatment for borderline personality disorder in prisons: three illustrative case studies. *The Journal of Forensic Psychiatry and Psychology, 18*(2), 160–180.

Nelson, S., Baldwin, N., & Taylor, J. (2012). Mental health problems and medically unexplained physical symptoms in adult survivors of childhood sexual abuse: an integrative literature review. *Journal of Psychiatric and Mental Health Nursing, 19*(3), 211–220.

Newburn, T., & Stanko, E. A. (2013). *Just boys doing business? Men, masculinities and crime*. London: Routledge.

Nhat Hanh, T. (1975/1991). *The miracle of mindfulness*. London: Rider.

NHS Commissioning Board (2013). NHS Standard contract for high secure mental health services (adults). Retrieved 24 August 2016 from www.england.nhs.uk/wp-content/uploads/2013/06/c02-high-sec-mh.pdf.

Nichols, W. C., & Everett, C. A. (1986). *Systemic family therapy: an integrative approach*. New York: Guilford Press.

Niveau, G. (2007). Relevance and limits of the principle of 'equivalence of care' in prison medicine. *Journal of Medical Ethics, 33*, 610–613.

Noh, M. S., Lee, M. T., & Feltey, K. M. (2010). Mad, bad, or reasonable? Newspaper portrayals of the battered woman who kills. *Gender Issues, 27*(3-4), 110–130.

Nolen-Hoeksema, S. (2001). Gender differences in depression. *Current Directions in Psychological Science, 10*(5), 173–176.

NOMS (National Offender Management Service) (2015). *National partnership agreement between the National Offender Management Service, NHS England*

and Public Health England for the co-commissioning and delivery of healthcare services in prisons in England 2015–2016. London: NOMS. Accessed 28 June 2016 from www.gov.uk/government/uploads/system/uploads/attachment_data/file/460445/national_partnership_agreement_commissioning-delivery-healthcare-prisons_2015.pdf.

Norcross, J. C. (Ed.) (2011). *Psychotherapy relationships that work: evidence-based responsiveness* (2nd ed.). New York: Oxford University Press.

O'Campo, P., Salmon, C., & Burke, J. (2009). Neighbourhoods and mental well-being: what are the pathways? *Health & Place, 15*(1), 56–68.

Office for National Statistics (2005). *Mental health of children and young people in Great Britain, 2004.* Basingstoke: Palgrave Macmillan.

Office for National Statistics (2013). *Crime survey for England and Wales 2011–2012.* London: Office for National Statistics.

Office for National Statistics (2014). *Crime in England and Wales, year ending March 2014.* London: Office for National Statistics. http://doi.org/Figure 3: Trend in Crime Survey for England and Wales violence, 1981 to year ending December 2014

Office for National Statistics (2015). *Compendium: crime statistics, focus on public perceptions of crime and the police, and the personal well-being of victims: 2013 to 2014.* Chapter 2: Public perceptions of crime. London: Office for National Statistics. Retrieved 28 August 2016 from www.ons.gov.uk/people populationandcommunity/crimeandjustice/compendium/crimestatistics focusonpublicperceptionsofcrimeandthepoliceandthepersonalwellbeing ofvictims/2015-03-26/chapter2publicperceptionsofcrime.

Office for National Statistics (2016). *Compendium.* Chapter 2: Homicide. London: Office for National Statistics. Accessed 7 September 2016 from www.ons.gov.uk/peoplepopulationandcommunity/crimeandjustice/com pendium/focusonviolentcrimeandsexualoffences/yearendingmarch2015/ chapter2homicide.

Ogata, S. N., Silk, K. R., Goodrich, S., Lohr, N. E., Westen, D., & Hill, E. M. (1990). Childhood sexual and physical abuse in adult patients with borderline personality disorder. *American Journal of Psychiatry, 147*(8), 1008–1013.

O'Hara, K., Forsyth, K., Webb, R., Senior, J., Hayes, A., Challis, D., Fazel, S., & Shaw, J. (2016). Links between depressive symptoms and unmet health and social care needs among older prisoners. *Age and Ageing, 45*(1), 158–163.

Olds, D. L., Henderson, C. R., Tatelbaum, R., & Chamberlin, R. (1986). Improving the delivery of prenatal care and outcomes of pregnancy: a randomized trial of nurse home visitation. *Pediatrics, 77*, 16–28.

Oosterhuis, H. (2000). *Stepchildren of nature: Krafft-Ebing, psychiatry, and the making of sexual identity.* Chicago, IL: University of Chicago Press.

Orme-Johnson, D. W. (2011). The use of meditation in corrections. *International Journal of Offender Therapy and Comparative Criminology, 55*(4), 662–664.

Orsillo, S. M., & Roemer, L. (2011). *The mindful way through anxiety.* New York: Guilford Press.

Ott, C. H. (2003). The impact of complicated grief on mental and physical health at various points in the bereavement process. *Death Studies, 27*(3), 249–272.

Otten, C. (1986). *A lycanthropy reader: werewolves in western culture*. Syracuse, NY: Syracuse University Press.

Owens, T. (2015). Disability and sex work. In M. Laing, K. Pilcher & N. Smith (Eds.), *Queer sex work* (pp. 108–114). Abingdon: Routledge.

Padesky, C. A., & Greenberger, D. (1995). *Clinician's guide to mind over mood*. New York and London: Guilford Press.

Panos, T. P., Jackson, J.W., Hasan, O., & Panos, A. (2014). Meta-analysis and systematic review assessing the efficacy of dialectical behaviour therapy (DBT). *Research on Social Work Practice, 24*(2), 213–223.

Parker, I. (2010). Psychoanalysis: the 'talking cure'. In M-J. Barker, A. Vossler & D. Langdridge (Eds.), *Understanding counselling and psychotherapy* (pp. 77–99). London: Sage.

Parkman, S., Davies, S., Leese, M., Phelan, M., & Thornicroft, G. (1997). Ethnic differences in satisfaction with mental health services among representative people with psychosis in south London: PRiSM Study 4. *British Journal of Psychiatry, 171*, 260–264.

Parks, S. A. (2015). Family therapy, the third wave and the day-to-day work of an outreach worker. *Context, 140*, 2–6.

Parliament (2016). *Moves towards a modern penal system*. Accessed 8 June from www.parliament.uk/about/living-heritage/transformingsociety/laworder/policeprisons/overview/modernpenalsystem.

Parrott, S., & Parrott, C. T. (2015). Law and disorder: the portrayal of mental illness in US crime drama. *Journal of Broadcasting & Electronic Media, 59*(4), 640–657.

Pasolini, P. (1975). *120 Days of Sodom* [Film]. Salò, Italy: Produzioni Europee Associati (PEA).

Patten, D. (2013). *Full 2012–13 TV series seasons ranking*. Retrieved 28 August 2016 from www.deadline.com/2013/05/tv-season-series-rankings-2013-full-list/.

Pavlov, I. P. (1941). *Conditioned reflexes and psychiatry*. New York: International Publishers.

Paylor, I. (2011). Youth justice in England and Wales: a risky business. *Journal of Offender Rehabilitation, 50*, 221–233.

Payne, M. (2006). *Narrative therapy*. London: Sage.

Peay, J. (2010). *Mental health and crime*. Abingdon: Routledge.

Peay, J. (2011). *Mental health and crime*. London: Routledge Cavendish.

Pederson, L. D. (2015). *Dialectical Behavior Therapy: a contemporary guide for practitioners*. Chichester: John Wiley & Sons.

Pereda, N., Guilera, G., Forns, M., & Gomez-Benito, J. (2009). The prevalence of CSA in community and student samples: a meta-analysis. *Clinical Psychology Review, 29*, 328–338.

Pescoslido, B., Monahan, J., Link, B., Steuve, A., & Kikuzawa, S. (1999). The public's view of the competence, dangerousness, and need for legal coercion of person with mental health problems. *American Journal of Public Health, 89*(8), 1339–1345.

Peters, R., & Wexler, H. K. (2005). *Treatment Improvement Protocol (TIP) Series 44. Substance abuse treatment for adults in the criminal justice system. DHHS*

Publication No. (MSA) 05-4056. Rockville, MD: Substance Abuse and Mental Health Services Administration.

Petrak, J. (2002). The psychological impact of sexual assault. In J. Petrak & B. Hedges (Eds.), *The trauma of sexual assault: treatment, prevention and practice* (pp. 19–44). London: Wiley.

Pezdek, K., Finger, K., & Hodge, D. (1997). Planting false childhood memories: the role of event plausibility. *Psychological Science, 8*(6), 437–441.

Pezdek, K., & Lam, S. (2007). What research paradigms have cognitive psychologists used to study 'false memory' and what are the implications of their choices? *Consciousness and Cognition, 16*, 2–17.

Phillips, C., & Webster, C. (Eds.) (2014). *New directions in ethnicity and crime.* Abingdon: Routledge.

Phillips, J. (director and writer), Kukura, A. (director and writer), Stein, A. M. (director) (2007). *The Dharma Brothers* [Film]. Boston, MA: Northern Light Productions.

Phillips, P., McKeown, O., & Sandford, T. (Eds.) (2010). *Dual diagnosis: practice in context.* Chichester: Wiley-Blackwell.

Philo, G., McLaughlin, G., & Henderson, L. (1996). Media content. In G. Philo (Ed.), *Media and mental distress* (pp. 45–81). Harlow: Addison-Wesley Longman.

Pilcher, K. (2016). Male sex work and society. *Rural Society, 25*(1). Retrieved 30 December 2016 from www.tandfonline.com/eprint/CFsuGEsF6PfAUQW5 NHyf/full#.V1FYaXzEQjk.twitter.

Pilgrim, D. (2008). Recovery and current mental health policy. *Chronic Illness, 4*(4), 295–304.

Pinquart, M., Oslejsek, B., & Teubert, D. (2016). Efficacy of systemic therapy on adults with mental disorders: a meta-analysis. *Psychotherapy Research, 26*, 241–257.

Piquero, A. R., Brezina, T., & Turner, M. G. (2005). Testing Moffitt's account of delinquency abstention. *Journal of Research in Crime and Delinquency, 42*(1), 27–54.

Plous, S. (Ed.) (2003). *Understanding prejudice and discrimination.* New York: McGraw-Hill.

Plummer, K. (1995). *Telling sexual stories.* London: Routledge.

Polaschek, D. L. L. (2012). An appraisal of the risk-need-responsivity (RNR) model of offender rehabilitation and its application in correctional treatment. *Legal and Criminal Psychology, 17*, 1–17.

Polaschek, D. L. L., & Reynolds, N. (2004). Assessment and treatment: violent offenders. In C. R. Hollin (Ed.), *The essential handbook of offender assessment and treatment* (pp. 201–218). Chichester: Wiley.

Poole, J., Jivraj, T., Arslanian, A., Bellows, K., Chiasson, S., Hakimy, H. ... Reid, J. (2012). Sanism, mental health, and social work/education: a review and call to action. *Intersectionalities: A Global Journal of Social Work Analysis, Research, Polity, and Practice, 1*, 20–36.

Pope, K. (2001). Sex between therapists and clients. In J. Worell (Ed.), *Encyclopedia of women and gender: sex similarities and differences and the impact of society on gender* (pp. 955–962). London: Academic Press.

Pope, K., & Vasquez, M. (2010). *Ethics in psychotherapy and counselling: a practical guide*. New York: John Wiley.

Pope, K. S. (1996). Memory, abuse, and science: questioning claims about the false memory syndrome epidemic. *American Psychologist, 51*, 957–974.

Pope, K. S., & Tabachnick, B. G. (1986). Sexual attraction to clients: the human therapist and the (sometimes) inhuman training system. *American Psychologist, 41*, 147–158.

Pope, K. S., & Vetter, V. A. (1991). Prior therapist–patient sexual involvement among patients seen by psychologists. *Psychotherapy, 28*, 429–438.

Porter, R. (2003). *Madness: a brief history*. Oxford: Oxford University Press.

Porter, S., Yuille, J., & Lehman, D. (1999). The nature of real, implanted, and fabricated memories for emotional childhood events: implications for the recovered memory debate. *Law & Human Behaviour, 23*, 517–537.

Price, C. (2006). Body-oriented therapy in sexual abuse recovery: a pilot-test comparison. *Journal of Bodywork and Movement Therapies, 10*, 58–64.

Price, C. (2007). Dissociation reduction in body therapy during sexual abuse recovery. *Complementary Therapies in Clinical Practice, 13*, 116–128.

Prichard, J. C. (1842) *On the different forms of insanity, in relation to jurisprudence*. London: Hippolyte Baillière.

Prins, H. (1995). *Offenders, deviants or patients?* London: Routledge.

Prins, H. (2010). *Offender, deviants or patients: explorations in clinical criminology* (4th ed.). Hove: Routledge.

Prison Reform Trust (2008). *Doing time: the experiences and needs of older people in prison*. A Prison Reform Trust briefing. [Online]. Accessed 7 June 2016 at www.prisonreformtrust.org.uk/ProjectsResearch/Olderpeopleinprison/DoingTimeexperiencesandneedsofolderpeople.

Prison Reform Trust (2015). *Prison: the facts*. Bromley Briefings Summer 2015. Accessed 9 June 2016 from www.prisonreformtrust.org.uk/Portals/0/Documents/Prison%20the%20facts%20May%202015.pdf.

Purser, R., & Loy, D. (2013). Beyond McMindfulness. *The Huffington Post*, 7 January. Accessed 30 January 2016 from www.huffingtonpost.com/ron-purser/beyond-mcmindfulness_b_3519289.html.

Putnam, F. W. (2003). Ten-year research update review: CSA. *Journal of the American Academy of Child and Adolescent Psychiatry, 42*, 269–278.

Quilliam, S. (2012). 'Will I be asked to have sex in the therapy room?' *Journal of family planning and reproductive health care, 38*, 264–267.

Raleigh, V., Irons, R., Hawe, E., Scobie, S., Cooke, A., Reeves, R., Petruckevich, A., & Harrison, J. (2007). Ethnic variations in the experience of mental health service users in England. *British Journal of Psychiatry, 191*, 304–312.

Rathod, S., Phiri, P., Harris, S., et al. (2012). Cognitive behaviour therapy for psychosis can be adapted for minority ethnic groups: a randomised controlled trial. *Schizophrenia Research, 143*(2–3), 319–326.

Raynor, P., & McIvor, G. (2008). *Developments in social work offenders*. Research Highlights in Social Work. London: Jessica Kingsley Publishers.

Read, R., McGregor, K., Coggan, C., & Thomas, D.R. (2006). Mental health services and sexual abuse: the need for staff training. *Journal of Trauma & Dissociation, 7*, 33–50.

Reavey, P., & Warner, S. (2006). *New feminist stories of child sexual abuse.* London: Routledge.

Reeves, A. (2010). *Counselling suicide clients.* London: Sage.

Reeves, A. (2013). *Challenges in counselling: self-harm.* London: Hodder.

Reeves, A. (2015). *Working with risk in counselling and psychotherapy.* London: Sage.

Reeves, A., McKee, M., & Stuckler, D. (2014). Economic suicides in the Great Recession in Europe and North America. *The British Journal of Psychiatry, 205*(3), 246–247.

Reeves, C. (2014). Criminal law and the autonomy assumption: Adorno, Bhaskar and critical legal theory. *Journal of Critical Realism, 13*(4), 339–367.

Regehr, C., Alaggia, R., Dennis, J., Pitts, A., & Saini, M. (2013). Interventions to reduce distress in adult victims of sexual violence and rape: a systematic review. *Campbell Systematic Reviews, 9*(3), 1–133.

Reid, J. A., Beauregard, E., Fedina, K. M., & Frith, E. N. (2014). Employing mixed methods to explore motivational patterns of repeat sex offenders. *Journal of Criminal Justice, 42*(2), 203–212.

Reiman, J. H. (2001). *The rich get richer and the poor get prison: ideology, class, and criminal justice* (6th ed.). Boston, MA: Allyn and Bacon.

Rellini, A., & Meston, C. (2011). Sexual self-schemas, sexual dysfunction, and the sexual responses of women with a history of childhood sexual abuse. *Archives of Sexual Behaviour, 40*, 351–362.

Renn, P. (2004). The link between childhood trauma and later violent offending. In F. Pfafflin & G. Adshead (Eds.), *A matter of security: the application of attachment theory to forensic psychiatry and psychotherapy* (pp. 109–144). London: Jessica Kingsley Publishers.

Ressler, R., Burgess, A., & Douglas, J. (1988). *Sexual homicide: patterns and motives.* New York: Free Press.

Rhodes, W., Kling, R., Luallen, J., & Dyous, C. (2015). *Federal sentencing disparity: 2005–2012.* Bureau of Justice Statistics Working Paper Series. Washington, DC: Bureau of Justice.

Rice, S. M., Fallon, B. J., Aucote, H. M., Möller-Leimkühler, A. M., Treeby, M. S., & Amminger, G. P. (2015). Longitudinal sex differences of externalising and internalising depression symptom trajectories: implications for assessment of depression in men from an online study. *The International Journal of Social Psychiatry, 61*(3), 236–240.

Richardson, S. (2015). *Sex itself: the search for male and female in the human genome.* London and Chicago, IL: University of Chicago Press.

Ring, S. (2012). Due process and the admission of expert evidence on recovered memory in historic child sexual abuse cases: lessons from America. *The International Journal of Evidence & Proof, 16*(1), 66–92.

Ringer, A., & Holen, M. (2015). 'Hell no, they'll think you're mad as a hatter': illness discourses and their implications for patients in mental health practice. *Health* (available online ahead of publication. http://doi.org/10.1177/1363459315574115).

Ritchie, K. (1989). The little woman meets son of DSM-III. *Journal of Medicine & Philosophy, 14*, 695–708.

Robb, G. (2003). *Strangers: homosexual love in the nineteenth century*. London: Picador.

Robinson, B. A., Winiarski, D. A., Brennan, P. A., Foster S. L., Cunningham P. B., & Whitmore E. A. (2015). Social context, parental monitoring and multisystemic therapy outcomes. *Psychotherapy*, *52*(1), 103–110.

Robinson, G., & Crow, I. (2009). *Offender rehabilitation: theory, research and practice*. London: Sage.

Robinson, S., Vivian-Byrne, S., Driscoll, R., & Cordess, C. (1991). Family work with victims and offenders in a secure unit. *Journal of Family Therapy*, *13*: 105–116.

Rodenburg, R., Benjamin, A., de Roos, C., Meijer, A. M., & Stams, G. J. (2009). Efficacy of EMDR in children: a meta-analysis. *Clinical Psychology Review*, *29*(7), 599–606.

Rodgers, N. M. (2011). Intimate boundaries: therapists' perception and experience of erotic transference within the therapeutic relationship. *Counselling and Psychotherapy Research*, *11*, 266–274.

Roediger, H. L., & McDermott, K. B. (1995). Creating false memories: remembering words not presented in lists. *Journal of experimental Psychology: Learning, Memory and Cognition*, *21*(4), 803–814.

Rogers, A., Harvey, J., & Law, H. (Eds.) (2015). *Young people in forensic mental health settings: psychological thinking and practice*. Basingstoke: Palgrave Macmillan.

Rogers, A., Harvey, J., Law, H., & Taylor, J. (2015). Introduction. In A. Rogers, J. Harvey & H. Law (Eds.), *Young people in forensic mental health settings: psychological thinking and practice* (pp. 1–19). Basingstoke: Palgrave Macmillan.

Rogers, C. R. (1957). The necessary and sufficient conditions of therapeutic personality change. *Journal of Consulting Psychology*, *21*(2), 95–103.

Ronen, T., & Rosenbaum, M. (1998). Beyond direct verbal instructions in cognitive behavioral supervision. *Cognitive and Behavioral Practice*, *5*, 7–23.

Rose, N. (2002). At risk of madness. In T. Baker & J. Simon (Eds.), *Embracing risk* (pp. 209–237). Chicago, IL: University of Chicago Press.

Rosenbaum, T., Aloni, R., & Heruti, R. (2013). Surrogate partner therapy: ethical considerations in sexual medicine. *Journal of Sex Medicine*, *11*(2), 1–7.

Rosenfield, S. (2012). Triple jeopardy? Mental health at the intersection of gender, race, and class. *Social Science & Medicine*, *74*(11), 1791–1801.

Rosenhan, D. L. (1973). On being sane in insane places. *Science*, *179*(4070), 250–258.

Rowan, J., & Jacobs, M. (2002). *The therapist's use of self*. Milton Keynes: Open University Press.

Rubin, G. S. (1993). Thinking sex: notes for a radical theory of the politics of sexuality. In H. Abelove, M. A. Baiale & D. M. Halperin (Eds.), *The lesbian and gay studies reader* (pp. 3–44). London: Routledge.

Rutter, D., & Tyrer, P. (2003). The value of therapeutic communities in the treatment of personality disorder: a suitable place for treatment? *Journal of Psychiatric Practice*, *9*, 291–302.

Saarni, C. (1999). *The development of emotional competence*. New York: Guilford Press.

Sacher-Masoch, L. von (1870/2014). *Venus in furs*. West Roxbury, MA: B&R Samizdat Express.

Sade, M. (1791/2005). *The complete Marquis de Sade*. (P. Gillette, trans.). Los Angeles, CA: Holloway House.

Sakala, S. (2014). *Breaking down mass incarceration in the 2010 census: state-by-state incarceration rates by race/ethnicity*. Accessed 17 September 2016 at www.prisonpolicy.org/reports/rates.html.

Salzberg, S. (2011). Mindfulness and loving kindness. *Contemporary Buddhism, 12*(1), 177–182.

SAMSHA (Substance Abuse and Mental Health Services Administration) (2016). *SAMSHA's National Registry of Evidence-Based Practices*. Rockville, MD: SAMSHA. Available at http://nrepp.samhsa.gov/01_landing.aspx.

Sanders, T. (2005). *Sex work: a risky business*. Cullompton, Devon: Willan.

Savage, M. (2015). *Social class in the 21st century*. Harmondsworth: Penguin.

Saypol, E., & Fraber, B. A. (2010). Attachment style and patient disclosure in psychotherapy. *Psychotherapy Research, 20*, 462–471.

Scheeringa, M. S., Weems, C. F., Cohen, J. A., Amaya-Jackson, L., & Guthrie, D. (2011). Trauma focused cognitive behavioural therapy for post-traumatic stress disorder in three-through six year-old children: a randomized control trial. *The Journal of Child Psychology and Psychiatry, 52*, 853–860.

Scheflin, A., & Brown, D. (1996). Repressed memory or dissociative amnesia: what the sciences says. *Journal of Psychiatry and Law, 21*(2), 143–188.

Schiraldi, G. (2009). *The post-traumatic stress disorder sourcebook: a guide to healing, recovery, and growth* (2nd ed.). New York: McGraw-Hill.

Schooler, J. W. (2001). Discovering memories in the light of meta-awareness. *Journal of Aggression, Maltreatment and Trauma, 4*, 105–136.

Schouten, R. (2010). Terrorism and the behavioral sciences. *Harvard Review of Psychiatry, 18*(6), 369–378.

SCMH (2002). *Breaking the circles of fear: a review of the relationship between mental health services and African Caribbean communities*. London: Sainsbury Centre for Mental Health.

Scott-Whitney, K. (2002). *Sitting inside: Buddhist practice in America's prisons*. Boulder, CO: Prison Dharma Network.

Scoular, J. (2010). What's law got to do with it ? How and why law matters in the regulation of sex work. *Journal of Law and Society, 37*(1), 12–40.

Scrambler, G. (2011). Stigma and mental disorder. In D. Pilgrim, A. Rogers & B. Pescosolido (Eds.), *The Sage handbook of mental health and illness*. London and Thousand Oaks, CA: Sage.

Sedlak, A. J., Mettenburg, J., Basena, M., Petta, I., McPherson, K., Greene, A., et al. (2010). *Fourth National Incidence Study of child abuse and neglect (NIS–4): report to Congress*. Washington, DC: US Department of Health and Human Services, Administration for Children and Families.

Seelau, S. M., & Seelau, E. P. (2005). Gender-role stereotypes and perceptions of heterosexual, gay and lesbian domestic violence. *Journal of Family Violence, 20*(6), 363–371.

Segal, Z. V., Williams, J. M. G., & Teasdale, J. D. (2002). *Mindfulness-based cognitive therapy for depression: a new approach to preventing relapse.* New York: Guilford Press.

Selvini-Palazzoli, M., Boscolo, L., Cecchi, G., & Prata, G. (1978). *Paradox and counterparadox.* New York: Aronson.

Serano, J. (2010). The case against autogynephilia. *International Journal of Transgenderism, 12*(3), 176–187.

Sewell, H. (2012). Race, ethnicity and mental health care. In P. Phillips, T. Sandford & C. Johnson (Eds.), *Working in mental health: practice and policy in a changing environment.* Abingdon: Routledge.

Sexual Offences Act (2003). *Sexual Offences Act 2003,* c42. London: HMSO. Accessed 30 March 2016 from www.legislation.gov.uk/ukpga/2003/42/section/39.

Shapiro, F. (2001). *Eye movement desensitization and reprocessing: basic principles, protocols, and procedures* (2nd ed.). New York: Guilford Press.

Sheehan, R., McIvor, G., & Trotter, C. (Eds.) (2007). *What works with women offenders.* Cullompton: Willan.

Shelton, D. (2010). Systemic psychotherapy in prison. In J. Harvey & K. Smedley (Eds.), *Psychological therapy in prisons and other secure settings* (pp. 130–149). Abingdon: Willan.

Shepherd, L., Heke, S., & O'Donovan, A. (2009). Psychosexual problems in patients attending two London sexual health clinics. *Sexual and Relationship Therapy, 24,* 29–60.

Shindel, A., & Moser, C. (2011). Why are the paraphilias mental disorders? *Journal of Sexual Medicine, 8*(3), 927–929.

Shivani, R., Goldsmith, R., & Anthenelli, R. (2002) Alcoholism and psychiatric disorders: diagnostic challenges. *Alcohol Research and Health, 26,* 90–98.

Shonin, E., Van Gordon, W., & Griffiths, M. D. (2015). Does mindfulness work? *British Medical Journal, 351,* h6919.

Shonin, E., Van Gordon, W., Slade, K., & Griffiths, M. D. (2013). Mindfulness and other Buddhist-derived interventions in correctional settings: a systematic review. *Aggression and Violent Behavior, 18*(3), 365–372.

Shuker, R. (2010). Forensic therapeutic communities: a critique of treatment model and evidence base. *The Howard Journal, 49,* 463–477.

Shulman, E., Steinberg, L., & Piquero, A. (2013). The age-crime curve in adolescence is not due to age differences in economic status. *Journal of Youth and Adolescence, 42*(6), 848–860.

Sieff, E. (2003). Media frames of mental illnesses: the potential impact of negative frames. *Journal of Mental Health, 12*(3), 259–269.

Siegrist, J., Benach, J., McKnight, A., Goldblatt, P., & Muntaner, C. (2009). *Employment arrangements, work conditions and health inequalities: report on new evidence on health inequality reduction, produced by Task Group 2 for the strategic review of health inequalities post 2010.* London: Institute of Health Equality. Accessed 7 September 2016 from www.instituteofhealthequity.org/projects/employment-and-work-task-group-report/employment-and-work-task-group-full-report.pdf.

Signorielli, N. (1989). The stigma of mental illness on television. *Journal of Broadcasting & Electronic Media, 33*(3), 325–331.

Silver, E., Mulvey, E. P., & Monahan, J. (1999). Assessing violence among discharged psychiatric patients: towards an ecological approach. *Law and Human Behavior, 23,* 237–255.

Silverstein, R., Brown, A., Roth, H., & Britton, W. (2011). Effects of mindfulness training on body awareness to sexual stimuli: Implications for female sexual dysfunction. *Psychosomatic Medicine, 73,* 817–825.

Simon, R. (1999). Therapist–patient sex: from boundary violation to sexual misconduct. *Psychiatric Clinics of North America, 22,* 31–47.

Singh, S., Burns, T., Tyrer, P., Islam, Z., Parsons, H., & Crawford, M. J. (2013). Ethnicity as a predictor of detention under the Mental Health Act. *Psychological Medicine, 44,* 997–1004.

Singh, S., Greenwood, N., White, S., & Churchill, R. (2007). Ethnicity and the Mental Health Act 1983. *British Journal of Psychiatry, 191,* 99–105.

Singleton, N., Meltzer, H., & Gatward, R. (1998). Psychiatric morbidity among prisoners in England and Wales: the report of a survey carried out in 1997 by Social Survey Division of the Office for National Statistics on behalf of the Department of Health. London: HMSO.

Skinner, B. F. (1965). *Science and human behavior.* New York: Simon & Schuster.

Smail, D. (1998). *Taking care: an alternative to therapy.* London: Constable.

Smallwood, K. (2015). *The London garrotting panic of the mid-19th century.* Retrieved 7 September 2016 from www.todayifoundout.com/index.php/2015/06/garrotting-panic-1850-insane-ways-public-reacted/.

Smedley, K. (2010). Cognitive behaviour therapy with adolescents in secure settings. In J. Harvey & K. Smedley (Eds.), *Psychological therapy in prisons and other secure settings* (pp. 71–101). Abingdon: Willan.

Smith, J. (2016). The Dame Janet Smith Review (The Jimmy Savile investigation report by Dame Janet Smith DBE). London: BBC. Available at www.bbc.co.uk/bbctrust/dame_janet_smith.

Smith, L., & Tucker, I. (2015). 'Mad, bad and dangerous to know': the pervasive socio-medical and spatial coding of mental health day centre spaces. *Emotion Space and Society, 14,* 1–29.

Smith, M. D., Grov, C., Seal, D. W., & McCall, P. (2013). A social-cognitive analysis of how young men become involved in male escorting. *Journal of Sex Research, 50*(1), 1–10.

Smith, R. (1981). *Trial by medicine: insanity and responsibility in Victorian trials.* Edinburgh: Edinburgh University Press.

Smith, R. (2007). *Youth justice: ideas, policy, practice.* Abingdon and New York: Routledge.

Smith, S. M., Gleaves, D. H., Pierce, B. H., Williams, T. L., Gilliland, T. R., & Gerkens, D. R. (2003). Eliciting and comparing false and recovered memories: an experimental approach. *Applied Cognitive Psychology, 17,* 251–279.

Smith, T., & Cape, E. (2017). The rise and decline of criminal legal aid in England and Wales. In A. Flynn & J. Hodgson (Eds.), *Access to justice and legal aid: comparative perspectives of unmet legal need.* Oxford: Hart Publishing.

Soyka, M. (2000). Substance misuse, psychiatric disorder and violent and disturbed behaviour. *British Journal of Psychiatry, 176,* 345–350.

Squires, P. (2008). *ASBO nation: the criminalisation of nuisance.* Bristol: The Policy Press.

Standing, G. (2011). *The Precariat. The new dangerous class.* London: Bloomsbury.

Stanley, S. (2012). Mindfulness: towards a critical relational perspective. *Social and Personality Psychology Compass, 6*(9), 631–706.

Starzynski, L. L., Ullman, S. E., Filipas, H. H., & Townsend, S. M. (2005). Correlates of women's sexual assault disclosure to informal and formal support sources. *Violence and Vicitms, 20*(4), 417–432.

Statistics Canada (2015). *Homicide in Canada 2014.* Retrieved 26 November 2015 from www.statcan.gc.ca/daily-quotidien/151125/dq151125a-eng.pdf.

Steadman, H. J., Mulvey, E. P., Monahan, J., Robbins, P. C., Appelbaum, P. S., Grisso, T., et al. (1998). Violence by people discharged from acute psychiatric inpatient facilities and by others in the same neighbourhood. *Archives of General Psychiatry, 55,* 109.

Steele, H., Steele, M., & Fonagy, P. (1996). Associations among attachment classification of mothers and their infants. *Child Development, 67*(2), 541–555.

Steinberg, L. (2007). Risk-taking in adolescence: new perspectives from brain and behavioral science. *Current Directions in Psychological Science, 16,* 55–59.

Steiner, B., Sanders, M., & Langevin, R. (1985). Crossdressing, erotic preference, and aggression: a comparison of male transvestites and transsexuals. In R. Langevin (Ed.), *Erotic preference, gender identity, and aggression in men: new research studies* (pp. 261–276). New York: Routledge.

Steller, M., & Boychuck, T. (1992). Children as witnesses in sexual abuse cases: investigative interview and assessment techniques. In H. Dent & R. Flin (Eds.), *Children as witnesses* (pp. 47–73). Hoboken, NJ: John Wiley & Sons.

Stern, D. (1985). *The interpersonal world of the infant: a view from psychoanalysis and developmental psychology.* London: Karnac.

Stevenson, C. (2010). Talking about sex. In C. Butler, A. O'Donovan & E. Shaw (Eds.), *Sex, sexuality & therapeutic practice: a manual for trainers and clinicians* (pp. 31–54). London: Routledge.

Stewart, D. (2008). *The problems and needs of newly sentenced prisoners: results from a national survey.* Ministry of Justice Research Series 16/08. London: Ministry of Justice.

Stith, S. M., Rosen, K. H., Middleton, K. A., Busch, A. L., Lundenberg, K., & Carlton, R. P. (2000). The intergenerational transmission of spouse abuse: a meta-analysis. *Journal of Marriage and Family, 62*(3), 650–654.

Stith, S. M., Smith, D. B., Penn, C. E., Ward, D. B., & Tritt, D. (2004). Intimate partner physical abuse perpetration and victimisation risk factors: a meta-analytic review. *Aggression and Violent Behaviour, 10*(1), 65–98.

Stoltenborgh, M., van Ijzendoorn, M. H., Euser, E. M., & Bakerman-Kranenburg, M. J. (2011). A global perspective on CSA: meta-analysis of prevalence around the world. *Child Maltreatment, 16*(2) 79–101.

Stotzer, R. (2008). Gender identity and hate crimes: violence against transgender people in Los Angeles County. *Sexuality Research & Social Policy, 5*(1), 43–52.

Straus, M. A. (2012). Blaming the messenger for the bad news about partner violence by women: the methodological, theoretical, and value basis of the purported invalidity of the conflict tactics scales. *Behavioral Sciences and the Law, 30,* 538–566.

Stronach, E. P., Toth, S. L., Rogosch, F., & Cicchetti, D. (2013). Preventive interventions and sustained attachment security in maltreated children. *Development and Psychopathology, 25*(4pt1), 919–930.

Sungur, M., & Gündüz, A. (2014). A comparison of DSM-IV-TR and DSM-5 definitions for sexual dysfunctions: critiques and challenges. *Journal Sexual Medicine, 11,* 364–373.

Svanberg, P. O. (1998). Attachment, resilience and prevention. *Journal of Mental Health, 7,* 543–578.

Swales, M. A., & Heard, H. L. (2009). *Dialectical behaviour therapy.* London: Routledge.

Swartz, M. S., Swanson, J. W., Hiday, V. A., Borum, R., Wagner, H. R., & Burns, B. J. (1998). Violence and severe mental illness: the effects of drug abuse and non-adherence to medication. *American Journal of Psychiatry, 155,* 226–231.

Swenson, C. C., Henggeler, S. W., Taylor, I. S., & Addison, O. (2009). *Multisystemic therapy and neighborhood partnerships: reducing adolescent violence and substance abuse.* New York: Guilford Press.

Sykes, G. M., & Matza, D. (1957). A theory of delinquency. *American Sociological Review, 22,* 664–670.

Symons, C., Khele, S., Rogers, J., Turner, J., & Wheeler, S. (2011). Allegations of serious professional misconduct: an analysis of the British Association for Counselling and Psychotherapy's Article 4.6 cases, 1998–2007. *Counselling and Psychotherapy Research, 11,* 257–265.

Szasz, T. S. (1961). *The myth of mental illness.* New York: Secker and Warburg.

Szasz, T. S. (1997). *The manufacture of madness: a comparative study of the inquisition and the mental health movement.* Syracuse, NY: Syracuse University Press.

Tafrate, R. C., & Mitchell, D. (2014). *Forensic CBT: a handbook for clinical practice.* Chichester: John Wiley & Sons.

Tang, S. (2012). The care pathway approach: a contemporary, inclusive, outcome-focused rationale for service provision. In P. Phillips, T. Sandford & C. Johnson (Eds.), *Working in mental health: practice and policy in a changing environment* (pp. 39–48). Abingdon: Routledge.

Tarnowski, T. (2007). Sexuality in chronic lung disease. *Nursing Clinics of North America, 42,* 631–638.

Taylor, I., Walton, P., & Young, J. (1973). *The new criminology: for a social theory of deviance* (reprinted). London: Routledge.

Taylor, P. J. (1985). Motives for offending among violent psychotic men. *British Journal of Psychiatry, 147,* 491–498.

Taylor-Johnson, S. (2015). *Fifty shades of grey* [Film]. New York: Focus Features.

Tee, J., & Kazantzis, N. (2011). Collaborative empiricism in cognitive therapy: a definition and theory for the relationship construct. *Clinical Psychology: Science and Practice, 18,* 47–61.

Tengström, A., Hodgins, S., & Kullgren, G. (2001). Men with schizophrenia who behave violently: the usefulness of an early- versus late-starter offender typology. *Schizophrenia Bulletin, 27*(2), 205–218.

The Howard League (2016). *History of the prison system*. Accessed 4 February 2016 from www.howardleague.org/history-of-prison-system.

The Timechamber (2007). *The asylums list*. Accessed 10 June 2016 from http://thetimechamber.co.uk/beta/sites/asylums/asylum-history/the-asylums-list.

Thimm, J. C., & Antonsen, L. (2014). Effectiveness of cognitive behavioral group therapy for depression in routine practice. *BMC Psychiatry, 14*, 292-014-0292-x.

Thornton, D. (2006). Age and sexual recidivism: a variable connection. *Sexual Abuse: A Journal of Research and Treatment, 18*(2), 123–135.

Thornton, D. (2010). Evidence regarding the need for a diagnostic category for a coercive paraphilia. *Archives of Sexual Behavior, 39*(2), 411–418.

Tighe, A., Pistrang, N., Cadagli, L., Baruch, G., & Butler, S. (2012). Multisystemic therapy for young offenders: families' 'experience of therapeutic processes and outcomes'. *Journal of Family Therapy, 26*(2), 187–197.

Tombs, S. (2016). *'Better regulation': better for whom?* London: Centre for Crime and Justice Studies. Accessed 7 September 2016 from http://oro.open.ac.uk/46999/.

Tombs, S., & Whyte, D. (2007). *Safety crimes*. London: Taylor & Francis.

Tombs, S., & Whyte, D. (2015). Introduction to the special issue on 'Crimes of the Powerful'. *The Howard Journal of Criminal Justice, 54*(1), 1–7.

Tosh, J. (2011a). The medicalisation of rape? A discursive analysis of 'paraphilic coercive disorder' and the psychiatrization of sexuality. *Psychology of Women Section Review, 13*(2), 2–12.

Tosh, J. (2011b). Professor Zucker's invitation as a keynote speaker to the division of clinical psychology annual conference: a response. *PsyPAG Quarterly, 79*(1), 14–19.

Tosh, J. (2015). *Perverse psychology: the pathologization of sexual violence and transgenderism*. London: Routledge.

Tosh, J. (2016). *Psychology and gender dysphoria: feminist and transgender identity*. London: Routledge.

Tosh, J., & Carson, K. (2016). A desire to be 'normal'? A discursive and intersectional analysis of 'penetration disorder'. *Intersectionalities: A Global Journal of Social Work Analysis, Research, Polity, and Practice, 5*(3), 151–172.

Towl, G. (2011). Forensic psychotherapy and counselling in prisons. *European Journal of Psychotherapy & Counselling, 13*, 403–407.

Trier, L. von. (2013a). *Nymphomaniac: Vol. I* [Film]. Hvidovre, Denmark: Zentropa Entertainments.

Trier, L. von. (2013b). *Nymphomaniac: Vol. II* [Film]. Hvidovre, Denmark: Zentropa Entertainments.

Trivedi, J. K., Tripathi, A., Dhanasekaran, S., & Moussaoui, D. (2014). Preventative psychiatry: concept, appraisal and future directions. *International Journal of Social Psychiatry, 60*(4), 321–329.

Turanovic, J. J., & Pratt, T. C. (2015). Longitudinal effects of violent victimisation during adolescence on adverse outcomes in adulthood: a focus on prosocial attachments. *The Journal of Pediatrics, 166*(4), 1062–1069.

Turner, G. (1996). News media chronicle, July 1995 to June 1996. *Australian Studies in Journalism, 5*, 265–311.

Turner, L., Whittle, S., & Combs, R. (2009). *Transphobic hate crime in the European Union*. Press for Change. Accessed 20 November 2015 from www.ucu.org.uk/media/pdf/r/6/transphobic_hate_crime_in_eu.pdf.

Twigg, J., Wolkowitz, C., Cohen, R. L., & Nettleton, S. (2011). Conceptualising body work in health and social care. *Sociology of Health & Illness, 33*(2), 171–188.

Tyler, A. (2014). Advertising male sexual services. In V. Minichiello & J. Scott (Eds.), *Male sex work and society* (pp. 82–105). New York: Harrington Park Press.

Tyler, A. (2015). M$M@Gaydar – queering the social network. In M. Laing, K. Pilcher, & N. Smith (Eds.), *Queer sex work*. Abingdon: Routledge.

Tyler, T. R. (2006). Viewing CSI and the threshold of guilt: managing truth and justice in reality and fiction. *The Yale Law Journal, 115*, 1050–1085.

Tyrer, R., Mitchard, S., Methuen, C., & Ranger, M. (2003). Treatment rejecting and treatment seeking personality disorders: Type R and Type S. *Journal of Personality Disorders, 17*(3), 263–268.

Tyron, G. S., & Winograd, G. (2011). Goal consensus and collaboration. *Psychotherapy, 48*, 50–57.

Uba, L. (2002). *A post-modern psychology of Asian-Americans: creating knowledge of a racial minority*. Albany, NY: State University of New York Press.

UK Council for Psychotherapy (2009). *Ethical principles and code of professional conduct*. London: UKCP.

UK Council for Psychotherapy (2011). *Ethical principles and code of professional conduct: guidance on the practice of psychological therapies that pathologise and/or seek to eliminate or reduce same sex attraction*. London: UKCP.

UK Council for Psychotherapy (2015). *Memorandum of understanding on conversion therapy in the UK*. London: UKCP. Available at www.psychotherapy.org.uk/UKCP_Documents/policy/MoU-conversiontherapy.pdf.

Valentine, G. (1996). Angels and devils: moral landscapes of childhood. *Environment and Planning D: Society and Space, 14*(5), 581–599.

Van der Kolk, B. A. (2014). *The body keeps the score: brain, mind, and body in the healing of trauma*. New York: Viking.

Van Ijzendoorn, M. H., Goldberg, S., Kroonenberg, P. M., & Frenkel, O. J. (1992). The relative effects of maternal and child problems on the quality of attachment: a meta-analysis of attachment in clinical samples. *Child Development, 63*, 840–858.

Vanwesenbeeck, I. (2001). Another decade of social scientific work on sex work: a review of research 1990–2000. *Annual Review of Sex Research, 12*, 242–289.

Vanwesenbeeck, I. (2013). Prostitution push and pull: male and female perspectives. *Journal of Sex Research, 50*(1), 11–16.

Veale, J., Clarke, D., & Lomax, T. (2011). Male to female transsexuals' impressions of Blanchard's autogynephilia theory. *International Journal of Transgenderism, 13*(3), 131–139.

Veling, W., Selton, J., Susser, E., Laan, W., Mackenbach, J., & Hoek, H. (2007). Discrimination and the incidence of psychotic disorders among ethnic minorities in the Netherlands. *International Journal of Epidemiology, 34*(4), 761–768.

Verhoeven, V., Bovijn, K., Helder, A., Pereman, L., Herann, I., Van Royen, P., Deneken, J., & Avonts, D. (2003). Discussing STIs: doctors are from Mars, patients from Venus. *Family Practice, 20*, 11–15.

Vetere, A., & Dallos, R. (2003). *Working systemically with families: formulation, intervention and evaluation.* London: Karnac.

Viglione, D. J., Blume-Marcovoco, A. C., Miller, H. L., Giromini, L., & Meyer, G. (2012). An inter-rated reliability study for the Rorschach performance assessment. *Journal of Personality Assessment, 94*(6), 607–612.

Vives, A., Amable, M., Ferrer, M., Moncada, S., Llorens, C., Muntaner, C., ... Benach, J. (2013). Employment precariousness and poor mental health: evidence from Spain on a new social determinant of health. *Journal of Environmental and Public Health, Journal of Environmental and Public Health, 2013*, e978656.

Vivian-Byrne, S. E. (2001). What am I doing here? Safety, certainty and expertise in a secure unit. *Journal of Family Therapy, 23*(1), 102–117.

Vogeltanz, N. D., Wilsnack, S. C., Harris, T. R., Wilsnack, R. W., Wonderlich, S. A., & Kristjanson, A. F. (1999). Prevalence and risk factors for childhood sexual abuse in women: national survey findings. *Child Abuse & Neglect, 23*, 579–592.

Volbert, R., & Steller, M. (2014). Is this testimony truthful, fabricated or based on false memory? Credibility assessment 25 years after Steller and Köhnken (1989). *European Psychologist, 19*, 207–220.

Vossler, A. (2010a). Contexts and settings. In M-J. Barker, A. Vossler & D. Langdridge (Eds.), *Understanding counselling and psychotherapy* (pp. 237–258). London: Sage.

Vossler, A. (2010b). Systemic approaches. In M-J. Barker, A. Vossler, & D. Langdridge (Eds.), *Understanding counselling and psychotherapy* (pp. 191–210). London: Sage.

Vrij, A. (2005). Criteria-based content analysis: a qualitative review of the first 37 studies. *Psychology, Public Policy and Law, 11*(1), 3–41.

Wahl, O. F. (1992). Mass media images of mental illness: a review of the literature. *Journal of Community Psychology, 20*, 343–352.

Wahl, O. F. (1995). *Media madness: public images of mental illness.* New Brunswick, NJ: Rutgers University Press.

Wahl, O. F. (2003). News media portrayal of mental illness: implications for public policy. *American Behavioural Scientist, 46*, 1594–1600.

Walby, S., Armstrong, J., & Strid, S. (2012). Intersectionality: multiple inequalities in social theory. *Sociology, 46*, 224–240.

Waldner-Haugrud, L. K., Gratch, L. V., & Magruder, B. (1997). Victimization and perpetration rates of violence in gay and lesbian relationships: gender issues explored. *Violence and Victims, 12*(2), 173–184.

Walker, S. (1997). When 'no' becomes 'yes': why girls and women consent to unwanted sex. *Applied and Preventive Psychology, 6*, 157–166.

Wallace, S., Nazroo, J. Y., & Becares, L. (2016). Cumulative exposure to racial discrimination across time and domains: exploring racism's long term impact on the mental health of ethnic minority people in the UK. *American Journal of Public Health, 106,* 1294–1300.

Wallin, D. (2015). *Attachment in psychotherapy.* New York: Guilford Press.

Walsh, E., Moran, P., Scott, C., McKenzie, K., Burns, T., Creed, F., Tyrer, P., Murray, R., & Fahy, T. (2003). Prevalence of violent victimisation in severe mental illness. *The British Journal of Psychiatry, 183*(3), 233–238.

Walsh, K., Resnick, H., Danielson, C., McCauley, J., Saunders, B., & Kilpatrick, D. (2014). Patterns of drug and alcohol use associated with lifetime sexual revictimisation and current posttraumatic stress disorder among three national samples of adolescent, college, and household-residing women. *Addictive Behaviours, 39,* 664–689.

Walter, B. (2015). *Our old monsters: witches, werewolves and vampires from medieval theology to horror cinema.* Jefferson, NC: McFarland & Company.

Wampold, B. E., & Imel, Z. E. (2015). *The great psychotherapy debate: the evidence for what makes psychotherapy work* (2nd ed.). New York: Routledge.

Ward, T., & Maruna, S. (2007). *Rehabilitation: beyond the risk paradigm.* New York: Routledge.

Ware, J., Marshall, W. I., & Marshall, L. E. (2015). Categorical denial in convicted sex offenders: the concept, its meaning and its implication for risk and treatment. *Aggression and Violent Behaviour, 25*(B), 215–226.

Wasarhaley, N. E., Lynch, K. R., Golding, J. M., & Renzetti, C. M. (2015). The impact of gender stereotypes on legal perceptions of lesbian intimate partner violence. *Journal of Interpersonal Violence.* Online ahead of Publication, 0886260515586370-. http://doi.org/10.1177/0886260515586370.

Wasco, S. M., Campbell, R., & Clark, M. R. (2002). A multiple case study of rape victim advocates' self-care routines: the influence of organizational context. *American Journal of Community Psychology, 30*(5), 731–760.

Watson, J. B., & Rayner, R. (1920). Conditioned emotional reactions. *Journal of Experimental Psychology, 3,* 1–14.

Watzlawick, P., Weakland, J. H., & Fisch, R. (1974). *Change: the principles of problem foundation and problem resolution.* New York: W. W. Norton.

Weatherburn, P., Schmidt, A. J., Hickson, F., Reid, D., Berg, R. C., Hospers, H. J., & Marcus, U. (2013). The European Men-who-have-sex-with-men internet survey (EMIS): design and methods. *Sexuality Research and Social Policy, 10*(4), 243–257.

Weatherston, D., & Moran, J. (2003). Terrorism and mental illness: is there a relationship? *International Journal of Offender Therapy and Comparative Criminology, 47*(6), 698–713.

Weeks, J. (2007). *The world we have won.* Abingdon: Routledge.

Weeks, J. (2016). *What is sexual history?* Cambridge: Polity Press.

Wei, M., Heppner, P. P., & Russell, D. W. (2006). Maladaptive perfectionism and ineffective coping as mediators between attachment and future depression: a prospective analysis. *Journal of Counselling Psychology, 53,* 67–79.

Weiner, I. B., & Greene, R. L. (2008). Psychometric foundations of assessment. In I. B. Weiner & G.L. R. L. Greene (Eds.), *Handbook of personality assessment* (pp. 49–75). Hoboken, NJ: John Wiley & Sons.

Weitzer, R. (2010a). Sex work: paradigms and policies. In R. Weitzer (Ed.), *Sex for sale: prostitution, pornography, and the sex industry* (pp. 1–43). Abingdon: Routledge.

Weitzer, R. (2010b). The movement to criminalize sex work in the United States. (Regulating sex/work: from crime control to neo-liberalism?). *Journal of Law and Society, 37*(1), 61–84.

Welfel, E. (2015). *Ethics in counselling and psychotherapy: standards, research and emerging issues* (6th ed.). Independence, KY: Cengage Learning.

Welsh, B., Berzins, K., Cook, K., & Fairley, C. (2002). Management of common vulval conditions. *Medical Journal of Australia, 178*, 391–395.

Westcott, H. L., & Jones, D. P. H. (1999). Annotation: the abuse of disabled children. *Journal of Child Psychology and Psychiatry, 40*(4), 497–506.

Weston-Parry, J. (2013). *Mental disability, violence, and future dangerousness: myths behind the presumption of guilt.* Toronto: Rowman & Littlefield.

White, M., & Epston, D. (1990). *Narrative means to therapeutic ends.* New York: W. W. Norton.

WHO (2000). *Gender disparities in mental health.* Geneva: World Health Organisation. Accessed 28 December 2016 from www.who.int/mental_health/media/en/242.pdf?ua=1.

WHO (2001). *Strengthening mental health promotion.* Geneva: World Health Organisation (Fact sheet, No. 220).

WHO (2004). *Promoting mental health: concepts, emerging evidence and practice.* Geneva: World Health Organisation, Department of Health and Substance Abuse, Victoria Health Promotion Foundation and University of Melbourne.

WHO (2006). *Defining sexual health: report of a technical consultation on sexual health, 28–31 January 2002.* Geneva: World Health Organisation. Accessed 10 January 2015 from www.who.int/reproductivehealth/publications/sexual_health/defining_sh/en.

WHO (2013). *Guidelines for the management of conditions specifically related to stress.* Geneva: World Health Organisation.

WHO (2014). *Social determinants of mental health.* Geneva: World Health Organisation. Accessed 7 September 2016 from http://apps.who.int/iris/bitstream/10665/112828/1/9789241506809_eng.pdf?ua=1.

WHO (2016). *Suicide.* Geneva: World Health Organisation. Accessed 30 May 2016 from www.who.int/topics/suicide/en/.

Widom, C. S. (1989). Child abuse, neglect, and violent criminal behaviour. *Criminology, 27*(2), 251–271.

Widom, C. S., Czaja, S. J., & DuMont, K. A. (2015). Intergenerational transmission of child abuse and neglect: real or detection bias? *Science, 347*(6229), 1480–1485.

Wilcox, D. T., Garrett, T., & Harkins, L. (2014). *Sex offender treatment: a case study approach to issues and interventions.* Chichester: John Wiley & Sons.

Williams, A. (2013). 'I was more culpable because I knew better': Moors murderer Myra Hindley admitted she was worse than Ian Brady because she understood right from wrong. *The Daily Mail.* Retrieved from www.dailymail.co.uk/news/article-2256492/Myra-Hindley-admitted-worse-Ian-Brady-understood-right-wrong.html.

Williams, J. M. (2016). *Three minute breathing space*. Accessed 30 January 2016 from www.oxfordmindfulness.org/learn/resources/.

Williams, J. M., & Penman, D. (2011). *Mindfulness: a practical guide to finding peace in a frantic world*. London: Piatkus.

Williams, L. M. (1994). Recall of childhood trauma: a prospective study of women's memories of child sexual abuse. *Journal of Consulting and Clinical Psychology*, 62(6), 1167–1176.

Williams, L. M. (1995). Recovered memories of abuse in women with documented child sexual victimisation histories. *Journal of Traumatic Stress*, 8(4), 649–673.

Williams, M., Teasdale, J., Segal, Z., & Kabat-Zinn, J. (2007). *The mindful way through depression*. New York: Guilford Press.

Willmot, P., & Gordon, N. (Eds.) (2011). *Working positively with personality disorder in secure settings*. Chichester: Wiley-Blackwell.

Wilmoth, M. C. (2007). Sexuality: a critical component of quality of life in chronic disease. *Nursing Clinics of North America*, 42(4), 507–514.

Wilson, D. (2014). *Pain and retribution: a short history of British prisons 1066 to the present*. London: Reaktion Books.

Wilson, M. (2010). *Delivering race equality action plan: a five year review*. London: Department of Health.

Winstok, Z., & Straus, M. A. (2014). Gender differences in the link between intimate partner physical violence and depression. *Aggression and Violent Behavior*, 19(2), 91–101.

Winter, S. (1999). *Freud and the institution of psychoanalytic knowledge*. Stanford, CA: Stanford University Press.

Wissink, I. B., van Vugt, E., Moonen, X., Stams, G.-J. J. M., & Hendriks, J. (2015). Sexual abuse involving children with an intellectual disability (ID): a narrative review. *Research in Developmental Disabilities*, 36, 20–35.

Wolf, M. R., & Nochajski, T. H. (2013). Child sexual abuse survivors with dissociative amnesia: what's the difference? *Journal of Child Sexual Abuse*, 22, 462–480.

Wolitzky-Taylor, K. B., Resnick, H. S., McCauley, J. L., Amstadter, A. B., Kilpatrick, D. G., & Ruggiero, K. J. (2011). Is reporting of rape on the rise? A comparison of women with reported versus unreported rape experiences in the National Women's Study replication. *Journal of Interpersonal Violence*, 26, 807–832.

Wolkowitz, C. (2011). The organisational contours of 'body work'. In E. L. Jeanes, D. Knights & P. Yancey Martin (Eds.), *Handbook of gender, work, and organization* (pp. 177–190). Chichester: John Wiley & Sons.

Worthington, R. (2012). Dealing with trauma as an intervention for aggression: a review of approaches and the value of reprocessing. *Journal of Aggression, Conflict and Peace Research*, 4(2), 108–118.

Wyss, S. (2004). 'This was my hell': the violence experienced by gender nonconforming youth in US high schools. *International Journal of Qualitative Studies in Education*, 17(5), 709–730.

Young, J., Klosko, J., & Weishaar, M. (2003). *Schema therapy: a practitioner's guide*. New York: Guilford Press.

Youth Justice Board and Ministry of Justice (2015). *Youth justice statistics 2013/14*. London: Ministry of Justice.

Zander, T. (2008). Commentary: inventing diagnosis for civil commitment of rapists. *Journal of American Psychiatry and Law, 36*, 459–469.

Zerubavel, N., & Wright, M. O. D. (2012). The dilemma of the wounded healer. *Psychotherapy, 49*(4), 482–491.

Zola, I. K. (2011). Medicine as an institution of social control. *The Sociological Review, 20*(4), 487–504.

Zona, M. A., Palarea, R. E., & Lane, J. (1998). Psychiatric diagnosis and the offender–victim typology of stalking. In J. Reid Meloy (Ed.), *The psychology of stalking: clinical and forensic perspectives* (pp. 70–84). San Diego, CA: Academic Press.

Zucker, K., & Bradley, S. (1995). *Gender identity disorder and psychosexual problems in children and adolescents*. New York and London: Guilford Press.

INDEX